Homemaking

GENDER AND GENRE IN LITERATURE
VOLUME 8
GARLAND REFERENCE LIBRARY OF THE HUMANITIES
VOLUME 1042

GENDER AND GENRE IN LITERATURE

BARBARA E. BOWEN, *Series Editor*

MOTHERS IN THE
ENGLISH NOVEL
From Stereotype to Archetype
by Marjorie McCormick

FEMALE HEROISM
IN THE PASTORAL
by Gail David

SOUTH AFRICAN FEMINISMS
Writing, Theory, and Criticism,
1990–1994
edited by M.J. Daymond

REDEFINING AUTOBIOGRAPHY
IN TWENTIETH-CENTURY
WOMEN'S FICTION
An Essay Collection
edited by Janice Morgan
and Colette T. Hall

AIDS NARRATIVES
Gender and Sexuality,
Fiction and Science
by Steven F. Kruger

GENDER IN THE THEATRE OF WAR
Shakespeare's Troilus and Cressida
by Barbara E. Bowen

THREE RADICAL WOMEN WRITERS
Class and Gender in Meridel
Le Sueur, Tillie Olsen, and
Josephine Herbst
by Nora Ruth Roberts

HOMEMAKING
Women Writers and the
Politics and Poetics of Home
edited by Catherine Wiley
and Fiona R. Barnes

Homemaking
Women Writers and the Politics and Poetics of Home

Edited by
Catherine Wiley
Fiona R. Barnes

Garland Publishing, Inc.
New York and London
1996

Library of Congress Cataloging-in-Publication Data

Homemaking : women writers and the politics and poetics of home /
    edited by Catherine Wiley, Fiona R. Barnes.
            p.   cm. — (Gender and genre in literature ; vol. 8)
    (Garland reference library of the humanities ; vol. 1042)
        Includes bibliographical references (p.).
        ISBN 0-8153-2055-8 (alk. paper)
        1. Literature—Women authors—History and criticism.   2. Women
    authors—Biography.   3. Home economics.   4. Politics and literature.
    I. Wiley, Catherine.   II. Barnes, Fiona R.   III. Series.   IV. Series: Gender
    & genre in literature ; v. 8.
    PN471.H66   1996
    809'.89287'09045—dc20   95–53746
                                                                  CIP

Cover drawing of *Kitchen Table* by Lisa Spivak.

Printed on acid-free, 250-year-life paper
Manufactured in the United States of America

Contents

Series Editor's Foreword   ix
Acknowledgments   xi
Introduction   xv

1   Perhaps the World Ends Here   3
     Joy Harjo

2   *Homeric* Resonances: Longing and Belonging in   5
     Barbara Kingsolver's *Animal Dreams*
     Roberta Rubenstein

3   Writing Home: The Bible and Gloria Naylor's   23
     Bailey's Cafe
     Amy Benson Brown

4   Beyond Silence   43
     Lisa Suhair Majaj

5   My Self, My Body, My World: Homemaking in the   53
     Fiction of Brigitte Kronauer
     Jutta Ittner

6   Home-Breaking and Making in the Novels of   71
     Elizabeth Jolley
     John O'Brien

7   Ironing Their Clothes   83
     Julia Alvarez

8   The Dream Detectives   85
     Clarissa Pinkola Estés

9   Penetrating Privacy: Confessional Poetry and the   87
     Surveillance Society
     Deborah Nelson

10   Remembering China in *Wild Swans* and   115
      Life and Death in Shanghai
            Cynthia F. Wong

11   Keeping House: A Meditation on the Possibilities   135
      of the Essay
            Rebecca Blevins Faery

12   Unfamiliar Ties: Lesbian Constructions of Home   145
      and Family in Jeanette Winterson's *Oranges Are Not*
      the Only Fruit and Jewelle Gomez's *The Gilda Stories*
            Ellen Brinks and Lee Talley

13   Harmony and Resistance in *L'Amour, la fantasia*'s   175
      Algerian Women's Communities
            Martine Guyot-Bender

14   Spices   201
      To Whom It May Concern   205
            Ama Ata Aidoo

15   Relocating Home and Identity in *Zami:*   207
      A New Spelling of My Name
            Jennifer Gillan

16   Wild Lessons: Native Ecological Wisdom in   223
      Ruby Slipperjack's Fiction
            Sylvia Bowerbank and
            Dolores Nawagesic Wawia

17   Nature, Spirituality, and Homemaking in   239
      Marjorie Kinnan Rawlings' *Cross Creek*
            Carolyn M. Jones

18   Guest to New York City   261
      Man on the Terrace   262
            Cheryl Fish

19   Jewish Women in the Diaspora   263
         Gabriele Kreis, translation and introduction
         by Ingeborg Majer O'Sickey

20   Home   277
         Velina Hasu Houston

21   Untitled Letter   283
         Charlotte DeClue (Kawashinsay)

22   Yes, Something *Did* Happen in My Childhood   285
         Margaret Randall

23   Imagined Communities in the Novels of Michelle Cliff   287
         Meryl F. Schwartz

24   Refusing the Poisoned Chalice: The Sexual Politics   313
         of Rita Ann Higgins and Paula Meehan
         Karen Steele

25   Zehra Çirak: Foreign Wings on Familiar Shoulders   335
         Marilya Veteto-Conrad

26   Helena María Viramontes' Homing Devices in   361
         Under the Feet of Jesus
         Cecelia Lawless

27   How We Did It, from *Scenes from a Childhood*   383
         Alison Hawthorne Deming

      Notes on the Contributors   385

Series Editor's Foreword

The Gender and Genre in Literature series participates in what Eve Sedgwick has called one of the two great "heuristic leaps of feminism": the recognition that gender is a structuring force for "nodes of thought" that may have nothing explicitly to do with gender at all. Genre might be considered one of these nodes of thought, even though the word itself is simply a more direct importation from the French of the word "gender." The Gender and Genre in Literature series seeks to advance a discussion already under way within feminist criticism on the role of genre in enforcing the gender hierarchy: publication itself has historically been a gendering activity, as has been the choice, for instance, of epic over translation, drama over diaries.

But the discussion of gender and genre goes beyond these distinctions to investigate how the notion of genre itself is changing shape under pressure from feminist and other interventions in humanist epistemology. New categories of writing—letters, journals, popular fiction, travel narratives, advertising, science—are demanding attention as literary genres, while the traditional genres are being reanimated by efforts to disrupt their alignments with patriarchy, compulsory heterosexuality, and white supremacy. A painful history has already shown that any attempt to consider gender oppression in isolation from other forms of oppression just reinforces the hierarchies already in place, so deeply are they institutionalized in the late capitalist world. Thus the Gender and Genre in Literature series, while arguing for the importance of gender as a category of analysis, seeks to develop a complex and multiple understanding of gender with which to resee written culture.

The present volume, *Homemaking: Women Writers and the Politics and Poetics of Home*, enters the critical discourse on gender by way of two of its most pressing issues: the politics of women's locations at the end of the twentieth century, and the division of experience into public and private. That the emergence of systematic feminist thought in the west coincided with the invention of "private life" should not surprise us. Feminist thinkers from Mary Wollstonecroft on were quick to realize that the designation of the public and the private, male and female, was key to the subordination of women. Since at least the eighteenth century feminists have fought not just to reverse the terms of the gendered opposition but to undo the oppositional structure itself: the personal is political, we have insisted; "the private is marked by a public potential, since it *is* the weave, or texture, of public activity," Gayatri Spivak has written. *Homemaking* extends this central current of feminist thought both by investigating the most privatized and feminized of all spaces, the home, and by challenging the boundaries that separate "private" and "public" literary genres.

Essays jostle with poetry, criticism with autobiography; *Homemaking* refuses to accept the rule of genre that would cordon off critical from creative writing. Writing of many kinds, the book argues, can participate in the necessary renegotiation and reconstruction of "home." But the collection also recognizes that home is made a generative place for some women at the expense of others; several of the contributions address the location of "home" within national and international structures of power. *Homemaking* brings together voices that are still rarely heard together: women from the Turkish *Gastarbeiter* community in Germany, from postcolonial Ghana, from working-class Ireland, from Jordan and China, from the feminist movement in Algeria and the American suburbs of the 1950s, from Jamaica and the African diaspora in North American cities. The result of their conversation is a new analysis of the powerful connection between "home" and writing, an analysis rooted in the feminist critique of private life, yet confident that home, as a place of community and connection, can be re-made.

Barbara Bowen
Queens College and the Graduate Center
City University of New York

Acknowledgments

A number of people helped us to produce this book. We want to thank especially Geoff March of the University of Colorado at Denver Computing Services, Rod Tanaka of the CU-D Mac Lab, Susan Linville, Michael Evans Smith, Jason Goldfarb, and of course, all of our contributors whose good humor and patience we appreciate.

Ongoing and eternal appreciation to Mary Stephens of the CU-D Department of English, whose last-minute technical assistance saved us more than once! Great thanks also to our series editor, Barbara Bowen, and finally, to the woman who saw this through from inception to reality, with grace and great skill, Claudia Hirsch of Garland Publishing.

The editors gratefully acknowledge permission to reprint or quote from:

Ama Ata Aidoo's "Spices" first appeared in *Field* No. 50, Spring 1994 and is © by Oberlin College Press.

Julia Alvarez, "Ironing Their Clothes" is from *Homecoming*, copyright © by Julia Alvarez 1986. Published by E.P. Dutton / New American Library 1986. First published by Grove Press.

Eavan Boland's poem, "Self-Portrait on a Summer Evening," is reprinted from *Outside History: Selected Poems 1980-1990* by Eavan Boland, with the permission of W.W. Norton & Company, Inc. Copyright © 1990 by Eavan Boland.

Nien Cheng, *Life and Death in Shanghai*, copyright © 1988. Published by Grove / Atlantic, Inc.

All translations of Zehra Çirak's poetry, by Marilya Veteto-Conrad, are with the author's permission.

From *Free Enterprise* by Michelle Cliff. Copyright © 1993 by Michelle Cliff. Used by permission of Dutton Signet, a division of Penguin Books USA Inc.

Michelle Cliff, *The Land of Look Behind*, in Meryl F. Schwartz's essay, is cited with permission from Firebrand Books, Ithaca, New York,

Give Back: First Nations Perspectives on Cultural Practice, Gallerie Publications in Vancouver, British Columbia, Canada.

Paula Meehan, "The Statue of the Virgin at Granard Speaks," in Karen Steele's essay, is from *The Man Who Was Marked by Winter* and is cited by kind permission of the author and The Gallery Press (County Meath, Ireland) / Eastern Washington University Press © 1991.

Excerpts from *Bailey's Cafe*, copyright © 1992 by Gloria Naylor, reprinted by permission of Harcourt Brace and Company.

John O'Brien's essay on Elizabeth Jolley was first published as "Myths of Domesticity in the Novels of Elizabeth Jolley" in *Elizabeth Jolley: New Critical Essays*, by Collins Angus and Robertson Publishers (a division of HarperCollins) in Australia.

Marjorie Kinnan Rawlings is reprinted with the permission of Scribner, a division of Simon and Schuster Inc. from *Cross Creek* by Marjorie Kinnan Rawlings. Copyright 1942 Marjorie Kinnan Rawlings; copyright renewed © 1970 Norton Baskin.

Reprinted from *Collected Early Poems: 1950-1970* by Adrienne Rich, by permission of the author and W. W. Norton & Company, Inc. Copyright © 1993 by Adrienne Rich. Copyright © 1967, 1963, 1962, 1961, 1960, 1959, 1958, 1957, 1956, 1955, 1954, 1953, 1952, 1951 by Adrienne Rich. Copyright © 1984, 1975, 1971, 1969, 1966 by W. W. Norton & Company, Inc.

From *Live or Die*. Copyright © 1966 by Anne Sexton. Reprinted by permission of Houghton Mifflin Co. All rights reserved.

From "To John, Who Begs Me Not to Enquire Further," *To Bedlam and Part Way Back* by Anne Sexton. Copyright © 1960 by Anne Sexton, renewed 1988 by Linda G. Sexton. Reprinted by permission of Houghton Mifflin Co. All rights reserved.

From "The Wedlock," *45 Mercy Street* by Anne Sexton. Copyright © 1976 by Linda Gray Sexton and Loring Conant, Jr. Reprinted by permission of Houghton Mifflin Co. All rights reserved.

Ruby Slipperjack, *Silent Words* is reprinted with permission from *Silent*

Introduction

As current battles over the definitions of home indicate, there is no one concept of home, nor is home a static "safe place" that can exist unchanged by shifts in time or space. The concept of home, much like the concept of identity, is a fertile site of contradictions demanding constant renegotiation and reconstruction. Home is not always a comfortable place to be, and despite Bernice Johnson Reagon's distinction between home and "coalition," we contend that home is always a form of coalition: between the individual and the family or community, between belonging and exile, between home as utopian longing and home as memory, between home as safe haven and home as imprisonment or site of violence, and finally, between home as place and home as metaphor. In the words of Rebecca Blevins Faery, the woman writer who makes a home, while at the same time questioning its value as an artificial bulwark against change, is a "dweller in contradictions" (139). In her first experiment with home-owning and homemaking, Faery learns, like Sylvie in Marilynne Robinson's *Housekeeping*, that undoing a home may sometimes be as significant an activity as making one. In her exploration of the essay form, Faery discovers that the writer writes from a momentary safe place, which is at once destabilized by outside interruptions and interventions.

We hope that this collection provides such a temporary place of safety for women writers and their readers. We have aimed for a coalition of many voices and viewpoints, all of them; however, engaged in investigations of how women make themselves at home both in the world and in language, in the realm of poetics as well as politics. These essays focus primarily on women's writings in the second half of the twentieth century, with a few exceptions, but range across the world in their geographic scope, thereby emphasizing the cross-cultural diversity of women's experiences. These women find a common arena in which to define and empower themselves in writing, at the same time providing a literary space in which the community of their readers can similarly make themselves at home. Living as we now do, in a world where new nations arise from the collapse of old political structures, the idea of home as a starting point and a returning haven becomes ever more attractive and yet paradoxically more difficult to attain. The writers represented here explore how women have adapted to rapidly changing demands on them to provide home for themselves as well as others who would join them.

We all must write from somewhere, but that place's stability is often illusory. Home is therefore not an endpoint, but a constant movement towards or reconfiguration of the self in a place. If exile is to be in flight from, then home is to move towards. In the continuum of home and exile, if exile contains dislocation, isolation, and individualism, then home incorporates connection, relocation, and community. Exile has been the more favored term of the two states in the literary tradition, with many writers and theorists valorizing the condition that Andrew Gurr terms "creative exile" (7). Similarly, the poet Breyten Breytenbach claims exile as a space that frees the imagination, for the exiled writer is "engaged with an elsewhere that cannot be reached" (71); and yet Breytenbach's discussion goes on to clarify that the writer endeavors to regain that "elsewhere" by writing home.

In her essay "Alibis and Legends: The Ethics of Elsewhereness, Gender and Estrangement," Jane Marcus gives a timely warning about the tendency to theorize homelessness into abstraction: "As we debate these issues intellectually and privilege homelessness as impulse to art, let us remember that our cities are full of the nonwriting homeless" (275); indeed, real homelessness should not be romanticized. Gabriele Kreis, for example, through a series of interviews with Jewish refugees in New York, exposes how it became the role of women not only to adapt and survive in a new society that their men found alienating but also to create homes and new roles for themselves. These women's struggles for survival and their heroic adaptations to a new world and new language offer a sobering look at the world of exiles, which Kreis describes thus: "The life of the emigrant is a life at the precipice of an abyss: it is a life of contingencies." Charlotte DeClue's "Untitled Letter" (283) likewise points to the vagaries of exile on American streets, while Cheryl Fish's poems explore the compromises necessary for cramped highrise living. Regardless of the shape of their homes, or lack of a home, women writers find ways to make a space for themselves. We contend that the recent emphasis on outsiderhood and otherness in women's lives and women's writing must ultimately give way to a renewed focus on selfhood and homemaking. Reconstruction should follow deconstruction, as women work to remake—and rewrite—themselves by privileging community and connection over separation and dislocation.

This fight for survival links the personal construction of identity with the more social project of construction of home: these two creative tasks focus on making us at home with ourselves and at home with others. This means that home is the site of a sometimes uneasy coalition between personal space and community life, between the normative restrictions of home and the individual's desire for independence and creativity. Identity politics and the politics of location are intimately linked, as Adrienne Rich explains in her influential 1984 essay, "Notes Towards a Politics of Location." In response to this, and to Minnie Bruce Pratt's autobiographical essay, "Identity: Skin Blood Heart," Chandra Talpade Mohanty and Biddy Martin contend:

> The relationship between the loss of community and the loss of self is crucial. To the extent that identity is collapsed with home and community and based on homogeneity and comfort, on skin, blood, and heart, the giving up of home will necessarily mean the giving up of self and vice versa. (209)

Many of the writers in this collection describe and analyze the struggle for co-existence necessary for women who decide to make homes in which to locate themselves and to affiliate with those who live with them. For the relationship between self and place is an interactive and changing one; the politics of where we locate ourselves is an integral factor in the construction of female identity and subjectivity.

The constantly shifting and reconstitutive nature of home makes it an excitingly dynamic and contingent concept. Chandra Talpade Mohanty describes this process as a "reterritorialization through struggle" (90), a concept clearly demonstrated by the protagonists in Michelle Cliff's novels, who strive to renegotiate and ultimately reconstruct the notion of home and homeland through political struggle, as they battle the colonialist ideologies that divide and enslave the inhabitants of Jamaica. Meryl F. Schwartz discusses Cliff's creation of "imagined communities" both within her texts and with the readers of her novels, showing us how storytelling and unearthing repressed histories can create coalitions that empower women to rethink the definitions and possibilities of family and home. As Lisa Suhair Majaj points out in her autobiographical essay, naming oneself and one's home involves eternal negotiation, with the voices that consign women to silence and with the historical circumstances that necessitate changing one home for another.

The struggle for home, and who controls its composition and role, is a subject taken up by Deborah Nelson in her essay on governmental surveillance policies in the Cold War era and the impact these invasions of privacy had on women's Confessional poetry. She investigates how women have managed to make homes in a contested space that is paradoxically both private and public domain. Nelson argues that Confessional poetry constitutes more than suburban narcissism, as it connects the paradoxical lack of privacy in the isolated suburban home to a lack of identity for the women who live there. The recent ongoing vituperative battles over who controls the home, and more importantly, the idea and ideologies of home, indicate how vital the arena of home is to our self-image as a society. For example, in May 1995, Ralph Reed of the Christian Coalition announced a ten-point social agenda for Congress that seriously inhibits women's efforts to remake home from a feminist perspective. The proposals focus on school prayer, abortion, "parental rights," and private charity as a replacement for welfare. Their subtext is "the family," which according to conservatives is nuclear, heterosexual, and male-dominated. New books such as David Blankenhorn's *Fatherless America* promote a return to a patriarchal family structure and advocate barring single women from using sperm banks, a move that would make it almost impossible for lesbians to become parents, since they are also disadvantaged by adoption laws. The home as represented in the rhetoric of "family values" echoes the stifling suburban unit immortalized by Betty Friedan in *The Feminine Mystique*: it is not a space that encourages women to be creative beyond, or in, the domestic realm.

Ellen Brinks and Lee Talley contend that lesbian couples confront a particularly challenging task in their efforts to construct home and family in the face of active, frequently hostile, religious and political opposition. Novels by Jeanette Winterson and Jewelle Gomez rely on "fantastic modes of representation"—evangelism and vampirism—in order to portray lesbian family ties as new and yet familiar. Often one kind of home, in life and in writing, must be destroyed to make another. Brinks and Talley describe the narrator of Winterson's lesbian *Bildungsroman* as breaking the walls of convention that both protect and limit women: the narrator builds a revised home and a revised family from the tradition she shatters.

If women do indeed choose to site themselves at home, then they need to reclaim control of its value and construction. This is a battle still being fought on the homefront, by women who give up paid work in order to care for their children, and who are then stigmatized by a society that regards child-rearing and housework as inferior women's work, unpaid and invisible. We need to interrogate notions that have been negatively inscribed, such as housework, for as Ann Romines explains in *The Homeplot*: "[h]ousekeeping is not only the unspoken, unvalued routine by which a patriarchal regime is maintained. It is also the center and vehicle of a culture invented by women, a complex and continuing process of female, domestic art." (14). This statement shows the dual value of housework in society, an issue taken up in Jutta Ittner's essay. Ittner examines how the contemporary German novelist and short story writer, Brigitte Kronauer, explores the divisions and interconnections of public and private space for the housewife. The first person narrators in Kronauer's texts, Ittner contends, map out the personal and communal dimensions of their homes through interdependent concentric rings of the self, the body, and the home. For these women, daily life is a continual recreation of home, which is both a rewarding and a frustrating occupation in its never-ending circularity. For example, in "The Dream Detectives," Clarissa Pinkola Estés imagines the liberatory aspects of laundry, while Julia Alvarez itemizes the personal empowerment hidden in the simple act of ironing, in her poem, "Ironing Their Shirts." The speaker's meticulous attention to the pleats and collars she presses is an expression of the familial love she feels for the wearers of these clothes.

Women write in order to negotiate the tensions between definitions of home as a material space and home as an ideal place. Acknowledging and working with this tension provides the basis for creativity, as Janet Zandy explains in her introduction to *Calling Home: Working-Class Women's Writings*:

> Home is a good place to begin. Whether it is a tenement, a barrio, a ghetto, a neighborhood, the project, the block, the stoop, the backyard, the tenant farm, the corner, four walls, or hallowed ground, finding a place in the world where one can be *at home* is crucial. Home is literal: a place where you struggle together to survive; or a dream: "a real home," something just out of one's grasp, or a nightmare: a place to escape in order to survive as an individual. Home is an idea: an inner geography where the ache to belong finally quits, where there is no sense of "otherness," where there is, at last, a community. (1)

Zandy's attention to home's collective identity is significant: the less than ideal space in which we live among others points to how we can learn, ideally, to be at home in our own skin. In between the tension of the poles of home as actual and home as ideal, much of contemporary women's writing finds its space. Sometimes writers look back nostalgically to a family home that now exists only in memory, as is the case for Chinese writers Jung Chang and Nien Cheng in Cynthia F. Wong's essay on *Wild Swans* and *Life and Death in Shanghai*. These writers fluctuate between loyalty to their former homeland and affiliation with the cultural values of their adopted homes in the west. Wong charts these women's strivings for cultural reconstruction and a new place to call home, which are haunted by the "wrath of the past" and inevitably informed by western ideologies of political and literary freedom. In a similar fashion, Audre Lorde's biomythography, *Zami*, is underpinned by Lorde's mother's remembrances of her Granadan home. And yet, like Ama Ata Aidoo's poem, "Spices," *Zami* is redolent with the nostalgic fragrances of a past homeland that can never be retrieved, except through memory and storytelling. Lorde's honest portrayals of her often-turbulent relationships with a number of powerful women create a community of women whose bonds are complex and fluid; in her essay, Jennifer Gillan explains how, through writing, Lorde becomes a "journeywoman" by continually piecing together a home and family in transition. In the poem, "School Note," Lorde writes that for the embattled, "there is no place / that cannot be / home nor is," underlining the paradox that home is potentially both anywhere and nowhere, an almost mythical place of infinite possibilities. And yet, at its best, home can be both a livable space and a creative state of possibility for the woman writer.

For writers live in two worlds—the creative inner world and the outer social one—or as Gertrude Stein puts it, in *Paris, France*:

> After all everybody, that is, everybody who writes is interested in living inside themselves in order to tell what is inside themselves. That is why writers have to have two countries, the one where they belong and the one in which they live really. The second one is romantic, it is separate from themselves, it is not real but it is really there. (2)

Stein envisions the writer's second home as an imaginative state that is both within and outside her; thus she visualizes the delicate balance for writers between "the home where they belong" (paradoxically not the one "in which they live really") and the "not real" one which for them "is really there." As a result, many writers juggle the imaginative space with the material place of home in order to create. Zehra Çirak, a poet who is the daughter of Turkish immigrants living in Germany, refuses the role of victim or outsider in her life and poetry, despite the publishers and critics who try to stereotype her as the Other. Marilya Veteto-Conrad's essay describes how Çirak confronts the increasingly violent racism and xenophobia in her adopted country, defiantly making herself at home in German language, literature, and society, while at the same time denouncing the excesses of nationalism. This uneasy tension between the writer's creative world and the sometimes inhospitable social world, and the occasional failures of both to sustain creativity, produces a state of instability for the woman writer that Emily Dickinson terms "Homelessness at Home." Like Çirak, another daughter of immigrant workers, Estrella in Helena María Viramontes' *Under the Feet of Jesus*, grasps the tool of language in order to construct a home for herself in an American society that denies her a home or guaranteed citizenship. In her discussion of Chicanas' necessary configurations of "home" as the "space in between," or as a building constantly under construction, as it were, Cecelia Lawless focuses on the central image of an abandoned barn, which Estrella adopts as a temporary home in the journey towards speech and selfhood.

How, then, does a woman make herself at home in language and literature? How does she, as Margaret Randall puts it in her poem, "Yes, Something *Did* Happen in My Childhood," "stake well [her] territory," (285) when that territory is so often a space of contestation and contradiction? Much has been written about how women have inserted themselves in the margins of literary traditions that have historically been male-dominated preserves, but we are more interested in this collection in how women have created bonds of community among themselves. How women writers have redefined male-dominated literary spheres to create their own traditions and territories is addressed most directly by Roberta Rubenstein and Amy Benson Brown. Rubenstein examines Barbara Kingsolver's *Animal Dreams* as an extension and revision of the Homeric tradition; the protagonist, Codi, searches for the submerged family history that her father, Homer Noline, has misrepresented. Kingsolver also renews the waste land legacy by portraying the central quester of her novel as female: Codi learns to make herself and her hometown of Grace, Arizona, whole by discovering "ground orientation," which is based partially on an American Indian conceptualization of home as a space in nature linking individuals to family and community. In Gloria Naylor's *Bailey's Cafe*, the master narrative is the Old Testament that her multiple women protagonists, Eve, Jessie Bell, Esther, and two Marys, dismantle and redesign in order to remake themselves. Naylor's characters reconstruct home, in Amy Benson Brown's terms, as a "textual half-way house" in a state of perpetual restoration, not an Edenic source.

In a different exploration of the spiritual dimensions of home, Marjorie Kinnan Rawlings and Ruby Slipperjack revise conventional theological associations of homemaking in their texts. Their homes pay attention to the harmonies of the natural world, rather than to the impositions of traditional religious "authorities." Rawlings constructed a way of life at Cross Creek in northern Florida that focuses on both the physical relationships and the spiritual rhythms of the self in interaction with her community. Carolyn M. Jones shows how Rawlings' quest for solitude in the "wilderness" was transformed into a necessary communion with her neighbors who understood the weather, the wildlife, and the land far better than she did. Native Canadian novelist Ruby Slipperjack's fiction is even more grounded in the land because, as Sylvia Bowerbank and Dolores Nawagesic Wawia assert, "for the Ojibway, land is life; food, shelter and even human community are all gifts of the land" (234). Their essay exposes the connection between home and the natural world by showing how the word "ecology" shares etymological roots with the Greek world for household. The environmental crisis facing our planet, then, makes individual privacy in the isolated home impossible, or at lest unethical. Bowerbank's and Wawia's central question—"How are we to learn to become native to our home places?" (224)—reverberates throughout this volume.

When women are traditionally described as the true natives of a nation, however, other problems arise for women writers trying to make themselves at home. In her essay on Irish women poets Rita Ann Higgins and Paula Meehan, Karen Steele shows how they, too, resist cultural and literary paradigms by challenging the Yeatsian convention of conflating Irish womanhood with the country itself. Steele discusses how Irish women were limited both politically and culturally by the purely symbolic role of women in Irish politics, which was echoed in their restricted roles as symbolic emblems in Irish poetry. Contemporary Irish women poets create deliberately ordinary images of women and address taboo topics in their work, in order to resist the romantic and oppressive Catholic and nationalist prescriptions. Throughout the centuries, the powerful ideological constructions of nationhood and womanhood have been symbolically and strategically linked by politicians, religious leaders, artists, and writers. Much like Irish women, Algerian women in Assia Djebar's fictionalized autobiography learn to subvert orientalist notions of Arab nationhood that picture Algeria as a woman's body ripe for conquest. In contrast to some western feminists' attacks on the place of women in the Arab world, Martine Guyot-Bender shows that the strong Algerian women's society, whose loss the narrator mourns, is a nurturing space in which communities of women pass on their culture to each other. Indeed, these enclaves protect their inhabitants from the men who would control or appropriate them, for in Guyot-Bender's words,"a women's community constitutes a solid wall against outsiders, be they Arab males of the tribe or French invaders." (180) In stark contrast to this appropriation of women in the national struggle for identity, John O'Brien demonstrates how Australian women have had to fight to create a space for themselves in the traditionally masculinist Australian culture and literary world. In Elizabeth Jolley's novels, her women protagonists undermine domestic myths that constrain women in their "place" at home, and they pursue new modes of self-construction within the domestic setting, as well as new ways of structuring female friendships and communities.

The question of location as a political reality in the definition of home reminds us all that where we are, or where we come from, places us within a power structure. This fact was brought home to us in the organization of this book, when Ama Ata Aidoo, the Ghanaian writer, included a manifesto of sorts with her poem, "Spices." This political statement is a companion piece to her poetic expression of the links between geography and identity in the different worlds to which she belongs. She has too frequently been exiled in the pages of poetry collections, included but ghettoized because of her race, ethnicity, gender, or politics. Such are the politics of publishing—and of the world. Velina Hasu Houston's personal essay illustrates one literal element of this problem, as she describes the difficulty in placing oneself when one's background, and thus physical features, are multi-ethnic.

Artificial barriers between women are many-faced. One of the ways in which we have attempted to break down boundaries between women's writings is to interweave critical and creative pieces in order to set them in dialogue; unfortunately, in our culture, critical and creative faculties are frequently polarized, a move that damages both sides. As editors, we have worked to make a home for many different women writers and writing styles; we are particularly delighted that we have two collaborative papers that, like our joint editorship of this volume, underscore the possibility for intellectual coalitions of women. This book, then, contains our "imagined community" of women writers seeking a home.

Ultimately, as all of these essays and poems make clear, writing is a form of self-discovery, in which the writer can (con)textualize herself, write herself into being, and locate herself on the page. Writing is a physical embodiment of our interventions in society; writing can ground us, and chart a way home that we might not otherwise be aware of. We have framed the contents of this volume with two poems, "Perhaps the World Ends Here" by Joy Harjo and "How We Did It" by Alison Hawthorne Deming. Harjo writes of the kitchen table as the heart of a home, simultaneously metaphor and metonym as it stands for and contains the real and the abstract home. The kitchen table can center women as writers by reminding us that a work space for domestic and intellectual work can be one and the same. Deming writes of her daughter's journey out of childhood, of the improvisations necessary in "Our ramshackle, / wind welcoming house," (384) improvisations women writers invent every day. Out of such contingencies and what are often makeshift homes, women create literary havens for upcoming generations of writers. Margaret Atwood's analysis of the cartographic and historical role of literature in shaping national identity also applies to the reconstructive aspect of women's literary culture:

> What a lost person needs is a map of the territory, with his [sic] own position marked on it so he can see where he is in relation to everything else. Literature is not only a mirror; it is also a map, a geography of the mind. Our literature is one such map, if we can learn to read it as *our* literature, as the product of who we are and where we have been. We need such a map desperately, we need to know about here, because here is where we live. For the members of a country or a culture, shared knowledge of their place, their here, is not a luxury but a necessity. Without that knowledge we will not survive. (18-19)

In the ever-changing tradition of women's writing, this collection seeks to sketch a cartographic picture of our literature, situating home, in all its possibilities, as the true north of the map.

Catherine Wiley
Fiona R. Barnes

WORKS CITED

Atwood, Margaret. *Survival: A Thematic Guide to Canadian Literature.* Toronto: Anansi, 1972.

Blankenhorn, David. *Fatherless America: Why Men Are Increasingly Viewed as Superfluous to Family Life.* New York: Harpercollins, 1995.

Breytenbach, Breyten. "The Long March from Hearth to Heart." Ed. Arien Mack. *Home: A Place in the World.* New York and London: New York UP, 1993. 65-79.

Dickinson, Emily. *The Complete Poems.* Ed. Thomas H. Johnson. Boston: Little, Brown, 1960. 652-53.

Friedan, Betty. *The Feminine Mystique.* New York: W.W. Norton, 1963.

Gurr, Andrew. *Writers in Exile: the Identity of Home in Modern Literature.* Brighton, Sussex: Harvester Press, 1981.

Lorde, Audre. "School Note." *The Black Unicorn.* New York: W.W. Norton, 1978. 55.

Marcus, Jane. "Alibis and Legends: The Ethics of Elsewhereness, Gender, and Estrangement." Eds. Mary Lynn Broe and Angela Ingram. *Women's Writing in Exile.* Chapel Hill: U of North Carolina P, 1989.

Mohanty, Chandra Talpade. "Feminist Encounters: Locating the Politics of Experience." eds. Michèle Barrett and Anne Phillips. *Destabilizing Theory: Contemporary Feminist Debates.* Stanford: Stanford UP, 1992. 74-92.

Mohanty, Chandra Talpade, and Biddy Martin. "Feminist Politics: What's Home Got to Do with It?" Ed. Teresa de Lauretis. *Feminist Studies / Critical Studies.* Bloomington: Indiana UP, 1986. 191-212.

Pratt, Minnie Bruce. "Identity: Skin Blood Heart." Eds. Elly Bulkin,

Minnie Bruce Pratt and Barbara Smith. *Yours in Struggle.* Brooklyn: Long Haul Press, 1984. 9-64.

Reagon, Bernice Johnson. "Coalition Politics: Turning the Century." Ed. Barbara Smith. *Homegirls: A Black Feminist Anthology.* New York: Kitchen Table, 1983. 356-69.

Rich, Adrienne. "Notes Towards a Politics of Location." *Blood, Bread, and Poetry.* New York: Norton, 1986. 210-32.

Robinson, Marilynne. *Housekeeping.* New York: Doubleday, 1980.

Romines, Ann. *The Homeplot: Women, Writing and Domestic Ritual.* Amherst, U of Massachusetts P, 1992.

Stein, Gertrude. *Paris, France.* London: B.T. Batsford, Ltd., 1940.

Zandy, Janet, ed. *Calling Home: Working Class Women's Writings.* New Brunswick, NJ: Rutgers UP, 1990.

Homemaking

1

Perhaps the World Ends Here

Joy Harjo

The world begins at a kitchen table. No matter what we must eat to live.

The gifts of earth are brought and prepared, set on the table. So it has been since creation, and it will go on.

We chase chickens or dogs away from it. Babies teethe at the corners. They scrape their knees under it.

It is here that children are given instructions on what it means to be human. We make men at it, we make women.

At this table we gossip, recall enemies and the ghosts of lovers.

Our dreams drink coffee with us as they put their arms around our children. They laugh with us at our poor falling down selves and as we put ourselves back together once again at the table.

This table has been a house in the rain, an umbrella in the sun.

Wars have begun and ended at this table. It is a place to hide in the shadow of terror. A place to celebrate the terrible victory.

We have given birth on this table, and have prepared our parents for burial here.

At this table we sing with joy, with sorrow. We pray of suffering and remorse. We give thanks.

Perhaps the world will end at the kitchen table, while we are laughing and crying, eating of the last sweet bite.

*Home*ric Resonances: Longing and Belonging in Barbara Kingsolver's *Animal Dreams*

Roberta Rubenstein

Home is the place where, when you have to go there,
They have to take you in.
Robert Frost, "The Death of the Hired Man"
(*Animal Dreams* 182)

You can't know somebody. . . till you've followed him home.
(*Animal Dreams* 231)

Get to a good place, turn around three times in the grass, and
you're home. Once you know how, you can always do that, no
matter what. (*Animal Dreams* 235)

Of the many resonances with "home" that structure Barbara
Kingsolver's *Animal Dreams*, surely the first and most powerful cue is
the allusive presence of Homer, whose story of quest and return is
embedded in his epic. The first point of view introduced in the novel is
that of Doc Homer, Cosima Noline's father and the man who, through
misguided pride rather than malice, has disguised and misrepresented
the identity of home for Codi since her earliest childhood. Doc Homer's
voice alternates with Codi's throughout the narrative, providing a double
perspective for the several intertwined narrative motifs. Moreover,
Kingsolver elaborates on her Homeric intentions early in the novel.
Codi and her younger sister Hallie represent not only complementary
embodiments of the quest but complementary dimensions of the
Odyssean universe: Cosima (Codi's full Spanish name) signifies "order
in the cosmos" while Halimeda (Hallie's full name) means "thinking of
the sea" (13).

Kingsolver structures *Animal Dreams* through three overlapping
narrative dimensions, each of which depends on the pattern of the quest
and / or the return home. The most fundamental is the emotional and
psychological cluster that concerns the central attachments and losses

in Codi's own family history and that represent her belated but ultimate recovery of her own lost self in the aptly named town of Grace, Arizona. Codi's mother died when she was three years old and her sister Hallie was only an infant. Although Codi has vague memories of her mother as a "strong and ferociously loving" figure (49), she remains "an outsider to . . . nurturing" (46), not even certain whether she witnessed or only imagined the helicopter that conveyed her mother—who died "before [it] could lift itself out of the alfalfa" (49).

Codi's widowed father has been nearly as absent to her from childhood. Although Homer Noline is the community's respected doctor, he is unable to heal his own family. Numbed by grief over the loss of his wife, he has remained in a state of perpetual mourning, raising his two daughters in a clinical, detached manner based more on the correct orthopedic shoes than on the expression of affection. His perception of his daughters as young children, expressed in the first section of the novel, underscores the way his own losses have continued to delimit the world for Codi (though not for Hallie). Recalling the two girls sleeping inseparably together like small animals huddling for warmth, Homer conflates their past and future lives, reflecting "how close together these two are, and how much they have to lose. How much they've already lost in their lives to come" (4).

Thus emotionally unparented from an early age, as children Codi and her sister had played a game they called "orphans," in which they fantasized about who in an anonymous crowd of people might be "our true father and mother[.] Which is the one grownup here that loves us?" (72). Codi's history of separation and loss continued into adolescence, when she grew to become nearly six feet tall; her acute self-consciousness about her height still makes her feel "out of place" (228). When she was fifteen, she became pregnant—by a Native American boyfriend who never knew of her pregnancy—only to lose the child during the sixth month. Her father, aware of both her pregnancy and the stillbirth, had even witnessed Codi's burial of the fetus in a dry river bed without ever revealing that knowledge or comforting her in her loss. Although at one point he recalls an imagined conversation with her—"do you know what you have inside you?" (98)—he had voiced neither those words nor any other acknowledgement of her condition.

Shaped by these fundamental losses of mother and of child, Codi regards herself as "bracketed by death" (50). In fact, her surname, "no-line," literally encodes her separation from generational continuity, one that is compounded by her erroneous belief (because of her father's creation of a false history) that her parents came from Illinois and therefore that Grace is not her true "home." Although she does not name her condition—the prolonged depression of unresolved grief—most of the early images of the narrative figure her emotional deadness: bones and skeletons, graves and graveyards. The actual skeleton that Codi finds in a storage room in the high school where she teaches biology signifies the emotional skeletons in the closet that she must discover as prelude to the reclamation of her past and her discovery of her way back home.

Poignantly and ironically, what brings Codi back to the "memory mine field" (46) of her home town is her father's accelerating memory loss. Each of the sections of the narrative told from his perspective demonstrates the dissolution of a sense of time, so that events from the past become indistinguishable from current events. Because he holds many of the secrets to his family's history, his mental erosion and confusion make Codi's quest more urgent and difficult. Codi, less adventuresome and less optimistic than her politically idealistic sister, suffers from a sense of estrangement. "I *was* a stranger to Grace. I'd stayed away fourteen years and in my gut I believe I was hoping that had changed: I would step off the bus and land smack in the middle of a sense of belonging . . . home at last" (12). Instead, she continues to feel "dislocated" (47); having "spent my whole childhood as an outsider . . . I'd sell my soul and all my traveling shoes to *belong* some place" (30, emphasis in original).

Like Codi's inner being, the land around Grace is at risk; a major stage in her eventual discovery of her true place as an "insider" in Grace is her political awakening to that fact. The people in the community talk about "poison ground" and orchard trees that are dying of "fruit drop" (63); concurrently, Codi ponders the mystery of her own "family tree" (173). Through her temporary job as a high school biology teacher, she accidentally discovers that the river water and the land are literally "dead" as the result of unchecked chemical pollution from a nearby mining operation.

Galvanizing the women of Grace to rally against the mining company by opposing the dam that would divert their river and perpetuate the pollution of their land, Codi also initiates her own inner restoration. When she explains to the women of the "Stitch and Bitch Club" that the river can be restored, "you'd think I'd commuted a death sentence" (178). One woman affirms the necessity of action, arguing that their menfolk won't see the struggle to reclaim their land in the same terms as the women do. "'They think the trees can die and we can just go somewhere else, and as long as we fry up the bacon for them in the same old pan, they think it would be . . . *home*.'" (179). Private and public history—the personal and the collective meanings of "home"—converge in the struggle to rescue the contaminated land and water. As Codi pursues her own past, attempting to tap her father's memories even as they recede from coherence, Kingsolver suggests that the land also remembers. Codi explains to her high school students, "'People can forget, and forget, and forget, but the land has a memory. The lakes and the rivers are still hanging on to the DDT and every other insult we ever gave them'" (255).

These two clusters of ideas—the intertwined explorations of personal and collective memory as each bears on the idea of "home"— in turn suggest the most mythically resonant dimension of *Animal Dreams*. The parallels between Doc Homer's and Codi's inner dis-ease and the disease of the land strongly intimate the symbolic motif of the wasteland, drawing loosely upon both T.S. Eliot's complex poem and its antecedent, the legend of the Fisher King whose sterility parallels the land's inability to flourish.[1] The cycle of death and fertility also appears in traditional and contemporary Native American narratives, most visibly in Leslie Marmon Silko's 1977 novel, *Ceremony*.[2] Although in Kingsolver's contemporary rendering of the story Doc Homer is not literally a king, he functions symbolically in the narrative as the ailing Fisher King, incapacitated by old age and accelerating memory loss. As Codi has understood her family's isolation from the community he serves, "everyone in Grace was somehow related except us Nolines, the fish out of water" (71). A figure of authority in the town, Doc Homer presides over life and death as both doctor and coroner. Moreover, he acknowledges his spiritual malaise. When, midway through the narrative, Codi confronts him with her discovery in the town graveyard—a gravestone that provides a central clue to her family's buried history—Doc Homer responds, "'Perhaps I am dead'" (169).

What gives Kingsolver's narrative its originality is the fresh embodiment of the wasteland legend through the creation of a female rather than a male quester, one who is also heir to the "king's" malaise. Codi Noline mirrors her father's emotional sterility, a condition compounded by the traumatic events of her own childhood and adolescence as well as her experience as an "outsider," painfully estranged from the community in which she grew up. Before she returns to Grace, "anaesthetized" by pain (89), she had maintained a sterile relationship with an emergency room surgeon named Carlo—"a man who reattached severed parts for a living" (38)[3]—ostensibly seeking but actually fearing genuine emotional attachment. Her only true attachment is to her sister, whom she idolizes, comparing herself unfavorably to Hallie at every opportunity. As she phrases it in one of many efforts to articulate the difference between herself and her sister,

> With tears in my eyes I watched whatever lay to the south of us, the land we were driving down into, but I have no memory of it. I was getting a dim comprehension of the difference between Hallie and me. It wasn't a matter of courage or dreams, but something a whole lot simpler. A pilot would call it ground orientation. I'd spent a long time circling above the clouds, looking for life, while Hallie was living it. (225)

Codi's own inner torpor is thus figured not only in the sterility of the land around Grace but in her sense of radical disconnection from it—her lack of "ground orientation."

In some versions of the wasteland legend, there is a third figure besides the injured king and the quester whose task is to aid in his recovery: a healer.[4] However, Codi needs healing as much as her father does; in Kingsolver's reworking of the legend under the influence of both classical Western and Native American mythologies, it is the quester herself, not the king, who is ultimately healed. Ironically, Codi, the daughter of a doctor, studied to become one herself until, during her residency in obstetrics-gynecology, she suffered a failure of nerve during a complex delivery and withdrew from further medical training. But neither Codi nor her father is a true healer. As Codi admits, her motives for studying medicine were less than altruistic; "I did it to win love, and to prove myself capable" (36). Rather, the role of healer falls to Loyd Peregrina, the Native American man who unknowingly impregnated Codi years before.

Loyd is in many ways Codi's antithesis. Although he too has suffered emotional losses of those close to him—his twin brother Leander, who died at about the same age that Codi lost her baby, and a wife who ran out on him—Loyd is sustained by his strong family attachments and his Native spiritual tradition. Deeply connected both to people and to the land, he has access to the deeper meanings of "home" and an understanding of the true order of the cosmos that Codi (despite her name) only slowly acquires through his nurturing affection for her. Loyd's name suggests his "alloyed" state: he is, like his endearing coyote-dog Jack (and like the mixed-race Tayo in Silko's *Ceremony*), of mixed blood: Pueblo, Navajo, and Apache. The different tribal legacies embody complementary orientations in the world, roughly—as Loyd characterizes them—"homebodies" and "wanderers" (213); he identifies himself not as an Apache, or wanderer (as Codi had assumed during their brief adolescent relationship) but as a Pueblo, or homebody. His role in the narrative as Codi's spiritual guide is encoded in his surname: *"peregrina,"* the Spanish word for "pilgrim."

Codi, at this point still believing that her family originated far from Arizona, concludes that she is a member of the "Nothing Tribe" (213);[5] elsewhere she is humorously characterized by her friend Emelina as the opposite of a homemaker, a "home ignorer" (77). Becoming more fully acquainted with Loyd only after she visits his extended family of nurturing mothers and aunts in the Santa Rosalia Pueblo, Codi discovers that "You can't know somebody . . . till you've followed him home" (231). In this context, Paula Gunn Allen has observed that among the Keres [Laguna] people,

> Failure to know your mother, that is, your position and its attendant traditions, history, and place in the scheme of things, is failure to remember your significance, your reality, your right relationship to earth and society. It is the same as being lost—isolated, abandoned, self-estranged, and alienated from your own life. (210-11)

Against Codi's defensive ethic of individual loss—"nothing you love will stay" (233)—Loyd Peregrina's healing teaching and concern for her enable Codi to discover her capacity for intimacy and a more encompassing meaning of home, where nothing is ever lost.

Kingsolver's creation of the sympathetic and "grounded" character of Loyd suggests her assimilation of a Native American conception of home, not as a regressive place but as a space in which one is linked to a larger community. In a number of novels by Native American authors, "coming home, staying put, contracting, even what we call 'regressing' to a place, a past where one has been before, is not only the primary story, it is a primary mode of knowledge and a primary good" (Bevis 582). Bevis adds that "'identity,' for a Native American, is not a matter of finding 'one's self,' but of finding a 'self' that is transpersonal and includes a society, a past, and a place. To be separated from that transpersonal time and space is to lose identity" (585).

The three assumptions of tribalism—"the individual is completed only in relation to others," "respect for the past," and "place"

(Bevis 587-8)—are all emphasized in Kingsolver's narrative: the white female protagonist, under the spiritual guidance of her Native lover, ultimately recovers the meaning of her past and discovers her place in the community. Repeatedly in *Animal Dreams*, affirmative Native American images and attitudes are placed in contrast with Codi's or her father's ambivalent or negative attitudes towards themselves; these distinctions further demonstrate Kingsolver's effective blend of Western and Native American mythologies. For example, in Homer's *Odyssey*, the weaver Penelope embodies the principles of loyalty and patience; in traditional stories common to both Pueblo and Navajo traditions, the weaver Spider Woman is celebrated as the creative principle itself. By contrast, in one of Codi's father's disjointed reveries, Doc Homer views himself as a destructive weaver; "his family is a web of women dead and alive, with himself at the center like a spider, driven by different instincts" (98).

As Codi's guide to the more positively interrelated web of the Pueblo universe, Loyd takes her to a secret location in the desert where ruins of ancient pueblo dwellings illustrate the connection between physical and spiritual spaces. When Codi asks him, "'Is there anything you know of that you'd die for?'" Loyd responds, "'The land'" (122). According to Paula Gunn Allen (herself of mixed—Laguna Pueblo and white—blood), the link with the land is

> the fundamental idea that permeates American Indian life; the land (Mother) and the people (mothers) are the same. . . . The land is not really a place, separate from ourselves, where we act out the drama of our isolate destinies. . . . Rather, for American Indians . . . the earth *is* being, as all creatures are also being: aware, palpable, intelligent, alive. (119)[6]

Significantly, Codi and her sister Hallie find themselves engaged in parallel political causes on behalf of the land: helping to save or rescue it from chemical pollution. Hallie, committed to changing the world, has gone to Central America to work with Nicaraguans to protect their land from American toxic agricultural chemicals. Although she never appears directly in the narrative, her voice enters it through her upbeat letters to Codi from Nicaragua. Several details in her epistolary communications explicitly mirror events in Codi's experience. For example, while Codi idealizes Hallie's mission as "saving people's lives" (121), she literally saves a life herself, rescuing her friend Emelina's baby from choking.

Not long after the conversation between Codi and Loyd at the pueblo ruins of Kinishba, they move toward sexual intimacy, as Codi acknowledges—in language that adumbrates the wasteland motif—"just being held felt unbelievably good, the long drink I'd been dying for" (130). Following their first lovemaking, Codi feels as if her body has been "renewed. I felt like a patch of dry ground that had been rained on" (130). Later, Loyd explains to her his conception of the relationship between being *home* and being *lost*: the spiritual location of oneself in the cosmos. As he expresses it,

> 'The greatest honor you can give a house is to let it fall back down into the ground. . . . That's where everything comes from in the first place.'
> I looked at him, surprised. 'But then you've lost your house.'
> 'Not if you know how to build another one. . . . The important thing isn't the house. It's the ability to make it. You carry that in your brain and in your hands, wherever you go.' (235)

Loyd stresses that, in contrast with Anglos, many of whom insist on taking their homes with them in the form of mobile trailers, Native Americans are like coyotes: "'get to a good place, turn around three times in the grass, and you're home. Once you know how, you can always do that, no matter what'" (235). He adds, "'It's one thing to carry your life wherever you go. Another thing to always go looking for it somewhere else'" (236). Codi, initially resisting Loyd's wisdom along with the vulnerability his affection for her exposes, admits to herself, "I wasn't keeping to any road, I was running, forgetting what lay behind and always looking ahead for the perfect home . . . where no one you loved ever died" (236).

Other images in *Animal Dreams* extend the correspondences between the quest for home and the wasteland motif while bridging the several dimensions of the narrative I have suggested: psychological or emotional, political, and mythic dimensions. Of these, the most prominent is that of vision / blindness. There are figurative eyes everywhere in *Animal Dreams*. According to local legend, the residents of Codi's community descended from the Gracelas, nine sisters who came from Spain to Arizona in the nineteenth century to marry miners; they brought with them a population of peacocks, the descendants of which roam wild in the orchards of Grace. Fittingly, in the collective effort to oppose the mining company dam that would divert the river away from their town, the female descendants of the Gracelas also are linked with the wild birds: they make and sell *papier mâché* peacock *piñatas* that incorporate the "eye" feathers from actual peacocks. Supporting the motif of spiritual quest that structures *Animal Dreams*, peacocks are associated with wholeness, immortality, and the soul (Cirlot 251).

The narrative counterpoint to eyes and vision is blindness. Recalling the Teiresias figure of Greek mythology who also appears in Eliot's *The Waste Land*, and perhaps also the Cyclops whom Odysseus blinds in the *Odyssey*, Codi suffers, if not actual blindness, a deeply-imbedded fear of it. Pertinently, she regards her sister Hallie, whose clear moral vision she envies, as "more precious than an eye" (46). Jesting to a colleague, she describes her teaching method as "'the blind leading the blind . . .'" (153). In a recurrent nightmare, she experiences "a paralyzing freeze frame: there's a shattering pop, like glass breaking, and then I am blind" (74). Later, she speculates that the dream is not simply about losing her vision but, even more terrifying, about losing herself, "whatever that was. What you lose in blindness is the space around you, the place where you are, and without that you might not exist. You could be nowhere at all" (204). Through this correspondence between loss of vision and loss of self, Kingsolver articulates a central connection between Codi's literal and spiritual placelessness: without a home, understood as an emotional and spiritual center, she can neither locate nor secure her place in the cosmos.

Only near the very end of the narrative, after Codi has progressed in her healing journey and has suffered the terrible loss of her sister, does she identify in her father's deceptive revision of the family's history the source of her nightmare of losing vision. Doc Homer's lifelong hobby of photography characterizes his scientific and yet counterfeit approach to life as he endeavors to "photograph the past" (138). Like his own contrived self-image, his carefully constructed photographic images are composed to resemble something other than the actual objects being recorded on film. Years earlier, he had used his camera in a self-initiated research project in which he documented the local genetic pool: as a result of generations of inbreeding, virtually every child born in Grace comes into the world with "whitish, marblelike" eyes that only later turn pale blue (42). The allusion to the "sea-change" of *The Waste Land*—in turn an echo of Ariel's song in Shakespeare's *The Tempest* ("Those are pearls that were his eyes" [I, ii, 401]) suggests the transformative processes that unify Kingsolver's narrative.

To document his findings, Homer Noline photographed each

newborn's eyes shortly after birth. Ultimately, Codi discovers her father's photographs of herself and Hallie as newborn infants and determines through these visual documents that, in contradiction to Doc Homer's falsified history of the family's Illinois roots, both of her parents were direct descendants of the Gracelas—in fact, second cousins who married each other, to their families' regret.

> I held the two photographs up to the light, mystified. The eyes were unearthly. We were two babies not of this world. Just like every other one in the stack of photos; two more babies of Grace. He was doing exactly the opposite of setting himself apart. He was proving we belonged here; we were as pure as anybody in Grace. Both sides. *Our mother's name was Althea. Her family despised him.* (284, emphasis in original)

When Codi's longstanding conviction of being an "outsider" gives way to the certain knowledge that she indeed belongs "inside" the community from which she has felt herself estranged, the old nightmare recurs as an illumination that literally blinds her: she "heard the broken-glass pop of the flash and went blind" (284). Her temporary blindness gives way to a deeper vision, in which she affirms her place in the interconnected web of life and generativity.

Indeed, the cycle of renewal in both organic and spiritual senses that underlies the wasteland legend is reiterated in *Animal Dreams* through the frequent juxtaposition of icons of life and death: blossoms and bones.[7] Images of orchards and flowering fruit trees, skeletons and graveyards, recur throughout the narrative, recalling that the wasteland legend (according to Weston) is rooted in fertility rituals. The Gracelas sisters, whose progeny populates the town of Grace, also allude to the three Graces of Greek mythology: the sisters Aglaia (brightness), Euphrosyne (joy), and Thalia (bloom) were fertility goddesses. Moreover, numerous folklore beliefs specifically equate death and burial rituals with fertility. According to Weston, "This view [may be] at the root of the annual celebrations in honour of the Departed, the 'feast of souls,' which characterized the commencement of the winter season, and is retained in the Catholic conception of November as the month of the Dead" (Weston 85).

In *Animal Dreams*, three specific references to or celebrations of the "month of the Dead"—All Souls' Day—occur at the beginning, middle, and end of the narrative, marking successive stages in Codi Noline's spiritual renewal and her journey home. The first appears as

the novel's opening sequence, "The Night of All Souls" (3-4), in which
Doc Homer's recollections of his young daughters are interwoven with
multiple images of graves, skeletons, corpses, and death. During the
second All Souls' Day, Codi accompanies several women of the
community and their families to the town cemetery. There, she
remembers that years earlier her father had prohibited her and Hallie
from participating in the annual celebration, remarking, "'Those great-
grandmothers aren't any of your business'" (16). Of course, the exact
opposite is true, as the identity of her relatives becomes Codi's urgent
business.

When she stumbles on the neglected gravestone of one Homero
Nolina, she begins to suspect her father's true connection to Grace. Her
puzzlement about the "no-line" of her family history—her sense of
exclusion from the hereditary line connecting generations both before
and after her—accentuates her acute longing for belonging:

> More than anything else I wished I belonged to one of these
> living, celebrated families, lush as plants, with bones in the
> ground for roots. I wanted pollen on my cheeks and one of the
> calcium ancestors to decorate as my own. (165)

Yet, through her discovery of her ancestors' Spanish surname, Codi
ultimately recovers her connection to her legitimate "family tree," as
Kingsolver further unfolds the narrative's imagery of fertility and
vegetation: the *nolina* plant is a desert species related to the yucca plant.
Producing a flower spike as large as a Christmas tree, it is capable—if
moisture is insufficient—of surviving for years between flowerings.[8] As
Codi slowly evolves from "*noline*" to "*nolina*," Kingsolver fittingly
signifies her potential for blossoming after an extended period of
dormancy.

One further important representation of the associations
between burial, fertility, and renewal concerns the death and interment
of Hallie. Earlier, Codi has characterized Hallie as "the blossom of our
family, like one of those miraculous fruit trees that taps into an invisible
vein of nurture and bears radiant bushels of plums while the trees
around it merely go on living . . . the *semilla besada*—the seed that got
kissed" (49). Inevitably, Hallie dies during the narrative, a victim of
kidnapping and terrorism in Nicaragua. Profoundly grieved by Hallie's
death, Codi regards herself not only as "a skeleton with flesh and
clothes and thoughts" (302) but also as "a hard seed beyond
germination" (307). Yet, symbolically, Hallie's death allows Codi to

assimilate the denied dimensions of herself—caring, passion, and vulnerability—that her sister embodied. As she articulates that psychological truth at the ceremonial funeral for Hallie, "Everything we'd been I was now" (328).

However, between the news of Hallie's death and her burial, Codi experiences a temporary failure of nerve stemming from fear of her growing attachment to Loyd. While airborne on her way to Denver in ambivalent escape, she discovers a decisive sign in the airplane's obligatory return to the ground for mechanical reasons. Her new perspective vividly corroborates the "sea change," as well as the evolution toward a Native American awareness, that has occurred in her. From the air, Codi initially observes the "bone-dry" (320) paths that mark the empty creeks. Then, in an image that suggests a baptism in vitality, she observes the

> watercolor wash of summer light [that] lay on the Catalina Mountains. The end of a depression is . . . as if you have been living underwater, but never realized it until you came up for air. I hadn't seen color since I lost Hallie. . . . Just past the railyard was a school where a double row of corn-colored school buses were parked in a ring, exactly like one of those cheap Indian necklaces made for tourists. Bright backyard swimming pools gleamed like turquoise nuggets. The land stretched out under me the way a lover would, hiding nothing, offering up every endearing southwestern cliché, and I wanted to get down there and kiss the dirt.
>
> I made a bargain with my mother. If I got to the ground in one piece, I wasn't leaving it again. (321)

At last recognizing her true home in her deeper connection to the land and its association with her own mother,[9] Codi returns to Loyd by train, suggestively "approach[ing] Grace from a direction that was new to [her]" (322). Just before she reveals her presence to him, she acknowledges her altered understanding of the relation between inside and outside: "I was on the outside, in a different dimension. I'd lived there always" (323).

Having begun to accept that she cannot participate fully in life without accepting the reality of loss and death, Codi makes Hallie's memorial service in Grace an occasion for celebration of her life rather than a somber rite emphasizing its cessation. By Hallie's own prior request, the body remains behind in Nicaragua, underscoring the fertility motif that unifies the narrative: "'she said Nicaragua could use the fertilizer'" (303). The ceremony takes place in early summer, in an orchard where peacocks eye people curiously from the trees and where "every tree . . . looked blessed" (324), signifying the restoration of fruitfulness that mirrors Codi's inner renewal as well as her recovery of a legitimate location on her own *Nolina* "family tree." Through her awakened capacity for love and her reunion with her community and its land, Codi herself becomes a *semilla besada*. Her sister's philosophy—"It's what you *do* that makes your soul, not the other way around" (334)—ultimately describes the growth of moral understanding that occurs in Codi.

Prompted by the memorial ceremony for her sister, Codi endeavors to lay to rest—and to reconnect with—the spirits of others she has lost. The enactment of the ritual reburial of her lost child, described both through Codi's intense emotion and Doc Homer's confused overlapping of past and present events, accomplishes the effect of occurring in a timeless present. Moreover, the equation between buried bodies and fertility links not only the wasteland motif but Eliot's poem in particular with Kingsolver's narrative. The lines from *The Waste Land*, "That corpse you planted last year in your garden / Has it begun to sprout? Will it bloom this year?" (ll. 71-72) reverberate in Codi's unknowing participation in precisely this cycle of death and renewal when, at fifteen, she buried the corpse of her stillborn child in a dry riverbed. Retracing those steps nearly twenty years later, she achieves reunion with the land and with her own inner being—that prematurely buried part of herself that might be characterized psychologically as her lost inner child—and ultimately begins to blossom.

A frequent motif in myths of quest and return (although one not explicitly present in the wasteland legend) is the quester's reconciliation with his or her parents; *Animal Dreams* concludes with these culminating reconciliations. The final celebration of All Souls' Day that concludes the novel extends these central correspondences between death and renewed life, quest and arrival home. Near the end of Eliot's *The Waste Land*, the Fisher King, with "the arid plain behind" him, wonders, "Shall I at least set my lands in order?" (ll. 425-426). Homer Noline, now deceased, has joined his Nolina ancestors in the cemetery where "the spirits of all those old bones [are] being tended by their children" (339). His daughter Codi rejoices that, on Homer Noline / Homero Nolina's behalf and in fulfillment of the auspicious name he gave her at birth, she'd "brought some order to his cosmos finally" (340).

More profoundly, the sense of motherlessness that has fueled Codi's protracted longing to belong is ameliorated through her discovery of a true community, "fifty mothers who'd been standing at the edges of my childhood, ready to make whatever contribution was needed at the time" (328). Through the nurturing support of many women—including her friend Emelina, who, when Codi first returned to Grace, offered her a place to live, and who provides a model of flourishing family life—Codi achieves the emotional wholeness to accept that "all griefs are bearable" (327).

On the final Day of All Souls that concludes the narrative, Codi visits the actual location from which her mother departed years before and realizes that she indeed had actually witnessed, rather than only imagined, the helicopter that rose with her mother's body. As Viola (another of her "fifty mothers") advises her, "'if you remember something, then it's true'" (342). Reborn at the symbolic age of thirty-three and pregnant with another child of her union with Loyd, Codi has relinquished her preoccupation with loss and death and begun to invest herself in the creation and fruition of life, turning her attention from past generations to future generativity. Fittingly, she surrenders her impacted grief at her mother's absence from her life: she recovers the memory of the helicopter carrying her mother at the moment of her death, "ris[ing] like a soul" (342). Having found her place within the community—and also within the state—of Grace, she affirms her "ground orientation" (225) and embraces, at last, her true home.

NOTES

1.   Eliot acknowledged his significant indebtedness to Jessie Weston's now-classic study of the Grail Legend, *From Ritual to Romance*, and to James Frazer's *The Golden Bough*. Weston posited the central elements of the Waste Land story: "a close connection between the vitality of a certain King, and the prosperity of his kingdom; the forces of the ruler being weakened or destroyed, by wound, sickness, old age, or death, the land becomes Waste, and the task of the hero is that of restoration" (23). Later she clarifies the sources of these legends in ancient rituals of fertility: "in the earliest, and least contaminated, version of the Grail story the central figure

would be dead, and the task of the Quester that of restoring him to life. . ." (120).

2.   In *Ceremony*, a young man of mixed Laguna (Pueblo) and white blood returns to his New Mexican pueblo after World War II and struggles with his profound feelings of loss and alienation, believing that he is somehow personally responsible for the multi-year drought in his area. Through various healing ceremonies of fertility and renewal, he is ultimately reconnected to the land and to himself. See "Boundaries of the Cosmos," in Rubenstein, *Boundaries of the Self: Gender, Culture, Fiction*, 190-202.

   At least one other Native American author, James Welch, incorporates the wasteland motif in his novel, *Winter in the Blood* (1974). See Kenneth Lincoln's analysis of wasteland parallels in Welch's narrative in *Native American Renaissance*, 153, 155, 162. Several other narratives by Native American authors represent an ailing protagonist whose cure comes as he recovers his tribal identity. See William Bevis, "Native American Novels: Homing In" (580-616).

3.   Carlo's vocation may be an ironic allusion to ancient fertility myths: the dismemberment and recovery of the "severed parts" of Adonis / Osiris were associated with rituals of renewal and fertility. See Frazer, 365-6, 378-9.

4.   ". . . the Doctor, or Medicine Man, did, from the very earliest ages, play an important part in Dramatic Fertility Ritual . . . that of restoring to life and health the dead, or wounded, representative of the Spirit of Vegetation" (Weston 109). In Silko's *Ceremony*, there are several healers, including the Medicine Man Betonie and the spirit woman, Ts'eh, through whose intervention Tayo re-connects with his Laguna tradition, participates in ceremonies of purification and renewal, and recovers from his inner deadness.

5.   The language echoes another Homeric event: Odysseus outwitted the Cyclops by identifying himself as "Nobody."

6.   Elsewhere Allen elaborates that, traditionally, Native American people believe that "all are linked within one vast, living sphere, that the linkage is not material but spiritual, and that its essence is the power that enables magical things to happen. Among these magical things are transformation of objects from one form to another, the movement of objects from one place to another by teleportation, the curing of the sick (and conversely creating sickness in people, animals, or plants), communication with animals, plants, and nonphysical beings (spirits, katsinas, goddesses, and gods), the compelling of the will of another, and the stealing or storing of souls" (22-3).

7.   The connection between organic and spiritual dimensions of growth is deeply imbedded in Kingsolver's own biography. A biologist by academic training, she has commented in an interview, "I think biology is my religion. Understanding the processes of the natural world and how all living things are related is the way that I answer those questions that are the basis of religion." She adds, "I think the Christian creation myth, which says the world was put here as a little garden for us to use, goes a long way in explaining how we've really devastated that garden. We feel this entitlement. We have about used up what there is to use, and yet we continue looking at nature in terms of what we can exploit—the idea that this mountain is put here for me to mine and get pumice out of so I can make stone-washed jeans. Feeling that morality has nothing to do with the way you use the resources of the world is an idea that can't persist much longer. If it does, then we won't" (*Backtalk* 147).

8.   According to Diana Kappel-Smith, "Nolinas are relatives of yucca. Their flower spike when fully unfolded in bloom is a fragrant, insect-infested affair the size of a family Christmas tree. These are not minor events, and they are not common. One ranger [in Joshua Tree National Monument, California] has a nolina in his yard that hasn't bloomed for 17 years." As a result of unusually plentiful rains during two previous winters, it produced three flower stalks in the same season (86).

9.   In Silko's *Ceremony*, the orphan Tayo also heals his inner split as he understands the association between the land and his own mother. See Silko 267 and Rubenstein 202.

WORKS CITED

Allen, Paula Gunn. *The Sacred Hoop: Recovering the Feminine in American Indian Traditions*. Boston: Beacon Press, 1986.

Bevis, William. "Native American Novels: Homing In." *Recovering the Word: Essays on Native American Literature*, Eds. Brian Swann and Arnold Krupat. Berkeley: U of California P, 1987. 580-616.

Cirlot, J.E. *A Dictionary of Symbols*. 2nd Ed. Trans. Jack Sage. New York: Philosophical Library, 1971.

Eliot, T.S. *Collected Poems, 1909-1962*. London: Faber and Faber, 1963.

Kappel-Smith, Diana. "Fickle desert blooms: opulent one year, no-shows the next." *Smithsonian* 25 (March 1995): 79-91.

Kingsolver, Barbara. *Animal Dreams*. New York: HarperCollins [1990], 1991.

Lincoln, Kenneth. *Native American Renaissance*. Berkeley: U of California P, 1983.

Perry, Donna. Interview with Barbara Kingsolver. *Backtalk: Women Writers Speak Out*. New Brunswick, NJ: Rutgers UP,1993. 143-69.

Rubenstein, Roberta. *Boundaries of the Self: Gender, Culture, Fiction*. Urbana: U of Illinois P, 1987.

Silko, Leslie Marmon. *Ceremony*. [1977]. New York: New American Library, 1978.

Weston, Jessie. *From Ritual to Romance*. [1920]. Garden City, NY: Doubleday, 1957.

3

Writing Home: The Bible and Gloria Naylor's *Bailey's Cafe*

Amy Benson Brown

No dew-eyed Dorothy longs for home in *Bailey's Cafe*, though the fantastic setting of Gloria Naylor's fourth novel offers an alternative realm, like Oz, where characters come to terms with their histories and confront questions of good, evil, and authority. Safely ensconced in the "whorehouse convent" which is Eve's boarding house, Esther, Jessie Bell, and two Mary's tell their stories of origins (116). Home, in each of the central women characters' stories, represents the site of the construction and control of women's identity and sexuality. Naylor's biblically informed imagination, however, constantly underscores the fact that the production of cultural meaning is always mythical and textual as well social and historical.

By casting her characters as biblical figures, Naylor claims the Bible as a mythical home, a point of origins for the interpretation of women's identity and sexuality in Western culture. Thus, Eve's boarding house, a "way-station" for troubled characters, symbolizes Naylor's revisionary narrative project: *Bailey's Cafe* offers a textual half-way house between the given homes of our culture and those yet to be imagined. This essay maps the architecture of this half-way house by tracing the design of its three 'stories,' or most prominent layers of signification. The first story of this new structure is founded on a critique of Genesis and some other first stories of our culture. The second story overlays and complicates the first by re-reading biblical characters through sexuality and claiming them as a site / cite of potential cultural change. While the first two stories overtly engage the biblical tradition as source, or originary home, the third claims an alternative ontology in African American interpretive and literary traditions that provides the foundation for re-making home.[1]

"In the Wake of Home"

Since the individual narratives of *Bailey's Cafe* all occur in the aftermath of racism, war, rape, and family disfunction, they seem to echo Adrienne Rich's question: "In the wake of home, what would comfort be?" (319). The first woman's story, that of Sadie, a drunken prostitute sustained only by her fantasies of domestic perfection, clearly underscores the centrality of understandings of home to the tales that follow. In her revision of Eve, Esther, Mary, and Jezebel, Naylor re-examines some of the oldest stories of our culture as the basis for revising home. Re-reading the Bible with a "hermeneutic of suspicion," an approach which distrusts the power dynamics and traditional interpretations of the ancient text, she creates a critique powerful enough to "rupture the habits of narrative order" or "break the sentence," of some of the formative myths of our culture.[2]

"Eve's Song" retells the Genesis narrative of Eve's creation, sin, and expulsion from the garden. Louisiana's lush and isolated delta serves as Eve's original home, but her story reveals the place to be less than Edenic even before her fall from paternal grace. Eve's adoptive parent, "Godfather," rules the miniature world of this small town with an iron fist. His need for absolute control is signalled by the trinity of his roles as the school's "book-keeper," the cotton exchange's "scale foreman," and the church's "preacher" that all represent his power as interpreter, measurer, and judge (85). Despite his omnipresence in the community, he is hostage to the opinion of the townsfolk, denying his adopted child physical affection just to quiet the gossips' baseless sexual innuendo (83-84). When he discovers Eve masturbating in the fragrant "peppermint-grass" (85), Godfather sends her naked and impoverished from his home and church. While "Eve's Song" recontextualizes Eden by re-locating the grand power play of myth in the petty despotism of small town life, it also engages several fundamental interpretive issues of the ancient text.

First, "Eve's Song" makes visible an act of appropriation naturalized in Genesis—the masculine appropriation of generativity, represented in the Bible by God's sole creation of humanity and his granting of fertility to the barren wives of the patriarchs:[3]

> Godfather always told me that since I never had a real mother or father and wouldn't be alive if it weren't for him, *he* would decide when I was born . . . whenever I'd ask what day was my birthday, he'd kept changing it year to year, month to

month. . . . He was patient that way, when he wanted to teach me a lesson. (82)

Godfather's insistence that he "made" Eve (90) and his refusal to reveal her birth date underscore the power dynamics of the biblical account of creation which elides the representations of feminine divinities from the older, oral traditions it revises to establish a monotheistic creation myth.[4] "Eve's Song" thus "literalizes" the originary scene of creation by re-writing the romantic moment of myth as a realistic document of power struggle, simultaneously revealing and remaking the political subtext of the story of the fall. As Margaret Homans argues, this strategy of literalization, which translates the abstract figure into an "actual event or circumstance" (30), exposes the opposition between the figurative, paternal Word and the literal but always absent maternal referent that enables the making of literary meaning. By literalizing the masculine-identified logos of Genesis, Naylor reveals this story, which Homans calls "the modern story of language," to be a fable (13). While the plot imitates the action of Genesis by tracing Eve's fall and expulsion, Naylor's hermeneutic of suspicion circumscribes and thus defuses the claim of biblical logos to absolute authority. The thunder of God shrivels to Godfather's grunting in the pulpit.

The absence of Adam and Lucifer in Naylor's version also exposes her own interpretive investment in the myth. If Milton explains 'God's ways to man,' Naylor examines the significance of Genesis to women. By stripping Eve's story of both her mate and Satan, she exposes the layer of the ancient myth that establishes the relationship of the fore-mother to paternal authority. Exiled from Godfather's realm, she is literally far removed from the law of the father, though she carries the father's 'word' inscribed within her. Thus, Naylor's retelling of Eve's fall and exile allegorizes the genesis of women writers' authority on the margins of paternal law.

Another aspect of Naylor's "literalization" of Genesis targets not the text but its popular construction and reception. Eve's sin has become synonymous in popular culture with sexuality, although that depends upon a stubbornly perverse reading of the text which clearly defines her disobedience as consuming the fruit of the knowledge of good and evil. Naylor's recasting of Eve's crime as masturbation reveals the common conflation of sin with sexuality and decriminalizes this original "sin" as the innocent, sexual self-exploration of a lonely adolescent.

If "Eve's Song" debunks the myth of an originary edenic home by confronting the sexualization of Eve's sin, "Sweet Esther"'s story debunks the myth of the sexual power of the enslaved woman.[5] Like the biblical Esther, the enslaved Hebrew princess who liberates her people by pleasing her captor King, Naylor's Esther feels like a "princess" in the relative opulence of her new home (96). Amid the new luxuries of fine china and a bed "trimmed with lace," the twelve-year-old "bride" does not immediately realize she has been sold by her brother to satisfy the sadistic sexuality of a wealthy farmer. Once she is able to name what they do in the cellar as "making evil," she buys her own body back by fulfilling her brother's bargain: for twelve years of her brother's food and board, she surrenders twelve years to the sadist's cellar (98-99). Unlike her biblical namesake, Esther can never secure the liberty of others, although she eventually finds refuge for herself in Eve's house. She considers murdering her torturer to spare "the other young girls waiting in line to sleep along in his pink-and-lace bed. The other girls with brothers." But she realizes that there "are just too many of them to kill. And there are just too many twelve-year olds" (99).

If "Eve's Song" allegorizes the marginalized writer's relation to the originary home, center, or source of authority, "Sweet Esther" allegorizes the crime of slavery in the cellar of American culture. As Naylor brings us into Esther's consciousness, we hear the dehumanizing labels that echo in her memory: "The black gal. Monkey Face. Tar. Coal. Ugly. Soot" (95). Though this story is set in the early twentieth-century, the "black gal" remains an object of exchange between men and subject to the will of her master. Thus, Esther's body evokes "the captive body" that Hortense Spillers argues "becomes a source of an irresistible, destructive sexuality" (67), and a site for pornotroping as Esther and her owner "make evil" in the basement. This revision of Esther's story not only debunks the myth of the sexually powerful slave, it also figures the repression of such scenes of abuse. Esther's attempt to articulate her experience is haunted by echoes of the command: "We won't speak about this Esther" (95-99).

In sum, the unspeakability of Esther's abuse evokes the unspeakability of the sexual violations of enslaved women and the legacy of slavery on constructions of African American women's sexuality. In the stories immediately following Esther's, Naylor articulates another repressed aspect of representations of sexuality, the construction of the virgin / whore dichotomy. In "Mary: (Take One)," the name 'Mary' signifies both the Virgin and Mary Magdalene. By collapsing these two into one character, Naylor's hermeneutic of suspicion here reveals how the identities of "virgin" and "whore," though often understood as essences, are socially constructed and mutually defining.

When the gorgeous Mary, a.k.a. "Peaches," enters Bailey's Cafe, a local pimp, Sugar Man, whispers what "every man" was thinking: she is "born to be fucked" (102). Despite her doting father's attempt to protect her by dressing her in Mary blue and even building a brick wall around their house, Mary ultimately fulfills the social script to which Sugar Man refers. Naylor's critique of this script, however, shifts the stage where the whore is revealed from the act of sexual intercourse to the act of gazing:

> Everywhere I turned I could see her. But what was she doing in my room? She was a whore and I was Daddy's baby. Every mirror outside told me what she was: the brown mirrors, hazel mirrors, blue mirrors, oval, round, and lashed mirrors of all their eyes when they looked at me. . . . (104)

Seeing the reflection of the "whore" rather than "Daddy's baby" in the eyes of her community radically destabilizes Mary's self-perception, or internal eye / I. Daddy's favorite child ultimately splits her identity to accommodate the sexualized self the suspicious social mirrors reflect. Naylor's metaphor, however, also suggests that Mary's original identity as the virginal "Peaches" was no more true or essential than the "whore" she later became since her father's devotion to her also reflects the larger culture's racist fascination for lighter skin: he is "color-struck," as his wife laments (102). Thus, the early love and security Mary felt in her father's brick-fenced home was merely the first mirror-trick, since it too reflected who she resembled, rather than who she was. Mary concludes that only if she "had been born into a world without mirrors" might there "have been a chance for a real home" (108).

The dream of a "real home," however, does not necessarily posit the existence of an identity previous to or entirely independent of social context. Rather, Mary's dilemma points to a gendered twist or additional layer to W.E.B. Du Bois's definition of racial double-consciousness as the "sense of always looking at one's self through the eyes of others."[6] A phrase Mary has heard since childhood—"that gal's got promise"—further reveals how the split between the virgin and whore in her identity belies no buried, whole self, but the establishment of identity through social contracts (104). "Promise," her potential value on the marriage or sexual market, implies not only value *to* someone but also value *for* something and thus provides the basis of a contract:

> . . .(I)n my mirrors I would try to see what she had promised
> them that would cause the heat to seep up through the rough
> denim of their pant legs. . . . —What have you promised
> them? I whisper to her. —You. You. You. (104)

At last, Mary's eye / I recognizes the "you" in the mirror as the whore who contracted this promise. With this depiction of the ability of the "promise" to organize Mary's identity, Naylor demonstrates how such social contracts actually constitute the individuals they purport to regulate.[7] In short, by demonstrating that whores are made, not born, Naylor ironizes Sugar Man's initial comment that Mary is "born to be fucked." As Mary's "I" fulfills the contract by surrendering her "you," her position as exchanger, rather than merely the object of exchange, frees her by chasing the "demon" from her "mirror" (105).

This liberation, however, is only temporary because the bifurcated self inevitably collapses into the singular somatic self; in other words, Mary may have two minds, but she only has one body. Mary's disgust for the "whore" turns to self-loathing when "very slowly over time" she realizes that she "actually enjoyed being held and touched" (107). Thus, Mary's story demonstrates how the virgin / whore dichotomy reinforces the essentialist assumptions behind the pattern of blaming female victims. Formerly, Mary knew that the "you" in the mirror "had always been a whore," but now she thinks "I was probably always asking for it" (107).

Since the contract has lost its power to maintain the split between virgin and whore in Mary's identity, she has to attack the force that "gave the lie" to that split—her own body. Smiling into the bathroom mirror, Mary destroys her reflection by cutting her face with a beer opener. This marking of her own body is an attempt to rewrite the implications of the virgin / whore script as she literally disfigures herself. Eve alone recognizes Mary's design: "only the scar" is "reflected" in Eve's eyes when she pronounces Mary beautiful.

Jessie Bell's story follows Mary's immediately, and further explores the difficulty of rewriting the cultural scripts of women's sexuality, particularly African American women's sexuality. While the hermeneutic of suspicion de-naturalizes the virgin / whore dichotomy by tracing the social construction of the identity of the whore in Mary's story, it denies the label altogether in Jessie's. Although she bears the ill fame of the biblical Jezebel, Jessie's sexual relations with her husband and female lover offer one of the novel's rare representations of mutuality and choice. By the novel's close, the sexually infamous Jessie is known especially for her virginal refusal of "gentleman callers" at Eve's "whorehouse convent" (116).

Like the biblical Jezebel, Jessie enters unfamiliar territory when she becomes associated with a King. Naylor transforms the power of the biblical King Ahab into the political dabbling of a socially prominent African American family, the "Kings." Like the Queen from Sidon, Jessie is a foreigner to the Kings' world; the crux of her difference here, however, is not ethnicity or nationality, but class. Naylor reconfigures Jezebel's sabotage of Israelite politics as Jessie Bell's resistance to the self-loathing social politics of the Kings. Like the biblical queen's persistent loyalty to the Canaanite gods of her people, Jessie maintains the integrity of her social roots and refuses to adopt what she calls the Kings' "religion": "White folks . . . were Uncle Eli's god. And it was a god I wasn't buying" (125).

Conservative elders in the King family, like Uncle Eli, never accept the iconoclastic girl from the docks, and their discouragement contributes to her divorce and disgrace when her drug abuse and long-term affair with a woman become public. If mirrors symbolize the forces blocking Mary's attempts to establish a "real home," the papers or the press symbolize the source of the destruction of Jessie's home. As she notes, she has "no friends putting out *The Herald Tribune*. And it's all about who's in charge of keeping the records" (118). Both Mary's social mirrors and Jessie's bad press represent the importance of naming, even as Naylor's engagement of the Bible and the cultural scripts of women's sexuality alters the signification of those names.

Furthermore, the construction of Jessie as a Jezebel reveals that the homes of origins in all of these tales are founded implicitly on heterosexual assumptions. While the white-worshiping elder King uncle never liked Jessie's independence, her fall as Jezebel comes about only after her arrest in a raid of a "dyke club" (131). For years, Jessie refused her husband's offer to welcome her "special friend" to their house, reasoning that "[m]y needs were my own. But so was my home" (125). By implicitly defining her relationships with women as 'not home,' she locates her lesbianism literally 'on the side.' With this representation of an alternative sexuality located outside the home, Naylor marks the function of the traditional family home to represent the boundaries of sexual identity. This is more readily apparent when the issue of Jessie's identity is seen as part of Naylor's larger pattern of reconfiguring conflicting identities by figuring them within a single individual. We have seen the formative war between the virgin and whore in the construction of Mary's identity in "Mary: (Take One)." Similarly, in the novel's closing story, "Mary: (Take Two)," identity categories again fuse within a single person. There, it is not sexuality, but race and ethnicity that is the locus of redefinition as Mariam, an Ethiopian Jew, is driven from her home. Jessie Bell's caring, consensual relationships with her husband and with her female lover offer the novel's only depiction of an adult sexuality free from coercion or prostitution, yet she too is driven from her home. By fusing the homosexual and heterosexual in Jessie Bell's character, virgin and whore in Mary's, and Black and Jew in Mariam's, Naylor questions the traditional construction and opposition of these pairs of identity categories.

When Jessie Bell can no longer maintain a public / private split in her sexual identity, she lands in the "the women's house of detention" where Eve eventually leaves her calling card. In addition to the address, however, Jessie, like all of Eve's borders, must know what she calls the "delta dust" to enter her sanctuary. It is this knowledge that calls forth the second 'story,' or layer of signification, in this novel's engagement of the Bible.

The Delta Dust

In Eve's thousand-year journey from Godfather's home, she literally finds new grounds for her identity in the lush lands of the delta. "The delta dust exists" she discovers, "to grow things, anything in soil so fertile its tomatoes, beans, and cotton are obscene in their richness" (90). In her own time of dryness and exile, the dust permeates her very pores, preserving and re-sculpting her:

> Layers and layers of it were forming, forming, doing what it existed to do, growing the only thing it could find in one of the driest winters in living memory. Godfather always said that he made me, but I was born of the delta. (90)

As an alternative agent of creation to the formative logos of Genesis, the delta dust symbolizes the creative impulse which constructs the second 'story' or way of re-making meaning in the half-way house that is Naylor's novel. If the first story rereads some of the founding narratives of our culture with suspicion, the second story permeates them with a fertile and enlivening desire, just as the delta dust re-makes

Eve.

As Alicia Ostriker has shown, reading the Bible with a hermeneutics of desire as well as a hermeneutics of suspicion allows the revisionist writer "to insert herself into the story by identifying its spiritualities with her sensualities, and by feminizings of the divine."[8] The resulting expansion of possible biblical interpretations leads in *Bailey's Cafe* to a postmodern foregrounding of the traditionally subterranean process of making meaning. In other words, the half-way house of Naylor's fiction always presents itself as a made thing, attempting not to authorize one biblical interpretation but to dislocate any single or unitary truth as the object of interpretation. Furthermore, Naylor's postmodern approach to the ancient texts of the Bible invites readers to similarly open up her own work. *Bailey's Cafe*, in fact, operates as a "plurisignant" text in which constantly shifting meanings can only be located on a "threshold," rather than formulated definitively in some "rigid structure."[9] It is this plurality of possible meanings, the very open-ended quality of Naylor's imagination, that finds in Eve traces of a divine fore-mother.

Eve's assertion that she was "born of the delta" rather than "made" by Godfather reverses the original masculine appropriation of generativity exposed by Naylor's re-reading of Genesis in "Eve's Song." Re-made by the delta, Eve represents an earth-mother, evoking the Near Eastern tradition of fertility goddesses which were written out of the creation myths when redactors of Genesis revised ancient and diverse oral traditions. Naylor's re-imagination of Eve represents a resurgence of the repressed feminine divine of the Bible.[10] As if in revenge for the repression of the feminine, Eve's re-created garden of Eden at her boarding house features a mutilated tree at its center. This castrated "stump" is encircled year round by flowers worthy of Georgia O'Keefe's brush, and Eve makes these lush lilies, traditionally associated with female sexuality, bloom in and out of season.

Beyond her extraordinary gardening ability and thousand-year life-span, several other aspects of Eve's character mark her as a female figure of the divine. Her refusal to justify herself, asserting that beyond "good or bad or what I am—I am" (85) echoes God's paradoxical self-description, "I Am That I Am." (Exodus 3:14). Furthermore, like Christ, she heals the afflicted, promising Mary's distraught father to one day return her to him "whole" (113). Similarly, she proves herself to be Jessie's savior by forcing her to confront her own demons (136). Despite her healing powers and compassion, Eve maintains a divine detachment that spurs Jessie to call her an "icy, icy Mama" (118). The strongest evidence of Eve's power, however, is to be found not in her deeds but in her voice.

In several chapters of *Bailey's Cafe*, italicized passages embedded in the character's own narration represent his or her internal voice.[11] These interior monologues provide insight into the characters' motivations and understandings of their own identities and histories. In short, these stream-of-consciousness interludes offer themselves as keys to unlocking the character's identity. Near the conclusion of Jessie Bell's story, Eve's interior monologue surfaces with the prophetic authority of the Bible itself (136).

This episode begins with a battle of biblical quotations that dramatizes conflicting approaches to interpretation. Sister Carrie, a hypocritical Bible thumper, takes some "poetic license" with a few of her favorite passages condemning Jessie's "vile affections" (134). Bailey notes that to hear Sister Carrie, "you'd think loose women were the only thing ever on the Lord's mind" and that Eve, Carrie's arch-enemy, can match her quote for quote, citing chapter and verse with flawless precision (134). Yet, after Eve seals her victory by reciting Ezekiel's condemnation of hypocritical "sisters," one more biblical recitation appears in the scene. Unlike the other appearances of biblical texts, this one does not offer itself as a quote referencing the Bible, but as an interior monologue referencing Eve.

Glossing Eve's healing of Jessie's addiction, the voice asserts: *when I passed by thee, and saw thee polluted in thine own blood . . . I said, Live; yea, I said unto thee when thou was in thy blood, Live* (original emphasis, 136). Indented and italicized like the interior voices of other characters, this interlude offers not another recitation of a biblical text, but a re-citation or re-location of voice and authority. With these words, the prophet Ezekiel describes his resuscitation and nurturance of Jerusalem, the city of God so often described in the Old Testament as unfaithful or a whore.[12] This passage, which simultaneously evokes the biblical prophet and Naylor's Eve, functions as what Bakhtin has termed a "hybrid construction," a unitary-seeming utterance which actually contains "two 'languages,' two semantic and axiological belief systems" (304). The indentation and italicization of this passage serve as the "compositional markers" which Bakhtin notes attribute the utterance to a "single speaker" yet highlight the dual reference of the words marked. Thus, this interior monologue is fundamentally dialogic in nature since the 'word' here, fusing Ezekiel and Eve, simultaneously presents both the authoritative discourse of the Bible and what Bakhtin calls the "internally persuasive word" (344-

346).[13] In short, the authority of biblical logos is inseparable from the authority of Eve's voice here.

Naylor's construction of Eve's voice in this passage epitomizes her larger, transformative revision of biblical texts through the hermeneutic of desire; in sum, this passage marks Naylor's reversal of the process of exile and her re-clamation of home. Furthermore, Eve's voice here concretizes and represents the signifying practice Naylor has deployed throughout. By re-contextualizing biblical texts in the stories of Eve, Mary, and Jessie Bell, Naylor dialogues with biblical myth, revises it, and gives voice to significations that have not been heard before. Finally, Eve's interior monologue points to the third 'story,' or over-arching layer of meaning-making, at work in *Bailey's Cafe*. Naylor's re-construction of a mythological and textual home is facilitated by and inseparable from her claiming of an alternative lineage in African American literary tradition.

"Betwixt and Between": Father Blues and Mother Hurston

The epigraph of *Bailey's Cafe* evokes the blues, a tradition invented by African Americans, as both muse and medium of Naylor's creation: "the blues open / a place never / closing: / Bailey's / Cafe." Each character's song is orchestrated as part of larger performance including the "vamp," the "jam," and the "wrap." While authors frequently metaphorize their work as music or the act of writing as singing, the blues offers a particularly apt metaphor for Naylor's narrative strategies. What better medium could there be for this narrative half-way house of "folks . . . in transition" (219) than the blues, which Houston Baker characterizes as a "scene of arrivals and departures," a "juncture," a "place betwixt and between" (7)?

But more significant than the stylistic or thematic parallels between Naylor's story-telling and the blues is the function of the blues as a "matrix" or "womb" of African American culture (Baker 3-4). As such, the blues tradition offers an alternative ontology, a discursive point of origin that, unlike the authorizing logos of Genesis, is uniquely African American. Essentially oral and communal, the blues, furthermore, are akin to the African American tradition of story-telling which provides an alternative base for authority to the informing logos of the white male tradition (Pryse 9). Like the musical tradition of the blues, the African American literary tradition of the "speakerly" text provides an alternative discursive point of origin for Naylor's novel.[14] Hearing the stories of the characters who frequent *Bailey's Cafe* in their own voices simultaneously underscores the singularity of each individual's history and the communal or choral effect of reiterated themes.[15] However, the use of this tradition of voice in *Bailey's Cafe*, like the use of biblical tradition, works toward disintegration and cacophony as often as it does toward integration and harmony. This dissonance, furthermore, represents another manifestation of African American literary tradition.

Karla Holloway asserts that "voice" in literature by African American women is "manipulated—inverted from its usual dimension and re-placed into non-traditional spheres (layers) of the text" (622). While this technique causes some "dislocation" of meaning, as evidenced by the indeterminacy of interpretation in Naylor's biblical revisions, the "thematic emphasis on the recovery of some dimension of voice" balances the "dispersion" of voice (623). In Mary's story, for example, the deconstruction of the virgin / whore dichotomy dislocates the interpretation of the Gospel's two Marys, but it enables Naylor's character's assertion of voice, as evidenced by Mary's marking or re-writing of her body. Thus, the conflicting tendencies of Naylor's biblical revision, driven by both suspicion and desire, finally articulate an authoritative, if complicatedly intertextual, voice. The shape of this voice is undoubtedly influenced by its roots in the oral traditions of African American biblical interpretation.

Both the hermeneutics of suspicion and desire take a very decided shape when seen in the context of American slavery. The Bible, after all, was used as tool in the domination of enslaved people, and ministers frequently dwelt on passages exhorting slaves' obedience. Yet, enslaved people combatted such sermonizing with the strength of their own "faith assertions" that lead them to "reject any teaching" that used the Gospels to justify slavery (Canon 31). Renita Weems also argues that the black church focused on texts that corroborated their own sense of identity, their "values and yearnings" (59). Furthermore, the criminalization of literacy required the oral circulation of biblical stories, which implicitly discouraged the story-teller's "allegiance to any official text, translation, or interpretation" (Weems 61). The half-way house of *Bailey's Cafe*, however, is not only built on the interpretive strategies and unique artistic forms of African American culture: this novel's third 'story' or layer of signification engages a specific, African American textual antecedent. *Bailey's Cafe*'s "signifying" on the Bible is intertwined with its dialogue and revision of another (pre)text, Zora Neale Hurston's *Moses, Man of the Mountain*.[16]

Since Alice Walker's discovery of Hurston as a literary

grandmother, her texts have functioned as ancestral homeplaces or points of literary origin for twentieth-century African American women writers. While some key tropes and topoi of Hurston's most acclaimed novel, *Their Eyes Were Watching God*, resurface in *Bailey's Cafe*, Naylor signifies on Hurston's re-telling of the life of Moses more directly. Signifying, as Henry Louis Gates, Jr., has demonstrated, involves claiming, re-naming, and ultimately re-vising aspects of the form and content of "black antecedent texts" (256). *Moses, Man of the Mountain* dislocates the traditional, Western understanding of Moses by offering a "black re-reading" of his struggles and powers informed by Hurston's study of Haitian and African folklore (Boi 115). Clearly, Naylor's revisions of Eve, Esther, Mary, and Jezebel follow Hurston by asserting race as a fulcrum of critique. The eruption of desire and its role in the construction of Naylor's own authority also has its roots in Hurston's novel.

Moses inspired Hurston because she saw that the African legends exalting his power arose from his privileged discursive position. Anyone can follow God's commandments, but who, Hurston asks in the preface "can talk with God face to face?" The conclusion of Hurston's preface links her explicit assertion of Moses's authority with an implicit assertion of her own. Moses's power "did not flow from the Ten Commandments. It is his rod of power, the terror he showered before all Israel and to Pharaoh, and THAT MIGHTY HAND. The Author" (xxii). The thundering emphasis in Hurston's capitalization of "THAT MIGHTY HAND" and the immediate assertion of her own role as author suggests that the hand here metonymically represents Hurston's own writing and authority. Note, however, that the conclusion omits Hurston's signature, the linguistic sign of her gender.[17] This omission marks the territory which Naylor, guided by a hermeneutics of desire, attempts to re-map in her novel.

Naylor signifies on Hurston's re-imagination of biblical myth by insisting on gender and race as a double fulcrum, or pivoting point of revision. Suspicious of the negative interpretations of Eve's sin or Jezebel's infidelity, Naylor sifts the original text, discerning a different story of immortal strength or stubborn independence. By contrast, Hurston's narrative evidences neither suspicion nor desire in its re-imagination of female figures. Her portrayal of Miriam, for example, as a bitter, petty, false prophet detracts from that figure's significance in the biblical account.[18] Hurston's sole investment in Moses as God's agent or authoritative 'right hand,' may relate to another aspect of Naylor's signifying upon *Moses, Man of the Mountain*.

While Naylor departs from Hurston's focus on and identification with a powerful male biblical figure and instead re-imagines several biblical women characters, she retains the posture of a male-identified, over-arching narrator. Hurston's self-presentation as "The Author" is echoed and refigured in Naylor's self-presentation as "Maestro." Just as Hurston elides the gender of her individual signature, opting instead for a universal or generic title (and thus a masculine title in the tradition of Western literature), Naylor dons a male persona in the voice of the "Maestro," Bailey, who introduces and orchestrates the individual women's solos. Thus, both authors cross gender lines in their figurations of their own authority.

The significance of this act, though, is shaped differently by the historical contexts of each work. While Hurston's gender crossing evokes the traditional, universalizing construction of authority as gender-neutral, Naylor's gender crossing attempts to construct her authority as gender-plural. Bailey's own story opens the novel and functions in concert with the only other man's story, that of "Miss Maple," to frame the chorus of women's stories. The two men's very different experiences of racism and World War II counter each other and implicitly offer a dialogue with the women's narratives on the theme of the construction of sexuality and identity.[19] Thus, Naylor's gender crossing reflects not a masking or evasion of the subject of gender, but an overt exploration of it in the womanist tradition which stresses the relation of gender and racial oppression.

Although, like *Moses, Man of the Mountain*, *Bailey's Cafe* asks "who can talk face to face to God," the implied conversation between divinity and humanity in the latter takes a different shape. Naylor's re-invention of Eve through a hermeneutics of desire rests on an identification of the "spirituality" of the text with her own "sensuality," the corporeal reality of her own person which is inevitably shaped by gender, race, class, and sexual-orientation, among other things.[20] It is perhaps this fundamental identification that allows the appropriation of biblical logos evidenced by the prophetic language of Eve's interior monologue. The voice of biblical authority which emerges as Eve's own voice recalls the "Voice" of "I Am That I Am" which functions as character in Hurston's text. Despite the fact of his divine empowerment represented by his phallic rod, Moses's dialogue with God is characterized by the dramatic distance of conversation: in other words, Moses speaks and listens to the "Voice." In Naylor's text, however, this external dialogue is reconfigured as dialogic interplay. In other words, 'talking with God,' or the authoritative discourse of the Bible, functions as a textual event in Hurston's novel but as an enabling (pre)text, or fundamental context for the creation of meaning, in Naylor's novel.

The transgression implicit in this shift in authority is dramatized in one of the final scenes of *Bailey's Cafe*. The mother of Mariam, the miraculously pregnant and mildly retarded virgin exiled from her strictly orthodox Jewish, Ethiopian community, enters the holy space forbidden to women in order to pray for her daughter. Her resolve not "to bargain with God" or "plead her goodness" mirrors this novel's insistence on dialogue, its aim to talk with God "face to face." Naylor's text, like Mariam's mother's prayer, demands "pure and simple justice" (156). Yet, the conclusion of this scene reflects the fear that accompanies this bold assertion of authority. The crowd of worshippers, shocked and disoriented by Mariam's mother's daring, push her over the "threshold . . . of no return"; she falls on the "sacrificial altar" and immediately "turns to stone" (157). Mariam's mother's fate, like that of Lot's wife, represents the punishment, the sacrifice, that many women fear will be demanded if they claim title to a portion of sacred ground, if they refuse to remain in exile. Significantly, Mariam herself dies soon after giving birth due to a failure of imagination, literally drowning in the flood of her own faulty mental conjuring (228).

Mariam's story, however, also evidences authorial daring along with fear by dramatizing Naylor's revisionist project in her attempt to "bear the word" differently. Mariam's narrative, titled "Mary: (Take Two)," offers another scene like that of "Eve's Song" where the abstract and figurative is literalized. While this strategy in "Eve's Song" produces an allegory of the genesis of the woman writer's authority in exile, the revision of the Virgin birth offers an allegory of one woman writer's own reproduction and delivery of meaning. The child born to Mariam represents the "Word, the embodiment of Logos" but his character, once again, offers a Bakhtinian hybrid construction.[21]

The miraculous infant inevitably refers to Christ and thus claims a textual origin or home in the Gospels. However, by sending baby George to Irene Jackson's shelter, Naylor links the ending of this novel to the beginning of the story-line of her earlier work, *Mama Day*. By claiming a previous novel as another textual source or home, Naylor rocks this baby in the cradle of her own fictional world. The identity of the miraculous infant is constructed between two frames of reference: the biblical Word and Naylor's word. While George's birth concludes *Bailey's Cafe* by marking the sad fact that some children are "brought forth in limbo" (227), Naylor's use of this "child of light" to weave together her own novels celebrates the potential of narrative to construct an imaginative alternative, or refuge from perpetual liminality. This final signification on a (pre)text that she herself has authored only marks the larger re-constructive process of the whole novel. Balancing suspicion of the traditional use of the Bible in representations of women's sexuality with an enlivening desire to re-write the Word in her own image, Naylor creates a text that, like the back door of Bailey's Cafe, opens into possibility. By claiming textual homes in the Bible and in African American discursive tradition, *Bailey's Cafe* reformulates both and demonstrates the long process of re-making home.

NOTES

I would like to thank Alicia Ostriker, Martine Brownley, and Julie Abraham for their generous readings and support during the writing of this essay.

1.   Naylor's biblical re-vision here functions like that of H.D., Alicia Ostriker, Jeanette Winterson and other twentieth-century women writers whose works both contradict traditional understandings of the Bible and simultaneously attest to new interpretive possibilities.

2.   See Alicia Ostriker on women's re-writing of the Bible and Rachel DuPlessis on women's re-writings of other canonical texts.

3.   See, for example, the case of Sarah (Genesis 21:1-7) and of Rebekeh (Genesis 25: 19-25).

4.   On the sources and process of the Bible's composition, see Robert Alter and Frank Kermode. On the erasure of the feminine, see Ostriker, 33-38.

5.   Delores Williams argues that African American women's literature, by engaging patterns of representing African American women's sexuality, defines an area that feminist theologies must confront to understand the complexity of women's oppression.

6.   Naylor begins her article, "Love and Sex in the Afro American Novel," with precisely this quotation from Du Bois.

7.   As Nancy Armstrong has argued, novels which reveal the rhetorical operations of such contracts undercut fictions of essential identity. Following Althusser, Armstrong stresses the function of the contract to regulate the identities of those who enter into it (31-35).

8.   Ostriker, 18. She further explains that writers who re-read the Bible with desire are projecting their concerns onto the text no more than any other exegete. Nor is the hermeneutics of desire a strictly feminist phenomenon; its creative dimension is intrinsic to all interpretation.

9.   Karla Holloway defines this built-in plurality of meaning as a fundamental characteristic of African American women's novels.

10.   See Ostriker's own revision of Freud in which she claims that the "Repressed of biblical narrative is evidently not the slain Father but the slain (and immortal) Mother," 15.

11.   See Bailey's interior monologue about World War II (23-26) and Sadie's internal reality of domestic order and security (72-76).

12.   Ezekiel 16:6. I am indebted to Walter Reed for help in locating this passage and for turning my thoughts to Bakhtin through his readings of biblical texts.

13.   Bakhtin also maintains that authoritative discourse, the "word of the fathers," is not double-voiced and thus cannot "enter into hybrid constructions" (342-344). While this may characterize the most extreme or perhaps ideal conception of authoritative discourse, the belief that writers' and readers' actual experiences of authoritative discourse can indeed be double-voiced is integral to my thesis.

14.   Henry Louis Gates, Jr. defines the "speakerly text" as one "whose rhetorical strategy is designed to represent an oral literary tradition" (181).

15.   Voice here reflects the double-voiced tradition of African American literature since it functions as both an expression of individual identity as a link to communal identity. See Gates's introduction, xxv.

16.   The strategic use of the Bible in slave narratives by nineteenth-century African American women may offer another interesting, if more distant, textual antecedent.

17.   Nancy Miller discusses the effects of asserting or withholding the woman writer's signature (73).

18.   Compare, for instance, Hurston's account of Miriam's role in the adoption of Moses (42-45) and as a leader of the Israelites (268-298) to the biblical account of her role in Numbers.

19.   In addition to contemporary attention to constructions of masculinity, the recent controversy about black women writers' portrayals of black men renders Naylor's male "maestro" a politically useful writing strategy. See Deborah McDowell's discussion in "Reading Family Matters."

20.   See Ostriker's definition of this "erotic" identification and re-reading (66).

21.   See Homans' definition of representations of the Virgin with Child as sites for re-making the meaning of bearing the "Word" (30).

WORKS CITED

Alter, Robert, and Frank Kermode, eds. *The Literary Guide to the Bible*. Cambridge: Harvard UP, 1987.

Armstrong, Nancy. *Desire and Domestic Fiction*. Oxford: Oxford UP, 1987.

Baker, Houston. *Blues, Ideology, and African-American Literature: A Vernacular Theory*. Chicago and London: U of Chicago P, 1984.

Bakhtin, Mikhail. *The Dialogic Imagination: Four Essays*. Ed. Michael Holquist. Austin: U of Texas P, 1981.

Boi, Paola. "Moses, Man of Power, Man of Knowledge: A 'Signifying' Reading of Zora Neale Hurston (Between a Laugh and a Song)." Eds. Maria Diedrich and Dorothea Fischer-Hornung. *Women and War: The Changing Status of American Women from the 1930's to the 1950's*. New York: St. Martin's Press. 107-125.

DuPlessis, Rachel Blau. *Writing Beyond the Ending: Narrative Strategies of Twentieth-Century Women Writers*. Bloomington and London: Indiana UP, 1985.

Gates, Henry Louis. *The Signifying Monkey: A Theory of African-American Literary Criticism*. New York and Oxford: Oxford UP, 1988.

Holloway, Karla. "Revision and (Re)Membrance: A Theory of Literary Structures in Literature by African-American Women." *African-American Review* 24 (1990): 617-631.

Homans, Margaret. *Bearing the Word: Language and Female Experience in Nineteenth-Century Women's Writing*. Chicago and London: U of Chicago P, 1986.

Hurston, Zora Neale. *Moses, Man of the Mountain*. 1939; rpt. Urbana: U of Illinois P, 1984.

McDowell, Deborah. "Reading Family Matters." Ed. Cheryl Wall. *Changing Our Own Words: Essays on Criticism, Theory, and Writing by Black Women.* New Brunswick and London: Rutgers UP, 1989. 75-97.

Miller, Nancy. *Subject to Change: Reading Feminist Writing.* New York: Columbia UP, 1988.

Naylor, Gloria. *Bailey's Cafe.* New York: Harcourt Brace Jovanovich, 1992.

———. "Love and Sex in the Afro-American Novel." *The Yale Review* 78:1 (1989): 19-31.

Ostriker, Alicia. *Feminist Revision and the Bible.* Cambridge: Blackwell P, 1993.

Pryse, Marjorie. *Conjuring: Black Women, Fiction, and the Literary Tradition.* Bloomington and London: Indiana UP, 1985.

Reed, Walter. *Dialogues of the Word: The Bible as Literature According to Bakhtin.* New York and Oxford: Oxford UP, 1993.

Rich, Adrienne. *The Fact of a Doorframe.* New York: Norton, 1984.

Spillers, Hortense. "Mama's Baby, Papa's Maybe: An American Grammar Book." *Diacritics* 17:2 (1987): 65-82.

Walker, Alice. *In Search of Our Mother's Gardens.* San Diego: Harcourt Brace Jovanovich, 1983.

Weems, Renita J. "Reading *Her Way* through the Struggle: African American Women and the Bible." Ed. Cain Hope Felder. *Stony the Road We Trod: African American Biblical Interpretation.* Minneapolis: Fortress Press, 1991. 57-77.

Williams, Dolores. "Black Women's Literature and the Task of Feminist Theology." Eds. Clarissa Atkinson, Constance Buchanan, and Margaret Ruth Miles. *Immaculate and Powerful: The Female in Sacred Image and Social Reality.* Boston: Beacon P, 1985. 88-110.

4

Beyond Silence

Lisa Suhair Majaj

But when we are silent
we are still afraid.
> (Audre Lorde, "Litany for Survival," *The Black Unicorn*. New York: W.W. Norton, 1978, 32)

I have tried to name the things which have frightened me in my life. Spiders. Shadows under my bed. The angry voice of my father. Air-raid sirens. My mother's weeping. Jet bombers overhead. The rising noise of arguments late into the night. A lamp lit during black-out. Recurring nightmares. The half-eaten body of my cat's first kitten. A cloudless sky black with explosions. The sharp sound of bullets striking rock. An Israeli soldier's command, "Come to one side." A man whose hand brushes my hips or breasts, grabs at my crotch. Rows of tanks rolling across a border. The sharp look, the slight doubletake, when I mention my Palestinian identity. Subtly hostile questions, indecipherable silences. A door which remained closed despite my desperate pounding, the stillness of death within. Proclamations of war. Racist scrawls across my possessions. Anonymous phone threats, anonymous mail. Red splashes of paint on the sidewalk marking spots where a rape has occurred: red paint at every corner. A man cursing women. A Jew cursing Arabs. An American cursing foreigners. Neo-Nazis brandishing swastikas. The sound of blows behind a wall. An airport overflowing with refugees. A man in a uniform, any uniform.

I could separate these fears into categories: those inspired by my troubled family life, by the implacable forces of war, by sexism, racism, violence. Thus separated, they seem more manageably distinct, more subject to control. The child screaming from a nightmare of terrible insects fears only her imagination, unlike the student knocked breathless by a bomb's enormous reverberation. The girl so trained in silence as to be rendered speechless is merely shy, unlike the frightened young woman called aside for strip-searching and questioning because her name marks her as Arab, whose silence emerges from a politically circumscribed and historically grounded unease.

Yet these distinctions are too simple: they neglect the subtle connections between violence and repression, the myriad tendrils interweaving victimization and the ways in which we learn to inhabit our lives as victims. Besides, the visceral experience of fear respects no such distinctions. The autumn I turned ten I was troubled by a recurring dream of falling. In my dream I would slip off the rocky edge of a cliff and plunge downward, air hurtling past my gesticulating limbs, my vision clouded with the yellow film of nausea. I would wake to radio static, disembodied voices floating across the room, the distinctive retorts of guns and mortars beyond the windows, and the nausea would return. This was Amman, Jordan: Black September, 1970. The Jordanian army had moved to expel the Palestinians. Our house was unpropitiously located between a building held by the army and an empty lot occupied by Palestinian fighters. Chips of stone littered the pavement below our window where bullets had struck the house. We huddled for weeks below window level without water or electricity, eating canned food and drinking our diminishing stock of warm Pepsi. To awaken from a dream of falling to this shrouded darkness punctuated with gunfire, the urgent, surreal cadence of radio broadcasts, my parents' worried murmurs, the muffled breathing of sleeping relatives who had fled their exposed second floor apartment to shelter with us, was to continue falling.

That October my mother, sister and I left Amman for the quiet safety of Hawarden, my mother's Iowa hometown. Excited, at first, by the endless grocery aisles of colorful junk foods, the countless television channels, I soon grew silent before the sea of strange faces in my fifth grade classroom, the curious, pitying eyes of adults in church, the looks that marked me *waif, stranger*. My first day at school I stood motionless while children swirled round me, shouting questions that blurred into taunts: Did I live in a tent? Ride a camel to school? Eat with my hands? When the confusion calmed, I settled into a routine of classes and recess and lunch, Saturday morning cartoons and Sunday morning church, ballasted by my grandfather's steady presence at the kitchen table where he drank one can of beer a day and listened to the corn index. Eventually, I made friends with two girls in my class. We played marbles, tag, tetherball; traded comics and fifth grade jokes; wrote in each other's autograph books. I never spoke of Jordan, of the bullet holes in the wall above my grandmother's bed, the burned-out rooms of her home, the mortar shells we collected in the streets during ceasefire. Certainly I never mentioned my memories of the 1967 war with Israel, which these more recent events inevitably evoked: the pressure of my mother's frantic hands pushing my head into her damp apron as we huddled beneath the sink, the fierce whine of the air-raid siren piercing the dusty summer air, the acrid taste of fear flooding my mouth. Anxious for acceptance, I joined instead in chatter about marbles and Barbie dolls, choir practice and sledding, allowing the indecipherable outlines of my life to fade into a haze of silence.

Nine or ten months later, when school was out and the war was over, I returned to my circumscribed life amid the dusty rose bushes and low stone homes of Amman, the city the ancient Romans had called *Philadelphia, city of brotherly love*. I heeded that year's injunction to silence well; my return to Jordan reinforced the lesson. Although Palestinian life after 1970 was indelibly marked by the massacres and expulsions of that year, I managed to maintain a level of ignorance due not just to my parents' careful protectiveness of my childhood, but also to my own resistance of unsettling knowledge. I did listen with awe to stories of hungry families setting their starving pets loose to forage in the streets. But I juxtaposed these tales to reassuring memories of a quiet Iowa year, a winter of snow, two new friends. Before I left Hawarden, my friends and I had exchanged addresses and promised to keep in touch. For a few years we wrote faithfully—their letters arriving months late, by boat, because they kept forgetting to send them air mail; their script large and round and clear, reminding me of the calm pace of Hawarden life. But then the letters stopped—around the time that one of them became pregnant, rumor had it by her uncle or cousin. She was married off shortly before her fifteenth birthday. I did not hear from her, or from my other friend, again.

Teen pregnancy, sexual assault, were as implausible to me then as gunfire ravaging Hawarden's quiet streets would have been. I was a girl who did not easily understand or accept violence; I wanted not to speak of such things, as I had not spoken of Black September, of the war. I wanted my life to be like a book, possessing coherence and closure. But by retreating into silence I rendered myself unable to articulate, and therefore to confront, the chaotic forces which pressed imperceptibly, irrefutably, upon my life. It is an old betrayal, silence: one too frequently chosen, for reasons we may or may not understand. When my friend stopped writing to me, did she stop speaking as well, thinking that wordlessness could protect her, cradling speech inside her like the child she was too young to carry? Her imposed or self-imposed silence was in its own way as stark a violation as the incest or rape which abducted her into a life with no horizon. I wonder, sometimes, if she ever reclaimed her voice, or whether that sheen of calmness sank her altogether.

Perhaps I only arrived at some semblance of adulthood when I began to understand the ways in which the quiet patterns of our daily lives are built upon semi-willed ignorance of the agony of people in different streets, different cities, different countries. This century has defined itself through massacres and expulsions: Armenians, Jews, Palestinians, Kurds, Bosnians—vast numbers of people exiled, murdered, leaving behind the translucent rubbish of ravaged lives. As an Arab American I find myself particularly attuned to Middle Eastern sufferings: Lebanese and Palestinian children riven by occupation and war; Iraqi children killed by bombs, by sanctions' hunger and disease; Lebanese villages crushed by Israeli air raids; Palestinian refugees still homeless after a half century of despair. What messages of fear will these children carry with them into their futures, scripted into the ligaments of their bodies, the shadows that hollow their eyes? And anguish knows no boundaries: a fierce current courses from South Central Los Angeles to South African townships, Sarajevo and Srebrnica to Khan Yunis and Gaza City. An undertone of horror echoes from women in Serbian rape camps, eyes and bodies taut with an unspeakable anguish, to deceptively ordinary American homes where someone whispers threateningly, "Don't tell."

Don't tell. It has taken me a lifetime to begin to understand the ways in which such words corrode, crushing palpable lives beneath the stone weight of fear. But who are we if we cannot speak out about what we have undergone, learned, become? We are the stories we tell about ourselves; our words map the spaces of home. Our experiences etch themselves into our faces, the lines of grief and joy becoming sharper with age; our lives are timbred with a resonance underscored by the surprisingly fragile bass note of sorrow. To remain silent is to deny the embodied selves which bear us, rooted stalks, into the world: to become complicit in our homelessness. It is to deny, as well, those other narratives which inhabit us—the people crushed by tanks or bombs or guns or simple despair, the eyes and hands and voices whose pleas bind us to our jointly human state.

My attempts at writing are haunted by the Palestinian and other Arab lives so rarely given media space in human, personal terms. Voices I do not know press upon me, reminding me of the betrayal of silence. But the task of confronting, on both a personal and political level, the outrages of history requires a measure of personal confidence difficult for one schooled in silence. Like other Arab Americans, I have experienced hostility upon speaking out: threatening phone calls, anonymous mail, destruction of property, racist accusations. When I attempt to testify to the lives beyond the brief images of despair or anger flashed across the screen, I stumble over my own wariness of an environment so resistant to acknowledging Arab concerns, grievances, homelessness.

This silencing not only reinforces my sense of exile as a Palestinian, but also makes it difficult to explore other aspects of Arab American experience. The imperative of speaking out about political realities often claims precedence over more personal negotiations. But important as it is to challenge the daily litany of violence, the burden of testimony can become a means of avoiding a more personal self-confrontation. There are unspoken stories caught beneath our tongues: words we don't always understand, a mixture of Arabic and English welling up from deep within, frightening in its intensity. We are Arab American—but what guides can help us negotiate this confluence of cultures? "I feel sorry for my Arab American students," an educator tells me. "They don't know who they are. They aren't American, they aren't Arab. They're nothing." I used to introduce myself as "half Palestinian, half American," moving in and out of these dual identities with the same rapidity and surreptitious fear with which I still tuck my Palestine map necklace inside my clothing when I wish to evade confrontation, or pull it out when I am weary of avoidance. Though I now insist on the facets of my identity as integrally interrelated, my articulation of selfhood against this landscape of homelessness is never a matter of simple affirmation, but rather of negotiation and renegotiation.

If I could, would I rewrite myself? Born in Iowa to an American mother and a Palestinian father, I grew up in Jordan as a hybrid child, absorbing diverse and contradictory cultural nuances: both from the American Community School, where mixed heritage children were often disparaged by the "pure" Americans, and from my Arab relatives and neighbors, who viewed my limited Arabic, my relatively fair skin and hair, and my American-inflected manners as marks of foreignness. Despite the fact that English was our language of communication, in my family behavior was judged by Palestinian norms. Repeatedly told by my relatives and by others that I was Palestinian, that identity is bequeathed from one's father, I was also told—often by the same people—that I was American, different, an outsider. Chastised for not speaking Arabic, teased when I did speak it, I learned to keep quiet, drawing as little attention to myself as possible.

In yellowing childhood snapshots I peer warily out at the camera, thick plastic glasses obscuring the expression in my eyes, one tip of my wiry braid in my mouth. I lived on the edge of language, surrounded by a swirl of Arabic and English, but came to words slowly. Even in my teens I lisped, my mouth moving awkwardly around s's as if they were foreign creatures. My own name pulled my speech out of alignment, and so I avoided naming myself whenever possible.

At some point I began to take solace in the written word. Though much of my childhood is a blur, certain memories emerge unbidden: lying sprawled on a hot tile sidewalk, absorbed in a bulky edition of *Moby Dick*; crouching in the crook of a cherry tree, too transfixed by a Narnia tale to heed my cramped limbs or my mother's repeated call to lunch. I loved reading, the magical cadence of words, the narratives that lifted me up and away from the anxiety of daily existence. Perhaps part of my pleasure came, too, from the sheer physicality of English, its square letters so distinct from the fluid forms of Arabic script, its sounds clear and plain—in contrast to the infinitely subtle differentiations of Arabic consonants, the difficult, arching *'ein* which coated the throat like *dibbes* [grape molasses]. Unlike Arabic, which seemed far too complex—something that attracts me now—English seemed simple, its possibilities hemmed in by a reassuring certitude. Overwhelmed by my uncertainty about where I belonged, I turned longingly to the structures of English for a sense of home.

Besides, reading—and later, writing—offered a means of negotiating the fears which had started to rise within me: my anxieties about the familial tensions regulating our lives, the insecurity instilled by Christian missionaries who convinced me I was not "saved," my incomprehension about my budding, swiftly repressed sexuality, my fear of the political events which erupted like fireballs in my childhood sky. In the fall of 1970 I read and reread *The Diary of Anne Frank*, lying on the floor away from the windows, oblivious to the muted spiral of my parents' tension. When gunfire started riddling our days, and the protected back room filled with unwashed bodies rustling incessantly through the long nights, I returned again and again to Anne's diary, clinging to the amazing durability and resilience of language I found there, the evidence that homelessness and fear could be narrated, and through narration transformed. During the long evenings I sat crosslegged just outside the circle of lamplight, where the adults played endless games of pinochle and gin rummy, telling stories to myself as I formed figurines out of candle wax, turning instinctively to narrative to ward off the edging knowledge of darkness.

Looking back, however, I see the seeds of my adult alienation in the disjunction between my reading life and my actual environment. The books that wooed me those early years were the classics of any American girlhood: *Black Beauty*; *The Lion, the Witch, and the Wardrobe*; *Anne of Green Gables*. My mother, secretary / librarian at the American school, would bring home stacks of newly arrived library books; I read these eagerly, turning the pages carefully so as not to dispell the aroma of newness. By the time I was twelve I had exhausted the school library. But these books merely reinforced my longing to be "really" American. They offered, moreover, no reflection of my own Jordanian life, no hint of a world east of Europe, of the land and culture which both bound me by its restrictions and claimed me, however tenuously, as its own. The American curriculum my teachers so assiduously followed taught me next to nothing about the Middle East. When my parents took us to see the ruins of Crusader castles at Karak and Ajloun, their massive stone structures invading the horizon, I knew the western narrative of the Crusaders' invasion and conquest, but could not begin to imagine what that epoch of history had meant for Arabs.

My knowledge about Palestinian issues was similarly limited. Palestine was never mentioned in my American classrooms, and my Palestinian relatives did not speak to me about their past. It may have been too painful, or perhaps they assumed that I would absorb Palestinian history by osmosis—something that did not happen, since their political discussions not only excluded me as a child and a girl, but also took place in Arabic. Much to my present dismay, the first book I read about the Palestinian-Israeli conflict was Leon Uris' *Exodus*: oblivious to its distortions, I was riveted by the novel's sensationalism. It never occurred to me to search for an Arabic novel in translation, a book of Palestinian history, an Arabic poem. Perhaps I should not have been so irritated, recently, with an Arab American student who replied, when I mentioned an anthology of Arabic poetry, that he "didn't know Arabs *had* poetry." After all, the gaps in his education are no starker than those in my own.

If this alienation occurred in Jordan, I can only guess at what growing up in the United States would have been like, where my identity as a Palestinian would have been even more tenuous. When I was a child I longed desperately to come to the United States, where I assumed I would "belong." Would I have had the fortitude to withstand the taunts of "terrorist," "sand nigger," "camel jockey;" the profound silences or open hostility with which attempts at discussing Palestinian history are still met? Or would I have attempted to slough off my Palestinian identity altogether, becoming ever more silent in an attempt to prevent disclosure?

When I write or speak, I embark on a complex negotiation with the multiplicity of selves I carry with me, the silence so profoundly engrained in me. Often I feel like a well-educated foreigner who is not quite fluent in her adopted language and culture—whether that culture is Arab or American. Each part of my identity—Palestinian, American, woman—requires acknowledgment, affirmation; makes it both possible and necessary to speak. Yet each one of these identities has silenced me at various junctures of my life. Marginalized by my American identity in Jordan, my silence was reinforced by a sense of shame as I began to understand the role the U.S. has played in Middle Eastern history. As a Palestinian in the United States, my attempts at articulation have been met with hostility, incomprehension, ostracism. In both cultures I have been silenced as a woman—a silencing not necessarily more repressive in Arab culture, merely different. And though in the Middle East I have experienced war and political violence, in the U.S. I fear sexual and physical assault in a manner I never did in Amman or Beirut.

I have wondered who I am writing for: Arabs, Americans, Arab Americans? But perhaps the question is better put: where am I writing from? For too long Arabs in the United States have had to stress what we are not: not ignorant peasants, bloodthirsty terrorists, wandering nomads; not harem girls, oppressed wives, seductive belly dancers; not oil-rich sheiks or evil emirs; not anti-Semites or anti-Christians. It is time, in contrast, to begin exploring who we are: women and men, straight and gay, parents, children, artists, scientists, teachers, grocers, lawyers, carpenters, doctors, singers, gardeners: individuals only partially contained by any category or label, whose lives challenge the easy simplicity of identification. Beyond the stereotypes which cling with a terrible tenacity lies the fluid, subtle complexity of lived experience. Only when we begin to speak of our realities will our own voices finally welcome us home.

Recently I participated in a "high ropes course," an activity which involved traversing a series of rope bridges and cables strung 30 feet in the air between trees. I began by scrambling up a bridge, balancing in a tree while switching to a safety rope. Then I turned to face a cable stretched through space across which I was expected to walk, and felt fear detonate within me: my body limp with nausea, my voice a congealed mass in my throat. I do not remember how I got myself onto, and across, that cable; I recall only my partner's voice calling up to me, distant yet comforting, "I'll catch you if you fall." And the fierce recognition, solid as a fist in my belly, that *I had paid too much already to fear.*

Silence does not disperse fear, does not eliminate it. Rather, it is our voices and actions in the face of fear which are transformative. Coming to language is a process not unlike walking that cable high in the air with nothing but space below. I write by feeling my way along words which shape the silence around them, impelled by a fierce awareness of the voicelessness which precedes me, the huge price I have already paid to fear. The farther I go the more I understand that words are not the tightrope on which we balance, but the steps themselves that carry us forward into the headiness of motion, toward the rearticulation of home. On one side of me lies the abyss of historical tragedy, against which my own voice threatens to disappear. On the other side is the trench of personal indulgence into which I can too easily fall. I move tentatively, testing my fragmented weight against voices that articulate the silence. As I move forward these voices become clearer. Many are Arab American, some only recently familiar: Elmaz Abinader, Diana Abu-Jaber, Etel Adnan, Joseph Geha, Lawrence Joseph, Joanna Kadi, Pauline Kaldas, D.H. Melhem, Deborah Najor, Naomi Shihab Nye, Therese Saliba, David Williams. Others are older companions, familiar and challenging: Gloria Anzaldúa, Mahmoud Darwish, Joy Harjo, Sahar Khalifeh, Maxine Hong Kingston, Audre Lorde, Toni Morrison, Adrienne Rich, Leslie Marmon Silko. With so many voices weaving the air into a shimmering mesh, who would not dare move forward into sound?

5

My Self, My Body, My World: Homemaking in the Fiction of Brigitte Kronauer

Jutta Ittner

Home is a place that can be sold, bought, and owned—or so the real-estate ads proclaim. Home is also where I belong, and where the world arranges itself around the here and now of my body. So as Robert Frost wrote, "it all depends on what you mean by home" (Hollander 27). Is it a fortress to be guarded against invasion by outsiders?[1] Is it a woman's workshop, walled in and commodified, a place filled with icons and consumer goods, the house beautiful (Wright 214)? A shelter for day-dreams, or private family utopia?[2] A mirror of myself and my longings—for stability in an alienating world, for a space that is safe, for a retreat where I can finally be myself all by myself, "chez moi"? In the four novels and more than fifty stories by Brigitte Kronauer, one of Germany's most acclaimed contemporary women writers, home is a typical setting. She makes housekeeping a central focus and theme of her writings, in her first novel *Frau Mühlenbeck in Her House*, and in many of her stories. For Kronauer's women characters, home extends from the self outwards to the world. At first its furnishings and the world may both seem alien to these women, but they work to reshape their domestic space as an organic whole, establishing a creative relationship between their public and private realms by their homemaking.

In her recent study *The Home Plot*, Ann Romines argues that there has always been women's fiction which presented homemaking as neither an Arcadia nor a trap. Instead, this fiction tells complex truths about the satisfactions and dangers of the domestic ritual in female lives. Little attention has been paid to this fiction, however. Domestic issues have often been dismissed as "nice safe subjects" by male critics, and sometimes denounced as "feminine nonsense" even by the women themselves.[3] Of course, for centuries one sign of the accomplished housekeeper has been the fact that she was never caught in the act.

When what was by definition imperceptible within the dominant male culture became visible, women's reactions showed that they also regarded their own domestic tasks as "literarily unmentionable acts" (Romines 15). In an ironic sense, housekeeping was still too close to home. Only recently has feminist scholarship begun to regard literature focusing on women's everyday lives as significant, without explaining it apologetically as, according to Annis Pratt, a "cautious, diversionary 'politico-economic strategy'" (Romines 8).

In Kronauer's fiction the homemakers cannot be rendered invisible, not even by a reader oblivious to women's issues. Her domestic heroines no longer hide their brooms, aprons, and cooking utensils the moment the door bell rings, but go about their daily lives center-stage. Kronauer focuses with what has been called "obsessive precision" on the daily drama of housekeeping (Dormagen 17). Instead of creating a plot, however, she carefully arranges two-dimensional snapshots to provide a dynamic progression. As she explains, "For me literary texts are above all sculpted, and their sovereignty is a result of the calculated relation and relatedness of their components."[4] In these snapshots, or even snippets, everyday reality is not just a backdrop for perception and reflection. We experience how inanimate objects become alive, how the visible and audible twist and turn, surrendering to the formation of a new reality before our eyes:

> It's only my room, my room, I say aloud, with all the furniture in its place, with air in between in complete stillness. It's only things, they won't look. It's only things, they don't mean me, and they're dead, I say aloud so they hear me. I slowly retreat to the door, so I hear it, so it's true, and fling it wide open. There's only the street, the street, I say aloud. (*Die Revolution* 95)

Kronauer's reality-bites are often neatly framed by statements alleging certainty. The first-person narrator is an omnipresent medium of perception—eye, ear, and pen—that watches and painstakingly describes every detail of the drama of housekeeping. But sentences beginning "I perceive . . . " simultaneously describe and reflect the description. The narrator's perception constantly moves around, blurring the transitions between off-stage and on-stage observations. Unless we follow her every move closely, we lose track of her:

> Something solid, too, drops to the ground. I hear a noise. With

a pillow she has pushed a hairpin from her bedstand. Below it some dustflakes move to new places. She is unbuttoning the pillow-cover, she is standing in front of the bed. In the three-part mirror everything appears slightly tilted, the pulled-back curtains are swaying. They're also swaying in reality. (*Frau M* 11)

In her description of this housewife changing the sheets, washing the dishes, or watering the flowers, Kronauer's narrator reveals herself to the reader as a counter-presence, juxtaposing two radically different women. Passages of the first-person narrator reflecting and scrutinizing herself alternate with passages of observing her neighbor, Frau Mühlenbeck, with a mixture of fascination and horror at her exemplary competence.

Throughout Kronauer's fiction, the narrators speak in the first-person singular. "This persona that narrates and offers varying perceptions, emotions, insights, will be called 'I', according to misleading and common practice" (*Die Revolution* 5) she warns her reader. Although they do not manifest themselves as characters, all these narrative voices that analyze their individual perceptions, thoughts, and feelings as they observe incessantly what is happening in their home might well belong to one person, a collective person who seems to have certain autobiographical similarities to the author. Kronauer's first novel circles around the two women—the narrator and the woman she observes—two examples of how to approach life and make oneself at home in the world. For one woman, the day is a series of tasks that she tackles with relish; for the other, everyday life is a chore she tries to avoid. Frau Mühlenbeck is in her fifties or sixties, ebullient and energetic, a vital person in control of her life and a born homemaker. The second woman is a teacher in her thirties, given to doubts and speculations, not at home in the world or in herself.

In this essay I select from Kronauer's vast collection of snapshots and reflections those that deal with these two complementary realizations of home, arranging them in two concentric circles from the innermost circle of the self to the outermost of public space. The self, the body, the home—this sequence seems to indicate that there is a distance between self and home. In Brigitte Kronauer's understanding, however, "home" is not any farther from the center than is the self, and her stories show how in the "circles of hominess" home is both personal and communal (Hollander 27). The self is always the center, but it radiates through the concentric circles, and magically draws all they contain towards it, making a home for the self that eventually includes a part of the world. Home in this sense is not a place, but a central force that forms and reflects the totality of life.

"Chez moi": the Center

"Chez moi," "zuhause," at home. Where am I at home, and how close to home can I be? At one both with itself and its space, a sleeping cat appears in Brigitte Kronauer's story "Day with Interruption and Opponent" ("Tageslauf mit Unterbrechung und Gegner," in *Die gemusterte Nacht* [*The Patterned Night*]). It is a "center of life" in the deceptive stillness of its surroundings, in its blackness indistinguishable from the black pillows on the couch. The narrator's musings about her cat express some envy: "I wondered how deep its unconsciousness was, if it did not exist for itself in those moments" (Tageslauf 104). Like most female narrators of Kronauer's stories, she is quite familiar with this merging of the internal and the external. But this state is admissible only as an exception in the short span of time between sleeping and waking, when her body is still "melted away below the covers," and has not yet taken shape ("Eine erfolgreiche Bemühung um Fräulein Block" ["A Successful Effort for Miss Block"] in *Die gemusterte Nacht*, 59). In this ephemeral state of pure being, the woman exists without any boundaries, undefined and unlimited, "afloat below the pillows, bodyless, invulnerable, irresponsible, weightless, and sizeless" (Block 60-1).

Equally unstructured are her surroundings. In the gray morning light all objects are still blurred, and the "day that has to be lived through" is still without shape. At such moments her only wish is to remain without time and contours (Block 60). But perceiving leads to active participation, and as her eyes wander aimlessly around in the blur, objects emerge, and the diffuse space takes on edges and boundaries. The irrevocable separation of the internal and the external has begun. The first item on the agenda of her daily tasks is to prepare herself to enact her role, like the woman in W.B.Yeats's "Adam's Curse" who laments that "To be born woman is to know— / Although they do not talk of it at school— / That we must labour to be beautiful" (ll. 18-20). So "once you've gotten up, breasts are the order of the day. Eye makeup, speaking in a high voice, immediately, undoubtedly to be recognizable as a woman by all." Kronauer's narrator is still floating, but she's aware that there is no excuse—"what other choices do I have, being a woman." Every instant of her day is filled with the "rules and duties and seriousness" of her sex (Block 60).

Later, at the end of her working day, she can finally return home and to herself. She retreats from the hustle and bustle into the shelter of her bed and seeps into the stillness of the covers. The schoolteacher narrator in *Frau Mühlenbeck in Her House* comes home with her ears still stinging from the noisy classroom. Only sleep will provide her with that deep sense of homecoming that would be called "tout chez moi," all at home in myself: "In the afternoon, for my nap, I want it warm and quiet. It's so good to know that one can rely on it; as if one ceased to live, silent as in the deep sea perhaps. One can ramify under the thick quilt" (*Frau M* 24). Buried in her pillows, hibernating as it were (*Frau M* 25), sleep and death have become almost interchangeable for her. But as an animal emerges from its winter stupor, and as her cat springs to life after a deathlike sleep, she gathers strength for her next encounter with the world. All by herself in her bed, as much a womb as a tomb, she is ultimately "at home." Here she will recreate her self in order to reach out and embrace the world.

Making a Home

How does a woman bridge that abyss between the inside and the outside so that she can say: "I live in the house as I live inside my skin?" (Levi 15). How can a woman appropriate all the accidental, strange objects that have accumulated in her home over the years? And how can she make the endless round of household tasks—the monotonous routine of cooking, cleaning, washing, and ironing—a part of herself?

In Kronauer's story, "Day with Interruption and Opponent," the cat helps a woman sense that home is not a prison but her own imaginative space. The narrator, trapped in deathlike apathy and inertia, watches the cat perform the miracle of transforming its space with its playful activity, and she senses her own capacity to become more alive. Cats constantly make themselves at home "in all sorts of regions and spaces, conforming and causing to conform in ever-renewing circumstances" (Hollander 42). The moment the cat awakes from sleep, it changes a room that was inanimate in its "terrible equality of things" into a world of its own that is teeming with life. The cat:

> immediately begins to fill my room; it pumps the air full of action and passion, full of goals, full of results, beginnings, conclusions, an order; suddenly, a past and a future, suddenly,

a sequence of events, a selection of things, it breaks down into
details the totality of the room and my person. (Tageslauf 106)

The cat makes the world its home by extending itself in space and
time—by "living forward" as Kronauer puts it. It has a direction and
stays on course. What is more, it takes possession of things, connecting
with them by making them into imaginary playmates, obstacles, or
opponents, whereas the narrator is paralyzed by her own inertia.
Another story, "The Miracle of a Hypothesis" ("Wunder einer
Hypotheses," in *Die gemusterte Nacht*), describes the efforts of a
woman to relate to her home space in much the same way as the cat
does. Here she succeeds in magically transforming a world so familiar
in its every detail and routine into a meaningful, living organism—her
home. As soon as she makes herself the center and goal of her living
space, the objects that had been accidentally standing side-by-side
reorganize themselves into the singular arrangement that is hers.
Through her each object is irrevocably changed, so that nothing remains
as it was: "With some concentration I succeed in throwing the
inconsequential details with a single thrust like dice onto a table, and I
make their accidental arrangement a result" (Wunder 112).

The room in which she moves becomes a witness of her
presence. Nothing in it will be the same again, so she will be felt even
after she has left it. By touching them, even by only looking at them,
she has made things into parts of herself. "Once and for all" she has sat
on the kitchen chair, and "irrevocably" she has used the scissors. This
picture in front of her becomes "a picture once looked at by me!"
(Wunder 115). "Nothing on this messy desk . . . will be coincidental
and at the same time not be special, not be meaningful" (Wunder 116)
for she has given purpose and singularity to chaos, coincidence, and
aimlessness by secretly relating the things and events to herself.
Evenings "will pass without me, but they will all refer to me. For they
all are connected with me, they are tied to a date—a before and after"
(Wunder 113). Every little change that she makes represents her.
Whoever enters her space will:

> look around at the furniture and plants existing side-by-side
> peacefully and without purpose. Suddenly something moves
> forward, suddenly this armchair will have moved to a different
> place . . . all of a sudden it will turn into the most important
> object in this soundless room. . . . So this is my armchair! So
> this is my place! (Wunder 114)

In "The Miracle of a Hypothesis" this transformation is achieved by an intellectual somersault, the woman's pale imitation of the magic worked by a playful cat's antics. In sharp contrast, Frau Mühlenbeck, the earthy heroine of Kronauer's novel, appropriates space without thought or effort. This archetypal "hausfrau" is at home as naturally and matter-of-factly as she breathes. Her presence instantly changes the place. Returning from her shopping, she fills the peaceful house with life—as the cat did in "Day with Interruption and Opponent." She moves in her space as actively as the cat, and each movement and step is clearly audible: "Instantly she had created a totally different atmosphere, and the space around her was toppled, turned upside-down . . . Now speed, liveliness, restlessness called the shots" (*Frau M* 208). To a German reader, Frau Mühlenbeck noisily entering the house and clumping up the stairs immediately suggests the familiar turn-of-the-century walkup apartment house where ten or more families live under the same roof, their kitchen smells wafting up the sweeping staircase from under every door and collecting on the top floor. Next-door neighbors participated in each other's lives, and over the years they got to know one another intimately. A mother may have been born in the same house in which she sees her children grow up; then after she has died there, they may move back in with their families.[5]

So it is not surprising that the schoolteacher narrator knows Frau Mühlenbeck and her habits almost as if they were living in the same rooms. Moreover, the narrator seems to be in her apartment a lot, so she also witnesses Frau Mühlenbeck's quieter moments. We learn that her neighbor knows how to rest, but unlike the narrator she never indulges in extravagant meditations. Once Frau Mühlenbeck has decided that her coffee break is over, she jumps up, pours what's left of the coffee into the sink, snaps both book and her glasses shut, and "in no time" has heaped the table with all the ingredients for making a cake, "moving with a lot of clattering and banging" (*Frau M* 79).

She is never without a target, and she makes straight for it, finishing all her tasks without getting distracted: "Her face shows satisfaction, her expression is intent, her lips widen somewhat, it is an interested, attentive smile, yes, she smiles, but she is too concentrated for a real smile, a beaming smile" (*Frau M* 79). She whistles or sings while she works on an eiderdown quilt, attacks the dust under the couch, or polishes a window-pane. And as the cat does, she approaches every object as if it were an imaginary opponent:

How black the dirt sits on the paper towel! . . . She looks at

> the stained towel with glee and disgust; that is, her mouth is smiling and emitting experienced cries of horror. . . . Apparently she feels encouraged and inspired to continue with her task. Her whistling becomes even perkier, again innumerable tiny drops of Ajax are attached to the pane, they immediately start running. They need to be stopped. No more whistling now, she puffs angrily, and her arm vigorously moves from left to right and up and down. (*Frau M* 115)

Eventually she prepares to give the window the final once-over, as if meeting a real opponent eye-to-eye for the final shoot-out:

> At last she steps back, scrutinizing with a stern face, obviously satisfied. She positions herself at a certain distance from the window-panes, her hands buried in the pockets of her apron, her head suspiciously lowered, as if lurking and lying in wait for some flaws, she jumps forward, there was a spot, now that is polished off too, then back with her hands in her pockets and serious and yet all of a sudden a long sigh, thoroughly satisfied, and she stays put in front of the window, solemn and composed. (*Frau M* 115-16)

Her life moves in the everyday circle of using, preserving, and restoring her home. The repetitive and amorphous housework doesn't seem monotonous to her. It structures her life as sunrise and sunset structure the day, so that one task is as meaningful as another, whether it is washing the windows, peeling potatoes, brewing coffee, or watering the flowers. The narrator watches her perform her tasks, and with an almost irritating precision describes Frau Mühlenbeck's domestic rituals as she "beats back chaos every day with her broom" (Romines 12-13). She includes even the tiniest detail of the battle against dust and decay. Her scrupulous descriptions convey the ordered singlemindedness of Frau Mühlenbeck's actions, the energy and even passion with which they are executed, and her satisfaction once her task is completed.

Simone de Beauvoir contends that the housewife "never senses conquest of a positive Good, but rather indefinite struggle against negative Evil" (451). Yet this housewife enjoys a good fight, and her sweeping force seems inexhaustible. Moreover, it is her fight and her turf; even the rules are her own. Her home is an extension of her self. So how could it be the antagonistic "other?" Because she lives the unity of self, body, and home, caring for her home means caring for herself.

She would never associate herself with Bachelard's poet, who by polishing a piece of furniture "creates a new object; increases the object's human dignity." But like him she "awakens furniture that was asleep," and thus "registers this object officially as a member of the human household" (Bachelard 67), her household—her world.

The Door into the World

A spotless window seems to remove the separation between the outside world and the home. So glancing out the window is an ambivalent experience for the many women narrators in Kronauer's stories who are not at home in their homes, even though they work constantly at making and preserving them. For them the window is a point of transition, opening the walls to the fascination of the outside while still offering protection, but at the same time the world threatens to invade their protective space. Boundaries between inside and outside blur as the narrators' eyes roam the infinite sky. Any house is both a cell and a world, as Georges Spyridaki describes it. Its walls "contract and expand as I desire. At times, I draw them close about me like protective armor. But at others, I let the walls of my house blossom out in their own space, which is indefinitely extensible" (qtd in Bachelard 51). In "The Miracle of a Hypothesis" Kronauer's narrator tries to make this bulging outside world a part of her own private world:

> But of course there are more important things, like looking out the dormer window. This truly perennial panorama! At first this too will only be any place at the window, this space taken by me which now thrusts itself forward, but then everything visible from this spot will follow, the whole horizontal across the neighboring yards, the tilted, tree-lined street cutting across the picture, the houses as far as the horizon, the sky, everything in this singular arrangement. They cannot but notice the importance, even the essence of what is complete, perfect, as if frozen. (Wunder 114)

She succeeds in enclosing the outside world within the frame by "freezing" it. Once frozen, she can transform it as she does the armchair she has moved, or the scissors she has just put down. She has integrated the view from the window into her space. As a part of herself it will be recognized by others as another item in her life-inventory.

In contrast to the above character's successful integration, the insecure narrator of "A Sort of Achievement According to Nature" ("Eine Art Leistung nach der Natur," in *Die gemusterte Nacht*) reacts to the experience of exposure by retreating. This woman, sensing the pull of the outside world and feeling threatened by it, changes what she planned to cook for lunch so she won't need to go out shopping. She keeps losing herself in day-dreaming, looking, and meditating—constantly merging her self and the world. In spite of her efforts to structure her day, the morning passes without her even noticing it:

> I put the newspaper aside, clean up the dishes and step for a moment to the kitchen window, then I'll jump over to the supermarket across the street. The birds are flying around in the foliage, black in the bright shade of the leaves, and from there into the fresh darkness of the shrubs. I realize that I have been standing like this for a while, leaning against the window, propped up with my hands between the flowerpots on the windowsill, sticking my head as far out as possible. . . . Suddenly I hear shrill children's voices as if in hectic excitement from a school yard close by behind some houses and five, six trees. I remember. . . . Then, suddenly, noon, so the morning is over and done with. (Eine Art 74)

In this story the narrator gives a detailed report of her abortive efforts to fulfil her domestic duties. She is, however, a writer as well as a housewife, and the reader witnesses how this writer-housewife doesn't get around to doing any of the things she had planned, because she cannot separate her self from the outside world. Life outside drowns the limited life within her four walls, so that at the end of the day she will have to throw some supper together, and the page in her typewriter will still be blank. Yet she does not see this as a failed day. Observing the changes of light and color has given her such a sense of fulfillment that she takes "a deep breath as if this rest were deserved after a day full of hard work and strain" (Eine Art 77). As Romines observes, "the woman who chooses to *write* domestic rituals is also enacting these tests and conflicts in the medium of her own life" (14). In this story Kronauer uses the classic literary device of writing about the act of writing, combining the two professions of the domestic artist in what seems to be an ironic autobiographical comment. The existence of the story demonstrates her success in one of her professions. Despite the distractions of the outside world, she has found enough private space to reflect on her confusion.

Of course, each society has its own rules for privacy. In Kronauer's German society, privacy is secured by closed doors even inside the house, by two layers of curtains and drapes as a shield against the outside, and by hedges, fences, and walls that keep the world at a distance. Curtains and hedges grant visual protection, but they cannot prevent the invasion of acoustic boundaries. If as Shirley Ardener contends, our map of significant space is identified by the gaze, it may not coincide with our map of significant sound zones (20). That is, our sense of private space does not start and end at our property line. In Germany city people live in each other's pockets, even when they are prosperous enough to own their own row-house or detached house. When the narrator in "The Crucial Moment" ("Der entscheidende Augenblick," in *Die gemusterte Nacht*) consciously tries to restrict her seeing and hearing to the piece of yard enclosed by the hedges and "not the tiniest little bit beyond" (Augenblick 61), she fails to maintain even an illusion of privacy. Time and again someone breaks the silence, walks past the hedge crunching the gravel, "and I fall for it again and think someone is about to come round the corner, because the sound is so close by. . . . A tiny shock, almost a scare" (Augenblick 63). Passersby violate her fragile visual and aural privacy. In the novel, Frau Mühlenbeck has a similar privacy problem. She has moved into a new house where the landscaping is modern, open, and "American." She recalls with horror how:

> You could never sit on the deck without being seen by the neighbors. From all directions you had the neighbors saying hello, even from above—our lodger. These greetings went on and on, it drove you crazy, this vigilance and friendliness from all directions at once! . . . I said thanks a lot for your generous landscaping, I want a fence or a wall, and when it's there, a hedge above it! . . . Today they are still saying hello all the time all over the neighborhood. Our yard is surrounded by a hedge too high for anybody to look over it, on all three sides, unmistakably a fortress. (*Frau M* 184)

Frau Mühlenbeck defends her territory forcefully and without hesitation. Salesmen don't even get a foot in her door, she ambushes dogwalkers, and she gleefully uses a form of trench warfare against the mailman until he stops cutting across her border of perennials. But whoever needs shelter will find her door open. From the safety of her "fortress" she spontaneously reaches out to people in need: a young homeless man gets a sandwich and a cup of coffee in her kitchen even though she later realizes with a shock how risky that was. When from the coziness of her warm kitchen she sees a young mother frantically pushing her baby carriage through the pouring rain, she opens the door wide and waves her in:

> Not a moment's hesitation! I am sure she'd been hoping for something like that. No words were wasted. She just barged in with her baby carriage all the way through the hall! As if now there was no time to be lost! A young scraggly thing, yellow hair, black spots all over her face and her neck, streaking from her eyes. I couldn't decide whether it was tears or the rain that had dissolved her makeup. The baby was squalling in its wet pillows. But first we closed the front door, and here it was dry. (*Frau M* 56)

Of course, this creates a lot of additional work, and some grumbling:

> When I was kneeling on the carpet and brushing off all that mud, I thought to myself: Dammit, why in with the whole baby carriage! As usual, the neighbors pretended they were deaf or blind or God knows what. That's just like you, same as ever, old Margarete! (*Frau M* 57)

Frau Mühlenbeck's openness contrasts with the wariness of her neighbors, and even more with the almost paranoid reaction of her observer. This narrator "stiffens with aversion" just watching people eat or talk noisily, and she is flooded with "hate against their compactness" if they sit too close to her in the train (*Frau M* 25). She has warm feelings for people only from the safe "friendly distance" of taking a walk on a Sunday morning, for example: "There I can look at them without any consequences. I have a real love of all humans, they all interest me, I can see something nice in all of them" (*Frau M* 25). Her sense of her self is so blurred and fragile that she even feels threatened by contact with her boyfriend, and she feels closest to him in a public space like a café. Frau Mühlenbeck, on the contrary, is fully and securely at home in her self, her body, and therefore in the world. Other women might feel the desire to make the world their home, yet shrink back when they sense how thin the line is between isolation and intrusion. She has no fear that somebody might trespass, so she can be open to people. She can commit herself without getting carried away, and without fear of being invaded. Her love for mankind is genuine, straightforward, and unsentimental.

This is most visible in the way she treats the vagrants who come by regularly. As she says: "We are loyal to each other, I've known them for years, they trust me. I could never send them away" (*Frau M* 103). Not only does she help; she is able to maintain the precarious balance between charity and condescension. One beggar, a regular who is almost a neighborhood landmark, never actually begs. Instead, he accepts contributions in a polite and dignified manner: "So it was today, again the bow, the ceremonious greeting, joy on my part that he's still there, so reliable and unchanged" (*Frau M* 103). But that day she can't help noticing that his old shoes have disintegrated. She recalls that in her basement there's a perfectly good pair of shoes that her husband doesn't wear, but how can she offer them without breaching their unspoken contract?

> You see, up to now there was this friendly closeness, no blathering, and we were both very comfortable with it. It wouldn't have crossed my mind to ask him how he lived. When someone lives the way he does, I respect it, and his clothes are part of it. But here I simply had to interfere, dignity or not! (*Frau M* 105)

She's very relieved when he accepts the shoes and leaves "with the usual 'Very kind of you!' and not a syllable more, a tad more cautious than usual, but as if nothing had happened" (*Frau M* 105).

"Sympathy is the recognition of someone else under the aspect of a common humanity," as David Bromwich writes in his interpretation of "The Old Cumberland Beggar" by William Wordsworth (139). If Frau Mühlenbeck's sympathy includes feeling *for* another person with respect and over distance, it excludes the possibilities of feeling *as* another person and of reciprocal feeling. She treats the beggar in the manner that Wordsworth commends:

> Where'er the aged Beggar takes his rounds,
> The mild necessity of use compels
> To acts of love; and habit does the work
> Of reason; yet prepares that after-joy
> Which reason cherishes. (ll. 98-102)

According to Frau Mühlenbeck's own reasoning:

If I see something like that, I could say just like them: None
of my business! But I just can't do that, it makes me nervous,
it has nothing to do with being Christian. I'm not "a
Christian." It just gets on my nerves to watch something like
that, it drives me crazy. . . . I like to give a hand, especially
when it's so easy. I feel good afterwards, and I can walk a
little straighter. (*Frau M* 128)

In the encounter of the beggar with the middle-class perfectionist
"hausfrau" the extremes of alienation and belonging are staked out.
Wordsworth's poem delves into the complexity of the concepts of home
and homelessness, and by doing so almost reverses their meanings. His
solitary beggar has no home—"his place knows him not"—but on his
rounds he connects with the people in the neighborhood. Through his
encounters he becomes the focus of this community, and he even works
a kind of magic. Their "acts of love" create in them a feeling of being
"turned around," as Wordsworth puts it. Their enclosed selves are
transcended as they reach out—a gesture that the neighbors in
Kronauer's novel are not ready to make. Indeed, they are so
preoccupied with themselves that they stare out at the pouring rain
without seeing the distraught young mother and miss their chance—not
only to act charitably, but to overcome their own isolation. Only by
opening their doors would they free themselves from their self-made
prisons and become at home in the world.

In that sense home is not a place because it extends from the
innermost self throughout the world. It manifests itself in the layers and
circles around us, and we create it anew every day by actively and
lovingly going about our daily lives. Not everyone's self is a castle,
however. In Kronauer's fiction the Frau Mühlenbecks are outnumbered
by the fragile and wary observers of life. Of course, many of her
readers aren't at home in themselves either. Some have a cat to help
them change meaningless space into a live, organic whole, like the
narrator in "Day with Interruption and Opponent." Others find their own
clever way, like the woman in "Miracle of a Hypothesis." Like the
schoolteacher in her novel they may feel the need to retreat to the
womb of their beds, so they can face the assault of humankind's
"compactness" against their fragility. The varying perspectives that
Kronauer's characters offer are all parts of one complex picture
portraying home as something that can be achieved yet cannot be
owned. If home is any sort of utopia, it is a collective, shared, global
utopia. So when Marguerite Duras describes how a woman "can't help

trying to interest her nearest and dearest, not in happiness itself but in the search for it" (48) she speaks of the happiness which lies in being at home in the self, in the body, and in the world.

NOTES

1. Theodor Adorno's comment, realistic in the 1930s, may be relevant to Germany today: "The caring hand that even now tends the little garden as if it had not long since become a 'lot,' but fearfully wards off the unknown intruder, is already the hand that denies asylum to the political refugee" (34).

2. According to Duras, "The house a woman creates is a Utopia. She can't help it—can't help trying to interest her nearest and dearest, not in happiness itself but in the search for it" (48, my translation).

3. Ernest Earnest and Joyce Carol Oates, quoted in Romines, 8ff.

4. *Aufsätze* 8. Since Kronauer's fiction has not yet been translated into English, I have made my own translations of the quoted passages.

5. Primo Levi illustrates his own "unnoticed but profound relationship" with a house when he says that "a short while ago, and with some discomfort, I realized that my favorite armchair occupied the precise spot where, according to my family tradition, I came into the world" (13).

WORKS CITED

Adorno, Theodor. *Minima Moralia: Reflections from Damaged Life.* London: NLB, 1974.

Ardener, Shirley, ed. *Women and Space: Ground Rules and Social Maps.* New York: St. Martin's, 1981.

Arnauer, Heinz Ludwig, ed. *Brigitte Kronauer.* Munich: Text+Kritik, 1991.

Bachelard, Gaston. *The Poetics of Space.* Trans. Maria Jolas. New York: Orion, 1964.

Beauvoir, Simone de. *The Second Sex.* Trans. and ed. H.M. Parshley. New York: Vintage, 1989.

Bromwich, David. "Alienation and Belonging." In Mack, *Home* 139-157.

Dormagen, Christel. "Versiegelt im leuchtenden Augenblick. Der lange Satz bei Brigitte Kronauer." In Arnauer, *Kronauer* 13-18.

Duras, Marguerite. *La Vie matérielle.* Paris: P.O.L., 1987.

Hollander, John. "It All Depends." In Mack, *Home* 27-46.

Kronauer, Brigitte. *Aufsätze zur Literatur.* Stuttgart: Klett-Cotta, 1987.

_____. *Frau Mühlenbeck im Gehäus.* Munich: *dtv* / Klett-Cotta, 1984.

_____. *Die gemusterte Nacht.* Munich: *dtv* / Klett-Cotta, 1989.

_____. *Die Revolution der Nachahmung Oder: Der tatsächliche Zusammenhang von Leben, Liebe, Tod.* Göttingen: Schlender, 1975.

Levi, Primo. "My House." *Other People's Trades.* New York: Summit, 1989: 11-15.

Mack, Arien, ed. *Home: A Place in the World.* New York: New York UP, 1993.

Romines, Ann. *The Home Plot: Women, Writing and Domestic Ritual.*
Amherst: U of Massachusetts P, 1992.

Wright, Gwendolyn. "Prescribing the Model Home." In Mack, *Home*
213-226.

6

Home-Breaking and Making in the Novels of Elizabeth Jolley

John O'Brien

The increasingly recognized novels of the contemporary Australian novelist Elizabeth Jolley have presented international readers with images of Australian women that are often both delightful and disturbing. On the one hand, Jolley repeatedly relies on age-old, traditional myths; on the other hand, she typically twists conventional ideas just enough out of proportion as to call them into question. In particular, the novels of Elizabeth Jolley, especially *Miss Peabody's Inheritance*, *The Well*, and *Palomino*, are rich with images of rustic domesticity. The idyllic surface, however, betrays a complexity that deserves detailed consideration. Sharing a self-conscious awareness of gender and myth, these three novels in particular benefit from a reading focusing on the ideological clash between feminism and the idea of "women's place" according to the Australian cultural tradition. In her consistent interest in domestic settings and in the similarities between the characters who inhabit them, Jolley both demystifies the traditional myth of domesticity and holds up, in *Palomino*, the possibility for alternative configurations of domesticity. Aimed at the level of individual consciousness, her charged scenarios hit home at the level of ideology where myth is most fundamentally challenged.

Historically, the home is the mythic cornerstone of Western male-centered cultural repression, as well as the focal point for the indoctrination of women. In Ruskin's sentimental glorification of the home, for example, the myth is a powerful one, and—like other dangerous myths—it justifies its existence under the guise of protection.[1] Charlotte Perkins Gilman is blunt: "The home, in its very nature, is intended to shield from danger; it is in origin a hiding place, a shelter for the *defenseless*" (qtd in Bell 395). That the ideology of domesticity depends upon the notion of female subservience is painfully clear, but its share in whatever constitutes Australian identity is more complex. At first glimpse, the Australian legend contradicts the stereotype of the defenseless woman. In the rugged bush, where resourcefulness was vital and husbands, to say the least, lacked a reputation for domestic co-operation, the women could hardly afford to be "feminine" in the Victorian sense.

The work of Henry Lawson offers a good example of the traditional representation of women in early Australian literature. Lawson's writing, which reflects so powerfully the core Australian national identity, is—on the surface, at least—atypical in offering a more careful consideration of women characters than is usual for early Australian literature. While his work reflects an interest in the role of women in the Australian bush, he nonetheless demonstrates the pervasive power of the traditional conceptions of women, ultimately presenting what it means to be Australian as decidedly masculine.[2] Though he may pay more attention to women in his work, Lawson is ultimately no advocate of androgyny. "No Place for a Woman," for example, shows the bush to be incompatible with traditional femininity, and the appreciation for women's accomplishments and strength under hardship is repeatedly overshadowed by expectations based on domestic associations. So, when the narrator first sees one bush home, his imagination constructs the absent wife from clues located well within the traditional myth: "The walls and the fire-place were white-washed, the clay floor swept, and the clean sheets of newspaper laid on the slab mantelshelf under the row of biscuit-tins that held the groceries. I thought that his wife, or housekeeper, or whatever she was, was a clean and tidy woman of the house" (249).

The "toughening" of the woman of the bush is a matter of necessity, and cultural sex roles, even in the unfriendly / unfeminine bush context, end up actually supporting tradition. In fact, if Lawson's women are empowered by the ambiguous freedom resulting from their abandonment and isolation, cultural perceptions of "woman's place" are not necessarily challenged. That place is still the home, and the women in the bush simply have the *additional* task of extra work outside the house. If the myths of traditional domesticity / femininity are discredited, it is primarily attributable to transporting the cult of domesticity to a bush context where "shelter" and "hiding places" are few and far between and the "defenseless" woman simply never lasts. In addition, the traditional myth of domesticity finds its way into Lawson's work in supporting the idea that the value of the bush woman is not in her assertive, aggressive femininity, but in the way she manages an impressive litany of masculine accomplishments. If she demands respect, then it is because she can behave so much like a man (for a woman). It is a contemporary writer like Jolley, employing both the traditional domestic myths and their variations, who shapes a more forceful resistance to patriarchal ideology.

Feminist scholars have long appreciated the value of the work of Roland Barthes in considering literary treatments of women in relation to myths of domesticity—most notably his focus on a text's potential to sabotage codes supporting ideological stances such as those that animate traditional domestic myths. Barthes provides the groundwork for re-reading classical texts in a way that calls into question codes that classify gender difference (138). By refusing to accept literary productions as transparent carriers of "content," Barthes interrogates myth in a way that Cheri Register argues is "one of the richest variants of feminist criticism." Being able, after all, to identify or expose mythic structures not only challenges existing patriarchal myths, but also makes it possible to "reimagine them female"—a process which Register calls "the reclamation of myth" (275). This dual focus on exposing and reimagining is, I argue, strikingly similar to Elizabeth Jolley's approach to domesticity in her novels, in particular her shared approach to what Barthes calls "demythification, the desire to reverse [a myth or stereotype], to blacken it, to read it inside out" (26). For Jolley, the myths she seeks to expose and re-imagine are those that rely on codified signs like the hearth, the home, and the kitchen to bolster the bourgeois myth of domestic tranquillity. In all the novels I will consider, the figure of the home is central. I will discuss *Miss Peabody's Inheritance* as an attack on domesticity, *The Well* as a study of the violence of repression, and finally *Palomino* as the novel which, in its portrayal of female friendship, offers the most vivid possibility for reimagining domesticity.

Miss Peabody's Inheritance presents, at times, a seemingly clear surface mirroring the domestic idyll conjured up in the dreamy lines about the girl in her "little hut in a little alpine field / And all her household things / Gathered in that small world" (63). One manifestation of this allusion to Goethe is the character of young Gwendaline Manners. Her name itself a Victorian echo, she acts in the novel as a negative example of the power of dominant ideology. Although Miss Thorne goes to great pains to take her on a trip to Europe and introduce her to the world at large, she recognizes that the girl is interested only in the domestic life: "All those years with the intellectual and musical background of Pine Heights . . . and the gel wants simply the kitchen, the ironing board and the baby bath" (76). Eventually Gwendaline accepts not just clothes from Mr. Frome, but a tote-bag for baby things and a marriage proposal. Convinced the girl has "had enough schooling for me," the persistent man speaks plainly: "I need a wife," he says, "it's as simple as that" (130-1). Gwendaline's world becomes as domestic as her fiancé's expectations.

Instead of relaxing into an easy, dominant mythic structure, however, the novel attacks the myth itself. The repressive nature of the home is epitomized by Miss Peabody's tyrannical, disabled mother who can even *hear* when the house needs dusting. In this novel more than the others, the stifling nature of the traditional home is starkly clear. Miss Peabody's father even made her "a dolls' house" to practice cleaning as a child: "And, when she was grown up and no longer had the dolls' house, she vacuumed and polished number 38 Kingston Avenue every weekend . . . [until] right under her mother's hopeful eyes, she turned into an old maid" (21-2).

Miss Peabody, then, doesn't just represent the grim side of the domestic myth. She lives it. Her life is "a series of clichés" (68), and her character in the novel is a study of the repression that is imposed by the "home-sweet home" ideology under which she was raised. Trapped in her home, she finds relief in her close friendship with a novelist, whose letters are "the greatest pleasure she had ever known" (99). Diana invites her into an alternative mythic world where the wildly exciting adventures of the novels and their exotic Australian author are staged. Even in the midst of her housework, she imagines the author of these homo-erotic adventure novels as Diana, the Goddess of the Hunt, "a tall woman grace[ful] and shapely about the neck and breast. She would wear tall riding boots" (8).

The inheritance of the title refers to more than the novel itself: it is also the gift of transgression that the dull domestic life of Miss Peabody has excluded, and that is why Dorothy is drawn to a novel like *Angels on Horseback*, which the novelist herself calls pornographic.[3] The novel-in-progress Dorothy receives in serial form is similarly naughty, at points reading like the silliest French erotica: "Ah! that's more like it. Oh wicked! Prickles! Shall I soap you? Of course you may do that again. As often as you like . . ." (11). Though reading about this "waterfight" disturbs Miss Peabody, it is, she vaguely senses, *exciting* to be disturbed in such a way. In the stiflingly non-transgressive myth she lives by, the most scandalous thing she can think to do is tell the office of her high blood pressure or buy metallic colored pantyhose, but in her vicarious enjoyment of the "schoolgirls gallop[ing] by on their strange, erotic, nocturnal adventures" (46), she is able to experience the thrill of movement she has been denied.

Along with resisting the domesticity that nearly strangles Miss

Peabody, the novel—especially the novel within-the-novel—is also playing with traditional and transgressive codes. The best example of the two combined occurs early in the novel when the ostensibly prim, proper, and benignly authoritative headmistress has her own novel reading interrupted by a mesmerizing display of sensual energy by Debbie, whose "long straight strong legs" (38) tempt Miss Thorne more than she would like. In a way that would please Barthes, Jolley takes the significance of the apron and reverses it and turns it inside out—all in the spirit of play: "For want of something to replace the immodest dress Matron has tied a domestic science apron tightly round the slender body . . . [She's thinking that] the aprons should be used more often; there was something virginal and attractive about them especially when worn next to the skin like this" (37-8). By the end of the young girl's blatantly seductive dance, not only is the meaning of the apron reversed, but so are the headmistress and student roles as well. Debbie is in complete control, receiving no punishment for her bold transgressions. The authority figure ends up having to speak more quietly than usual to disguise her trembling voice.[4]

Dorothy herself discovers the arbitrary and conflicting nature of mythic signification. When she studies the name Diana, she learns that it is full of built-in contradiction, to the point that the name means "both the Goddess of Virgins and the Goddess of Birth." Eventually, she concludes that the contradictions "make the Goddess human" (73), and in that single phrase lies much of what Jolley's novels accomplish, not just the subversion of traditional myths, but the discovery of a system of non-traditional codes that people living beyond tradition—all her primary characters—can embrace without punishment or shame. At the end of the novel, Dorothy makes a break by leaving the house at Kingston Avenue for Australia, for her a sign of transgression and possibility, and in doing so she is aware that to be free necessitates escaping the confines of home and myth. When she is capable of "putting Kingston Avenue out of her mind completely," she senses "enormous possibilities" and wonders if the appropriately named Miss Flourish might accompany her to Diana's farm.

The Well dramatizes the most tragic of consequences, a novel in which the domestic idyll is most romantically portrayed and most fully believed. Living in their isolated cottage, Kathy and Miss Harper enjoy every variety of domestic ritual. They wash and brush each other's hair, cultivate a little garden, enjoy evening storytelling, and even share late night lingerie parties, until—"entirely alone, together and happy" (39)—they realize that three years have slipped by unnoticed. In particular, the kitchen is central to their existence. They enjoy a vast collection of "innumerable cookbooks" (39) and on nothing less Victorian than a wood stove indulge in wondrous meals. Quite unlike the housework that so torments Miss Peabody, these women share an exceptional passion for domestic duties, especially cleaning and cooking. Under an erotic spell familiar to readers of Jolley, the authoritative figure, Miss Harper, falls for the young girl and trades her interest in the land and business for a life of pure pleasure organized around the tasks of the home. The outside world is dismissed with the help of a few checks to convenient charity organizations.

However, the smooth surface of the idyll itself is as deceptively tranquil as the repressive pleasantries of Victorian domesticity. Where *Miss Peabody's Inheritance* investigates stagnation and missed opportunity, *The Well* unearths the real violence of domestic repression, exposing a domestic idyll selfishly and ruthlessly enforced by Miss Harper. The cage Miss Harper provides is a gilded one, but George Bernard Shaw's use of the metaphor is still an accurate description of what is wrong with this home.[5] As becomes clear to the people in the town and to Mrs. Borden, Kathy is overprotected by Miss Harper. Even Kathy's best friend, Joanna, is perceived as a rival who is appropriately described in figurative terms suggesting a threat to domestic cleanliness: "Hester was vague in her mind about the life this other girl could have had but it was dirty and infected and should be kept away from the freshness and purity of their own lives" (45).

Miss Harper's most intense fears relate to the man Kathy inadvertently runs down and kills. Through his weird "after-life," he represents more than just the danger of theft and violence; he becomes the man she fears will inevitably steal Kathy away from the shelter of home and hearth. He is also suggestive of the young girl's own sexual desires which up to this point have been kept in a child-like state of "dainty innocence" (150), with vague fantasies of marrying the man of her dreams. In short, the mysterious man is a threat to all that domesticity holds dear as it is constructed and enforced by tradition in general and Miss Harper in particular.

The eerie voice from the well, the "spirit of the beast that goeth downward to the earth" (11), may not be "real," but the effect on Kathy certainly is. Miss Harper already fears marriage for Kathy, which she imagines in bestial terms, and finally she decides that Kathy must simply never leave: "She could not think of Kathy going away, not just yet. Not yet. Not ever" (162). Consequently, when the dead man surrealistically speaks, the reader's confusion as to whether he is actually alive is dwarfed by what the resurrection might mean. Kathy accepts his marriage proposal and his sexually suggestive talk, and she even begins, like Gwendaline, thinking about stocking up on baby supplies. It becomes similarly obvious to Miss Harper that Kathy's sexual awakening directly threatens her own idyll of domestic bliss.

The novel is resistant to the extent that it dramatizes vividly the price of imposing one's own domestic tranquillity on another. In illustrating the point, Jolley makes use of powerful symbolism in the figure of the well. For Miss Harper, the well is the "beast" she remembers from the Bible, the beast of her own sexuality, "those ugly places, unvisited, somewhere further on, far off and lower down beyond the end of the track. Places where Hester had never wanted to go" (151). In the irony of semiotic play, the well for Kathy represents the potential and vague eroticism of a sexuality not feared but anticipated. Therefore, with this cacophony of meanings, all converging at the well site, Miss Harper decides that the well must be permanently sealed if the idyll is to be restored. After a violent struggle with the floating corpse, she returns to the shelter of the cottage to wake Kathy with the offer of some freshly baked scones. Miss Harper denies the physical and symbolic cruelty of her action by pretending a smooth surface of domestic paradise, trying to fill the home with the "warm safe smell of baking" (110).

In *Palomino* the myth of domesticity is not just attacked but confronted with the notion that traditional domestic myths may be transformed in such a way that traditional myth is reclaimed to become a healthy idyll of feminine friendship. At first glance, *Palomino* may seem to suggest not so much a dialectic change, but a more radical reversal of gender roles. In Andrea's relationship to Laura, Jolley seems to invert a traditional male / female relationship. Upon closer analysis, there is no simple reversal. If Laura, because she is the property owner, is more "masculine," it is a role constantly contradicted by her often-mentioned innocence and weakness. Instead of a simple reversal of roles that would leave the hegemonic structure intact, their relationship is, like Diana's name, a complex mix of destroyed and reimagined myth. Andrea remembers Laura's "long deep kiss of possession" more for its tenderness than any impression of masculine proprietorship (189), and while their rustic home retains the traditional sense of home as shelter, there is a uniquely feminine inscription.

Jolley reimagines mateship's masculine codes of violence, abandonment, and alcohol in feminine terms (even down to the walkabout equivalent in the repeated European trip motif in her novels), but *Palomino* most powerfully forges an alternative myth of domesticity in the opportunities it finds in female friendship. Carroll Smith-Rosenberg's study of close relationships between nineteenth century women identifies such strong resistance in Victorian life, but in Jolley there is a distinct dialectic change. Where Victorian women had close relationships within or in spite of their subordinate role, in *Palomino* the female friendship is imagined more within the contemporary tradition of the feminist utopia, existing without men at all. In this way, one could say that the codes are not reversed or even abandoned, but reclaimed in the shape of a new idyll—perhaps a more determined effort at what was suggested in Miss Peabody's fantasies.[6]

What makes Laura's relationship with Andrea utopian in comparison with the others in Jolley's novels is, initially, the relative lack of sexual repression. It is there to be sure—especially for Laura early in the novel. Still, even if there is restraint, where the other two novels record painful self-denial and suppression of same-sex attraction and love, *Palomino* offers an example of a lesbian relationship with open physical and emotional expression that, by the end of the novel, no longer tolerates the "imprisoning of passion" (197).

Another reimagined aspect of conventional formulations of domesticity relates specifically to the possibility of open communication. In the other two novels, as in Lawson's male-female relationships, communication is always constrained, repressed, or encoded (as in the case of Diana's letters). In *Palomino*, there is a blunt honesty located far outside the masculine tradition. The openness in *Palomino*, the exchange of intensely personal secrets that makes up the bulk of the novel, is in deep contrast to silences resulting from the ideologically encouraged belief that "the home-bred brain of the woman continually puzzles and baffles the world-bred brain of the man" (Bell 396). The bond itself breaks old codes and establishes new ones. For Laura and Andrea, "it's the ideal of an Idyll. . . . Transparently simple. Isn't this how it is? Instead of wars and politics we are concerned with a friendship between two women, with the harvest from the land and with the birth of a baby" (219).

Miss Harper and Miss Thorne never transcend the masculine authority-role and consequently ruin their potential relationships in the complexities of domination, manipulation, and repression. Miss Peabody never escapes those traditional constraints that stifle the possibility of freedom. Both *Miss Peabody's Inheritance* and *The Well*, however, end on a somewhat positive note. Miss Peabody is about to engage herself in her inheritance, and even Miss Harper makes an effort toward a limited social engagement in the final scene with Mrs. Borden and her children. Thus, there is a hint at the end of both novels that the protagonists will find some new direction through writing (creation as an alternative to repression, destruction, or stagnation). They may even, in writing, find a way to transform their lives in the way illuminated in *Palomino*.

Elizabeth Jolley emphasizes that the most appropriate site for resisting traditional domestic mythology / ideology is within the self, which explains, in part, the distinct psychological perspective in her novels: "The world is threatened by the evil and the stupid. The only hope is the individual conscience which defies a meaningless mass morality" ("Author's Statement" 214). The feminine friendship in *Palomino* is not part of a larger desire to change society; as in *The Well*, these women want little to do with the larger world. However, the novel demands recognition of the fact that the masculine cultural codes from even before the Victorian cult of domesticity can be fought most effectively where such myths live on. The self is where dominant ideology does the most damage, under cover of seemingly transparent complicity in which repression and alienation deny a valuable sense of identity. So it is with the self that Jolley places her hope in *Palomino*, with the image of wholeness and love:

> We are not making any laws. Our world together is an isolated one. We are not imposing a structure which is harmful to anyone or out of harmony with other structures. Simply we are living here together. I am managing my small farm and you are having a holiday to recover from the illness brought on by malnutrition. We have come to know one another very deeply. I can't see that there is anything wrong. (193-4)

Diane Bell's *Generations* comes closest to extrapolating the significance of these individual structures when she concludes that "constructions of self, forged in the little worlds of home, give form to our cultural understandings of the socio-economic structures of 'the big world'" (qtd in Matthews 101). From the clash and entanglement of cultural codes, stereotypes, and subconscious survival tactics, Jolley invents a new context in which it is possible for a cage to be "reimagined" so that bird / cage metaphors may eventually be outdated and emancipation may finally and completely be achieved.

NOTES

1.   Ruskin voices the typical Victorian myth: "This is the true
        nature of home—it is the place of peace; the shelter, not only
        from all injury, but from all terror, doubt, and division . . . and
        wherever a true wife comes, this home is always round her.
        The stars only may be over her head, the glow-worm in the
        night-cold grass may be the only fire at her foot, but home is
        wherever she is; and for a noble woman it stretches far round
        her, better than ceiled with cedar or painted with vermilion,
        shedding its quiet light far from those who else were
        homeless" (qtd in Vicinus 31).

2.   As one might expect, nationalist songs and poems are
        especially blatant in their exclusion of women (Arthur Adams'
        "The Australian," for example), and when women are included,
        things don't get much better:

> Oh, Willie, dearest Willie,
> I'll go along with you,
> I'll cut off all my auburn fringe
> And be a shearer too.
> I'll cook and count your tally, love,
> While ringer-o you shine
> And I'll wash your greasy moleskins
> On the banks of the Condamine. (qtd in Palmer 63)

        Sociologists   like   Maureen   Baker   have   characterized
        contemporary Australia as still in the grip of myths of male
        domination and home-bound femininity (Hornadge 203).

3.   The title may be a play on the title of Coventry Patmore's *The
        Angel in the House*, but with these "Angels of the Hearth"
        sporting horses and riding boots.

4.   Like the use of the apron here, in other works, Jolley plays
        with domestic signs. In "Woman in a Lampshade," for
        example, an innocuous household item is transformed into
        something very different when worn on the head. It becomes
        a collapse of opposites (domestic tranquility when in its proper
        place; crazy perversity when worn): "It was like a garden-party

hat only more foolish because it was, after all, a lampshade. To wear the lampshade suggested the dangerous and the exotic while still sheltered under a cozy domesticity" (138).

5. Shaw's discussion of the metaphor in 1891 is similar to the conclusion reached here, that liberation must occur at the level of feminine consciousness: "If we have come to think that the nursery and the kitchen are the natural sphere of a woman, we have done so exactly as English children come to think that a cage is the natural sphere of the parrot: because they have never seen one anywhere else. . . . The sum of the matter is that unless Woman repudiates her womanliness, her duty to her husband, to her children, to society, to the law, and to everyone but herself, she cannot emancipate herself" (qtd in Finney 197).

6. Mellor's discussion of the resistant value of feminist utopian writing is especially appropriate here: "It attempts to describe and thus undermine the mythic power of a prevailing ideology or false consciousness. . . . It then offers a variety of alternative ways of structuring society which liberate both men and women from a masculinist ideology of false consciousness" (243). Mellor invites a comparison with Jolley's repeated use of male intruders, isolated settings, and female affinity with nature.

WORKS CITED

Barthes, Roland. *The Pleasure of the Text*. New York: The Noonday Press, 1975.

Bell, Linda A. *Visions of Women*. New Jersey: Humana Press, 1983.

Finney, Gail. *Women in Drama: Freud, Feminism, and European Theatre at the Turn of the Century*. Ithaca: Cornell UP, 1989.

Jolley, Elizabeth. "Author's Statement." *Australian Literary Studies* 10:2 (1981): 214.

_____. *Miss Peabody's Inheritance*. New York: Penguin, 1983.

_____. *Palomino*. New York: Persea Books, 1987.

_____. *The Well*. Victoria: Penguin, 1986.

_____. *Woman in a Lampshade*. New York: Viking Penguin, 1983.

Hornadge, Bill. *The Australian Slanguage*. Victoria: Methuen, 1987.

Lawson, Henry. *The Collected Stories of Henry Lawson*. Victoria: Penguin, 1981.

Matthews, Jill Julius. "'A Female of All Things': Women and the Bincentenary." *Australian Historical Studies* 23:91 (1988): 101.

Mellor, Ann K. "On Feminist Utopias." *Women's Studies* 9 (1982): 241-262.

Palmer, Vance. *The Legend of the Nineties*. Victoria: Melbourne UP, 1972.

Patmore, Coventry. *The Angel in the House*. London: J.W. Parker, 1856.

Register, Cheri. "Literary Criticism." *Signs* 6:2 (1980): 268-82.

Smith-Rosenberg, Carroll. "The Female World of Love and Ritual: Relations Between Women in Nineteenth-Century America." *Signs* 1:1 (Autumn 1975): 1-29.

Vicinus, Martha, ed. *Suffer and Be Still: Women in the Victorian Age*. Bloomington: Indiana UP, 1972.

7

Ironing Their Clothes

Julia Alvarez

With a hot glide up, then down, his shirts,
I ironed out my father's back, cramped
and worried with work. I stroked the yoke,
the breast pocket, collar and cuffs,
until the rumpled heap relaxed into the shape
of my father's broad chest, the shoulders shrugged off
the world, the collapsed arms spread for a hug.
And if there'd been a face above the buttondown neck,
I would have pressed the forehead out, I would
have made a boy again out of that tired man!

If I clung to her skirt as she sorted the wash
or put out a line, my mother frowned,
a crease down each side of her mouth.
This is no time for love! But here
I could linger over her wrinkled bedjacket,
kiss at the damp puckers of her wrists
with the hot tip. Here I caressed complications
of darts, scallops, ties, pleats which made
her outfits test of the patience of my passion.
Here I could lay my dreaming iron on her lap. . . .

The smell of baked cotton rose from the board
and blew with a breeze out the window
to the family wardrobe drying on the clothesline,
all needing a touch of my iron. Here I could tickle
the underarms of my big sister's petticoat
or secretly pat the backside of her pajamas.
For she too would have warned me not to muss
her fresh blouses, starched jumpers, and smocks,
all that my careful hand had ironed out,
forced to express my excess love on cloth.

8

The Dream Detectives

Clarissa Pinkola Estés

In our neighborhood, when women dream,
pot roasts rise over the rooftops,
crock-pots float out through kitchen windows—
off they go into the speckled blue.
Girdles of pink rubber with garters flapping
went their way heavenward, and
pointy circle-stitched brassieres aim and launch,
vaulting ahead of black-crusted ovens.
The oak floors that moaned, "wax me, wax me,"
creak apart, and stave by stave glide upward
'til they are flying in formation.
Wax jars, rags caked with gudj, boxes of suds dust,
ebb and eddy up there along with crystal and china—
the kind that must be scalded in order to come clean.
Oil stains unseated from garage cement
levitate like thin black doilies.
And the heavy wicker baskets of wet sheets,
and the lead lids of canning jars,
and the rakes and knives, and
the interchangeable chemicals
for hair and face and floor,
and all the black nighties and eye-lash curlers—
all these rise up into the sky
'til the heavens are filled
with the arsenal of women's work.
Now, there are metal planets
spinning on silver forks,
and entire lingerie galaxies.
There are novas beaten by a billion whisks,
and a Milky Way kept coiled
by a trillion wooden clothes-pins.
And all the gifts that women hated,
and all the gifts they never wanted,

all the bad husbands,
all the rotten children,
all of them floated up and up.
And the dreamers, the billions of women dreamers
awaken in the morning with everything gone,
not a mop-dreadlock left.
They lie to the dream detectives,
"Oh! It must have been a robbery,
why when I wasn't looking,
someone kidnapped everything.
Oh, oh my."

9

Penetrating Privacy: Confessional Poetry and the Surveillance Society

Deborah Nelson

Ideologically, family behavior may remain 'the most private and personal of all areas of behaviour, almost totally free from external supervision and control'; in practice it is anything but, and it is out of this discrepancy between ideal and real families, the one with simple and natural rights, the other propped up by a mass of civil, political and social sealing wax, that modern female sexual citizenship emerges. (Evans 245)

Home is our spy pond pool in the backyard,
the willow with its spooky yellow fingers
and the great orange bed where we lie
like two frozen paintings in a field of poppies.
(Sexton, "The Wedlock," ll. 29-32)

Confessional poetry needs to be reevaluated in the context of the highly charged political debate about privacy in which it arose. Critics of this poetry claim that the dark terrain the confessional poet explored was a private plot, nothing more than the suburban half acre that symbolized middle class life. Called private, narcissistic, and self-indulgent, confessional poetry has seemed the antithesis of sixties protest poetry that spoke to and for those embattled in the civil rights and anti-war movements.[1] However, the political debates central to America's redefinition of itself in the Cold War are not exhausted in these two movements; the debate over the right to privacy has also figured as one of the most volatile political controversies of the Cold War era. From *N.A.A.C.P. v. Alabama*[2] in 1958, to *Griswold v. Connecticut*[3] in 1965, to *Roe v. Wade*[4] in 1973, and *Bowers v. Hardwick*[5] in 1986, each decade's most significant privacy decision has echoed the political questions of its time and offered a site in which the definitions of private and public could be disputed. Moreover, since the right to privacy has primarily sheltered domestic liberty, protecting such areas as child rearing, contraception, and marriage, the battles waged over privacy have metonymically represented the conflicts over gender and sexuality that have marked the post-war era.

The period between 1960 and 1966, when the legal privacy debate focused almost exclusively on the privacy of the home, also witnessed an unprecedented exposure of the domestic sphere in such landmark confessional works as Anne Sexton's *To Bedlam and Part Way Back*, *All My Pretty Ones*, and *Live or Die*, Sylvia Plath's *Colossus* and *Ariel*, Adrienne Rich's *Snapshots of a Daughter-in-Law*, Allen Ginsberg's *Kaddish*, John Berryman's *Dream Songs*, with Robert Lowell's *Life Studies* in 1959 and W.D. Snodgrass's *Heart's Needle* in 1958 immediately preceding them. That this confessional moment should occur simultaneously with an outbreak of concern about the loss of privacy in the home suggests a contradiction. However, I propose that we read this apparent paradox as instead a parallel that reveals the irreconcilable tensions of Cold War domestic ideology. If we characterize both privacy and confession as issues of self-disclosure—who chooses if or when to make information about the self available and to whom—then the articulation of a right to privacy works with rather than against the explosion of confessional writing as responses to a pervasive sense of surveillance.[6] Confession, placed in the context of invasive scrutiny of the home, would seem to pre-empt surveillance by appearing to expose the desired secrets. The right to privacy, seen in the context of transgressive revelations about the home, would appear to censor the domestic realm by idealizing the withdrawal of private life from public scrutiny.

The pervasive sense of surveillance arose out of the paradox of what Elaine Tyler May has called "containment" ideology—i.e. that the home provided a defense against the insecurity of Cold War nuclear diplomacy (10-11). The excessive political importance this containment philosophy placed on the home necessitated its surveillance in order to guarantee compliance with the political ideals it was meant to represent. That is to say, the security offered by the private home could only be assured by violating its privacy. In contrast, by designating the home as the cradle of personal liberty and the cornerstone of democratic self-governance, the legal community paradoxically defined the home as *a*political. The Supreme Court in particular sought to protect the home as a wholly private sphere in order, it was said, to preserve liberty in the face of an increasingly intrusive organized society. However, as the private home rose in political importance as the crucible of democratic citizenship—the symbol and locus of the liberty denied to the subject of a totalitarian government—it was simultaneously denied a place in public discourse as anything but an ideal. Since the home of domestic ideology was, therefore, principally a metaphor and a contradiction, a figure for conformity as well as for libertarian individuality, exposing the metaphor of the ideal home as the fantasy that it was meant undermining a cherished ideological bulwark against totalitarianism.

While elevating domesticity to a sacred and quintessentially American virtue, the idealization of the home silenced the experience of women, the citizens who were to occupy this realm as their exclusive domain. In this context, their anti-metaphorical representations of the home placed women confessional poets at the crossroads of the politicization of the home, its silencing, and its surveillance. In order to enter the public sphere, women writers had to violate privacy and confront the myths of the private home as a source of liberty and even, ironically, of privacy itself. Writing from within the home about the home, these poets not only changed literary decorum, but they transformed a central political metaphor, legitimizing the discussion of what went on inside the home and making that discussion a reasonable concern of public discourse. In keeping with the 1960's radical questioning of American at-home authority and ideology, women poets like Sylvia Plath, Adrienne Rich, and Anne Sexton provided evidence that the threat was no longer just "out there," it was also "in here," and its very containment was unfitting the home for its political purpose. Confessional poetry's contribution to public discourse was the dismantling of domestic ideology through the act of exposure itself, through the self-disclosure of that which should have been the subject of surveillance.

With the 1959 publication of *The Eavesdroppers*, a series of academic studies and journalistic exposés describing the encroachments on privacy from government, big business, higher education, medical research, and computer databases began to reach wide audiences.[7] Within the context of these popular, and sometimes apocalyptic, discussions of privacy, the Supreme Court heard an increasing number of cases in which the home was invaded. These cases presented a diversity of violations from literal invasion, as in the case of *Mapp v. Ohio*,[8] where police entered a private home without a warrant, to metaphorical intrusion, as in the case of *Poe v. Ullman*,[9] where Connecticut's statute banning contraceptives opened the door for police trespass of bedrooms. Yet, despite the perceived encroachments on individual privacy during the Cold War, privacy was hailed as one of the characteristic rights of a democracy, one that defined "America" in opposition to the Soviet Union. The right to privacy became during the sixties an extremely important symbol distinguishing American democratic government from the police state, despite the totalitarian practices the U.S. government employed in order to defend itself against totalitarianism. Nevertheless, while privacy was a right of enormous importance, to actually seek or make use of it invited suspicion from neighbors and, occasionally, government agencies like the FBI.[10]

The omnipresence of surveillance in Cold War society was converting the notion of confession as a sacrament into the perception of confession as a criminal act. In the context of the invasive scrutiny of private life, Sylvia Plath, a poet who is rarely considered political, connects the pervasiveness of surveillance in ordinary life to this transformation of confession. The following poems written in 1962, for example, "The Other," "Words Heard, by accident, over the phone," "The Detective," "The Courage of Shutting-Up," "A Secret," "The Jailer," "Purdah," and "Eavesdropper," some of which were marked for inclusion in the *Ariel* collection, illustrate an extraordinary sensitivity to surveillance and the assault on privacy.[11] In these works, metaphors of policing, interrogation, and spying make the home a crime scene, and so a subject of surveillance. In terms similar to the Court's explanation in *Mapp v. Ohio* that an invasion of privacy constituted a "coerced confession," Plath's poem, "The Other," reveals the overdetermination of guilt that results from surveillance:

> The police love you, you confess everything.
> Bright hair, shoe black, old plastic,
> Is my life so intriguing?
> Is it for this you widen your eye-rings? (ll. 7-10)

There may be no crime to confess to ("Is it for this you widen your eye-rings?"), but it does not matter; everything—"bright hair, shoe black, old plastic"—constitutes evidence of a crime, everything contributes to the confession. When surveillance is never identified, the questions are always controlled by the observer. The watched have no idea what they might be confessing because they have no idea of what they are suspected. Plath then shows how omnipresent surveillance takes interpretation further out of the hands of the observed when she quickly shifts position from criminal to investigator, from confessor to interpreter. As if making an arrest, she begins her interrogation:

> Open your handbag. What is that bad smell?

It is your knitting, busily

Hooking itself to itself,
It is your sticky candies. . . . (ll. 14-17)

From the evidence she collects, Plath supplies her own answers, offering the interpretation that should be supplied by the silent defendant. Because both the questions and the answers are supplied to the confessor, the interpretation of the watchers is all that matters.

In Plath's "Eavesdropper" this climate of suspicion moves from official surveillance to infect personal relationships. In this poem in which neighbors spy on one another, the confessional poem becomes a hall of mirrors in which the watcher and the watched cannot be distinguished:

Do not think I don't notice your curtain—
Midnight, four o'clock,
Lit (you are reading),
Tarting with the drafts that pass,
Little whore tongue,
Chenille beckoner,
Beckoning my words in—
The zoo yowl, the mad soft
Mirror talk you love to catch me at.

How you jumped when I jumped on *you*!
Arms folded, ear cocked,
Toad-yellow under the drop
That would not, would not drop
In a desert of cow people
Trundling their udders home
To the electric milker, the wifey, the big blue eye
That watches, like God, or the sky
The ciphers that watch it. (ll. 28-45)

As she watches "you" reading, the reader watches her in the "mad soft / mirror talk you love to catch me at." Not only is Plath caught looking at herself, this "mirror talk" is the words he reads—her confessional poems. "How you jumped when I jumped on *you*!" reverses the watcher and the watched again. Plath watches him watch himself in her writing, creating an endless series of reflections in which each regards him / herself watching the other. This mirrored watching allows each to keep the other and the self in view, all the while policing the self while appearing to police the other. Moreover, this mutual regard, this double scrutiny, takes place beneath another all watching force: "the big blue eye / that watches, like God, or the sky / the ciphers that watch it." Beyond their individual surveillance, a larger investigation is taking place, one that, "like God or the sky," is simply inescapable. And yet, once again, the doubling redoubles as the watcher—blue eye, God, or sky—watches the "ciphers" watch it. By using the word "cipher"—which can disguise meaning or indicate the lack of meaning—Plath suggests both the coding of their behavior and its meaninglessness. This endless watching ultimately becomes exposed as a futile and paralyzing process for it only reveals more surveillance.

The decentralization of surveillance and suspicion that Plath's poem reflects flourished in the post-war growth of the suburbs, which, while placing the private home at the center of American consciousness, simultaneously enforced homogeneity and conformity. By the mid-fifties, fifty percent more Americans owned their own home than in the pre-war years (Davison 188), and the building of single-family dwellings was continuing apace. GI mortgages and William Levitt's application of the techniques of mass production to the building of homes made home buying accessible to citizens of even modest means (Halberstam 136-39). Mass-produced privacy was the paradox of the day. Intensifying this paradox, the marketing of single-family homes stressed white Anglo-Saxon conceptions of privacy and domesticity while these same suburbs enforced an ideal of the American nuclear family through the convenience of neighborhood surveillance.[12] As Adrienne Rich imagines in "September 21," the house itself served as an instrument of surveillance rather than a refuge from scrutiny.

> Wear the weight of equinoctial evening,
> light like melons bruised on all the porches.
> *Feel the houses tenderly appraise you,*
> *hold you in the watchfulness of mothers.*
>
> Once the nighttime was a milky river
> washing past the swimmers in the sunset,
> rinsing over sleepers of the morning.
> Soon the night will be an eyeless quarry
>
> where the shrunken daylight and its rebels,

loosened, dive like stones in perfect silence,
names and voices drown without reflection.

Then the houses draw you. Then they have you.
(ll. 1-12, emphasis mine)

What begins as benign and even fond attention—the "houses tenderly
appraise you / hold you in the watchfulness of mothers"—becomes
threatening by the end of the poem: "Then the houses draw you. Then
they have you." It seems that the comfort offered by the houses does
not protect the speaker from the blind and self-obliterating night,
("names and voices drown without reflection"), but instead threatens to
absorb her. Instead of returning to the bosom of the watchful mother,
the houses "have you," as if "you" could not escape. In like manner, the
suburbs were understood to absorb individuality, to homogenize each
family in the tremendous pressure to conform to the norms of the local
community. In other words, the suburban home, while marketed as a
source of privacy, was in fact a place defined by surveillance.

For Anne Sexton, as for most women of her generation, the
home was not a private place at all. However, because it offered little
opportunity for adult communication, for public or political discourse,
it was not really public in any significant way just as it was not private
in any meaningful way.[13] We can see this paradox of mass-produced
privacy in Sexton's "Self in 1958," a poem written in 1958 and revised
in 1965:

> What is reality?
> I am a plaster doll; I pose
> with eyes that cut open without landfall or nightfall
> upon some shellacked and grinning person,
> eyes that open, blue, steel, and close.
> Am I approximately an I. Magnin transplant?
> I have hair, black angel,
> black-angel-stuffing to comb,
> nylon legs, luminous arms
> and some advertised clothes.
>
> I live in a doll's house
> with four chairs,
> a counterfeit table, a flat roof
> and a big front door.

Many have come to such a small crossroad.
There is an iron bed,
(Life enlarges, life takes aim)
a cardboard floor,
windows that flash open on someone's city,
and little more.

Someone plays with me,
plants me in the all-electric kitchen,
Is this what Mrs. Rombauer said?
Someone pretends with me—
I am walled in solid by their noise—
or puts me upon their straight bed.
They think I am me!
Their warmth? Their warmth is not a friend!
They pry my mouth for their cups of gin
and their stale bread.

What is reality
to this synthetic doll
who should smile, who should shift gears,
should spring the doors open in a wholesome disorder,
and have no evidence of ruin or fears?
But I would cry,
rooted to the wall that
was once my mother,
if I could remember how
and if I had the tears. (ll. 1-40)

The second stanza of the poem describes the suburban structure that underlies so much of Sexton's work: "I live in a doll's house / with four chairs, / a counterfeit table, a flat roof / and a big front door. / Many have come to such a small crossroad." For Sexton, it was the inevitable position of this doll in the doll's house to live a paradox—to dwell entirely within the walls of the home, which, though completely divorced from the public, is neither private nor individual. Although no reference to a "doll's house" can fail to recall Nora's exit, in Sexton's poem the speaker seems immobilized, caught in the gunsights of an oppression, "(. . . life takes aim)," so generalized as to defy naming. The feeling of being a watched target extends beyond the threshold of her home so that, unlike Nora, she cannot simply close the door behind her to escape. If "*life* takes aim," there is no outside to escape to nor inside to hide within; there is only an overpowering sense that every action is monitored and that a wrong move could draw fire. From her position trapped in her doll's house, "windows . . . flash open on someone's city / and little more," offering no more than a glimpse of "someone's city"—a city and therefore a public world so far removed from her own life that she cannot even name whose city. Even so, this unknown city is the only view from her window.

To a large extent, this diffuse sense of surveillance was built into the structure of the suburban home itself. As Jane Davison writes in *To Make a House a Home*, the "open design" in the architecture of small suburban homes did away with doors and separate rooms, maximizing the sense of space while minimizing the opportunity for privacy. Along with this architectural elimination of privacy, Davison argues that the advocacy by women's magazines of "family togetherness" made women "wonder what was so private about life in homes. . . " (188). Betty Friedan diagnosed the results of such a loss of privacy when she associated the open plan in contemporary houses with the problem of the "feminine mystique." As she said in 1963, the open plan, since it did away with privacy, forced woman "to live the feminine mystique. . . . There are no true walls or doors . . . she need never feel alone for a minute, need never be by herself. She can forget her own identity in these noisy open-plan houses" (246). This correlation between the physical structure of the house—its absence of personal privacy—and the psychic structure of women—their loss of personal identity—governs confessional poetry as well. The loss of personal identity, which derived from a loss of privacy, gave birth to an autobiographical mode of writing which appeared to construct the personality of the poet obsessively while eschewing any notion of privacy. Compounding the lack of privacy within, the scrutiny of the home from without further dissolved the binary between public and private, obscuring the line between voluntary self-disclosure and forced confession. The open door of Sexton's last stanza symbolizes the suburban mandate to be open, which is the most effective surveillance of the home because the housewife who made an exhibition of her openness policed herself. What is demanded by Sexton's unnamed observer is clear: "what is reality / to this synthetic doll / who should smile, who should shift gears, / should spring the doors open in a wholesome disorder / and have no evidence of ruin or fears?" (156). Sexton implies that "they" demand a fiction of openness, which exposes a pretense of health; she is permitted some "disorder" only so long as it is "wholesome." Most important, the openness conveys that there is nothing to hide, which is all the more oppressive for it necessitates a willingness to be observed. In these terms, confessional poetry would seem to be the open door, and as such, a submission to surveillance through self-exposure.

Nevertheless, Sexton turns this openness inside / out and instead uses it as her most effective disguise. On the one hand, her "disorders" are never "wholesome" and so she defies the unstated agreement to reveal only that which is not secret. On the other, the fiction of openness is always misread as the transparent fact of openness. The confession which appears to "tell all" hides all the more effectively for telling only some, and so renders a paradoxical privacy. As a result, Sexton can appear to comply with the imperative to be open—all the while subverting it—by taking advantage of one of confessional poetry's defining tropes: the fiction of sincerity. Sexton's ironically triumphant exclamation "They think I am me!" attests to the success of this impersonation, which is nothing more than playing herself seamlessly. Instead of claiming another role, Sexton consistently acknowledges that she herself is the role, and that therefore she has no sincere self to reveal. However, while she clearly deceives "them," she does so through a fiction of sincerity, her most artful disguise, which begins to erode her own sense of reality. When she asks "what is reality to this synthetic doll. . . ?" she suggests that the complete erasure of privacy does away with truth as a component of confession; the confessor not only does not tell the truth, she can no longer distinguish what that truth might be.

The poem, "Live," in which Sexton responds directly to criticism of her confessional work, addresses the limitations of the fiction of sincerity. The second stanza reads:

> Even so,
> I kept right on going on,
> a sort of human statement,
> lugging myself as if
> I were a sawed-off body
> in the trunk, the steamer trunk.
> *This became a perjury of the soul.*
> *It became an outright lie*
> *and even though I dressed the body*
> *it was still naked, still killed.*
> It was caught

in the first place at birth,
like a fish.
But I played it, dressed it up,
dressed it up like somebody's doll.
Is life something you play?
And all the time wanting to get rid of it?
And further, everyone yelling at you
to shut up. And no wonder!
People don't like to be told
that you're sick
and then be forced
to watch
you
come
down with the hammer. (ll. 19-44, emphasis mine)

For Sexton, nakedness is also a disguise, one among the many that she employed to create the "perjury of the soul" that is her confession. Yet, her lament that ". . . even though [she] dressed the body / it was still naked, still killed," attests to the power of the confessional label which makes every costume appear "naked"—that is, transparent, literal, real—and so "killed," that is metaphorically dead and dead to metaphor. Regardless of the fact that she describes her work as a "perjury" and an "outright lie," the consistent reading of her work as pure confession denied it a metaphorical status, which is to say, the status of poetry. Rather than giving in to "everyone yelling at you to / shut up" in the belief that they are reading a confession rather than a poem, Sexton attempts to shift her "human statement" from confession, implying guilt, to testimony implying witness. This idea of witness is carried through in Sexton's explanation that "People don't like to be told / that you're sick / and then forced / to watch / you / come / down with the hammer." This watching, however, is complicated by the warning that she's sick and the idea that her watchers are forced. In what way does Sexton "force" "them" to watch? Who or what compels them to watch her "come down with the hammer?" This belief that watching is not a choice but a requirement forces us to understand the confessionalism of Sexton's work as response to a sense of widespread and unavoidable surveillance. In the case of the open door of the suburban home as with the self-revelation of the confessional poem, the watching will happen. "They," it appears, must watch.

On one level, therefore, confessional poetry echoes the sense of omnipresent surveillance that we find in other discourses. For example, in his 1966 dissent from *Osborn v. U.S.*, *Lewis v. U.S.*, and *Hoffa v. U.S.*,[14] Justice Douglas, the Supreme Court's most fervent champion of the right to privacy, provides a succinct and dramatic retrospective of the assaults on privacy that had provoked widespread concern and condemnation. This trio of cases, all of which revolved around privacy issues, brought into focus the dangers of the surveillance society. Douglas begins his dissent by declaring that:

> We are rapidly entering the age of no privacy, where everyone is open to surveillance at all times; where there are no secrets from government. The aggressive breaches of privacy by the Government increase by geometric proportions. (323)

He continues, sketching a harrowing portrait of the "age of no privacy" by citing examples from the Senate Committee on the Judiciary's 1965 hearings on "Invasions of Privacy":

> Secret observation booths in government offices and closed television circuits in industry, extending even to rest rooms, are common. Offices, conference rooms, hotel rooms, and even bedrooms . . . are 'bugged' for the convenience of government. Peepholes in men's rooms are there to catch homosexuals. . . Personality tests seek to ferret out a man's innermost thoughts on family life, religion, racial attitudes, national origin, politics, atheism, ideology, sex, and the like. Federal agents are often 'wired.' . . . They have broken and entered homes to obtain evidence. Polygraph tests of government employees and of employees in industry are rampant. The dossiers on all citizens mount in number and increase in size. Now they are being put on computers so that by pressing one button all the miserable, the sick, the suspect, the unpopular, the offbeat people of the Nation can be instantly identified. (323-324)

While I have not reproduced Douglas' complete record of invasions, I quote him at some length because his catalogue is as wide-reaching as it is well-documented. Moreover, the interpretation Douglas places on the government's dossier system, that "all the miserable, the sick, the suspect, the unpopular, the offbeat people of the Nation can be instantly identified," indicates that mind control rather than crime control was perceived as the principal motivation for government surveillance. The

Senate Committee studying the abuse of police state tactics by government agencies provides ample evidence for Douglas to conclude in a footnote that "Government is using such tactics on a gargantuan scale and has become callous of the rights of the citizens" (324, footnote 9). Furthermore, a brief inspection of this list indicates that law enforcement was not the only perpetrator of offensive intrusions into private life; big business, education, and bureaucracy were all complicit in invading the "sacred" space of the home.

On another level, however, the home in women's confessional poetry disputes the Court's notion of a "sacred" or private space untainted by public interests. In *Griswold v. Connecticut*, the 1965 decision which struck down Connecticut's prohibition against the use of birth control, the Court erected a constitutional right to privacy that would protect the home from scrutiny and consequently interference from the public realm. Douglas, speaking for the majority, argued that "The present case . . . concerns a relationship lying within the zone of privacy created by several fundamental constitutional guarantees" (480). This zone, which is the home, represented an absolute *a priori* privacy that could be reclaimed by imposing legal barriers to surveillance. By relying on the 1886 case *Boyd v. U.S.*,[15] the Court implicitly invoked Victorian notions of public and private spheres and even the recurring image in privacy cases of a "man's home as his castle." Likewise, the home Justice Harlan described in *Poe v. Ullman* in 1960 and reiterated in *Griswold* is a political metaphor that gathers ideological gravity from the layers of abstraction that both idealize and mystify:

> If the physical curtilage of the home is protected, it is surely as a result of solicitude to protect the privacies of the life within. Certainly the safeguarding of the home does not follow merely from the sanctity of property rights. The home derives its pre-eminence as the seat of family life. And the integrity of that life is something so fundamental that it has been found to draw to its protection the principles of more than one explicitly granted constitutional right. (551)

The language that Harlan used points to the fundamentally metaphorical character of his construction of the home. "Sanctity," "seat of family life," and elsewhere "sacred," all indicate that the ideal privacy being lost in the view of the Court is an abstraction born of traditional conceptions of the home as a male retreat from public life.

That contraception should be the arena in which the Court

defined the right to privacy tells us about the fears for specifically male privacy that lie behind this right. Douglas's famous image from *Griswold v. Connecticut*—"Would we allow the police to search the sacred precincts of marital bedrooms for telltale signs of the use of contraceptives" (480)?—echoes his earlier imagined invasion in *Poe v. Ullman*: "If we imagine a regime of full enforcement of the law in the manner of an Anthony Comstock, we would reach the point where search warrants issued and officers appeared in bedrooms to find out what went on" (651). In both cases, it is the *imagined* presence of the policeman in the bedroom that elicits the right to privacy. What we can see is that the Court perceived the Connecticut statute legitimating the surveillance of the bedroom to be more threatening in the context of a heightened awareness of invasions of privacy. In other words, the very real possibility of this penetration—both the ability and willingness to survey the bedroom—was documented in court cases, popular exposés, and legislative hearings, and this documentation compelled the Court to establish the home as the sacred zone of the right to privacy.

It is the way that Douglas conceives of the invasiveness of the birth control statute that indicates the feared loss of male prerogative behind the invasion of the bedroom. Douglas's footnote to his imagined enforcement of the law, officers appearing with warrants in bedrooms, relates Connecticut's contraception statute to another invasive law. He notes:

> Those warrants would, I think, go beyond anything so far known in our law. The law has long known the writ of *de ventre inspiciendo* authorizing matrons to inspect the body of a woman to determine if she is pregnant. This writ was issued to determine before a hanging whether a convicted female was pregnant or to ascertain whether rightful succession of property was to be defeated by assertion of a suppositious heir. (651)

Douglas's reading of the invasiveness of the Connecticut statute bears investigation. In his interpretation the "writ of *de ventre inspiciendo* authorizing matrons to inspect the body of a woman to determine if she is pregnant" is less invasive than a warrant to enter a bedroom. By his standards, the intrusion into the bedroom "goes beyond anything so far known in our law." Yet, it is difficult to equate the inspection of a woman's body, particularly to verify pregnancy, with the invasion of the bedroom, much less to perceive the bedroom's trespass as the more troubling violation. What we can determine from Douglas's use of this analogy, however, is that the bedroom is at least as private to a man as her body is to a woman. The house, then, or at least the bedroom, becomes analogous to the woman's body. To allow the police to penetrate the bedroom is to allow them to figuratively penetrate the man's body. That the woman's body can be literally invaded, in fact that the policing of her body makes up a long tradition in "our law," demonstrates that women's privacy is not truly at issue in birth control cases like *Poe v. Ullman* and *Griswold v. Connecticut*, but rather it is the father's privacy that is being defended. The surveillance of the woman's body for the purposes of patriarchy—to determine inheritance—is a legal legacy that reemerges in *Roe v. Wade* in the incarnation of the doctor who has replaced the matron.

In these dissents, we can see that the privacy safeguarded as a newfound constitutional right is the privacy of the patriarch whose moral autonomy is challenged by the paternalism of the state. The public intervention in the home represented by the state prohibition against contraception mocked this patriarchal authority, which was maintained through a rigid distinction between public and private. The blurring of the boundaries of public and private represented for the Court an improper contamination of the private sphere with public concerns, as if those concerns manifest themselves only in the physical intrusion of the home. Therefore, the Court reasserts patriarchal privilege when it redraws the boundaries between public and private. In contrast, Sexton's poems about the home denied the possibility of an *a priori* privacy and repositioned the home as a social, rather than private, territory, one which was political because implicated in public concerns, but private only insofar as it was isolated from public forums. Defined by its lack of privacy, the home of the confessional poets is neither properly public nor safely private.

The analogy between the home and the woman's body in Douglas's footnote reappears in "Housewife," a poem in which Sexton fuses "house" and "wife" in order to show the effects on men and women of a too intimate identification between women and the metaphorical home. In the poem, the transformation of the woman into the house makes the intrusion into the house or body a similar violation while at the same time, the collapse equates the disclosure of the private home with the exposure of the body.

> Some women marry houses.
> It's another kind of skin; it has a heart,
> a mouth, a liver and bowel movements.

The walls are permanent and pink.
See how she sits on her knees all day,
faithfully washing herself down.
Men enter by force, drawn back like Jonah
into their fleshy mothers.
A woman *is* her mother.
That's the main thing. (ll. 1-10)

The merging of the woman with the house determines the man's relationship to the private. Unlike Douglas's or Harlan's vision of the man's position in the home, Sexton's line "Men enter by force, drawn back like Jonah" suggests that men have a very temporary (as opposed to "permanent") presence in the house and that their position inside is unnatural. Their entry "by force" evokes a rape and the analogy to Jonah, the disobedient prophet who was expelled from the whale three days after his ingestion, reminds us of men's withdrawal from the home rather than their coexistence in it. The unnaturalness of their position inside the home becomes clearer when we find that they are drawn into their "fleshy mothers." For a man, to be inside the house is to be inside the mother, which provides two equally uncomfortable alternatives: he becomes either a child or an incestuous rapist. With this invocation of the mother, the structure of the house completely disintegrates—public and private, inside and outside intertwine, generational divisions disappear ("a woman *is* her mother"), and history draws to a halt. Instead, there is an endless cycle of transgression that perpetually returns to the beginning—the mother. From this perspective, the home is the world not of adult citizens but of mothers and children; it is a nursery where independent adults do not exist.

The poem works by literalizing the word "housewife," defining it first as the wife of a house—"some women marry houses"—and then, as the wife who is a house. Just as the poem begins by describing "some women" and concludes by defining all women ("A woman *is* her mother."), so too does the woman who marries a house inevitably become that house. Initially, the woman remains separate from the structure: "It's another kind of skin; it has a heart, / a mouth, a liver and bowel movements"—indicating that while the house is a body, it is not clearly human, nor specifically female. However, with the line "the walls are permanent and pink," the house is no longer "it," comfortably separate from the woman and so the distinction between the woman and the house begins to break down. By the time we "[s]ee how she sits on her knees all day / faithfully washing herself down," the woman has completely merged with the house and as a result, we are privy to her most intimate moments—we see her bathing—and so distinction between the public and private no longer exists external to the woman as the threshold to the home. Instead, she has internalized it and so the only private space left to her is that which is within the body. All spaces external to the body have become public spaces. When the woman becomes the house and internalizes the public / private boundary, she is both exposed and silenced. What's more, her transformation marks the moment of the reader's and speaker's *dis*-identification with the subject of the poem. For the first time, the speaker addresses the reader with an imperative, "see," shifting the relationship to the woman from one of possible identification to one of observation. We are explicitly instructed to become voyeurs, and as a result, the poem takes place at a distance from the woman. Because reader and poet speak about, but no longer with or to her, becoming the house has excluded her from the public discourse the poem engages. As Sexton shows, this disconnection of the woman from public discourse was one of the results of marking the threshold of the home as the border between public and private and then idealizing privacy. While men risked committing violence by crossing into the private sphere, they could move and speak freely beyond the threshold of the house. As a result, the prohibition against violating privacy did not leave men voiceless. In contrast, women, whose whole existence in the Cold War 1950s and early 1960s was defined within the walls of the home, were left silent with the prohibition against disclosing the private. Furthermore, the internalization of the threshold meant any entry by a woman onto the public stage would be perceived as a kind of exposure. Privacy would always be violated when women, who are defined as wholly private, speak about their lives.

Anne Sexton's "For John Who Begs Me Not To Enquire Further," written in 1959 and Justice Harlan's dissent in the 1960 Supreme Court opinion, *Poe v. Ullman*, form a dialogue about the relationship of the private to public discourse. *Poe v. Ullman*, a forerunner to *Griswold v. Connecticut*, was a case brought by a married couple, a married woman, and their doctor which asked the court to grant declaratory relief from the Connecticut statute prohibiting the use of birth control. Though *Poe* was held by the majority on the court to be non-justicible (meaning that the court could not rule on it) because they perceived no imminent threat to the appellants, Justice Harlan's dissent became a crucial building block in the formation of constitutionally protected privacy. Taken from precisely the same historical moment, Sexton's poem and Harlan's dissent present divergent conceptions of the relationship of private life to public discourse. Harlan's vision of privacy aspires to a complete silencing of private life and retains the strict binary opposition between public and private that fifties Cold War ideology held in place. Sexton, in contrast, maps out the territory *between* the public and the private, acknowledging both the uselessness and the impossibility of maintaining a rigid division between the two.

Justice Harlan's 1960 dissent in *Poe v. Ullman* addresses the suitability of private life, particularly sexuality, for public discourse. Harlan finds the statute unconstitutional not because it criminalizes recreational (as opposed to procreational) sex but because it would require criminal prosecution which would, more ominously, necessitate testimony about private matters. His dissent reads:

> Precisely what is involved here is this: the State is asserting the right to enforce its moral judgment by intruding upon the most intimate details of the marital relation with the full power of criminal law. Potentially, this could allow the deployment of all the incidental machinery of the criminal law, arrests, searches and seizures; inevitably, it must mean at the very least the lodging of criminal charges, a public trial, and testimony as to the *corpus delicti. Nor could any imaginable elaboration of presumptions, testimonial privileges, or other safeguards alleviate the necessity for testimony as to the mode and manner of the married couples' sexual relations, or at least the opportunity for the accused to make denial of the charges.* (498, emphasis mine)

It is frequently instructive to read the way that justices shift from the issue at hand to a more troubling issue at the margins of the case they are adjudicating. Like Douglas, who imagined the policeman's invasion of the marital bedroom, Justice Harlan also imagined what *might happen* but what, in fact, did *not* happen in *Poe v. Ullman:* married couples testifying about their sex life. For Harlan the mere possibility of this testimony justifies striking down the Connecticut statute. Yet, the reason that this statute stayed on the books from 1879 to 1965 was that such testimony was never indeed compelled; the law, not enforced in the home, functioned only to prohibit the distribution of contraceptives by birth control clinics. Furthermore, married couples rarely testified on their own behalf or even attached their names to briefs, hence the use of pseudonyms—Poe, Doe, and Roe—in all the landmark birth control cases. In fact, the only names associated with birth control and abortion cases are those of clinic operators and doctors, providers rather than users of birth control.

Justice Harlan does not deny that the state traditionally regulated the morality of its citizens; he claims that all civilized societies do that. Nor does the Justice trouble himself over whether regulating family size is a rational implementation of state power. Instead, Harlan finds that forcing testimony about private conduct, even if the testimony consisted of no more than a denial of the criminalized behavior, would constitute an unjustifiable exercise of state power even though regulating the private behavior would not. The violation is intolerable to him for he sees the physical home, sanctified as the "seat of family life," as fundamentally outside of the realm of public discourse and he cannot envision any kind of procedural safeguard that would prevent its disclosure. What Harlan and later Justice Douglas conclude is that the ineffable importance and "sacred" nature of private life necessitate silence about it. On the one hand, private matters derive their sacredness from being so intimate that they are withdrawn completely from public view. On the other, withdrawing from public view is what makes private life so sacred. In any case, the mutual reinforcement of sacredness and privacy necessitates that private life remain unvoiced or else risk pollution.

The court argued that private life, however, not public discourse would be compromised whereas critics of confessional poetry, like John Holmes, Sexton's first mentor and teacher, believed that public discourse suffered from its contamination with the trivialities or tragedies of private life. In response to his warning not to publish her first collection of poems, *To Bedlam and Part Way Back*, Anne Sexton wrote a personal letter defending the publication of her confessional work and enclosed the poem that was her poetic manifesto and, ultimately, her critique of privacy: "For John Who Begs Me Not To Enquire Further."

> Not that it was beautiful,
> but that, in the end, there was
> a certain sense of order there;
> something worth learning
> in that narrow diary of my mind,
> in the commonplaces of the asylum
> where the cracked mirror

or my own selfish death
outstared me.
And if I tried
to give you something else,
something outside of myself,
you would not know
that the worst of anyone
can be, finally,
an accident of hope.
I tapped my own head;
it was glass, an inverted bowl.
It is a small thing
to rage in your own bowl.
At first it was private.
Then it was more than myself;
it was you, or your house
or your kitchen.
And if you turn away
because there is no lesson here
I will hold my awkward bowl,
with all its cracked stars shining
like a complicated lie,
and fasten a new skin around it
as if I were dressing an orange
or a strange sun.
Not that it was beautiful,
but that I found some order there.
There ought to be something special
for someone
in this kind of hope.
This is something I would never find
in a lovelier place, my dear,
although your fear is anyone's fear,
like an invisible veil between us all . . .
and sometimes in private,
my kitchen, your kitchen,
my face, your face. (ll. 1-45)

In addition to its private circulation, Sexton also published the poem in her first collection and so it became a public affirmation of her decision to break down the barriers between public and private. Many feminist critics have read "For John . . . " as Sexton's clearest expression of her motivations for writing poems which dealt openly and even flamboyantly with subjects that cross over from the autobiographical into the secret and shameful, subjects such as suicide, madness, adultery, menstruation, abortion, incest, and domestic violence. Yet we can see, given the reservations articulated by John Holmes, that Sexton was responding to a question of what both poetry and public discourse could represent.

In "For John" Sexton mocks the narcissism of her confessions as "the narrow diary of [her] mind," "the cracked mirror," and "[her] own selfish death," bitterly but ironically exclaiming that "It is a small thing / to rage in your own bowl." Yet this rage is not a small thing, rather the bowl is, and the bowl is glass, a transparent fishbowl, an instant metaphor of exposure. As we can see from the next lines, her revelations do not remain private, and hence, they are no longer insignificant personal matters but rather, as Alicia Ostriker claims in *Seduction and Theory*, "transpersonal" (157). In the first crossing from one private domain to another—"Then it was more than myself; / it was you, or your house / or your kitchen"—the rage that would be small in one's own bowl repeatedly assaults the private space of the reader / John Holmes, insisting through repetition on identification—"you . . . your . . . your." This identification with the reader returns in the final lines of the poem, no longer echoing, searching for a response, but instead rendering a precise symmetry that admits no evasion: "my kitchen, your kitchen, / my face, your face." Not only does Sexton construct an analogy between face and kitchen, an unexpected alignment that links the private zone of the kitchen with the private *and* public self of the face, she suggests that the reader cannot disavow this identification. Though it happens "in private," the lessons of the confession inevitably find their way behind the "invisible veil between us all. . . ," which is the barrier imposed by the reader's fear of identification. It is not, after all, the irrelevance of her work that motivated John Holmes to attempt to silence Sexton, but rather his identification with her that unnerved him. Sexton intimates that the motive for shrouding private life under a "veil" is the resistance to identifying with writers who make us anxious, particularly women writers, with whom she suggests male readers will identify if they would permit themselves to do so. So when she discarded her veil, refusing to disguise herself by adopting more appropriately "public" subjects and forms, she forced an intimacy and identification that changed the face of contemporary poetry.

The revelations of self and of private life, symbolized by the "house" and the "kitchen," make up what Carolyn Forché has called the "social," that intermediate ground between the private and the political (31). We can see that Sexton's justification depends on speaking the private, but not simply *in* private. Private matters, according to this poem, do not need a public forum because they move inexorably from home to home through the power of identification. And yet the circumstances of the publication—she addresses her reader in the public domain of a collection as well as in the private sphere of a letter—remind us that Sexton does in fact need a public forum, in this case a publisher willing to promote her work, and that it is the impending publication of her work that finally moves John Holmes to express his distaste and discomfort. At issue for Sexton, and for many of her readers, both sympathetic and suspicious, is the appropriateness of her subject—private life—for public discourse.

The title "For John Who Begs Me Not to Enquire Further" echoes Sophocles' *Oedipus*, a reference Sexton suggests in the epigraph she chose from a letter Goethe wrote to Schopenhauer making reference to Jocasta's desire for Oedipus "not to enquire further." As Alicia Ostriker points out, this reference to Oedipus positions Sexton in the traditionally male role of truth-seeker and public figure while placing Holmes in Jocasta's conventionally timid female role (156). Furthermore, Diane Middlebrook explains his timidity as Holmes' own guilt over his wife's suicide, a guilt Sexton unconsciously exploited in her response to his complaints that her poetry gave nothing to the reader (98-100). But, though each critic notes Sexton's role as Oedipus and each remarks on the quest for a "transpersonal" aesthetic, neither considers the political implications of this choice of frame for her poem. Oedipus is not merely a "transpersonal" figure; he is a political figure. What's more, *Oedipus* is a drama that revolves around the relationship of private sin to political health. It is the city's suffering, after all, that prompts Oedipus to search out and divulge his private transgressions. This complicated link between political health and private morality had long been a staple of Cold War ideology as Elaine Tyler May has shown. This allusion indicates that Sexton was aware of the political implications of her personal revelations and that her manifesto, at least as part of her collection, does not depend on a personal motivation for writing. In other words, it is not just John Holmes to whom she writes.

Opponents of confessional poetry and the framers of constitutional privacy shared a common desire to keep what happened in the home outside of public discourse. Taking up positions akin to

John Holmes', later critics like Paul Breslin, Charles Altieri, and Walter Kalaidjian could not appreciate how the exposure of the inadequacies or mythologies of the home contributed to a public and political debate.[16] Similarly, Harlan's development of the right to privacy depended on maintaining the sanctity of the home, whose image could only be tarnished by public testimony about private sexual behavior. For these writers and thinkers, the public and private spheres remained pure only insofar as each could be distinguished from the other and this distinction could only be sustained by preventing *private* life from becoming a subject of public discourse. However, confessional women poets' construction of the home irrevocably changed the threshold between public and private. Their display of suburban domesticity de-idealized the home and made clear that it was no longer, nor had it ever been, an absolute retreat from public concerns. Moreover, by deconstructing the home, they were able to engage in public debate with new authority and so to redefine the subjects deemed public. The debate over privacy in the sixties, by paradoxically legitimating the exposure and discussion of private life, helped women to cross the threshold into the public arena and eventually to lobby for their own right to privacy, represented however ambivalently by *Roe v. Wade*. And perhaps the effect of this open house continues, though in ways less frightening because now familiar. Julie Iovine's 1994 *New York Times Magazine* article on home design states that "the line between public and private, once absolute is not only shifting but dissolving. In its place is the possibility of a comfort zone where public and private overlap, share the same elements and create a new sense of community" (21). It appears that opening the home to the public and the public to the home continues to demand a reimagination of both.

NOTES

1.   Walter Kalaidjian's extensive critical history of contemporary
       poetry offers a thorough retrospective on the perception of
       confessional poetry as a "private" art (10-32). Kalaidjian's
       contention that confessional poetry "led to a poetic solipsism
       at the end of ideology and 'beyond' politics" (14) needs
       revision if we remember that privacy itself was one of Cold
       War America's defining political controversies. Many feminists
       literary critics have, of course, long argued the political
       relevance of confessional poetry.

2.   357 U.S. 449 (1958).

3.   381 U.S. 479 (1965).

4.   410 U.S. 113 (1973).

5.   478 U.S. 186 (1986).

6.   While I have not drawn directly on Foucault's theories of
       surveillance and confession, I am certainly indebted to his
       landmark studies *Discipline and Punish: The Birth of the
       Prison*, and *The History of Sexuality, Volume One: An
       Introduction*.

7.   See Samuel Dash. In 1962, Morris Ernst's *Privacy: The Right
       to Be Let Alone* began to define a constitutional right to
       privacy; in 1964 two best-selling books—Myron Brenton's *The
       Privacy Invaders* and Vance Packard's *The Naked
       Society*—alerted the nation to the perils of the surveillance
       society; in 1967, Alan Westin's *Privacy and Freedom* took a
       comprehensive look at privacy from anthropological, legal, and
       philosophical perspectives; in 1968 Bernard Spindel's *The
       Ominous Ear* described the sophistication of wiretapping and
       its widespread use; and in 1969, *On Record: Files and
       Dossiers in American Life* (ed. Stanton Wheeler) revealed the
       kinds and amounts of information the government compiled in
       dossiers on private citizens while Jerry Rosenberg declared *The
       Death of Privacy*. *Roe v. Wade* in 1973 and the Privacy Act
       and the Freedom of Information Act of 1974 transformed the

context of the privacy debate as did the gradual acceptance of a certain base level of surveillance in American society.

8.   367 U.S. 643 (1961).

9.   367 U.S. 497 (1961).

10.   According to Benita Eisler, in the logic of the "mushroom cloud" of personality tests administered to school children and job applicants alike, "[s]olitude and solitary pursuits were not only worrisome in themselves; such preferences pointed to other, still more dangerous tendencies" (37).

11.   It is well known that Plath's selections for *Ariel* were amended and reordered after her death by her husband / editor, Ted Hughes, omitting, as Marjorie Perloff has argued in *Poetic License*, poems that revealed Plath's anger over his infidelity. While I find Perloff's reading persuasive, these poems also have intriguing political readings. Furthermore, there are indications throughout her work that Plath was sensitive to her political context. The introduction to *The Haunting of Sylvia Plath* by Jacqueline Rose is perhaps the most complex working through of Plath's political and historical awareness.

12.   Both Jane Davison and Myron Brenton associate privacy with "Anglo-Saxon" norms. Throughout her discussion of twentieth-century architecture, Davison remarks on the nostalgia for supposedly Anglo-Saxon ideals manipulated by architects and housing developers. Brenton argues that "[t]hroughout modern history man—in particular Anglo-Saxon man—has bitterly resisted any attempt to encroach too greatly on his privacy" (225). Given the culturally specific nature of privacy, we should recognize that the privacy endorsed by the Supreme Court and deconstructed by confessional poets derived from Anglo-American roots.

13.   Anita Allen defines the concept of "meaningful privacy" in *Uneasy Access: Privacy for Women in a Free Society*.

14.   385 U.S. 323, 87 S. Ct. 439 (1966).

15.   116 U.S. 616 (1886).

16.   See Paul Breslin and Charles Altieri for their critiques of confessional poetry's refusal to engage public issues.

WORKS CITED

Allen, Anita. *Uneasy Access: Privacy for Women in a Free Society.* Totowa, NJ: Roman and Littlefield, 1987.

Altieri, Charles. *Enlarging the Temple: New Directions in American Poetry during the 1960's.* Cranbury, NJ: Associated UP, 1979.

Brenton, Myron. *The Privacy Invaders.* New York: Coward-McCann, 1964.

Breslin, Paul. *The Psycho-Political Muse: American Poetry Since the Fifties.* Chicago: U of Chicago P, 1987.

Dash, Samuel. *The Eavesdroppers.* New Brunswick, NJ: Rutgers UP, 1959.

Davison, Jane. *To Make a House a Home: Four Generations of American Women and the Houses They Lived in.* New York: Random House, 1994.

Eisler, Benita. *Private Lives: Men and Women of the Fifties.* New York: Franklin Watts, 1986.

Ernst, Morris. *Privacy: The Right to Be Let Alone.* New York: Macmillan, 1962.

Evans, David T. *Sexual Citizenship: The Material Construction of Sexualities.* London: Routledge, 1993.

Forché, Carolyn, ed. *Against Forgetting: Twentieth-Century Poetry of Witness.* New York: W.W. Norton, 1993.

Foucault, Michel. *Discipline and Punish: The Birth of the Prison.* Trans. Alan Sheridan. New York: Vintage, 1979.

____. *The History of Sexuality, Volume One: An Introduction.* Trans. Robert Hurley. New York: Vintage, 1978.

Friedan, Betty. *The Feminine Mystique.* New York: W.W. Norton, 1963.

Halberstam, David. *The Fifties.* New York: Villard Books, 1993.

Iovine, Julie V. "The New Comfort Zone." *New York Times Magazine Part 2* (2 October 1994): 21.

Kalaidjian, Walter. *Languages of Liberation: The Social Text in Contemporary American Poetry.* New York: Columbia UP, 1989.

May, Elaine Tyler. *Homeward Bound: American Families in the Cold War Era.* New York: Basic Books, 1988.

Middlebrook, Diane. *Anne Sexton: A Biography.* Boston: Houghton Mifflin, 1991.

Ostriker, Alicia. "Anne Sexton and the Seduction of Audience." Ed. Diane Hunter. *Seduction and Theory.* Urbana: U of Illinois P, 1989. 154-169.

Packard, Vance. *The Naked Society.* New York: D. McKay, Co, 1962.

Perloff, Marjorie. *Poetic License.* Evanston, IL: Northwestern UP, 1991.

Plath, Sylvia. *The Complete Poems.* Ed. Ted Hughes. New York: Harper and Row, 1981.

Rich, Adrienne. *Snapshots of a Daughter-in-Law 1954-1962.* New York: W.W. Norton, 1967.

Rose, Jacqueline. *The Haunting of Sylvia Plath.* Cambridge: Harvard UP, 1991.

Rosenberg, Jerry. *The Death of Privacy.* New York: Random House, 1969.

Sexton, Anne. *The Complete Poems.* Boston: Houghton Mifflin, 1981.

Spindel, Bernard. *The Ominous Ear.* New York: Award House, 1968.

Westin, Alan. *Privacy and Freedom.* New York: Atheneum, 1967.

Wheeler, Stanton, ed. *On Record: Files and Dossiers in American Life.* New York: Russell Sage Foundation, 1969.

Remembering China
in *Wild Swans* and *Life and Death in Shanghai*

Cynthia F. Wong

Vera Schwarcz describes a Chinese dancer who is struggling with a piece of rope on the theater stage, and she observes that the movements enact the force of an emphatic bond which twentieth-century China exerts on those who try to leave the homeland.[1] The dancer's wild gesticulations at first seem to represent both his despair at being held back in China and his hope for establishing new roots in a foreign land, but as the dance proceeds, the message becomes more complicated:

> He's trying to make his way to a distant door, to cross its freedom-promising threshold. He tries to cut memory's umbilical cord, to be born anew. But he collapses on the way to the emancipation that lies beyond all mother tongues. The young man is left embracing the unbreakable tie—the history that cannot be forgotten, the dreams that cut like knives. (86)

The dancer is *on the verge* of a liberation, but instead, he surrenders to an inevitable fate: "left embracing the unbreakable tie," he submits to an impossibility of forgetting China and an improbability of easy assimilation in a new homeland. Even those who make it across the physical threshold still carry with them "the history that cannot be forgotten." The dancer's struggles stress to those both at home and abroad that departure is a physical condition always shrouded by the fact of obligation—whether psychological or emotional—to the homeland.

Beyond the borders of their motherland, the Chinese participate in a universal quest to reestablish their cultural identities in spite of—and more often, because of—their home country. Determined to sever the umbilical cord binding themselves to China, those abroad inevitably encounter the wrath of the past as they construct a liveable present. Although those abroad may desire an "emancipation that lies beyond all mother tongues," a freedom that presupposes disengagement from both their place and language of origin as they establish new roots, they find that China herself remains with them. Schwarcz characterizes the quest for cultural redefinition as both private and collective, and she adds a warning to those who stray too far from their recollections of the homeland:

> Exiled from the home country, they partake of the bittersweet feast of migrants throughout history: They pass the fixed borders of inherited knowledge in search of new—even if dangerous—insights about the maternal world left behind. (86)

Both Jung Chang in *Wild Swans* (1991) and Nien Cheng in *Life and Death in Shanghai* (1986) cross these borders by writing their autobiographical texts in a foreign language (English), and they reconstitute stories about China which reveal their strong desires to cut from or to forget the past they left behind.[2] Each reconstructs a new home in the act of writing about the old home; subsequently, each deals with the psychological burden that their homeland exerts on their remembered experiences.

Jung Chang's stories, written in London when the author was in her late thirties, are about her grandmother's concubinage to a warlord and her mother's political transformations both towards and away from Communism at various epochs of Mao's rule; the stories depict Chinese historical events unfolding in the twentieth-century and emphasize how, as women, Jung Chang's ancestors manifest the radical spirit which will characterize the author's own life story in the later part of the book, culminating with her departure from China at the age of twenty-six. All three women have pivotal roles in the narrative; all make heroic and dangerous decisions which go against Chinese norms, and all emerge as victors of their own destinies. Seen in the writer's western context, however, the women's actions are praiseworthy, rather than anarchic, a view maintained by Chinese culture.

A similar unfolding of unconventional Chinese female behavior characterizes Nien Cheng's story, which focuses on the Cultural Revolution of the 1960s, when the author is already in her fifties. Where Jung Chang praises her grandmother and mother (while offering sleight-of-hand criticism of her father and other males), Nien Cheng mourns the loss of her actress-daughter in what she supposes was a botched-up arrest, where authorities viciously, but perhaps unintentionally, murdered the young woman during an interrogation.

Nien Cheng's own experiences focus on her years in a Chinese prison, following her arrest as a "capitalist roader." Since the charges against Nien Cheng are never more specific than that she had social and cultural liaisons in the west, her imprisonment is particularly senseless to a western reader. When Nien Cheng leaves China for the west at the end of her book, she conveys the relief of liberation to her reader, who understands the departure as Nien Cheng's way of managing grief about her dead daughter and her now-alien homeland. Similarly, when Jung Chang leaves China for Great Britain, the reader celebrates her opportunity for a western education, a dream beyond all hope in Communist China. Importantly, both women write in the English language to western audiences, as if such transgression would emphasize their exiled states and their subsequent pain of remembering the homeland. By focusing on Chinese injustices from a western perspective, and by highlighting the plight of women, their texts might be received favorably in the new homes.[3]

Both position their narratives from a western point of view as they remember China under Mao, because then they are able to critique the motherland from their estranged positions. As their narratives progress, though, the reconstruction of an oppressive China emerges less as an effort to offer social criticism and more fully as the writers' struggle not to abandon completely the meaning of and bond to the homeland; criticism moves towards commemoration, and estrangement moves toward a desire for reconciliation. The return to China becomes both subject of their narratives and the reason for tension found in their writing. Both women insist at the outset of their texts that the events are "real" and recorded chronologically, "just as they occurred," and both insist on the truthful reflection of remembered experiences. The women situate their personal stories against political history, with China herself serving as a structuring device for the texts; China is indelibly etched in the consciousness of the two women. What new (or dangerous) knowledge they procure abroad eventually emerges less as a scathing dismissal of the motherland and more as critique of twentieth-century politics in general. Their texts suggest a personal nostalgia for a China before the advent of Maoism, or for the period of the May Fourth movement at the turn of the century when intellectuals argued for western idealism as one response to the decimation of imperialism.[4] The May Fourth intellectuals who advocated foreign influence for addressing internal problems may be seen as the predecessors of exiles like Jung Chang and Nien Cheng, who found their new homes in the west. Those who participated in the literary revolution of 1917 found inspiration for their stories beyond China's own border, but they also found it necessary to return—either physically as in the case of the May Fourth writers, or psychologically in the cases of Jung Chang and Nien Cheng—to the homeland.

Both women progress from merely describing events to narrating their significance; they therefore move from simply recording situations to analyzing, later even criticizing, their manifestation and consequences. This movement is both personal and literary, and it suggests the ways China-as-homeland structures and motivates the texts. In her provocative study, *Woman and Chinese Modernity*, Rey Chow states that in the May Fourth period, "discussions of literature increasingly centered on 'realism,' which was to win major support from writers in the decades to come because it represented the principle that literature could not be divorced from life" (40). Both Jung Chang and Nien Cheng make a similar assertion through their insistence on their texts' realism, even though considerable lapses of time between experience and narrative may call into question veritable representation. Chinese writers of the 1920s, having returned to China after an educational sojourn to the west, practiced what Chow calls a "disinterested realism" in that "literature should *in itself create* the truthful social vision by capturing history in its whole" (Chow's emphasis 42). Realistic narratives, we recall, "depict life as it is" and emphasize concrete, rather than abstract details; they are also characterized by use of objective, rather than subjective or opinionated facts, and they involve "a doctrine of natural causality . . . [which embodies] inclusive presentation of all the factors that influence life."[5] However, Jung Chang's and Nien Cheng's declarations of their veracity of representation give way to a literary reprisal that also occurred with the May Fourth writers. Specifically, as Chow observes, realistic writers were excited not so much by the possibility of redefining literature per se; what moved the narrative act also moved the literary texts and had more to do with the writers' growing awareness of change in China and abroad:

> What emerged was hence the view that "literature is literature." However, as the course of history shows, this independent status of literature, which was assimilated from the readings of Western literature and infused with a Western sense of humanism, led not to an aestheticism in China but rather to the ideal of literature as a new agent for social change. (42)

Seen in light of Jung Chang and Nien Cheng who wrote their texts abroad, Chow's assessment of May Fourth writers applies to the two women's remembrances of China. Like their May Fourth predecessors, both women reveal their loyalty to China through western forms which might capture both this regard for the homeland and a desire for social transformation of her cultural practices. However, their idealistic approaches bear further examination, especially since, unlike the May Fourth writers, both remained abroad rather than returning home.

In speaking their personal stories against a historical context, both women examine the implications of the private against the public, the tale of home and self against the story of the homeland. Both indicate that actual experience and the later act of narration coincide and that this correspondence will enable them to present accurately not merely the facts of their own lives in the painful period but the truth about Maoist politics as well. They criticize the homeland through this evasive strategy, because open condemnation of China or her policies constitutes an act of defiance deplored by the values they themselves hold dear. In other words, denunciation of the homeland is a renunciation of self, a value prescribed by China herself. Writing their stories in a foreign tongue, away from China in the west, the women find themselves struggling with competing values about self: in order to possess selfhood, an emblem of western individualism, they must first forget the fact of China's atrocities so as not to denigrate the country which first gave them a sense of self. For in China, loyalty to self is synonymous with loyalty to one's country, even if loyalty to the country of origin eventually becomes circumscribed by that for the country of their resettlement; in China, mother and motherland come first, for these represent the true home. In the west, Jung Chang and Nien Cheng express in their texts the struggle with these two senses of loyalty to both old and new countries, real and made homes. They inevitably confront a condition that L. Ling-chi Wang describes as the "inseparable bond between the Chinese abroad and their cultural roots in China" (181), a bond that is especially noticeable when those abroad resettle in a new country and feel a kinship with the new influences. The emotional tension characterizes both Jung Chang's and Nien Cheng's autobiographical texts and becomes the basis for their representation of Chinese history and their personal stories "through a release of sensual details whose emotional backdrop is often that of entrapment, destruction, and desolation."[6]

In remembering China, then, both Jung Chang and Nien Cheng express the force of their Chinese identities, even as they present texts which seem ostensibly to help them sever ties to the homeland. The objectivity and natural causality they seek in their realistic texts make way for subjective and analytical explanations, finally producing texts interpreted according to their growing (negative) assessments about China. I would like to suggest that their texts nevertheless commemorate China, both the homeland and the past, despite the authors' proclamation to forget the pain of particular periods represented in their texts. As Schwarcz puts it, "To commemorate the past is an act of repossession. It bestows ongoing value, it claims unending relevance for the event that is being called to mind" (90). In this manner, the texts themselves serve in the end to represent the writers' struggle with a refusal to forget the homeland and with an insistence on interpreting her historical past in the best light possible. While their texts do not reveal overtly the "homeland longing" described by Hsin-shen C. Kao, they do indicate the writers' inability, or perhaps a subconscious unwillingness, to lay to rest the importance of China and of being Chinese.[7] The commemoration of China is also significant in light of the writers' assertion of self in the new country. Rather than offer wholesale criticism of China, the narrative texts express the writers' desire for continuity through these essential passages: from China to the west, from political oppression to freedom, from being the subjects of history to being writers or makers of new versions of history. Each passage represents for the writers a renewed understanding of China and the legacy she bestows upon her kin.

Both Jung Chang and Nien Cheng emerge as keepers and defenders of an older China which has disappeared. They mourn the destabilization and internal fragmentation caused by twentieth-century politics. They acquiesce to Chinese rulers in the early stages of Communism as a sign of their native willingness to conform; they respond to their rulers as obedient Chinese. Their western texts, however, reveal their later self-critical attitude towards this early tendency to follow their leaders without question. Their acceptance and eventual rebellion, their early devotion and later criticism all evolve through time and reflect directly the historical legacy of China herself. As women, the first terms (acceptance and devotion) become important signifiers of their family roles inscribed for their gender in China, while the second terms (rebellion and criticism) manifest years later in the actual writing of their texts in the west; in the second stage, their texts also assert their individual assessment of political events, an assertion which challenges their proscribed submissiveness in China. Jung Chang's narrative, in particular, sets forth the historical movements which begin at the turn of the century, the period marking the start of the end of imperial rule and also marking the concubinage of Jung Chang's maternal grandmother to a warlord general. Jung Chang's subsequent narrative reveals the major political movements which chart the destiny of China and the fate of her family.

The criticism of Chinese history in Jung Chang's book follows from the "course of liberalization" (508) she identifies as an important result of speaking out against political atrocities and making such events known to the rest of the world, which in this case means the English writing and speaking countries. Her narrative therefore begins, as does twentieth-century Chinese politics, with an account of the collapse of imperial rule in the early 1900s. However, China eliminated one form of totalitarian policies by eradicating the feudal monarchy, but then she also had to deal with the efficacy of new versions of absolutist rule which followed. The autocratic governments of the Kuomintang and the Communists attest to a united, although perilously divisive, ideology against imperialism; the division led to the fiercest civil strife in this century. The emphases of both the Kuomintang and Communists on a fervent nationalism, an aversion to foreign aggression and influence, and internal self-strengthening gave way to a long line of "programs" initially aimed at empowering the common people. When Mao took official power in 1949, the people first regarded his leadership with awe and praise.[8] As Jung Chang's narrative shows, however, the way his politics eventually impinged upon private lives had devastating consequences for the country. In particular, Jung Chang's assessments of Mao's role in history analyze the relationship of politics and everyday existence:

> In the days after Mao's death, I did a lot of thinking. I knew he was considered a philosopher, and I tried to think what his "philosophy" really was. It seemed to me that its central principle was the need—or the desire?—for perpetual conflict. The core of his thinking seemed to be that human struggles were the motivating force of history, and that in order to make history [,] "class enemies" had to be continuously created *en masse*. . . . He ruled by getting people to hate each other. In doing so, he got ordinary Chinese to carry out many of the tasks undertaken in other dictatorships by professional elites. . . . In bringing out and nourishing the worst in people, Mao had created a moral wasteland and a land of hatred. But how

much individual responsibility ordinary people would share, I
could not decide. (495-6)

Jung Chang's assessment is much like Nien Cheng's in *Life and Death
in Shanghai*, where criticism of Mao is always considered in light of
general philosophical speculations about what it meant to live in China
during that particular period:

> Constant change is an integral part of the Communist
> philosophy. For the entire thirty-eight years of Communist rule
> in China, the Party's policy has swung like a pendulum from
> left to right and back again without stop. Unless and until a
> political system rooted in law, rather than personal power, is
> firmly established in China, the road to the future will always
> be full of twists and turns. The wanton use of personal power
> such as Mao wielded during the Cultural Revolution may yet
> turn back the clock. Factional struggle for power among the
> new leaders is almost a certainty, though there will be an
> interval of superficial unity while each man consolidates his
> position. The Chinese people will continue on the sidelines,
> allowed to speak only with an affirmative voice. (543)

Significantly, both women seem to avoid making direct comparisons
with national devastation and their private situations. They concentrate
on analyzing Maoism in a general way towards the end of their
narratives; their focus on Chinese humanity, as opposed to an obsession
with personal grief, lends credible objectivity to their accounts.
However, it is important to point out that both Jung Chang and Nien
Cheng were also excluded from what Mao's government could provide
for people like them; declared as "capitalist roaders" through their
family's association with ideas and practices antithetical to Maoism,
both women "earned" their unwelcome status in China. Properly
speaking, their exiles were the inevitable results of Mao's politics.
      Away from the center (China) that had produced their
existence, both women examine the status of the Chinese nation and
their Chinese selves. In this respect, both reconfigure the parameters of
the homeland according to the memories they conjure up while in the
new home, the west. The narratives are an attempt to define their
Chinese roots and identity, both the way these inform their true home
(China and Chinese views) and the way these will provide them means
to choose a destiny abroad or, in other words, to make a new home.

Their non-fictional texts are exported from their remembrance of China and their deeply held conviction that it is important each commemorates her from a vantage point of tactful criticism of Communism, the politics which forced their exiles. Both accounts emphasize cultural upheavals and their impact upon their family members, but both authors appear deeply divided at times in their loyalties to family and State. The seeming equivocation stems from their making a transition from one nation to another, from situating their remembrances at the limit of two distinct cultures, East and West, and from remaking one home to another. Jung Chang writes in her epilogue that after leaving China, ten years passed before she began her narrative. Similarly, Nien Cheng writes her story after a considerable lapse of time has occurred. Significantly, both write their accounts in the language of the new culture and after each received prodding encouragement from western friends interested in their versions of China. Because their intended audiences exist outside China, their narratives are both literal and figurative acts of translation. In speaking of the old and past (China) in the new and present (West), their texts are therefore also transgressive acts that move them beyond the motherland and the mother tongue.

Both writers capture their sense of the important temporal transitions and indicate how they make the emotional and physical passage away from the homeland. Nien Cheng expresses her love of western freedom in the context of her regard for Chinese history:

> Back doors in America lead only into people's kitchens. When I am with others, I can speak candidly on any subject without having to consider whether my remarks are ideologically correct or to worry that someone might misinterpret what I have said. . . . The death of my daughter and my own painful experience during the Cultural Revolution can never be forgotten; even writing about it is traumatic.
> . . . But I persisted in my effort. I felt the compulsion to speak out and let those who have the good fortune to live in freedom know what my life was like during those dark days in Maoist China. (538)

Jung Chang's narrative tone has some of Nien Cheng's poignant resonance. In her epilogue, she uses a similar image which symbolizes her physical and emotional passages:

> The door of China has been opening wider and wider. . . .
> Between 1983 and 1989, I went back to visit my mother every
> year, and each time I was overwhelmed by the dramatic
> diminution of the one thing that had most characterized life
> under Mao: fear. (507)

In both texts, the women cross the "freedom-promising threshold"
(Schwarcz), even though it means leaving behind their beloved
homeland. Both exemplify the two ways they survived the Cultural
Revolution: by her mode of narration and the way each structures her
text. The completion of their stories is evidence that bodily survival was
accomplished, since both escaped political persecution and death in
order to write about the events. Both also survive in order to traverse
the limit of their national identities and establish new citizenship in
English-speaking countries, where their texts are received with great
empathy. Both use the English language in ways which allow them
literal transgression of their native lands and tongues; both employ
English as a way to combat western perceptions about Chinese
communism. However, in writing abroad in a foreign language, they
exclude from their audience those who still reside in China, perhaps
those who are undergoing similar fates that their texts describe. In this
regard, their texts fall short of their own expectations for social change
within China; like their May Fourth predecessors, they saw change as
something imported from elsewhere, such as the west. Ironically, once
in the west, Jung Chang and Nien Cheng felt their best efforts to speak
about China required that they remain abroad.

What both writers accomplish in their narratives has less
directly to do with polemics than with ordering events so that they can
repossess their own regard for China; in this way, they can pass along
their reverence to western readers already sympathetic to democratic
ideals or critical of socialist ones. Certainly, both suffered unjustly by
western standards for their social positions in the regime, but in the
context of Chinese politics, their experiences in the motherland were in
accord with their social positions and the politics of the time. Writing
their texts for the western audience meant they were able to represent
their pasts in the new contexts of western homes; writing meant they
could pass from being subjects of Mao's politics to being scribes of
new cultural selves. Nien Cheng's narrative of her six and a half years
in a Shanghai prison for vaguely specified crimes deserves a reader's
compassion. The experience itself represents about one tenth of her
actual life, but it takes place over half of the narrative text and is

therefore accorded an importance without realistic proportions to the rest of her life. Located at the center of her book, the prison scenes serve to structure the writer's consciousness (ie: her hope for redefining self), rather than to represent objectively the course of Chinese history. It is in this period of "ample time," Nien Cheng tells us in her author's opening notes, that she was able to "recall scenes and conversations in a continuing effort to assess their significance." Similarly, the majority of Jung Chang's book is devoted to the life experiences of the author's grandmother and mother, experiences reinterpreted over time and through the perceptions of other people as well, so that their "realism" comes less from the author's empiricism than her ability to synthesize multiple stories. In proper chronological fashion, though, Jung Chang's own personal story comes in the last six of the twenty-eight chapters of the book. The last chapter, entitled "Fighting to Take Wing," encapsulates a spirit of escape and freedom, as opposed to constriction and limitation bestowed by Chinese politics. Though they are compassionate accounts of unfortunate circumstances, both texts must be viewed as highly personal accounts and versions of what occurred in China under Mao. What social change they might have hoped to inaugurate as a result of speaking their stories has less to do with overtly criticizing Maoism than with reinterpreting their experiences under general humanist—more specifically, western liberal—principles of existence.

Only by escaping China can both writers begin to make discernible progress in shaping these life stories and, thus, translate the experiences for western audiences. To accomplish this narrative task, both examine their lives according to western ideals of freedom. Immediately after taking flight, Jung Chang writes, "I avoided thinking about the China I left behind" (506). In an apparent effort to avoid sentimentalizing life in China, both women choose to transmit their stories years after the fact with much distance between eastern and western experiences. It is the passage of time and the separation of space which endows the writers with the strength to remember how things "really" and "actually" occurred; importantly, this passage of time occurs in their western resettlement. Whether their stories will bring about new knowledge to western readers and social change to China, however, remains to be seen.

As direct descendants of the May Fourth movement, both Nien Cheng and Jung Chang advocate revising ancient Chinese philosophy and combining these with western knowledge to address contemporary concerns. As a young woman in the 1930s, Nien Cheng must have benefitted directly from the insights of May Fourth intellectuals who sought to import fresh (foreign) ideas in solving the nation's problems. Nien Cheng herself travelled abroad and learned of different cultures besides China, thus broadening her intellect. But her situation is by no means common to all in China, a fact she acknowledges early on in her book. Her devotion to Chinese culture and history, shown in scenes where she mourns the destruction of Chinese artifacts and books collected over time, is an effort to sustain an attitude about culture that is foreign to most in China. In one scene, she manages to persuade young Red Guards to cease destroying her porcelain pieces and says, "Although members of the proletarian class did not appreciate value, they understood price" (77). Knowing that it would be possible to exchange the art for hard currency in the open foreign market, the Red Guards give in to Nien Cheng's financial logic. Consisting mostly of members from the peasant classes, the Red Guards "understood price" and not cultural value, a difference which sets them distinctly apart from the cultivated Nien Cheng, their class enemy.

For Jung Chang, devotion to China originated from her parents' own political involvements. Her father supported Communist ideology from its inception and passed along his beliefs to the family. Jung Chang herself came of age during the Cultural Revolution and was a Red Guard for a time. Her desire to travel abroad coincided with her critical reflection of China under Mao. Several unpropitious delays did not prevent her from embarking to Great Britain in 1978 at the age of twenty-six to begin a promising academic career, first as a doctoral student at York University and later as professor at London University. Like Nien Cheng, Jung Chang procured a rare and unique opportunity to leave the homeland; writing of their experiences to a Chinese audience would seem profoundly foreign, perhaps even traitorous, to those who lack both means and opportunity in Communist China to do what Nien Cheng and Jung Chang accomplished.

Both women reveal in their writing a desire to retrieve some lost presence still rooted somewhere in China, although both express contentment in their new homelands, places of receptive and comprehending audiences. While mostly stoical in tone, the texts nevertheless suggest a melancholy that reveals the authors' wish to connect the hopeful present in a foreign land to an irretrievable but indelible past in China, where both lost so much. To do so, however, would mean acknowledging the uniqueness of their present lives and indicating how their experiences in a foreign homeland opposed those of the common Chinese. In writing their texts, the women writers are able to commemorate China according to this desire for continuity, but with genuine doubt about ever rejoining those in China, since their personal lives set them apart from those remaining in the homeland. It is this poignant aspect of their texts which I find most revealing of their own sense of what it means to be Chinese, whether in China or abroad, whether under tumultuous or peaceful existences.

Specifically, L. Ling-chi Wang observes that the Chinese have very precise terminology to symbolize the "genesis and maintenance of life" (182). Wang indicates that the word *gen* (roots), for instance, is found in the two paradigms which name the history and life of Chinese abroad: *yeluo guigen* "characterizes the Chinese abroad as fallen leaves that must eventually, even *inevitably* return to their roots in the soil of China" while *luodi shenggen* "depicts them as seeds sown in foreign soil, taking root wherever they have emigrated" (183). In the two opposing terms, *gen* remains constant and reminds the Chinese of his or her biological and ancestral roots; *gen* bestows a sense of permanent identity to the individual, one which denotes both personal and national selfhood, or their sense of belonging to a homeland. Nien Cheng expresses both her joys and regrets in the new settlement, and she establishes her sense of self in *gen* which speaks her oppressed condition in China:

> The United States of America is the right place for me. Here are Jewish survivors of the Holocaust, dissidents of repressive regimes who had been imprisoned, boat people from Vietnam, and political tyranny. Among people like these, I do not feel alone. Since I settled in Washington, D. C., I have been accepted by the American people with unreserved friendliness. I have found old friends and made new ones. My only regret is that my daughter, Meiping, is not here with me. (539)

Jung Chang also notes a dramatic transformation between China and the West in stating her new roots:

> I have made London my home. . . . [in] 1982, when I decided to stay in Britain, it was still a very unusual choice. Thinking it might cause dilemmas in her job, my mother applied for early retirement, and was granted it, in 1983. But a daughter living in the West did not bring her trouble, as would certainly have been the case under Mao. (507)

Both Nien Cheng and Jung Chang, as *luodi shenggen* sowing new seeds in foreign soil, make the west their new homes, but they do so with a refusal to forget the motherland and an insistence on remembering those left behind. Had they been able to produce a clean slate in their present conditions, they might have felt less a compulsion to remember China in a way which fails to denounce her recent past.

I have avoided an interpretation of Nien Cheng's and Jung Chang's texts which emphasizes a *Chinese* perspective largely because they do not write their stories from this view. Had they intended such a perspective, they would have written in Chinese, the language of the homeland. Instead, I have examined their stories of China written from a newly established *western* situation, because it is from this angle that the emotional tensions about their sense of self emerge most clearly. Loyalty and guilt are coterminous; in order to remain true to the homeland, they must acknowledge their own privileged opportunity to leave her oppression. Both women have strong loyalty to the motherland, but it is also true that both have accepted western influences, such as liberalized views about freedom and expression, which have influenced the way each presents her story. In this respect, they found solace for expression from the philosophy inherited by the May Fourth intellectuals, but they will most likely remain in the west until China—if ever—embraces western and foreign influences.

Without resorting to rhetorical questions about how East and West have determined western narratives about eastern experiences, it is possible to indicate here that Nien Cheng and Jung Chang first identified their subjugation to China under Mao.[9] That Chinese women should have the audacity to occupy a historian's role, much less a social critic's, might have been incomprehensible before Mao. Ironically, what they and their families endured during the Cultural Revolution in effect provided them the compulsion to find a new home in which to write their stories. As antagonists of Mao's China, it would have been impossible to write without both spatial and temporal distance between the homeland and the new home. That the situation happened to be the west for both women indicates something important about their eventual exiles. In their stories about the motherland, both women stress the importance of the *feminine*. Jung Chang writes about her maternal lineage and fairly ignores her paternal legacy; Nien Cheng laments the loss of her daughter to a great and painful extent, at times causing her to actively disregard the possibility of ever living with another human being.[10]

Like other "migrants throughout history" (Schwarcz), Nien Cheng and Jung Chang document their *personal* histories and partake of the universal quest to establish new homes. While they rely on Chinese historical dates and facts to support their narratives, they are primarily concerned with sharing the tragedies experienced by their own households during the period of Maoism. Because they cannot generalize their experiences to all Chinese, their narratives fall short of making full political reform possible; ultimately, such energy towards social change may not be in their own agendas. Like other liberal humanist texts which emphasize commonalities shared by other beings on earth, their narratives achieve a highly personalized representation of life in China under Mao. In this manner, both writers perhaps resurrect in their texts the oldest Confucian philosophy about self-cultivation through inner autonomy, a principle which perceptively and subtly contradicts Maoist ideology. Such contradiction could come only from a new context, a new home, or they risk being regarded as enemies of the state. Bound to their origins, however, they finally are unable to completely break from her ties; they feel obliged to recall her from a perspective which refuses to criticize her explicitly. In the new land, a new birth is possible only with such connection to the homeland, providing each writer with an unbreakable bond to their true homes, their true selves.

NOTES

1.   See "No Solace from Lethe" for Schwarcz's description of the performance entitled "Threshold: A Dance Theater of Remembering and Forgetting" that was performed at the La Mama theater in New York one year after the 1989 shootings at Tiannanmen Square.

2.   The Chinese place the family name (what we in the West call the "last name") before the given name. I have used the authors' full names throughout this essay given the similarities of their family names. I also have used the Western inversion of their names.

3.   I taught Nien Cheng's book in two classes at a mid-sized
        public midwestern university (1991), and students saw the
        book as a validation of Communism's irrational policies while
        they admired the author's resilience and endurance. Others who
        have read Jung Chang's book tell me they find the narrative
        exhilarating and the author's perspective refreshing; some
        attribute their positive regard for the book to the "sad but
        uplifting" experiences of the author.

4.   See Jian Bozan et al. for a Chinese perspective on the May
        Fourth movement. Most Western historians agree that this
        movement marked an end to feudal monarchism, or
        imperialism, and that it drew China's attention to the world
        beyond. The Chinese emphasize her "patriotism" in warding
        off Western aggression; they underplay the part about Western
        cultural influence, as this passage from Bozan et al. makes
        clear: "Generally speaking, the intellectuals who preached the
        New Learning at this time were sincerely desirous of learning
        something useful from Western culture. Although their social
        theories still retained some poisonous traces of Chinese
        feudalism and even contained the slave ideology of
        imperialism, they were actuated by a desire to save China"
        (138).
                Intellectual debates more often center around the
        significance of the movement as a whole, as Ying-Shih Yü
        indicates. For Yü, the May Fourth era began with the literary
        revolution of 1917, and this period has been called the "New
        Culture Movement," the "Renaissance," and the
        "Enlightenment," terms which imply "a particular historical
        interpretation regarding the nature and significance of the
        movement" (130). For this essay, I call attention to what May
        Fourth intellectuals regarded as the importance of importing
        western values and ideas to China, what Vera Schwarcz
        identifies as the "utility of looking beyond China's borders for
        sources of Chinese renewal" (94). This view is closer to what
        Jung Chang and Nien Cheng accomplish in writing their texts
        about China.

5.   See Wallace Martin for a fuller discussion of the literary
        realism and convention in contemporary narratives.

6.   See Chow, 85, for her discussion of "Modernity and Narration—in Feminine Detail." I would like to point out that in my analysis of the texts of Jung Chang and Nien Cheng, I do not see these two women writers engaged with the literary and historical projects associated with modernity, which entailed some eradication of the past in order to arrive at what Chow, quoting Paul de Man, depicts as "a true present" (86). As I pointed out earlier, these two writers still struggle with veritable representation along the tenets of literary realism, aspects emphasized by the May Fourth writers.

7.   See Hsin-sheng C. Kao for a comparison of Chinese overseas writers and writers in exile. What Kao calls "nativism as the mark of culture" may characterize the work of Jung Chang and Nien Cheng: "There are some writers who write in a foreign language but whose works cannot take leave of the people and affairs in China" (15).

8.   It is important to point out that Mao was responsible for instigating programs aimed at equality for all citizens, including women. Ironically, though, men and women also suffered equally under the programs.

9.   Here, I am thinking of Rey Chow's discussion of Julia Kristeva's book, *About Chinese Women*, which Chow indicates returns discourse about China to square one: "Even though Kristeva sees China in an interesting and, indeed, 'sympathetic' way, there is nothing in her arguments as such that cannot be said without 'China.' What she proposes is not so much learning a lesson from a different culture as a different method of reading from within the West. For, what is claimed to be 'unique' to China is simply understood as the 'negative' or 'repressed' side of Western discourse" (7).

    This is the tautology I seek to avoid in my discussion of the two narratives: neither writers seek to provide a "method of reading from within the West"; neither do they seek to turn China, in many ways their beloved motherland, into the 'negative' or 'repressed' of the Western logos. In doing either of the above, they would be canceling out the possibility of a cultural redefinition which I find so important to their narrative tasks.

10.   The maternal family is very important to Jung Chang's narrative, as the subtitle of her text shows. In the genealogy she provides at the beginning, she identifies each of her mother's family with their given names; in the same chart with her father's family, she indicates her paternal grandparents as "Mr. and Mrs. Chang" and, with the exception of a beloved aunt who is her father's sister, all of her father's siblings are identified anonymously as "seven others."

WORKS CITED

Bozan, Jian, Shao Xunzheng, and Hu Hua. *A Concise History of China*. Beijing: Foreign Languages Press, 1986.

Chang, Jung. *Wild Swans: Three Daughters of China*. New York: Simon & Schuster, 1991.

Cheng, Nien. *Life and Death in Shanghai*. New York: Penguin, 1988.

Chow, Rey. *Woman and Chinese Modernity: The Politics of Reading Between West and East*. Theory and History of Literature 75. Minneapolis: U of Minnesota P, 1991.

Kao, Hsin-sheng C. *Nativism Overseas: Contemporary Chinese Women Writers*. Albany: State U of New York P, 1993.

Martin, Wallace. *Recent Theories of Narrative*. Ithaca: Cornell UP, 1986.

Schwarcz, Vera. "No Solace from Lethe: History, Memory, and Cultural Identity in Twentieth-Century China." *Daedalus* 120 (1991): 85-112.

Wang, L. Ling-chi. "Roots and Changing Identity of the Chinese in the United States." *Daedalus* 120 (1991): 181-206.

Yü, Ying-shih. "The Radicalization of China in the Twentieth Century." *Daedalus* 122 (1993): 125-150.

Keeping House:
A Meditation on the Possibilities of the Essay

Rebecca Blevins Faery

> When one looks from inside at a lighted window, or looks
> from above at the lake, one sees the image of oneself in a
> lighted room, the image of oneself among trees and sky—the
> deception is obvious, but flattering all the same. When one
> looks from the darkness into the light, however, one sees all
> the difference between here and there, this and that. Perhaps all
> unsheltered people are angry in their hearts, and would like to
> break the roof, spine, and ribs, and smash the windows and
> flood the floor and spindle the curtains and bloat the couch.
> [Marilynne Robinson, *Housekeeping*]

I

I had, it seemed, to my surprise, terror, and delight, bought a
house. It was high summer, July of 1988, the peak of a season of
dazzling heat and soul-wrenching drought. As I drove between Iowa
City and Dubuque, where I was teaching a seminar, I watched the corn
in fields on either side of the two-lane highway shrivel relentlessly week
by week under the baking sun until I heard, or thought I heard, as I
drove, a very high-pitched keen or wail coming from the corn, begging
for rain.

Moving day arrived when the seminar ended, according to plan.
During the weeks I was away teaching, assorted carpenters and dry-wall
workers and plumbers and painters had executed my preliminary plans
for turning the house into my own. It was—is—a grand house, old and
possessed of great dignity, so I had a lot to work with: high ceilings,
wide mahogany pocket doors at once dividing and connecting all the
downstairs rooms, multiple tall windows looking out on a wide lawn
with room for a terrace, a garden, a grape arbor, a bed of multi-hued
lilies. A house full of promise, of possibilities.

The unpacking and settling-in were a strain in the dry heat, well over a hundred degrees day after sizzling day. Indulging a fantasy which my new identity as owner of this grand house allowed me, I adopted in interludes the persona and habits of a woman of leisure and splurged on a Yucatan hammock, which I hung between an old box-elder and a leaning cedar not far from the back porch. I took refuge in their shade when fatigue overtook me, swaying as I read. The novel in my hands, as I recall myself in those moments through the screen of memory, is Marilynne Robinson's *Housekeeping*.

Mornings I rose, made coffee, soothed the cat out of her nervousness at waking in a house whose unfamiliarity she had daily to confront anew, and set to work to establish the cleanliness and order I've been taught to believe is next to godliness. My domestic inclinations I gave full rein: this was my home, my haven, nest, stay against the confusion of impermanence, each room a stanza of the poem to fixity I was trying to make of the enterprise. I had married this house with enthusiasm, and I took up the familiar role and tasks of house-wife with an energy made vigorous by commitment. "I was born to live in this house," I said to my friends in the romantic flush of love for my new home; "I intend to stay here forever."

It must be understood, for this tale to make any sense at all, that I have yearned all my adult life for permanence, for "home," for a long commitment to a place, a dwelling that would house me securely and comfortably in return for my love and attention, its walls my fortress against flux and fortune's whims. Yet every home I've had I've lived in only briefly; I've been, despite my longings, a woman forever on the move. Or, more precisely, several women, simultaneously and in succession, and all of them on the move.

In the heat of that summer, I was making another stab at it. I labored in splendid isolation toward splendid order in the arrangement of furniture, pictures on the walls, dishes in the cupboards. This finely articulated distribution of my possessions soothed me into pretending that I was indeed protected from the shifting boundaries of identity, from the fraying and unraveling that are the lot of us all.

The dissonances between my determined housekeeping and the interpolations of lazy late-afternoon hours of suspended reading of *Housekeeping* did not escape me. The novel drew me away from my busy-ness to the still hours in the swaying hammock, drew me with its exquisite sentences, its elegiac tone, its visions that all efforts to stop the flow of time, change, displacement, discomposing are fruitless. It's a vision I share, indeed advocate. The difference is that the women in the novel act on that knowledge. I, on the other hand, sometimes at least, act as if I *don't* believe it, though I do. In the novel, Sylvie knows that something means to undo a house, so she opens the doors and windows and lets the undoer in. She underscores the silly futility of housewifely saving and storing by collecting useless things—empty cans, old newspapers—and arranging them neatly against the walls of all the rooms. Sylvie refuses the bourgeois ideologies of "home" with all their attachments to class privilege, ideologies that confine women within the predictable roles and ordered spaces of domesticity; she embraces the road rather than the cottage beside it. I try to do these things too, in my own way. But I, on the other hand, dweller in contradictions, also batten down, hunker, and hope.

II

In their essay "Feminist Politics: What's Home Got to Do with It?" Biddy Martin and Chandra Talpade Mohanty use their reading of another essay, Minnie Bruce Pratt's "Identity: Skin Blood Heart," to consider the political ideologies of "home": house, family, kin, community in the immediate sense; personal identities grounded in race, class, gender, sexuality, convictions and claimed affinities in the wider sense. And while the following passage from Martin and Mohanty addresses Pratt's remarkable essay alone, I offer it as a perspective on the possibilities of the essay in general:

> [The essay] is a form of writing that not only anticipates and integrates diverse audiences or readers but also positions the narrator as reader. The perspective is multiple and shifting, and the shifts in perspective are enabled by the attempts to define self, home, and community that are at the heart of Pratt's enterprise. The historical grounding of shifts and changes allows for an emphasis on the pleasures and terrors of interminable boundary confusions, but insists, at the same time, on our responsibility for remapping boundaries and renegotiating connections. These are partial in at least two senses of the word: politically partial, and without claims to wholeness or finality.

The essay as a performance of reading. The essayist as reader. The reader of essays as reader. All readings contingent, partial, multiple, shifting. Nothing is fixed, and nobody has a corner on truth.

When Samuel Johnson in his famous *Dictionary* defines the essay as "a loose sally of the mind; an irregular, undigested piece," I at least suspect the privileging of reason over feeling, intellection over intuition. It is the article or treatise which earns from Johnson an implicit description as "a regular, orderly composition," the thing the essay, by his definition, is not. What makes for the difference? The meanderings, for one thing, of the essayist's persona, made precedent by Montaigne. A "composition" requires the writer's subjugation to a monumental discourse. The essay is written by somebody who sallies into a subject loosely, leaving—or making—holes that are not knitted up, carrying along and exploring the myriad possible specificities of the writer's experience and identity. The essay rests on perspective, on the position of the essayist within the web of culture. It allows the essayist to say, "This is how the world looks to *me*, from my particular place in it." The essay has, then, the potential for being at least an inroad, if not indeed an attack, on monumental discourse because as a form it negotiates the split between public discourse—formal, ordered, impersonal, knowing, with pretensions to universality and fixity, and private utterance—tentative, personal, questing, provisional. If the "composition" is an edifice, the essay is a nomad's tent. It moves around.

The essay, then, is and has been a form open to the articulation of estrangements and contradictions, a place for expressing the strains, differences, rejections as well as connections experienced by those who feel or have felt particularly marginalized by the discourses which have composed the dominant social text. I am thinking here of writers like James Baldwin, Nancy Mairs, Alice Walker, Audre Lorde, Minnie Bruce Pratt, and many others who have recognized in the essay a potential site for the operations of contesting discourses and have used it to explore and construct in language the multiple perspectives which variant experiences and identities produce.

Virginia Woolf, for instance. Think of all those polite essays she wrote about her reading and published in the *Times Literary Supplement*. Think of how comforting, how comfortable they are, spoken from the privileged position of a woman of means, of well-placed family, of culture. And then think of others, *A Room of One's Own* and *Three Guineas*, in which she speaks from a position as outsider, attempting to undo the cultural stories that have placed her there, on the margins, because of her gender. Such writing from the margins is "guerrilla writing," a phrase I read recently and have not been able to forget. In the terrain of monumental discourse, such pieces are eruptions of personal presence based on shifting experiences and identities, eruptions that aim to dis-compose the power relations that reside in textuality. And such moments are accomplished not only *by* particular essays within the field of more orderly forms of writing; they occur also *within* essays, as in Woolf: in "Professions for Women," when that-which-cannot-be-said about a woman's experience of her body slips away like a fish escaping a line. Or in "The Moment: Summer's Night," when an imaged scene of domestic violence—"He beats her"—intrudes upon and contrasts with the cultivated civility of the narrator and her companions. Or in "22 Hyde Park Gate," which closes with the astonishing revelation of the sexual abuse Woolf and her sister were subjected to by their half-brother. Is Woolf in these texts violating her own dictum that the purpose of the essay is "to give pleasure"? What sort of pleasure can we get from scenes of wife-beating and forced incest and the taboos against expressing bodily experience? Perhaps the pleasures of heresy—the thing Adorno calls "the law of the innermost form of the essay." And the pleasures of heresy are not small. Carl Klaus has aptly termed the essay an "antigenre, a rogue form of writing in the universe of discourse." I would elaborate only to observe that the essay can be, has been, rogue or heretical not only in form but also in effect. As "antigenre," it has the capacity to work against, even to undo, the presumptions that have structured western discourse.

Look, for another example, at what is happening in the realm of conventional academic writing. A couple of years ago, a friend gave me a copy of Jane Tompkins' essay "Me and My Shadow" in an effort to help me out of a difficult period of inability to write. I read about Tompkins' anger at the "straitjacket" of the suppression of the personal voice and personal experience in academic writing, about the "two voices" she felt within her, one of which had been systematically silenced. I read her plea for redressing the damage done by the conventions of intellectual discourse, a plea based on the conviction that readers "want to know about each other":

> Sometimes, when a writer introduces some personal bit of story into an essay, I can hardly contain my pleasure. I love writers who write about their own experience. I feel I'm being nourished by them, that I can match my own experience with theirs, feel cousin to them, and say, yes, that's how it is.

Yes, I said to myself as I read, a seemingly endless stream of tears rolling down my cheeks—whether tears of grief, or joy, or both, I'm still not clear—yes, that's how it is.

Sometimes, though, the voice relating personal perspective and experience in an essay draws me, excites me, because what I read challenges rather than confirms my own experience and thus opens up for me new perspectives on the world. Then my response is not "That's how it is," but "Is that how it is?" If I am to act in the world in a way that attempts to respect and accommodate differences, I need to know what the world is like not only for people who are in some way like me, but also for people who are in some way different. I must be taught as well as teach. Patricia Williams, a black feminist legal scholar, begins an essay on commercial transactions by telling the story of the rape and impregnation at age twelve of her great-great-grandmother by the girl's white owner. The essay, "On Being the Object of Property," is a dazzling poetic display which inserts the continuing personal pain of such a heritage into the affect-less tradition of legal scholarship and thereby unsettles that tradition. It links Williams' meditations on her personal and racial histories, her experiences of race and gender in a hierarchical culture, with legal issues like the "Baby M" case and the forced sterilization of women of color. The essay accommodates passages like this one:

> There are moments in my life when I feel as though a part of me is missing. There are days when I feel so invisible that I can't remember what day of the week it is, when I feel so manipulated that I can't remember my own name, when I feel so lost and angry that I can't speak a civil word to the people who love me best. Those are the times when I catch sight of my reflection in store windows and am surprised to see a whole person looking back. Those are the times when my skin becomes gummy as clay and my nose slides around on my face and my eyes drip down to my chin. I have to close my eyes at such times and remember myself, draw an internal picture that is smooth and whole; when all else fails, I reach for a mirror and stare myself down until the features re-assemble themselves like lost sheep.

The passage is a metaphoric description of the dis-composing effect of monolithic racist and sexist discourses on Williams, and of the composing effect of her own writing, in which she reconstructs—*re-*

members—a self, however momentary, however *partial* in both senses of the word: invested with self-interest and without claim to finality. Williams' writing simultaneously composes herself and discomposes conventional discourses which in a variety of ways deny her. She makes use of the literary qualities of language, whose task, in their origins in the oral traditions of poetry, was to make memorable the stories of the tribe or culture in order to assure they would be repeated and thus not forgotten. Williams' essay is a frontal attack on the master's house, a stream of words aimed at eroding the rock of oppression at the foundation of culture. Her essay insists that there is never just one story; rather, there are many stories which can and must be told, which must be heard. In this essay Williams, like Sylvie in *Housekeeping*, is an undoer. And that cannot be a futile effort because, as James Baldwin, filled with simultaneous despair and desperate hope, writes in his beautiful essay "Nothing Personal," "For nothing is fixed, forever and forever and forever, it is not fixed; the earth is always shifting, the light is always changing, the sea does not cease to grind down rock."

What the pedagogical implications of such a view of the essay might be I have considered here hardly at all, and then only indirectly. Certainly the form itself has been an outsider in the institution of literary studies, relegated mostly to the composition classroom where, too often, its essential qualities of perspective and personal voice have been masked or even banned. What could happen if we admit the "antigenre" not only into our polite and scholarly forms of writing, but also into the rigidly generic classrooms and hallways of our educational institutions—what Nancy Mairs calls "the ivory phallus"—I can scarcely imagine. I know I'd like to be around to watch.

III

So. What did I leave out of my story of buying a house, of my attempts to shore up its walls against some imagined ruin? Some of the reasons. I belong, by race and by family tradition, to a propertied class, where owning a house stands in direct equation with respectability. It is my toehold. Also because I am a woman who came of age in an era when "home" was woman's sphere, even when she's also the "head of household." Also because I've been, most of my adult life, relatively rootless, following along after one man, one life plan, in flight from others. Now, my children grown and gone, I become paradoxically even more obsessive about a "nest."

If you wonder why I of all people proved so susceptible to the seductions of "home" with all its attendant ideologies, I can tell you only and simply that I am a woman partially constructed by such ideologies.

But perhaps I've painted an overly romantic picture of the house and my relation to it. It's been almost two years now, after all, since I moved in, two years of mild winters and early springs and one temperate summer. Like all love affairs, this one has lost some of its glow. The house is still grand, I admit; but water pipes burst, the roof leaks, the porches sag. The deep and dark waters of the lake at Fingerbone reach all the way to Iowa and lap at my edges. The house is after all less comfortable, less comforting than I had hoped, and other yearnings have started to surface. I manage to muster, twice a year, the thousand dollars to pay the property tax. But I feed the squirrels that eat holes in the eaves to winter over in the attic, though my more prudent friends urge me to trap them humanely and move them out, into the country west of town.

And I think I forgot to mention that I share the house—and not just with my cat. In fact I live only in those hardly-discrete rooms of the first floor, rooms that flow liquidly one into another. In the upstairs apartment are Karen and Wayne, their black cat and their books. Wayne writes novels, Karen makes poems, so on our good days, all of us are more preoccupied with meanings than with maintenance. In the spare parking place next to the alley, a huge and ancient Buick appears several days a week beside my tenants' Toyota. The Buick is ventilated with rusted-through holes the size of my fist. It belongs to Alex, broad-faced member of the Mesquakie tribe from the settlement over at Tama. He wears a long braid down his back, a feather in his black felt hat; he won a dance competition, he told me, at a pow-wow on the shores of Lake Michigan just a few months ago. Karen and Wayne mentioned casually once that he was "visiting"; instead, I think he lives there with them on the days he needs to be in Iowa City to go to school. They don't tell me that because, I suppose, they think the same impulse that led me to lay a brick terrace and plant lilies would make me exercise a white law and kick him out. But I say nothing. I'm learning to live with, live through contradictions, even learning to love them. I grow weary of defending territory to which I'm not sure I can lay just claim. And I want to be an undoer too, as well as one of the undone. I want this house to be open. Alex, when he sees me in the yard, greets me and calls me "the landlady." The term gives me a start, especially coming from him. Whose home is this, anyway?

I know, I know, it is in some sense mine. But I can give it up. And surely someday, some way or other, I will.

NOTE

The texts cited in this essay are: T. W. Adorno, "The Essay as Form," in *New German Critique*, 1984; James Baldwin, "Nothing Personal," in *The Price of the Ticket*, 1985; Carl Klaus, "Essayists on the Essay," in *Literary Nonfiction*, ed. Chris Anderson, 1989; Nancy Mairs, *Remembering the Bone House: An Erotics of Place and Space*, 1989; Biddy Martin and Chandra Talpade Mohanty, "Feminist Politics: What's Home Got to Do with It?" in *Feminist Studies / Critical Studies*, ed. Teresa de Lauretis, 1986; Minnie Bruce Pratt, "Identity: Skin Blood Heart," in Bulkin, Pratt, and Smith, *Yours in Struggle*, 1984; Marilynne Robinson, *Housekeeping*, 1981; Jane Tompkins, "Me and My Shadow," in *New Literary History*, 1987; Patricia Williams, "On Being the Object of Property," in *Signs*, 1988; Virginia Woolf, "Professions for Women," in *The Death of the Moth and Other Essays*, 1942; Woolf, "The Moment: Summer's Night," in *The Moment and Other Essays*, 1948; Woolf, "22 Hyde Park Gate," in *Moments of Being*, 1976.

12

Unfamiliar Ties: Lesbian Constructions of Home and Family in Jeanette Winterson's *Oranges Are Not the Only Fruit* and Jewelle Gomez's *The Gilda Stories*

Ellen Brinks and Lee Talley

If a number of twentieth-century women writers creatively invest in the idea and representation of home, it is not because home, in the conservative sense, provides a haven or refuge from terrifying realities that lie outside it. Our essay will outline the difficulties and rewards that a particular group of women writers—self-identified lesbians—articulate by writing about home. The challenges they face are necessarily different from those of heterosexual women. Even respecting the most obvious differences of race, class, age, or geographical location among lesbians, the pervasiveness of homophobia means that society routinely (with legal sanction and precedent) refuses lesbians the rights to home and family and makes the expression of these ties very difficult, if not impossible. Few other social groups in the U.S. experience this specific kind of unjust, although legalized, oppression.

Unlike heterosexual couples, lesbian couples cannot be legally married. They cannot, with certainty, will their property or the care of their persons to their partners. They are frequently denied child custody, or if they have a child together, they must resort to additional legal measures to insure that their partners will be recognized as legal guardians in the event of their own death.[1] Beyond this, lesbians document countless acts of material violence to their persons, homes, and private property. Existing statutes in many states allow police to invade lesbian and gay homes and arrest their inhabitants for illegal sexual practices.[2] Numerous ballot initiatives currently pending in the United States threaten to legalize housing and job discrimination on the basis of sexual orientation.[3] In such a hostile climate, "home" is anything but secure for lesbians.

Indeed, home and family all too frequently function as sites where society's own antagonisms collectively come out. Arrogating power in the name of a "family values" ideology, conservative political movements constrict the acceptable vocabularies and meanings of home. This powerful, organized homophobia attempts to produce the illusion of one desirable family: a white father and mother with (ideally) blond children.[4] Such rhetoric illuminates the interconnections between racism, sexism, and heterosexism and explains why some gay families become intensely private, invisible, and separate from the public sphere. Thus, real social violence gives rise to the need for privacy and security that resembles, but needs to be distinguished from, internalized homophobia. Yet the result is the same: queer family ties are kept in the closet.

These secluded homes do become havens for some lesbians. Yet one cannot ignore the Victorian overtones that a privatization of family life implies. In addition, lesbians may find themselves bound to a language that betrays or silences them. Some lesbians describe their family and home life in public by hinting about *housemates* and *best friends*, instead of the words heterosexuals freely use, *girlfriend*, *partner,* or *lover*. Others simply remain silent, unable to trust society with a relationship that for too many represents the unspeakable (expressed in the "don't ask, don't tell" mentality). Most lesbians assess who can be trusted in the work place or in public gatherings.

Beyond these forms of seclusion and silence, however, lesbians also create visibly different homes and extended families. Many of the emotional ties between lesbians are conventional, like friendships with other women. Others are unfamiliar in a predominantly heterosexual society: women who choose a lifelong partner based on sexual and emotional intimacy while consciously rejecting motherhood; women who become parents, either alone or with a partner, without recreating the father-mother dyad; women who become aunts and godmothers to the children of these partners; women who remain close friends with former lovers after the relationship is over and a new one begun; and lesbians who make homes for themselves alone or in nonmonogamous relationships.[5] Beyond these unfamiliar relations between women, lesbian homes are often distinguished by an acute historical awareness of the gay men and lesbians before them who shaped homes and families under even more restrictive conditions. Lesbians are also conscious of their attachment, nostalgia, frustration, and ambivalence towards their homes of origin, that is, the family and communities that raised them.

Today, many lesbian writers are reappropriating the notion of home.[6] Given the contested nature of "home" in First World

Eurowestern culture today, their aesthetic endeavors cannot be taken as anything other than political. These creations are the results of local, national, and international gay rights activism—activism that has afforded and continues to give lesbians greater aesthetic freedoms to imagine their lives. Within the context of a large body of artistic work, this essay takes a more narrow focus and explores the artistic and political issues addressed by two writers, British author Jeanette Winterson and American writer Jewelle Gomez, as they revise conventional notions of home and family. We do not claim that their works are representative, but choose them because they complicate the meanings of the lesbian home by using highly original narrative modes and rhetorical strategies.

Jeanette Winterson's *Oranges Are Not the Only Fruit* and Jewelle Gomez's *The Gilda Stories* lie generically and thematically at opposite poles. Winterson's novel is an autobiographical, lesbian coming-of-age story set in an English evangelical home, while Gomez's science-fiction fantasy spans two hundred years in the life of a lesbian vampire. Both writers flesh out lesbian definitions of home and family within very specific communities, challenging their culture's overarching, pervasive heterosexual assumptions and models. Acutely aware of literary language and the storyteller's generative voice, these writers revise familiar modes of discourse—ones all-too-often associated with, or used to locate and contain, the dangers of homoerotic desire, such as Biblical texts, fairy tales, Victorian literature, and vampire fiction.

Winterson's overt (and radical) challenge to her readers lies in asking them to imagine a coming-of-age and coming-out narrative permeated with evangelist Christian discourses that typically describe homosexuality as an abomination. The intertextual references to the Biblical story of Ruth and the chapter headings from the first eight books of the Bible indicate more than a clever literariness or parodic subversion on Winterson's part, however.[7] They function as an ongoing allegorical touchstone for the heroine Jeanette's (and the reader's) experience of her self and home of origin. As Winterson's "signature," these religious languages or narratives shape her personal and artistic identity and testify to her literary lineage, asking the reader to see a kind of family resemblance. She thus bears witness to the liberating aspects of her heroine's fundamentalist upbringing without simplifying the myriad ways it betrays and punishes her.

Out of this ambivalent legacy, she incorporates forms that provide the source material for some of the most conservative gender and sexual roles for women and finds their emancipatory voices. Familiar narratives become estranged as Winterson splices Jeanette's coming-of-age story with fairy tales, fantastic sequences, Arthurian legend, and new readings of Charlotte Brontë's *Jane Eyre* and Christina Rossetti's "Goblin Market." Jeanette works with words to make sense of her family of origin. Despite betrayals that many would find unforgivable, Jeanette's loyalty parallels Winterson's debt to, and understanding of, the importance and enduring effects of received literary forms—her verbal homes of origin. Challenging conservatives who like to present the family as well as the oldest and most sacred literary forms as fixed and unchanging, *Oranges* testifies to their mutual flexibility and transformative potential. Winterson's novel formally mirrors her protagonist's development, as her hybrid literary forms *collectively*—not individually—"house" family without defining its totality.

Winterson's own evangelical background also informs the world of her protagonist, Jeanette. Representing a life-style many would assume antithetical to lesbianism, Jeanette / Winterson nonetheless shows the centrality of words and narrative structures to evangelism and to her work as a writer. Fundamentalist religion gives language an originary capacity (Jesus was the Word of God made flesh) and from this religion Jeanette inherits a profound appreciation for language's generative powers as she refashions her understanding of family. When the child Jeanette learns to read the world for God's signs—in other words, subversively in the eyes of a secular society—, she is learning about language's capacity to create reality in different forms. The church, her alternate, extended family, emphasizes such creation in their acts of conversion: making the "Heathen" believe its members' stories of salvation. Its own means of reproduction, conversion yields a larger family without physical reproduction. This example provides Jeanette with the command of persuasive and performative language. By the novel's end, these imaginative strategies enable Jeanette to accept lesbianism as "normal," return home after familial betrayal, and reconstitute home and family from the discursive vantage point of a writer / prophet.

Oranges Are Not the Only Fruit begins with a chapter aptly titled "Genesis." Like the biblical Genesis that describes the world's beginnings, it calls attention to Jeanette's origins. By appropriating one of the oldest and most influential ordering narratives of Judeo-Christian culture, Winterson starts her novel as a staged revolt against evangelism's literal interpretation of the Bible as Truth. She turns "the

Beginning" on its head as she uses it to describe her mother's birth / conversion story and her own birth. Simultaneously, she incorporates the New Testament plot of the nativity. This overlapping of origins, Adam's / Jesus' / her mother's / her own, deconstructs the biblical Genesis where God creates one man and chooses one tribe, one family, then finally one patriarch, Abraham. *Oranges* makes biblical origins about women and matriarchal history, since father and son do not exist in this world. Jeanette even denies her father's existence to her first lover Melanie, when she says: "'I haven't [a father] either'" (83). The remaining seven chapters of the novel, named after the next seven books of the Old Testament, narratively recreate the Old Testament as personal autobiography. This humorous parody revises Judeo-Christian notions of family and home to include its newer and less familiar members.

Winterson's creative use of these biblical stories reflects the project both Jeanette and her mother Louie embark upon as well. The narrative collage points to the inadequacy of any single text or genre that purports to define a specific identity. Further, the novel rejects the binary oppositions that underlie many of our cultural fictions: oppositions such as "man / woman," "white / black," "heterosexual / homosexual," or "good / bad," for example.[8] The paradigms Louie erects at the beginning of the story illuminate the inadequacy of such oppositions. Jeanette writes how her mother

> had never heard of mixed feelings. There were friends and there were enemies:
>
> Enemies were: The Devil (in his many forms)
>   Next Door
>   Sex (in its many forms)
>   Slugs
> Friends were: God
>   Our dog
>   Auntie Madge
>   The Novels of Charlotte Brontë
>   Slug pellets
> and me, at first. (3)

Winterson calls attention to how much Louie divides Jeanette's world, fragmenting it by listing the items vertically, literally isolating each entity. By not staying on the "proper" list of friends, Jeanette is an enemy. Yet by looking closer at these oppositions, their idiosyncratic potential for subversion becomes apparent. Despite the pain her eventual shift entails, her move aligns her with enemies and their capacity for multiple meanings. Considered demonic by her mother for her "deviant" sexual practices, Jeanette resembles the devil in her use of language, since it too appears in many forms. Note, however, that Winterson places Jeanette in neither category. She thus situates her in the non-binary realm "of many forms," somewhere beyond the opposition of friend (Self) or enemy (Other). Her acceptance of "mixed feelings" is central to her acceptance of her lesbianism, since a lesbian by definition cannot fit comfortably into a binary view of the world.[9]

Ironically, Jeanette's capacity for mixed feelings and non-binary thought can be attributed to her mother's teachings. The above list, for all Louie's claims to divide the world into two camps, breaks down into an amazing plurality, so that her set of oppositions (friend / enemy, God / Devil, Slug / Slug pellets) deconstructs in light of the other entries. For example, our dog and next door are no more opposites than the novels of Charlotte Brontë are with sex (in its many forms). Unlike an unbeliever or conventional believer, Louie teaches Jeanette "to interpret the signs and wonders that the unbeliever might never understand" (17). As Jeanette recounts:

> I learnt about Horticulture and Garden Pests via the slugs and my mother's seed catalogues, and I developed an understanding of Historical Process through the prophecies in the Book of Revelations, and a magazine called *The Plain Truth*, which my mother received each week. 'It's Elijah in our midst again,' she declared. (17)

On the basis of this bizarre confluence of texts, Jeanette begins to see the world in non-traditional ways. Combining millennialism and historicism with her mother's hilarious and overly literal interpretations of the world ("It's Elijah in our midst again"), Jeanette creates a heady confusion of epistemologies.

Mother and daughter embark on this interpretive project with their church. Louie raises Jeanette to spread the word of God, thereby enlarging their religious family, and more importantly, to believe in her own voice. Part of this training to become a missionary involves understanding and manipulating the powers of language. Since evangelists believe it is their duty to spread the Word / Truth of God, this power / knowledge is inextricably linked to their religion. Winterson depicts the church as an organization devoted to language, disseminating many stories, quite literally "marketing" salvation through the construction of narratives. As Jeanette explains, they have aids like "the action kit, which had been specially designed by the Charismatic Movement Marketing Council. [It] explained that people are different and need a different approach. You had to make salvation relevant to them, to their minds" (35). Thus, the members address a larger audience, and Jeanette learns early on about story-telling's power as a medium for addressing different readers.

She also learns revolutionary reading strategies from certain members of her church. In the second chapter, "Exodus," chronicling Jeanette's exodus from her mother's home to school, Winterson parodies the Israelites' flight from Egypt. In the Bible, Moses is invaluable to the Israelites, since he explains God's Word. In Winterson's second chapter, the elderly, "testifying" Elsie becomes a feminist Moses of sorts, one of Jeanette's most important teachers. Elsie encourages Jeanette's extraordinary creativity, one that goes unrewarded at school where teachers and peers are mystified and disturbed by her imaginative play with religious themes. Elsie continues her mother's reading lesson by stating, "what looks like one thing . . . may well be another," but adds a cautionary note to her mother's rule of interpreting the wor(l)d (30). She teaches Jeanette the importance of looking inward or beyond appearances, despite other people's opinions:

> 'Some folk say I'm a fool, but there's more to this world than meets the eye. . . . There's this world,' she banged the wall graphically, 'and there's this world,' she thumped her chest. 'If you want to make sense of either, you have to take notice of both.' (32)

Elsie stresses the interplay between the physical and emotional worlds.

Elsie guides Jeanette out of traditional patriarchal religion in part by reading her works such as Christina Rossetti's "Goblin Market," a poem expressing a homoerotic desire that strengthens home and family. In this poem about literal and figurative forbidden fruit, a girl (Laura) ignores her sister Lizzie's warnings: "We must not look at goblin men, / We must not buy their fruits: / Who knows upon what soil they fed / Their hungry thirsty roots" (4). Disregarding these prohibitions and the cautionary tale about the unfortunate girl named Jeanie (a version of Jeanette's name), who dies from eating goblin fruit, Laura buys the fruit with a lock of her hair, devours it, and then proceeds to waste away until her (good) sister Lizzie saves her. Lizzie tries to buy more fruit, but the Goblins pelt her with it instead, ultimately forcing Laura to eat, lick, and kiss the fruit off her. Upon her return Lizzie cries:

> . . . 'Laura,' up the garden.
> Did you miss me?
> Come and kiss me
> Never mind my bruises,
> Hug me, kiss me, suck my juices
> Squeezed from goblin fruits for you,
> Goblin pulp and goblin dew.
> Eat me, drink me, love me;
> Laura, make much of me. . . . (19)

Ironically, the oral eroticism between the two girls is supposed to re-establish the centrality of home and family: the Rossetti poem ends with the two sisters grown into virtuous Victorian women. They, in turn, tell this story to their own children, teaching them to be good children who honor home and family by heeding the prohibitions in the stories told to them. More importantly than the questionable containment of lesbian desire though, Elsie indirectly displays her own acceptance of same-sex relationships, something Louie is incapable of doing.

The most important lesson about language and family that Elsie shares, however, is their endless possibility for renewal. Jeanette remembers the lines from William Butler Yeats's "Lapis Lazuli" that Elsie reads to her: "All things fall and are built again / And those that build them again are gay" (30). Elsie teaches Jeanette that the walls that fall are eventually rebuilt, and that those who rebuild or refashion them are the fortunate ones (note the suggestive pun on "gay"). Throughout the novel, Winterson writes of literal and figurative walls that divide and stigmatize people, as well as those appropriate to personal boundaries, such as the imaginary chalk circle she draws to protect her soul (113). All these stories, however, point to the possibility of rebuilding family, even if the "walls" that uphold and define it must be broken first.

The central story about finding family and home that Louie rewrites is Charlotte Brontë's novel, *Jane Eyre*. Louie's version of the novel reinforces what she wants her daughter to learn about family: that it is *not* based on blood ties but upon choice. Although Jane finds true "blood relatives" in Brontë's text, Louie tells Jeanette that Jane marries the cold, passionless St John, the missionary. Louie neatly valorizes missionary work in her own version—a suspicious vocation in *Jane Eyre* because it represents life without passion—and erases Jane's already existing familial bond with St John, her cousin. Holding up her own *Jane Eyre* as a mirror for Jeanette, Louie willfully uses it to reshape her daughter's sense of self and their church family. Like Jane, Jeanette is an orphan (note that Jeanette is a variation on the name Jane). And as the reader learns, Louie too is orphaned. Disowned by her family for marrying down, "after a while [Louie manages] to forget that she'd ever had any at all. 'The church is my family,' she always said whenever [Jeanette] asked about the people in the photograph album. And the church was [Jeanette's] family too" (37).

Louie's revisionary work gives Jeanette a precedent for liberating home and family from the biological, and therefore, heterosexual, models of family as opposed to those based upon choice. Louie problematizes the cultural weight accorded to blood relations and raises her to view sexual reproduction as fornication (i.e., degenerate). *Oranges Are Not the Only Fruit* depicts a strangely "barren" world. Except for Jeanette and the family next door (known more for their sex than their offspring), there are no families with children represented in the novel. Sexual reproduction is literally and figuratively disrupted. Instead, the reproduction of the church family is the central focus of Louie's world and work, and she closely nurtures and monitors its growth. Besides the church's travelling revival shows, every Sunday the family listens to the world report for the numbers of converted "Heathen." Since age peers can convert one another in religious reproduction, generational (and therefore conventional, hierarchical) differences between adults and children are erased: all church members are perceived to be equal.

Louie is particularly invested in nonbiological constructions of family because they allow her to have a family and to replace the one that disowned her. Louie envies the Virgin Mary for "getting there first," for making a *divine* word flesh without engaging in sexual intercourse (3). Louie, in turn, makes Jeanette, her adopted "foundling" daughter flesh with a set of *adoption papers* that describe her conception without "the jolt beneath the hip bone" (3, 5). Louie moves Jeanette's birth story into her disembodied fantasy. Like her willful imposition of her passionless version of *Jane Eyre* upon Jeanette, the denial of Jeanette's birth mother becomes a massive betrayal. When the older Jeanette, "literate and curious . . . [decides] to read it for [herself as] a kind of literary pilgrimage," she tells the reader her discovery: "Jane didn't marry St John at all. . . . [S]he goes back to Rochester.

[This] was like the day I discovered my adoption papers while searching for a pack of playing cards. I have never since played cards, and I have never since read *Jane Eyre*" (74-75).

Louie's emphasis on choice-based models frees her from essentialist ideas about family, but this freedom comes at a price. Louie narrows her model exclusively to the spiritual family. She denigrates motherhood when she cruelly describes Jeanette's birth mother as a "carrying case," telling Jeanette that *she* (Louie) is her mother. Traumatized, Jeanette relates feeling uncertain for the first time in her life: "uncertainty to me was like Aardvark to other people. A curious thing I had no notion of, but recognized through second hand illustration. . . . I was very upset. Uncertainty was what the Heathen felt, and I was chosen by God" (100). Jeanette identifies herself as one of the Heathen, for they are the ones "unsaved" and "blind," made unsure of meaning and their own emotions in the face of Louie's absolute claims to Truth. The ambivalence Jeanette feels for her birth mother and for Louie's fierce maintenance of their own family, although painful, allows Jeanette to contemplate the idea of family as appearing "in many forms."[10]

Jeanette learns of her adoption in the chapter "Numbers," named after the biblical book where the chosen people are pictured as "faithless, rebellious, and blind to God's signs" (*New Oxford Bible* 160). She discovers not only her mother's betrayal of her birth mother and *Jane Eyre*, but of Louie's blindness to her own desire. Louie's brushes with rebellion include a love affair with a Frenchman and the suggestion of lesbianism. Louie thus offers her the figurative fruit of homosexuality: for some time a *woman's* picture resides in the "Old Flame" section of her scrapbook (36). The visual image, even though removed, is a literalization of Otherness and other possibilities, which cannot fail to suggest the luscious fruits of the "Goblin Market" and the biblical forbidden fruit. Like the good sister Lizzie and Jeanette's visionary demons, Louie continually offers Jeanette oranges. She thereby initiates her into the multiplicity of sexual and textual meanings, despite her valiant, if contradictory, attempts to suppress bodily reproduction and passion.[11]

Louie more fundamentally betrays Jeannette by rejecting her lesbianism in the "battle" recounted in the chapters "Joshua" and "Judges." The Bible details the Battle of Jericho, in which both the good and bad suffer until the righteous blowing on a trumpet tumbles the walls and good triumphs over evil. Important to *Oranges* is the falling of walls in Jeanette's battle. The walls that "protect" and "limit"—those upholding the patriarchy and conservative notions of family—fall in "consequence of blowing your own trumpet" (112). Jeanette makes the walls fall; as a lesbian, she dares to define herself outside the patriarchal and heterosexual order. Winterson deconstructs the sex / gender binaries, literally causing them to tumble down by situating her heroine outside the walls of sexual difference, or heterosexuality (112). Louie, the pastor, and other church members perform an exorcism in an attempt to rebuild those walls. When Jeanette's sexual desires resist "the cure," they force her to leave home. This exile makes Jeanette rethink her own identity (in its many forms), her understanding of language (in its many forms), and the possibility of home.

In her final chapter "Ruth," Winterson writes allegorically—with a self-styled fairy tale and stories about the dissolution of King Arthur's court—of Jeanette's decision to leave her family of origin. Winterson plumbs the impact of Louie's betrayal, building upon the plot of Ruth and reinforcing the lesson of familial loyalty by telling that lesson three times. In the Bible, Ruth is loyal to her mother-in-law in extraordinary ways, following her to a new land once Ruth's husband dies. Instead of beginning the chapter with stories of Jeanette's exile and eventual inclusion into a foreign family and home, as a parallel to the Biblical text might suggest, Winterson embarks with the fairy tale of Winnet Stonejar, an anagram for Jeanet[te] Winterson.

Winnet leaves the only home she knows and her father, a wicked wizard. Homesickness literally strikes her down, and she is found close to death by a wise woman from a nearby village "who understood the different types of sorrow and their effects" (153). She is taken in by the villagers but is never quite at home there, since she is always reminded of her otherness, her exile. The villagers speak a different language than Winnet's native tongue, but know of her father and his dangerous powers. Winnet longs to speak of her past, but the villagers expect her to be quiet and not to question either the present or the past. Even though Winnet knows of her father's insanity and the evils he had created, she longs to discuss it. Ultimately she leaves again, journeying to a distant city where people will presumably let her speak and transform her exile into a point of departure that neither suppresses nor silences the past.

Winnet's problem mirrors Jeanette's, as she finds herself in a culture that relegates fundamentalists and lesbians to its verbal margins. Thus, the task of finding a home in exile is doubly difficult, since Jeanette's religious past and her sexuality awaken in others the desire to silence her. Jeanette refuses this silence by employing another narrative to tell her own story. She uses familiar Arthurian legend, specifically Perceval's struggle to return to King Arthur's court—a mythic family of chosen members that defines the unified nation, "England"—to imagine her inclusion in British society. When she leaves her mother's, however, the temporary home that Jeanette finds is literally a home for "Others." She chooses to work at a local mental hospital because it comes with "a room of [her] own" (158). Her self-conscious evocation of a literary mother, Virginia Woolf, suggests a familial resemblance between the two writers: namely, their adoption into a family of women writers in the face of personal struggle.

In the room of her own that *is* home, Jeanette begins to explore and articulate a relation to her family of origin through a complex net of narrative modes and rhetorical strategies. Like the Bible chapters that title each era of Jeannette's life, the reader senses Jeanette's power over the wor(l)d, knowing that words' meanings, as in the New Testament, are the site for beginnings. When she writes of the difficulty of naming, for example, Jeanette acknowledges the power of language not just to reflect, but to create reality as well. She describes the vast "unknownness of my needs," plumbing the depths of the desire for family and for familiar surroundings, and she also expresses the lack of trust and fear due to the magnitude of her mother's betrayal (170).

Just as Winnet, Perceval and Jeanette all seek a family, so does Louie. The church family she had chosen is close to dissolving, rocked by scandals of theft and adultery. By the end of the novel, Jeanette and Louie mirror one another in their similar struggles to reclaim home and family where there appears to be none left. Although Jeanette demonstrates her own ability to create family, Winterson chooses to close with Louie's words. The voice of the missionary and mother signifies an uneasy peace in the recognition of disturbing similarities and powerful ties between mother and daughter. With a new transistor radio Louie broadcasts the Word, calling out, "This is Kindly Light calling Manchester, come in Manchester, this is Kindly Light" (176). Like Jeanette, she continues to create her family, undaunted by geographical obstacles and even by the dramatic and powerful dissolution of her church home. She even works as a consultant to other families who have "lost" children to homosexuality. Finally, Jeanette visits Louie's home at the end of the novel, trying to find a way to acknowledge her bond with her mother.

Although mother-daughter relations and conservative Biblical interpretation structure the novel's conflicts, Jeanette's mother and church family teach her subversive reading strategies: discursive vantage points for rebellion and creation. These reading strategies ultimately enable mother and daughter to imagine home as a place that can accommodate them, despite ideological differences and personal experiences that affect their chosen families. They help Louie reclaim her own life after her daughter's "betrayal" and allow Jeanette to direct and wield the language of her betrayers in the service of her own attempts to make a new home.

At the end of the novel, rather than becoming a missionary as her mother intended, Jeanette describes a more problematic relationship to the world and language. While a missionary spreads the Word of God, narratives grounded in a transcendental "Truth," Jeanette describes herself as a prophet. A prophet speaks of the present and the future in words that are inherently unstable and untested:

> I could have been a priest instead of a prophet. The priest has a book with the words set out. Old words, known words, words of power. Words that are always on the surface. Words for every occasion. The words work. They do what they're supposed to do; comfort and discipline. The prophet has no book. The prophet is a voice that cries out in the wilderness, full of sounds that do not always set into meaning. The prophets cry out because they are troubled by demons. (161)

Jeanette is a prophet "troubled by demons," having no "book with the words set out" and "lacking words for every occasion." Jeanette / Winterson's words will not "comfort and discipline" like the priest's. It is here, at the end of *Oranges*, that the prophet Jeanette begins her quest for new family.

Jewelle Gomez's *The Gilda Stories* also refashions narrative to include visions of family that upset traditional ideas of domesticity, desire, parenting, and intimacy. As wildly disparate as they appear to be, lesbianism, evangelical religion, and vampirism have a profound common denominator, one that allows us to find points of commonality between these two very different novels. Our secular, heterosexist cultural imagination fears conversion to any one of these groups, since they are seen as fostering "unnatural passions" and promoting their way of life. Coming out and coming of age—even for a vampire—are forms of conversion. They entail the revision of inherited languages that describe the self and family relationships. Not out to convert others, however, Winterson and Gomez flesh out the idea of family to explore the transformative experiences of lesbianism.

Jewelle Gomez transforms literary conventions by creating a literary heroine, Gilda, closely allied with lesbian erotics—the female vampire. Since her early appearances in Samuel Taylor Coleridge's *Christabel* (1797), Sheridan LeFanu's *Carmilla* (1871), and Bram Stoker's *Dracula* (1897), the female vampire's assertive exploration of unconventional sexuality has upset cultural assumptions about femininity. She is all-too-willing to sacrifice the stable generational or reproductive dynamics of the heterosexual family. Imagined as socially death-defying yet domestically death-dealing, female vampires undermine the nuclear family by luring off or killing its members. They become the fascinating and repulsive creatures that society unsuccessfully attempts to destroy in order to preserve "the home" and the institution of marriage and motherhood. In *The Gilda Stories*, Gomez complicates this inherited discourse with a runaway African American slave-turned-vampire as her protagonist. Beginning as a slave narrative, Gilda's stories from 1850 to an imagined 2050 trace a vampiristic lesbian diaspora through the novel's material and discursive search for a new home and family. Because the black lesbian and the creature of the shadowy margins, the vampire, suffer from the lack of a visibly defined social identity, Gomez affiliates them as culture's "anti-subjects," or paradigms of the "outsider" in society.

Gilda's fantastic life as a vampire, however, makes personal history comprehensible in part through an embodied social history of black lesbianism. As she assumes different personas over two hundred years in diverse American geographical locations and social worlds, Gilda's interactive work of building family and home is figured through the blood exchange, in which Gilda shares dreams and stories subconsciously with her "victims" or partners. Gomez thus complicates the relationship between the vampire and her victim. In a sexually and subjectively transformative act with connotations of maternal nurturing, Gilda creates a mutuality based on difference, not the one-way, deadly exchange imagined in traditional vampire lore. Common or mixed blood is not perceived as tainted, and it becomes her anti-racist and anti-homophobic legacy.

Unlike *Oranges, The Gilda Stories* begins with the death of the mother. Named at first simply Girl, the runaway slave and protagonist of the novel also loses her home, a slave shack on a Mississippi plantation. Without security, privacy, comfort, or possibility of ownership, this debased version of home reveals the extent to which the domestic sphere (as an ideal) has historically been a white privilege. Girl, however, clings to an idea of home as the memory of lived experiences, the richly inviting, sensual ones tied to her mother's presence: the "teasing pinches," her "starchy dough smell," the "crackling of the brush as [she rakes] the bristles through the Girl's thicket of dark hair before beginning the intricate pattern of braided rows," and her "large black hand" clutching Girl's own (9).

The recollections of physical and emotional intimacy resurface in the synaesthetic images of Girl's dreams. As she dreams of this lost home at the novel's opening, her mother's lost origins arise as well: the Fulani "home across the water . . . [had] a natural rhythm of life without bondage" (11, 10). Merging her own history with her daughter's life, Girl's mother passes on to her the oral stories and legends that record a Fulani lineage. They are her spiritual legacy. Seen in relation to their *double* dispossession—the denial of the right to possess material property as women and as African Americans—, these words and images of her mother's cultural tradition become the *symbolic property* that the slave owners cannot confiscate or control. They give her a historical identity or family that transcends the dehumanizing one imposed by slavery, sustaining her while she is a slave and a runaway. This heritage is incorporated deep into Girl's subconscious.

Girl soon learns, however, that the security of this inheritance, like her mother's life, is tenuous. She acknowledges that this Fulani past is riven with gaps: it is a fragmentary, collective creation "pieced together from many different languages" (10). Gomez frustrates the reader's desires for a "pure" heritage or homeland, figured as the uninterrupted tie to the mother or the mother's peoples. She aligns this historical discontinuity of African American identity with its communicative experiences as well. Whether she is dealing with translation, storytelling, or memory, Girl must face her mother's and her own ability to forget: the verbal loss of family and home.

In part, Girl's amnesia signals the psychological defenselessness and danger always already present in slavery and exacerbated by her mother's death. This deft equivalence is figured in the novel within a single dream. When Girl forgets her past, her own life is endangered:

> She tried to remember what her mother had said about the world as it had lived before this time but could not. The lost empires were a dream to the Girl, like the one she was having

> now. She looked up at the beast from this other land, as he
> dragged her by the leg from the concealing straw. (11)

The dream-memory of an imminent rape exposes the precariousness of
the mother-daughter bond. The lost homeland is reduced to a
disappearing "dream" within a frighteningly "real" nightmare. In
response to the rapist "beast from the other land," however, Girl finds
another maternal legacy providing for her safety. Girl's mother gives
her the capacity to defend herself with force: "In sleep [Girl] clutched
the hand of her mother which turned into the warm, wooden handle of
the knife she had stolen when she ran away" (9). Her mother's *vital*
transfer occurs when the warm hand of maternal care and safety
metonymically slides to the warm knife, the knife Girl with which kills
her rapist, at least in her dream. Her mother transforms slavery's brutal,
sexualized injury of women into Girl's knowledge that she can wield
violence herself, as a weapon for her self-protection and survival.
Violence characterizes the system of slavery, and here it shapes the
physical and psychic escape from it. Gomez thus makes Girl's murder
of her rapist into a metaphor for the possibility of birthing herself out
of slavery:

> He started to enter her, but before his hand finished pulling her
> open . . . she entered him with her heart which was now a
> wood-handled knife. . . . She felt the blood draining from him,
> comfortably warm against the now cool skin. It was like the
> first time her mother had been able to give her a real bath. . . .
> Now the blood washing slowly down . . . was like that bath—a
> cleansing. . . . The Girl moved quietly, as if he had really been
> her lover. . . . Looking down at the blood . . . she felt no
> disgust. It was the blood signaling the death of a beast and her
> continued life. (11-12)

Altering the conventional sexual organization of the scene, Girl
penetrates the man with her knife / phallus. Her rape turns into his
murder—a rebirth wrested from the sexualized violence of his life and
an institution which originally birthed Girl and her sisters. Girl's
appropriation of a traditionally male power, the power to penetrate,
suggests the aptness of her future calling as a vampire, itself another
rebirth, as we shall see.

Girl's "birth" enacts a revenge for the rape and physical abuse
of generations of African American women by white men and the

children that were born out of this brutality. Girl is a terrorized child, prematurely compelled to mother herself before she has the physical and emotional maturity to do so. Significantly, the vampire Gilda, Girl's surrogate mother, finds her in her barn during this dream-flashback to the rape and moves to protect her. What Gilda offers Girl is a new home and family, one whose first gift is a warm cleansing bath, like her mother's baths and the bath with the rapist's blood after her premature birth in the barn.

At Gilda's upscale brothel, "the Woodard place," Girl finds herself part of a larger collective of women, unusual in many ways, not the least of which is the presence of a mistress and the absence of a master. Situated on the outskirts of the town (outside the control and surveillance of conventional family values), the Woodard place playfully inverts social hierarchies of domestic labor and property-ownership. There, liveried men wait on women who by choice refuse the marriage bond and achieve physical, intellectual, and financial independence. Gilda herself adopts a decidedly "queer" identity, with her nocturnal rhythms and her ambiguous gender, dressing at times as a man, at others as a woman. As one woman in the house confides to Girl, Gilda is beyond nameable social identities or recognizable family ties: "After all the time I been here I still don't know who Miss Gilda is. . . . I don't know who her people is" (36).

During her years at the Woodard place, before becoming Gilda's vampire daughter and inheriting Gilda's name after her death, Girl begins to comprehend just how unstable home is through those closest to her, Gilda and her partner, Bird. Home is a place that they, too, have lost, but also something that they recreate. Bird, a Native American who has escaped a smallpox epidemic, the slavery of the reservation, and rejection by her tribal family, transforms exile into belonging, homelessness into family. Before Bird leaves the Woodard place to reclaim a home within her tribe (unsuccessfully, as it happens), she reawakens Girl's repressed memories of her mother. Bird becomes a foster mother for Girl as she teaches her to read and write, expanding her mother's legacy from a purely oral into a *textual* one and inspiring the same kind of physical and intellectual exchange her birth mother had:

> Another reason she enjoyed the lessons was that she liked the way Bird smelled. . . . The soft scent of brown soap mixed with the leather of her headband and necklace created a familiar aura. It reminded the Girl of her mother and the strong

smell of her sweat. . . . The Girl rarely allowed herself to miss her mother or her sisters, preferring to leave the past alone. (20-21)

Girl recovers the Fulani dance rhythms as she translates her maternal memories into her act of telling. She "rocks slightly . . . rewoven into that old circle of dancers . . . [and pours] out the images and names, proud of her ability to weave a story" (39). Bird becomes Girl's midwife to a voice of maternal connection and inheritance.

Gilda finds that she too can reclaim her own suppressed maternal inheritance through Girl. Gilda sees in Girl "a younger self she barely remembered," a glimpse of her origins three hundred years ago (16). In a recovered memory of displacement, of bonds severed in slavery and diaspora, Gilda connects herself to both Girl and Bird:

> With her eyes closed she could slip backwards to the place whose name she had long since forgotten, to when she was a girl. She saw a gathering of people with burnished skin. . . . The spiced scent of their bodies was an aura moving alongside them as they crossed an arid expanse of land. . . . She held the hand of a woman she knew was her mother. . . . All that seemed left was the memory of a scented passage that had dragged her along in its wake and the dark color of blood as it seeped into sand. . . . Even there, in that mythical past she could no longer see clearly, she had moved nomadically from one home to another. . . . She opened her eyes . . . smiling as her own past dissolved. . . . She wanted to look only forward, to the future of the Girl and Bird. (18)

With her emphasis on the future, Gilda suggests that the emerging family of Girl, Gilda, and Bird is more than blood ties or a similar historical experience (one that includes the spilling of blood, a mother's death, and forced exile). Formative as these experiences turn out to be, to define family solely along these lines would situate it in an unalterable relation to the past. Gilda's concept and experience of family responds to the past as the common ground for a possible future, just as Gomez's narrative incorporates the history of slavery and current racism to launch her depiction of a family situated in the future.

Gomez begins her story, as we all begin our lives, with the presence of the mother. While these maternal connections assert their undeniable claim on the daughter's self-understanding, Gomez suggests that they are only a part of her identity. Bird, Gilda, and Girl find themselves separated from their mothers and communities of origin—in a sense, their "mother earth"—but these homeless daughters resist the debilitating aspects of exile in their own lives. As vampires they carry the soil of their birthplace (vampiric birthplace, that is) in the carefully sewn hems of their garments. Despite their travels, through this act they become the most rooted of creatures, never far from or able to forget their homes of origin. Similarly, while physical and psychic violence, forgetting, and alienation powerfully define the diaspora, making orphans out of its children, it creates a powerful need to imagine other kinds of family. Unfortunately, as Gilda discovers, her need for a home is matched by an ignorance of how to find it. What family lessons can these daughters claim from their mothers' lives, lives characterized by a bondage that disavows or breaks familial bonds? Girl's, Gilda's, and Bird's answer is tied to historical necessity, their own resolve, and the unique possibilities that vampirism offers. Gilda and Bird become the Girl's vampire parents and create a new family line. The blood bond, that is, the vampire's bite, literalizes their new relationship and the multiple connections of "family" they have already begun to form.

By virtue of the motif of exile and her characters' search for a new home, Gomez foregrounds an embodied point of intersection between a diasporic, lesbian, and vampiric identity. *The Gilda Stories* acknowledges the cultural legacy that links the vampire's homelessness and the marginal social position occupied by the "homosexual," one well documented in filmic and literary criticism to date.[12] Vampires represent the perverse and deviant, not only because of their homoerotic tendencies, but because of their associations with other "aberrant" forms of exchange as well. In their cultural representations, vampires make visible and contain within their stigmatized figures the dangers of sexual excess (eg., the sexually voracious Lucy in *Dracula*), capitalistic greed, contagion, bad mothering, psychic debility, or the pathological collapse of boundaries between self and other.[13] The encounter with the vampire is characterized as a one-way or intransitive exchange that leads the victim from intense erotic desire to a wasting sickness and finally to death, destroys familial (and therefore patriarchal) generational dynamics by replicating its homoerotic "evil." Traditional vampiric reproduction occurs at the cost of individual life and the dissolution of the victim's family.

While she retains the erotic longings and pleasures of their bite, Gomez rejects the cultural equation of the vampire with anti-familial forces. She specifically motivates Gilda's odyssey through two centuries as the quest to find a new home and family. Gilda soon discovers that two very different kinds of vampires exist, some who kill their victims by draining their blood in the conventional way (these vampires seem to prefer heterosexuality, too) and those who, like her, do not take life. The family Gilda joins over the course of her life is created by a radical manipulation best explored here through the novel's defining activity and metaphor, the blood exchange.

In *The Gilda Stories*, there are two types of blood exchange: one that makes family or cements an already existing family tie, and one that takes place as the vampire feeds. Bird and Gilda, after a one-hundred year separation, reaffirm their kinship tie in the blood exchange that literalizes family and desire:

> Gilda's was a full body, and Bird was enthralled by the reality of it. She sliced beneath the right breast and watched through the thick darkness, the blood which stood even thicker against Gilda's dark skin. She hungrily drew the life through her parted lips into her body. . . . This was a desire not unlike their need for blood. . . . It was not unlike lust, but less single-minded. She felt the love of motherly affection, yet there was more. As the blood flowed from Gilda's body into Bird's they both understood the need—it was for completion. They had come together but never taken each other in as fully as they could, cementing their family bond. Gilda felt the life flowing from her. . . . Bird pulled Gilda across her chest and sliced the skin beneath her own breast. . . . She pressed Gilda's mouth to the red slash, letting the blood wash across Gilda's face. Soon Gilda drank eagerly, filling herself, and as she did her hand massaged Bird's breast, first touching the nipple gently with curiosity, then roughly. She wanted to know the body that gave her life. Her heart swelled with their blood, a tide between two shores. To an outsider the sight may have been one of horror: their faces red and shining, their eyes unfocused and black, the sound of their bodies slick with wetness, tight with life. Yet it was a birth. (139-140)

With its transgression of numerous cultural taboos, the narrator anticipates that this bloody scene may provoke "horror" in an onlooker. Gomez is not out to shock her readers gratuitously with the scene's graphic nature. The violation of deep-seated cultural beliefs contributes powerfully to what makes this passage disturbing, even horrific.[14]

Gomez addresses the taboo that denigrates the female body and bodily fluids as "dirty" (especially during menstruation) and repudiates it with a lesbian oral-sex / birth scene where women's bleeding is represented as life-giving and erotically charged.

Further, Gomez problematizes the incest taboo that underlies the construction of family. Since Bird was originally this Girl / Gilda's "mother" and Girl / Gilda consciously chose to be created by the first Gilda as a companion for Bird, Gomez challenges the incest boundaries that divide family members from one another. There is no stable I / you or individuated identity given the way vampires bond as family. In relation to Bird, this Gilda is simultaneously Girl and Gilda, i.e., daughter and lover. In Bird and Gilda's eroticism, they experience what it is to be a mother, sister, infant, child and lover in relation to their partner (and to themselves). She suggests that the predominantly Oedipal (heterosexual) understanding of sexuality and family erects intersubjective boundaries that limit, even preclude, intimacy and an experience of difference. Bird and Gilda discover a different kind of birth into relational identities. Gomez's emphasis here on generative potential is significant ("Yet it was a birth," 140). While she repeatedly returns in the novel to the experience of mothering or being mothered, with the mature Girl, Gilda, and Bird, this experience occurs with peers outside of a biologically determined mother-child relationship. Gomez does not idealize women for their reproductive capacity—an idealization that historically has masked women's exploitation within patriarchal culture—but for their regenerative experiences with other women. Since female vampires / lesbians do not conceive children within the nuclear family, they cannot be used to maintain and sustain paternal names, lines, or properties. They experience being born and giving birth as adults, creating, as it were, a horizontal line of kin, or a chosen family.

The second form of exchange in *The Gilda Stories*, the one that occurs during feeding, also differs from the traditional vampiristic one. The blood feeds life to the vampire, but the vampire gives a gift in return. In Gilda's world, there is a subjective transitivity implicit in the feeding process. Her bite penetrates body and mind; in a kind of psychosomatic conversation, Gilda explores the subconscious thoughts and dreams of her "victim," imparting herself in exchange for the blood she takes:

> There is a joy to the exchange we make. We draw life into
> ourselves, yet we give life as well. We give what's needed—
> energy, dreams, ideas. It's a fair exchange in a world of

cheaters. . . . In our life, we who live by sharing the life blood of others have no need to kill. It is through our connection with life, not death, that we live. (45)

Gilda explains the difficulty of conveying an act that has no imaginative precedent in culture's existing narratives: "There are only inadequate words to speak for who we are. The language is crude, the history false" (43). Vampirism, in this sense, is reciprocal nourishment, or a gift exchange.

The physical transfusion of blood figures the circulation of ideas and a rejection of mind / body dualism: it figuratively stages a world where different racial, ethnic, and sexual identities are not ghettoized (or essentialized) but instilled in acts of physical and psychic nourishment. When Gilda and her kind travel the roads at night, they create a diverse intersubjectivity. Their story becomes an allegory for a genuinely multicultural world. The novel continually poses the questions: where does the vampire's body / mind begin and end? where does the "victim's"? In the same way that family can no longer remain an isolated and self-sustaining unit, neither can home. Given the impossibility of detecting a vampire's bite and given their nomadic existence, many families are unknowingly linked through the blood exchange.

The reciprocity established in the vampire's feeding co-exists with Gomez's imagined other homelands. When Gilda moves to San Francisco in 1890, the second stop on her two-hundred year pilgrimage, she discovers kin in a "queer" vampire community already in existence—the circle of the gay Sorel and his friends. Sorel opens her mind to a global gay and lesbian family and offers her the safety to come out of that other "slavery" she experienced in Louisiana, a closeted lesbian identity: "Wherever we are we must expect each other. This is a family lesson we've learned well" (61). At the same time, Sorel differentiates between the bonds of queer sexuality and the intimate bond formed through the blood exchange that creates family. The motivations to create family need to be carefully examined, and family should never be forced or gained through manipulation: "To choose someone for your family is a great responsibility. It must be done not simply out of your need or desire but rather because of a *mutual* need" (69, emphasis added). Sorel's advice arises from the egregious errors of his own experience: Eleanor, the beautiful, narcissistic vampire he creates, understands family as the succession of her temporary possessions, trophies attesting to her power, while

Samuel, another member of this "dysfunctional vampire family," is a killer vampire of Eleanor's creation. Their violent deaths by murder and suicide haunt this utopian fiction and make Gilda wary and sensitive to her motivations as she seeks her family.

As Gilda lives in different African American social worlds or homelands, her identity as a queer vampire intersects with, but is never identical to, these communities of which she is a part: as a farmer in a freed black community in Rosebud, Mississippi in 1921; as a beautician in a transitional neighborhood of Boston's South End in 1955; as an actress in an off-Broadway theater group in 1971; as a musician in New York in 1981; and as a writer in Hampton Falls, New Hampshire in 2020, before her last journey, the escape to Machu Pichu in a dystopian 2050. Gilda learns about race solidarity and the cohesiveness born out of political struggle, but she also realizes that the homes she makes for herself in various communities frequently do not include lesbians when they point to their members.

The other family Gilda finds is the group of artists that accompany her through the last century represented in *The Gilda Stories*. It is Gilda the writer of romances, though, who exchanges ideas with her readers in an act that bears an uncanny resemblance to the exchange of feeding. Her choice of the romance genre is telling, for it has long been associated with female readers and writers, shuns elitism by aiming for a broad audience, and places a high value on the reader's pleasure. Her pen name, Abby *Bird*, recalls Bird's gift to her of the written word and the many languages she and Bird had to master as a means of survival and as a precondition for homemaking—in other words, their multilingualism. When her romances spread across the country, she enters into her readers' minds through her text, feeling out their thoughts and dreams with her stories. In return, her voice is contained or incorporated within her readers. Thus, Gomez aligns Gilda's writing with her vampiric identity and family, but interestingly makes a subtle shift away from the direct contact and agency implicit in vampire's feeding. She mediates the influence instead through writing, a displaced form of contact. While the act of feeding was imposed upon an unconscious "victim," Gilda's readers are active participants in the exchange. This shift expresses the mutuality integral to family.

As Gilda's life as a vampire lengthens over decades, her identity disperses and extends over numerous incarnations and relationships: "She saw now not just herself but a long line of others who had become part of her as time passed. The family she had *hungered for* as a child was hers now. It spread across the globe but was closer to her than she had ever imagined possible" (223, emphasis added). The satisfaction of familial desire denied her by slavery and described as one of the most basic human needs is now satisfied. Transgressing the limited bounds of the individual, Gilda understands her identity as a part of history, global yet intimate, embodied but transitive, fragmentary and adaptive: "Each new era had somehow slipped in around her and she'd adapted to it rather than thinking of herself as separate from it, *part of another line of history*" (216, emphasis added). Part of numerous lines of history (history too has its families and family resemblances), Gilda's transgenerational vampiric identity helps her understand the creation of home and family as greater than the individual. Gilda's lives—their wealth of lived events, interpersonal relationships, and collective identities—become a treasury of stories, a new home bequeathed to her readers.

Gomez and Winterson carefully shape Gilda's and Jeanette's life-stories from the revisionary wealth inherent in the fantastic literary modes of vampirism and evangelism. Poetically and politically fashioning domestic spaces that incorporate and welcome "unnatural" passions, both novels expand our understandings of personal and social identity. Thus, while they write of contested practices that historically construct "the family," they also provide their heroines with a recovered sense of home and a kinship that is not based on blood ties but on choice. If readers find themselves startled by Jeanette's visit home at the end of *Oranges* or disturbed by the violation of boundaries in *The Gilda Stories*, we can only say that imagining new families frequently proves unsettling. Both authors reject traditional and static representations of home with their emphasis on the inclusion of radically "other" identities into the family.

Winterson's and Gomez's inclusion of difference points to the culturally constructed nature of existing family models that stigmatize certain individuals and social groups. As private, domestic spaces come under fire from reactionary groups, the expression of a wide range of experiences becomes an important political strategy. Gomez and Winterson offer a home to their lesbian protagonists, like the activists who carve out a place for queer expression and imagination. As writers, they bring attention and criticism to bear upon a culture that typically renders gays, lesbians, and bisexuals silent and invisible. Their fantastic modes of representation suggest to the reader that what is unfamiliar may in fact be closest to home.

NOTES

1.   At the present time in the US, Hawaii alone recognizes same-sex marriages as legal. For the complex legal issues involved in same-sex partnerships and parenting, see: Denis Clifford, Hayden Curry, and Robin Leonard; April Martin; and the booklets on Second Parent Adoptions, Legalizing and Protecting Partnerships, Artificial Insemination, and Foster Parenting and Adoption published by the National Center for Lesbian Rights (870 Market St., Suite 570, San Francisco, California 94102).

2.   According to the 1993 Annual Report of the Gay and Lesbian Task Force, the number of anti-gay violence and victimization crimes reported nationally was 1813. This includes murder, assault, arson and vandalism, harassment, hate group activity, police abuse, prison violence, campus violence, and AIDS related violence. These figures do not, of course, reflect the actual amount, since surveys show that only a fraction of hate crimes are reported. An excellent study on the sociology of homophobic crimes is Gary David Comstock's *Violence against Lesbians and Gay Men*. Sodomy laws are still in effect in twenty-three states, of which six specifically criminalize homosexual sodomy alone: Arkansas, Kansas, Maryland, Missouri, Montana, and Tennessee.

3.   Conservative grass-roots activism makes the battles over city and county ordinances the main battleground for gay and lesbian civil rights at the present time.

4.   For work that explains the complex intersection of racism, sexism, and homophobia, see Marilyn Frye and Cherríe Moraga.

5.   See also Anndee Hochman.

6.   In the burgeoning field of gay and lesbian fiction and non-fiction, the following works and anthologies testify to the increased visibility of queer domestic spaces: Nancy Andrews; Phyllis Burke; Lilian Faderman; Frederick Bozett; Bennett L. Singer; John Preston; *Is the Homosexual My Neighbor? A*

Positive Christian Response; Suzanne Sherman; Ellen Lewin;
A Member of the Family: Gay Men Write about Their Family;
and Kath Weston.

7.   To avoid confusion, we refer to the character in the novel as
      Jeanette and the writer of the same name as Winterson. When
      we use the construction Jeanette/Winterson, we are deliberately
      invoking both identities.

8.   Note that these words also carry cultural value in addition to
      defining themselves against another word. Man is defined
      against woman, and the color white is defined *against* the
      color black. If you think of how our culture, both sexist and
      racist, then thinks about these pairs, you'll note that the third
      pair connotes "normal" versus "deviant" sexual practices. The
      fourth pair fills out the set, calling attention to the fact that our
      culture privileges the straight, white man side of the
      constructions. These pairings of words ultimately help our
      culture order itself, however wrongly, and are called binary
      oppositions, since they define themselves against one another.
      For further reading on the intersection of power and language,
      and a good summaries of current literary and linguistic theory,
      see Deborah Cameron.

9.   Monique Wittig argues that since woman is defined
      oppositionally to man, a lesbian—a woman who defines herself
      by / through other women—cannot define herself according to
      the binaries that order our world. She concludes that "a lesbian
      is not a woman" in her essay "The Straight Mind."

10.   At this point in her life, Jeanette is unable to relinquish her
      desire for her "real" mother. Given western culture's
      investment in birth / biological relatives as opposed to adopted
      or constructed ones, the young Jeanette does not, despite
      Louie's attempts, separate her "biological" from "real" mother.

11.   Nell Gwynn was the historical figure who said, "Oranges are
      not the only fruit." Dubbed the "protestant whore," she was
      Charles II's mistress and was loved more by the public than
      his legitimate wife. In addition to complicating ideas about
      authentic family members, the constant references to her—via

oranges—allude to the power of the monarchy, women's sexual power, and the ability to weave history and fiction together.

12.   An anthology of lesbian fiction devoted to the figure of the female vampire recently appeared: *Daughters of Darkness: Lesbian Vampire Stories*, ed. Pam Kesey, includes a very useful bibliography of filmic and literary representations of the vampire. A number of critical articles explore the connection between vampirism and homoeroticism. See especially: Sue-Ellen Case; Christopher Craft; Bram Dijkstra; Ellis Hanson; and Eve Sedgwick. The work of gay male critics or critics exploring male homoeroticism in relation to the vampire tends to focus on the figure of the vampire as a homophobic metaphor for AIDS, while lesbian writers tend to use the female vampire as a model of transgressive sexuality.

13.   While the works in the previous note call attention to the vampire's homoeroticism, the following essays explore the vampire's disturbance of acts of exchange: see Joan Copjec; Daniel Pick; John Allen Stevenson; and Franco Moretti for Count Dracula as a metaphor for uninhibited capitalistic greed.

14.   The endurance and popularity of supernatural fictions attests to their power to entertain but also to the advantages and possibilities they offer for critique: their unreal modes of depiction reject the status quo of realistic modes of representation and thus, the world those realistic modes represent.

WORKS CITED

Andrews, Nancy. *Family*. San Francisco: Harper, 1994.

Bozett, Frederick, ed. *Gay and Lesbian Parents*. New York: Praeger, 1987.

Burke, Phyllis. *Family Values: A Lesbian Mother's Fight for Her Son*. New York: Vintage, 1994.

Cameron, Deborah. *Feminism and Linguistic Theory*. London: Macmillan, 1985.

Case, Sue-Ellen. "Tracking the Vampire." *differences* 3.2 (Summer 1991): 1-20.

Clifford, Denis, Hayden Curry and Robin Leonard. *A Legal Guide for Lesbian and Gay Couples*. Berkeley: Nolo Press, 1994.

Comstock, Gary David. *Violence Against Lesbians and Gay Men*. New York: Columbia UP, 1991.

Copjec, Jean. "Vampires, Breast-Feeding, and Anxiety." *October* 58 (1991): 24-44.

Craft, Christopher. "'Kiss Me With Those Red Lips': Gender and Inversion in Bram Stoker's *Dracula*." *Representations* 8 (1984): 107-33.

Dijkstra, Bram. *Idols of Perversity: Fantasies of Feminine Evil in Fin-de-siècle culture*. Oxford: Oxford UP, 1986.

Faderman, Lilian. *Odd Girls and Twilight Lovers*. New York: Penguin, 1991.

Frye, Marilyn. "On Being White: Towards a Feminist Understanding of Race and Race Supremacy." *The Politics of Reality: Essays in Feminist Theory*. Freedom, CA: The Crossing Press, 1983.

Gomez, Jewelle. *The Gilda Stories*. Ithaca: Firebrand Books, 1991.

Hanson, Ellis. "Undead." Ed. Diana Fuss. *inside / out*. New York: Routledge, 1991. 324-40.

Hochman, Anndee. *Everyday Acts and Small Subversions: Women Reinventing Family, Community, and Home*. Portland, OR: The Eighth Mountain Press, 1994.

Is the Homosexual My Neighbor? A Positive Christian Response. New York: Harper Colllins, 1994.

Kesey, Pam, ed. *Daughters of Darkness: Lesbian Vampire Stories*. Pittsburgh: Cleis Press, 1993.

Lewin, Ellen. *Lesbian Mothers*. Ithaca: Cornell UP, 1993.

Martin, April. *The Gay and Lesbian Parenting Handbook: Creating and Raising Our Families*. New York: Harper, 1993.

A Member of the Family: Gay Men Write About Their Family. New York: Plume, 1992.

Moraga, Cherríe. "From a Long Line of Vendidas: Chicanas and Feminism." Ed. Teresa de Lauretis. *Feminist Studies / Critical Studies*. Bloomington: Indiana UP, 1986. 173-190.

Moretti, Franco. "Dialectic of Fear." *Signs Taken for Wonders*. London: Verso, 1983.

The New Oxford Annotated Bible with the Apocrypha (Revised Standard Version). Oxford: Oxford UP, 1977.

Pick, Daniel. "Terrors of the Night: *Dracula* and Degeneration." *Critical Quarterly* 30 (Winter 1988): 71-87.

Preston, John, ed. *Hometowns: Gay Men Write About Where They Belong*. New York: Plume, 1991.

Rossetti, Christina G. *The Poetical Works of Christina G. Rossetti*. Vol 1. Boston: Little, Brown, and Company, 1905.

Sedgwick, Eve. *Between Men: English Literature and Male Homosocial Desire*. New York: Columbia UP, 1985.

Singer, Bennett L., ed. *Growing Up Gay / Growing Up Lesbian: A Literary Anthology*. New York: New Press, 1994.

Sherman, Suzanne, ed. *Lesbian and Gay Marriage: Private Commitments, Public Ceremonies*. Philadelphia: Temple UP, 1992.

Stevenson, John Allen. "A Vampire in the Mirror: The Sexuality of Dracula." *PMLA* 103 (1988): 139-49.

Weston, Kath. *Families We Choose: Lesbians, Gays, Kinship*. New York: Columbia UP, 1991.

Winterson, Jeanette. *Oranges Are Not the Only Fruit*. London: Pandora Press, 1988.

Wittig, Monique. "The Straight Mind." *Feminist Issues* 1 (Summer 1980): 205-206.

13

Harmony and Resistance in
L'Amour, la fantasia's Algerian Women's
Communities

Martine Guyot-Bender

The fate of Muslim women has been a subject of great concern for feminist activists inside and outside Islamic countries. Islamic laws consider women inferior to men and not deserving of equal status: sequestration, illiteracy, inheritance laws, and repudiation are only some issues that have prompted sympathy and closer examination of the lives they live (Achour 227-249). In 1959, Frantz Fanon linked the indignation of the French public at women's second class status as a means to justify the French expansionist and missionary agenda in Algeria. Commenting on the French urge "[de] faire honte à l'Algérien du sort qu'il réserve à la femme" [(to) throw shame on the Algerian man of the type he reserves for the woman] (19), Fanon considered encouragements made by the colonists to Muslim women to reject the "sujétion séculaire" [century-old servitude] an obvious strategy for breaking down the originality and the integrity of the Algerian people and culture (19-20).

Similarly, a number of contemporary critics interested in the way westerners envision non-western cultures warn all observers again about the tendency to analyze non-western situations according to western values.[1] They point out that general accounts of Muslim cultures, well-intentioned as they might be, rarely present the true variety of social contexts and situations, and instead offer sets of cultural stereotypes. In particular, broad statements still typically reduce the complexity of Muslim women's position in society to overwhelming dissatisfaction and suggest, for example, that rivalry and power struggles are unavoidable among women forced, because of traditional family structures, to live under the same roof.[2] Recently, however, scholars have recognized that those women have, over the centuries, found their own strategies to manage confinement and forced cohabitation.

Rather than producing homogenized generalizations, recent studies of Muslim women's struggles for survival and empowerment de-emphasize the Islamic cultural determinant in favor of a focus on individual experiences. The recent volume *Muslim Women's Choices*, for example, challenges "public opinion in the West [which] generally ignores this diversity and is largely influenced by deep-rooted assumptions that Islam is a monolithic religion controlling all aspects of its adherents' lives" (1). The authors focus on variety and individual experiences, rather than on stereotypical assumptions and group experiences, ultimately exploring how "Islamic women in diverse Muslim communities and societies live out their lives" (19). In her study of polygamy in two narratives written in French by Algerian novelists, *Ombre sultane* by Assia Djebar and *La Chrysalide* by Aicha Lemsine,[3] Denise Brahimi suggests that feminine sorority coexists within competition. This approach is, I believe, a valuable one to counter reductionist examinations in which women appear completely powerless and sometimes lifeless. I will follow a path similar to Brahimi's, observing, in another of Assia Djebar's books, *L'Amour, la fantasia*, the strengths women derive from a life mostly devoted to homemaking.

This narrative is commonly regarded as a harsh criticism of the sex-segregated society in rural Algeria. Winifred Woodhull, for example, recently wrote: "Without question, Djebar's novels are feminist and highly critical of women's situation in Algeria" (79). This affirmation does not take into account the complexities of women's positions in Muslim societies. Without minimizing the oppression to which they are subjected, I want to suggest that a series of episodes in *L'Amour* also illustrates ways in which women have resisted oppression both from Algerian men and from the French colonists through mutual support and collective strength. My reading constitutes a limited case study rather than yet another generalization on the status of "the Algerian woman." Contrary to previous analysis of *L'Amour, la fantasia*, I will focus on textual instances where home-related issues of the Sahel rural setting of the text are presented in a more positive way than is most often pointed out by Djebar's critics. I will also examine the main narrator's tension between the desire for, and the rejection of, a traditional Muslim mode of life for women; while illustrating the women's confinement in the rural setting of her childhood, she also exemplifies longing for the support these women's groups offer. Yet, before doing so, I want to highlight some important issues of representation found in *L'Amour*.

"Homemaking" is not the primary topic of *L'Amour, la fantasia*. The ostensible subject of this non-linear text is the integration of past histories, both historical and personal: historical in the evocations of the invasion of Algeria by the French in 1830 and the Independence War in the mid-twentieth century, and personal in the evocations of the main narrator's childhood in Algeria, along with reflections on her position as an immigrant in France. The complex and overlapping "plots," the absence of linearity, and the play among different narrative voices make the task of summarizing *L'Amour* an arduous one. For Brahimi who wrote the post-face, it is a "tissage subtil" [subtle weaving] (261). Indeed, this "tissage" materializes in the multiple textual subdivisions: "parties" [parts], "chapitres" [chapters] (alternatively numbered and unnumbered, titled and untitled), and "mouvements" [movements]. Despite this visible fragmentation, the text is highly structured. In the first two parts, which constitute half of the book, chapters alternate between autobiographical and historical storylines. The autobiographical chapters focus on the narrator's childhood in the Sahel and memories of her first years in France, and the historical chapters relate episodes of the invasion of Algeria in 1830. The third part, which constitutes the second half of the book, is composite as well. It interweaves transcriptions of interviews made by the main narrator of two women's oral recollections of the Algerian revolution which ended on Algeria's independence in 1962, together with additional reflections of the same narrator's status as a resident of France with a traditional Arabo-Berber background.

The first person of the autobiographical chapters shares many features with the author, although no autobiographical claim is made by her until the very end of the text: "L'autobiographie pratiquée dans la langue adverse se tisse comme fiction" [autobiography practiced in the adversary tongue weaves itself as fiction would] (247).[4] Throughout the text, the anonymous narrator examines her place as a bilingual speaker. On the one hand, she benefitted from the French presence by gaining independence as well as by accessing the world of writing closed to many Algerian women. On the other hand, this independence separated her from her family's women. She was sent at an early age to a French school by her father who himself taught there, then went to a French boarding school, and eventually moved to France where we understand she is now residing. Her visits to her native region and memories of her adolescent life lead her to ponder her own childhood, her status as an "outsider" to the society she evokes, as well as the status of those women who, unlike her, remained in the village.[5]

In one part of the text, autobiographical reflections alternate
with fragmented recollections of the Independence War gathered by the
narrator from Chérifa and Djennet, two women witnesses of and actors
in this historical period. The two testimonies are the result of many
layers of interpretation from the two speakers' memory (by definition
affected by the action of time), from their oral discourse in Arabic, from
the main narrator's double translation into both written discourse and
French. Here, Djebar provides what Fanon wanted to see happen:
"donner sa voix au peuple algérien" [to give one's voice to the Algerian
people] (5). Yet, she goes beyond the claim made by the sociologist for
whom the Algerian voice remained essentially male: in *L'Amour*, the
Algerian voice is exclusively a woman's voice.

This multiplicity of voices gives the reader access to an equal
multiplicity of points of view, although the narrator makes clear that she
manipulates each one of them. The dominant discourse of victorious
French officers' written testimonies projects the mythical and romantic
representation of Algeria's physical and cultural traits, the "produit
d'imaginations fumeuses et pétries de fantasmes" [emerging from hazy
imaginations and built on fantasies] (Fanon 12), found in late nineteenth
and early twentieth-century orientalist painting, as the opening citation
from painter and novelist Fromentin announces. Numerous descriptions
implicitly attributed to the French officers indicate the effects of
imagination and fantasies on observation, and how art influences the
way a reality is perceived, thus altering the vision of one's environment.
As Fanon in particular had already remarked about the colonialist vision
of Algeria, the whole country was, for these soldiers, clearly associated
with a woman's body (16):

> Devant l'imposante flotte qui déchire l'horizon, la Ville
> Imprenable (Alger) se dévoile, blancheur fantomatique, à
> travers un poudroiement de bleus et de gris mêlés. Triangle
> incliné dans le lointain et qui, après le scintillement de la
> dernière brume nocturne, se fixe adouci, tel un corps à
> l'abandon, sur un tapis de verdure assombrie. La montagne
> paraît barrière esquissée dans un azur d'aquarelle.
> [Facing the imposing fleet that reaps the horizon, the Invincible
> City (Algiers) unveils itself, ghostly whiteness, through a
> powder of mixed blues and grays. A leaning triangle in the
> distance and which, after the last glimmering of the nocturnal
> haze, fixes itself smoothed, in the manner of an abandoned
> body, on the rug of green vegetation. The mountain appears,

a sketched wall in a pastel-blue horizon]. (Djebar 18, my translation throughout)

This French officer's vision (or is it the one the main narrator imagines?) is inscribed in the context of the orientalist fetishist painting. On the one hand, terminology associated with art appreciation such as the "poudroiement de bleus et de gris," "verdure assombrie," "azur d'aquarelle," detaches the landscape from its physical boundaries and makes it a mere subject of representation. On the other hand, the way in which the author of the quotation refers to the female body frames the status of the allegorical Muslim woman: "la Ville Imprenable se dévoile" [the Invincible City unveils herself] assimilates the city to the assumed mystery (thus desirability for the European man) of the veiled woman who makes herself available to men; "blancheur fantomatique" [ghostly paleness] refers to its mysterious purity and quality (she is the unknown to be explored and conquered); "tel un corps à l'abandon" [like a body in abandon] gives the vision of the city (and the implied woman) the erotic connotation of an act of possession to be consummated soon. Fanon saw in this type of representation "l'attitude dominante . . . un exotisme romantique, fortement teinté de sensualité" [the dominating attitude . . . a romantic exoticism, tinted by sensuality] (25). The French soldier who wrote this description was clearly influenced by the familiar representation of harem women of orientalist painting: Algiers was a place / woman ready to be taken by him.[6]

Counterbalancing such romantic and dominating views found in the historically oriented chapters of *L'Amour*, Djebar's interviews and transcription of women's testimonies supply an alternative voice to the written voice of history books, most commonly a male colonizing voice. Indeed, Chérifa's and Djennet's tales about the Independence War provide rare insiders' point of view, which take into account the daily experience and struggles of a population dominated by a foreign power. There, we discover a new dynamics of home: a marginal yet effective means of resistance and empowerment.

In the intersecting of discourses between the French soldiers' view of Algeria and the narrator's own view of her culture, "homemaking" is a strong but ambivalent leitmotif in *L'Amour, la fantasia*. It appears throughout the text in the narrator's reflections and questions about her cultural background and her own place on the margin of this culture. It also emerges from the narrator's informants' recollections. Both discourses point to the restrictiveness of Algerian women's place in society, while simultaneously revealing their strengths

(Woodhull 5). My examination concentrates on two kinds of episodes: on the main narrator's hesitation between rejection of and attraction to a traditional mode of life she criticizes and has abandoned and on illustrations of the power arising from confinement during the colonial period and the Revolution. I will first focus on the connotations of home and on the dynamics among women within that home, before taking a closer look at the narrator's place as an outsider to these communities. In Djebar's fragmented portrayals, support among women exists. In the autobiographical segments, the women's community emerges as an autonomous functioning structure while in historical testimonies women use women's specific tools to support men's wars. In both cases a community of women constitutes a solid wall against outsiders, be they Algerian males of the tribe, or the French invaders.

Arabo-Berber homes in L'Amour, la fantasia

In the background of the text stand the equivocal women's communities of rural Algeria. Readers of *L'Amour* get glimpses of these communities through the eyes of the French soldiers both during the invasion of Algiers in 1830 and during the Algerian Revolution in the 1950's; through the eyes of the adolescent and later the adult main narrator; and through the eyes of the women witnesses and resisters during the Revolution. Perceptions vary greatly depending on the observer's position vis à vis the wall separating women from men. In their testimonies, the French officers commonly relegate women to the position of belongings of the village, "les tribus se réfugient en cas de nécessité, avec femmes et enfants, troupeaux et munitions" [tribes take refuge when necessary with their women and children, herd and munitions] (83). On the other hand, women refer to themselves as a "people" (51), a social group whose strong identity reflects the common definition of the term: "an entire body of persons who constitute a community or other group by virtue of a common culture, religious, or the like" (Random House 1000).

The communities evoked in *L'Amour, la fantasia* seem to share many features with the traditional rural tribal Muslim societies historian Albert Hourani discusses in his *History of the Arab Peoples*, even those of two or three centuries ago.[7] "The basic unit," Hourani writes, "was the nuclear family of three generations of women: grandparents, parents and children living together in village houses or in the woven tents of the nomads" (105). According to Fanon they were "homogène[s] et quasi-monolithique[s]" [homogenous and quasimonolithic] (83). Hourani adds that men were in charge of outside work and transactions, and women were in charge of cooking, attending to the house and to the education of young children, and were under the protection of the male head. What the historian refers to as "the tribe" closely resembles *L'Amour*'s social structures built on the regrouping of several families with a common name or a common ancestor. "The house, a microcosm organized by the same opposition and the same homologies which order the whole universe, stands in a relation of homology with the rest of the universe" remarked sociologist Pierre Bourdieu about this setting (143). Indeed, within the "tribe," each home was a reflection of the others, thus creating a mirror-like effect where repetition of the same basic family model reinforced the accepted cultural standards: a prominently hierarchical and monolithic social model where gender specificity and segregation dominated (Ahmed 116-17).

This system of gender segregation based on the separation between men's spheres and women's spheres has complex ramifications. Segregation restricts women's field of action in the outside world, while creating a rather homogeneous society within the individual homes, as well as homogeneity among the collective village. In fact, with the exception of the narrator and her mother, women in *L'Amour* seem rather accepting of a social model that protects the specificity of their culture.[8] While these restrictions obviously deny women access to the outside world, to the world of transactions, and economical and political dominance, separation also acts as a means of preserving a traditional style of life from outsiders, as it did during the colonial period. It constituted "un garde-fou" (149) [a parapet] according to Djebar's discussion of the harem.

Indeed, *L'Amour* suggests many ways in which women inside homes empowered themselves, both in regard to Algerian men and to the French. The physical space of the home, its rituals, and the mingling of generations participate in the making of the "people" of women. The privacy of the homes where adult women spend most of their time constitutes a clearly confining space in the narrator's perception, a limitation which translates in the physical depiction of women in the narrator's childhood rural environment. Spatial limitation appears throughout the text: "trois jeunes filles [qui] sont cloîtrées au milieu d'un hameau du Sahel que cernent d'immenses vignobles" [three young women cloistered in the middle of a hamlet of the Sahel surrounded by endless vineyards] (22). In addition, references to the invisibility of women, those "frêles fantômes" [fragile ghosts] (23) alternate with mentions of the institutionalized inferiority of the "femmes reléguées" [relegated women] (53). The main narrator's own memory of childhood days spent in the courtyard carry the feeling of being a "fugitive," for instance when she and her cousin transgressed the allowed boundaries on their way to the communal bakery. The home is beyond doubt a prison.

Yet, life exists within these boundaries, and the text counterbalances such visions of confinement with suggestions that the same space is nonetheless a productive one. Central to this double value of the home is the evolution of the narrator's emotions from initial relief, when her father sent her to the French school, to explicit regret for the community she had left, when she realizes she has lost some of her heritage. Leaving the village first meant gaining a freedom probably coveted by many girls of her age. At an adult age, this separation meant isolation from the support group this family initially constituted. Spatially and linguistically removed from her familiar and tight community in the Sahel, she remembers having first appreciated the concrete rupture with the all-women environment which would infringe on her freedom. Her father provided her with greater independence and formally freed her from "le cercle des aïeules" [the circle of elder women] (36), often considered as the embodiment of the cultural and religious pressure on women. Furthermore, this separation allowed her to substitute writing for the oral means of communication most common for rural women of the narrator's childhood (Fanon 83). But, since everything is a "trade off," this initially liberating separation later gives way to a nostalgic longing for the "ambiance" of the house and the courtyard she was once eager to leave.

The narrator soon comes to realize that a house is not unlike the soul, as she considers the pleasure that can arise from the quaintness of a home, then or now. All parts of the text, autobiographical, historical and oral testimonies, offer scattered but repetitious illustrations of paradise-like homes, centers for harmony and / or power. While in the historical chapters she imagines the bliss women enjoyed during evenings spent on the terraces before the invasion, "leur royaume" [their realm] (20), she also remembers her own ecstasy when finding relief from the heat inside the cool house: "la demeure est spacieuse. Multiples chambres fraîches, ombreuses, encombrées de matelas empilés à même le sol, de tentures sahariennes, de tapis tissés autrefois par la maîtresse de maison. . . ." [the house is spacious. Numerous cool rooms, shady, encumbered by mattresses piled up on the floor, Saharan curtains, rugs once hand-woven by the lady of the house . . .] (22).

Such comfort is a source of unmixed feelings shared by the whole community:

> Pour moi comme pour mon amie, il restait évident que la plus belle maison, par la profusion des tapis, par la soie chatoyante des coussins, était sans conteste 'la nôtre.' Les femmes, chez nous, issues de la ville voisine célèbre pour ses broderies, s'initiaient à cet art à la mode déjà au temps des Turcs.
> [For me and my friend, it was obvious that the most beautiful house, by the profusion of rugs, by the shiny silk of the cushions, was obviously 'ours.' Women in our community originally from the nearby town were initiated to this art already fashionable under the Turks]. (38)

Within the walls, she sees the marks of her cultural background, untouched by the French. She is fully conscious of the reassuring decor in which art and functional objects mingle, a decor elaborated by hands of the past to which contemporary hands are still adding on for the future, thus creating a tangible link between the generations of women. The pride she and her community take in their specific skills and in the timeless impact they have on their physical environment leads to the visible condescension with which women of the narrator's family often commented on "le coin reculé de la campagne française" [the corner of the French back country] (38), the original home of one of their French visitors.[9] The careful management of the Arabo-Berber space the narrator now mourns constitutes the manifestation of women's specific knowledge and creativity, a realm of sharing and teaching of skills. This space develops a coherent and harmonious continuum, thus becoming the metaphor for achievement and success of women within their limited role in society.

The adolescent narrator was raised in a community where homes are cultural markers. Her curiosity about the difference between her culture and the French colonial culture focuses not so much on the individual colonists who lived in her village, but on the interior of the French homes she could sometimes glimpse through the window (she remembers that she was never invited inside the house, while the French woman walked into her family's courtyard quite freely). For her, objects truly revealed the presence of an Other in the heart of her native village:

Je regardais le corridor qui ouvrait sur d'autres pièces. Je devinais le bois luisant des meubles dans la pénombre; je me perdais dans la contemplation de la cochonnaille suspendue au fond de la cuisine; des torchons à grands carreaux rouges semblaient, ainsi accrochés, un pur ornement; je scrutais l'image de la Vierge au dessus d'une porte. . . . Le gendarme et sa famille me paraissent soudain des ombres de passage dans ces lieux, et par contre ces images, ces objets, cette viande devenaient les vrais occupants.

[I would look in the hallway that opened on other rooms. I guessed the polished wood of the furniture in the dark; I would sit there contemplating the hams hanging from the kitchen ceiling; towels with large red checkers seemed, hanging this way, pure ornamentation; I observed the Virgin Mary picture over one of the doors. . . . The policeman and his family are suddenly no more than passing shadows in these places, and on the contrary these images, these objects, this meat were becoming the real occupants]. (38)

The girl is intrigued by objects foreign to her native culture and religion. While the accumulation of furniture and wood floors mark a mere aesthetic difference, the ham hanging from the ceiling and the Virgin Mary picture both emphasize the incompatibility of cultures based on such different beliefs as Islam and Christianity. Such culturally marked spaces were the real intrusion in the village. Thus, when the French were expelled from Algeria in 1962, their houses were dismantled and emptied of the hidden and unfamiliar objects, the very symbols of cultural colonization and violation of the local culture. A real cultural exorcism took place: "tout ce décor, autrefois tapi dans l'ombre de demeures à la fois ouvertes et inaccessibles, se trouva déversé sur les trottoirs" [the whole decor, once hidden in the shade of homes both open and inaccessible, was thrown out on the sidewalks] (38). The victory over the colonizing forces and the return to political independence are, in *L'Amour*, symbolized by the reclaiming of spaces and homes.

L'Amour's women in their homes

As suggested in *L'Amour*, rural life was considered "regressive" (51) both by the French colonists and by urban Algerians who more readily accepted French modes of life and the comforts of modernization. Yet, the closed rural homes constitute a protected locus for preserving the local culture and traditions from the outside world. This protection has been pointed out by observers of the Muslim world outside the Maghreb, such as Rosemary Ridd who has described Muslim women's communities which, in the apartheid system of the Cape in South Africa, "provided people with substance, self-respect and a refuge from the apartheid" (92) as well as Deborah Pellow's similar observations in her essay, "Solidarity among Muslim Women in Accra, Ghana." Members of gender-segregated environments, both critics observe, have the potential to develop strong support systems, similar to the one the adolescent narrator of *L'Amour* experienced during animated women's celebrations:

> Dans les fêtes de mon enfance, les bourgeoises sont assises écrasées de bijoux, enveloppées de velours brodé, le visage orné de paillettes ou de tatouages. Les musiciennes développent la litanie, les pâtisseries circulent, les enfants encombrent les pieds des visiteuses parées. Les danseuses se lèvent, le corps large, la silhouette tranquille. . . . Je n'ai d'yeux que pour ma mère, que pour mon rêve sans doute où je me représente adulte, moi aussi dansant dans cette chaleur. Les rues de la ville sont loin; les hommes n'existent plus. L'éden reste immuable: danses lentes, visages mélancoliques qui se laissent bercer. . . . [In the celebrations of my childhood, the bourgeois women are sitting covered with jewels, wrapped in embroidered velvet, their faces decorated with sparkles or tattoos. The women musicians slowly start the litany, pastries circulate, children run around the decorated guests. The dancers get up, with their wide bodies, and a tranquil figure. . . . I cannot detach my eyes from my mother, from the dream where I see myself as an adult, also dancing in this heat. The town streets are far way; men do not exist anymore. Paradise is timeless; slow dances, melancholic faces that allow themselves to be rocked. . .]. (233)

The everlasting edenic and magical atmosphere of such exclusively feminine events protected the young observer from the outside threats of streets and men, and reassured her, at least temporarily. Although some of the autobiographical episodes of women's celebrations are not as heartwarming as this one, many illustrate equally comforting associations between home, harmony and resistance. In addition, typically feminine home-related activities like milking the goat or preparing meals are not, in *L'Amour*, insignificant or merely laborious chores. Whenever mentioned, they reveal a valuable *savoir-faire* that only the women from within the community can achieve. Such expertise applies, for example, to evocations of the nanny's secret herbal remedies, embroidery and weaving, the mixing of the henna, ritual songs for important occasions and, of course, cooking.

Yet, harmony among women is more apparent in their human relationships. Complicity between women of all ages is a major factor in *L'Amour*. Within the structure of small nuclear families most common in western cultures, one rarely finds two individuals of the same age. On the contrary, in an extended family like the one in *L'Amour, la fantasia*, the daily proximity of women of the same age under the same roof allows for shared experiences. The main narrator's memories are filled with women functioning in groups: "jeunes filles et femmes de la famille, des maisons voisines et alliées, rendent régulièrement visite quelque sanctuaire. . . . Des groupes piailleurs se répandent dès lors, dans la campagne proche" [young girls and women of the family, of neighboring or allied homes, regularly render themselves to some sanctuary. . . . Chirping groups invade, then, the nearby countryside] (146). Indeed, women's communities in *L'Amour* constitute microcosms of all the cycles of life, a space where the cohabitation of several generations render the different phases of life visible and public. In western homes, daily contact is usually restricted to, at most, two generations, parents and children. Quite contrarily, in homes where extended families cohabit, privacy is replaced by more extensive contact, and, at night, one can hear: "[Les] chuchotements des aïeules aux enfants dans le noir, aux enfants des enfants accroupis sur la natte, aux filles qui deviendront aïeules" [(the) whispering of the elders to the children in the dark, to the children of children squatting on the grass mat, to the girls who will become elders] (203).

The most pleasing memories for the narrator are of her grandmother, who is synonymous with security and stability. She carries with her images of times she and the older woman spent comforting each other, through, for example, intimate rituals like evening feet rubbing. She remembers the impact her companion's death had on her and a recurrent dream, a nightmare in reality, in which the loss of the loved one translated into the loss of a home: "Je cours, je dévale la rue cernée de murs hostiles, de maisons desertées" [I run, I rush down the street surrounded by hostile walls, by deserted houses] (221). The dreamer sees herself escaping in the streets of the town, as if the whole notion of a home had collapsed with the disappearance of the older woman. Other women of her lineage who marked her childhood include the warmhearted aunt with whom she seeks tranquility:

> Un refuge me restait: quitter la maison bruyante, dédaigner l'arbitrage de ma mère et de ses amies, occupées le plus souvent à des travaux de broderie. Je me réfugiais chez ma tante paternelle. . . . Elle me cajolait et me faisait entrer dans sa plus belle pièce où un haut lit à baldaquin de cuivre me fascinait. . . . Elle me réservait confitures rares, sucreries, parfums déversés sur mes cheveux et sur mon cou.
>
> [I had one refuge left: to leave the noisy house, leaving behind the discussions between my mother and her friends, most often busy embroidering. I took refuge with my paternal aunt. . . . She would comfort me and let me in her most beautiful room where a high canopy brass bed fascinated me. . . . She would keep for me rare jams, sweets, perfumes poured on my hair and my neck]. (203)

Such explicit bonds between women of different generations also arise from alliances between women of the same generation.

Indeed, each generation constitutes its own community. In the intimacy of closed rooms, secrets are shared and education takes place at all ages: "les jeunes filles cloîtrées écrivaient des lettres; des lettres à des hommes; à des hommes aux quatre coins du monde; du monde arabe naturellement" [the cloistered young women wrote letters; letters to men; men from all over the world; the Arab world naturally] (24). The solitude usually attached to the writing of letters becomes a joint enterprise in which the young women combine ingenuity in a common effort to reach the outside world, to overcome their confinement. But this process goes beyond the imaginary seduction of foreign men. It embodies a shared thrill of bending rules, surmounting danger and obstacles, a sort of seduction of one another: a complicity that only a shared experience can build.[10] Living together, the cousins have similar questions, desires for exploration, and together construct answers to the "mysteries" of the outside world. Growing up and slowly discovering adult life in such a communal setting will bring these girls a life-long complicity. They prepare, in their endeavor, to become the next group of adult women dancing in unison at celebrations, and later perhaps, the "cercle des aïeules" for the next generations of girls, insuring the continuity of the community.

In some cases, the text makes feminine complicity a factor of cross-cultural exchange. Although contact between Arabo-Berber households and French households was limited, *L'Amour, la fantasia* illustrates mutual respect that women from both backgrounds had for their homemaker's role and their *savoir faire*. When the narrator's mother and her French friend, the policeman's wife, trade recipes, it is more than the technique or the practical aspects of cooking a meal they exchange, it is expertise in comparable domains. When they share their disappointment with their respective husbands, "ces hommes" [these men] (38), inept in choosing the right knitting needles or the ideal fruit and vegetables when shopping for their wives, they affirm domination in the space they are given to rule as well as men's status as outsiders and amateurs. But then, when they are back in their own homes, protected by their own walls, they resume their conversations about cultural differences.

Le cercle des femmes often transforms the courtyard into a forum where not only home-related but also cultural identity topics are discussed because "les conversations importantes étaient féminines" [the significant conversations were among women] (51). While Djebar's narrator remembers standing on the doorstep of the French house, halfway between desire and rejection, she also carries in her memory bits of conversations affirming Arabo-Berber cultural pride and the inferiority of French women:

> La plupart [des femmes] que notre pays asservi a tentées savent seulement traire une vache à leur arrivée ici! Si ensuite elles se civilisent, c'est parce qu'elles trouvent ici force et richesse.
> [Most (women) tempted by our dominated country only know how to milk a cow when they arrive here. If then they become more civilized, it is because here they find strength and wealth]. (39)

The Algerian way of life must have had a stronger impact on the "uncivilized" French women who settled there than on themselves, the women nurtured in Algeria's rich culture and religion. Displacement and exile did not apply to them, but to the French women who had lost some of their identity in their home country and were in search of a community. The notion of civilization, as the quotation indicates, is a relative and subjective one. Contrary to the European tendency to look down upon non-western ways of life, the village women are unambiguously proud of their heritage, and see how the French women try to imitate it. Such pride emerges, for instance, when they discuss young women's behavior regarding men. It also appears in the "la pureté 'Arabe'" ['Arabic' purity] (39) the elders were always seeking which enticed the narrator's mother to switch back to the "purisme traditionnel" [traditional purism] (51) when she was in their presence. Because their world remained rather closed to the foreign eye, women preserved a mode of life very similar to the one before the colonial period. During the years of French domination, the home was a space of passive resistance, hardly altered by contact with another culture. The relative stability of Algerian rural homes during the 130-plus years of colonial domination illustrates the misconception in the notion of change introduced by the French presence. As *L'Amour* shows, women kept away from the written language and from extensive contact with the French, and were consequently less affected than men by the imposition of another language and the transformation of society. Closed walls preserved a traditional way of life, thus supporting the relation between seclusion and nationalism.

Confinement within the house does not, however, translate into a lack of interest in public affairs, as the fragments on the Independence War, especially Djennet's testimony, suggest. There, we see homes used as political resistance centers, and women transforming their traditionally housebound functions into tools of opposition against the French colonists, an opposition that did not involve carrying weapons and physically fighting other soldiers, but rather the strength found in collective energy. Gender segregation did not prevent solidarity between men and women when it came to fighting for the community at large. Djennet prides herself on having served the revolution by providing shelter, food, and comfort to warriors. There is no ambiguity in her tale about the significance of her role: "la 'révolution' a commencé chez moi, et elle a fini chez moi" [the Revolution started in my home and was concluded in my home] (170) she affirms twenty years after the end of the conflict.[11] Although she lived in fear because of the consequences that the presence of revolutionaries in her home could bring her, she considered her farm, her bread wood-stove, the very walls of her home, as the ultimate space of resistance. Her patriotic determination made her accept the pain of seeing her house burnt three times by the French, and, responding to the sarcasms of a neighbor's criticism, to profess her role as resister: "J'accepte d'aller jusqu'à la mort" [I am ready to die for it] (172).

Homemakers like Djennet used the skills they knew best to support the war. They sewed uniforms to give the *maquisard* group the appearance of an army and they fed the refugees: "Nous allions apporter la semoule aux Frères. Nous cherchions dans la forêt où l'entreposer. Il fallait aussi trouver où la pétrir, où la préparer" [we took grain to the Brothers. We had to find a place to stock it. We also had to find a place to knead it, to prepare it] (187). She prides herself on the meaning her home had for the *maquisards*, and turns the room where they find refuge into a sanctuary:

> Ils prirent l'habitude de venir, de dîner, de veiller, puis de repartir pour la nuit. Dans la journée je gardais cette pièce vide. Il m'arrivait de me dresser sur son seuil et de me dire: 'Cette chambre où entrent les fils de la Révolution deviendra verte, verte, verte, comme une pastèque fermée, et les murs, un jour, ruisselleront tout entiers de vapeur rosée!'
> [They used to come, to dine, to stay, then to leave in the night. During the day, I kept this room empty. It happened that I stood on its doorstep and thought 'This room where the sons of the Revolution come will become green, green, green, like a closed watermelon and one day, a pink haze will stream down the walls!'] (201)

All layers of the past retold, the narrator's and Djennet's, focus at some point on women and their homes, or on women and other women. In doing so, Djebar has constructed a vision of Algerian homes that contains enviable parts. Women's lives are not seen only through the lens of oppression, but also through the lens of a liveable reality. These lives include harmony and solidarity among each other and toward the Algerian community, a harmony and solidarity that the narrator seems to be lacking in her Western experience.

Away from and within the community

As an adult observer, Djebar's narrator feels she has lost crucial everyday contact with this community, and has herself participated in the slow dissolution of such ancestral social structures. The sense of liberation she first felt when breaking away evolved, over time, into a sense of loss. Often she implicitly compares her life as a resident of France to women's lives in the communities of her childhood. As Fanon had warned in 1959, and as theories of post-colonialism now accept, she recognizes the conflict from which she issues. The French presence allowed her to break away from a system that did not permit women access to the economical and political world. It allowed her to gain an education, freedom to go about as she pleases, to benefit from modernity and obviously to become a scholar able to cast a potentially dominating outsider's gaze on a culture that was once hers. On the other hand, the French presence has also caused her family environment to change greatly, and to reject a traditional way of life (Tucker 195).

Retrospectively, as an adult narrator, she realizes the significance of even small deviations from the communal codes she knew as an adolescent. She remembers the confusion caused among the women of the family when the father, gone on a business trip, addressed a letter directly to the mother instead of to the son, and the elders' disapprobation when her mother used her husband's first name when referring to him instead of using the traditional third person masculine pronoun. Her parents, connected to the French community through the father's profession, tried in their way to bend some of the oppressive customs of their "tribe." Such transgressions, she understands now, contained an element of danger and disgrace for the other members of the community. The "culprits" (her parents), adopting foreign customs, put the whole community in danger of disintegration, by rejecting aspects of a community that functioned mainly on auto-reinforcement. Needless to say, the narrator's voluntary displacement to France, the colonizers' home, constituted an indisputable transgression and created a gap between her and her family that would only grow wider with time.

And yet, life in France, where the narrator now resides, has not completely erased the family traditions still echoing in her mind. Celebrations are particularly reminiscent of the dynamics of women's home communities. As the narrator rushes through the stages of preparation for her own wedding in Paris, everything, from the decor to the composition of the assembly, draws on images of the past, or of how things would have been, had she not left Algeria. The tension between rejection of, and desire for, traditional customs emerges from the juxtaposition of two wedding ceremonies, a juxtaposition which implicitly invites the reader to establish a comparison between the two events. The first one, entitled "La mariée nue de Mazouna," [The Naked Bride of Mazouna] is the imaginary tale of an 1845 sumptuous traditional ceremony with its "cortège de plus d'une centaine de cavaliers," [retinue of over one hundred horsemen] its "fantasia des cavaliers berbères," [fantasia of berber horsemen] its "cortège nuptial," [wedding retinue] the "palanquin de la mariée, précédé de cinq ou six cavaliers" [the bride's litter, preceded by five or six horsemen] (107), with the profusion of rituals, preparations, costumes, decoration, voices and joyous confusion. It contrasts sharply with the austerity that surrounds the simple ceremony of the narrator's own wedding in the Paris of the 1960s, in the midst of the Independence War.

The freedom of movement she enjoys in her student life in France, so unlike the confinement of the women of her native village, does not, at the time of the wedding, compensate for the constraints of her Parisian environment. The spacious rooms of the Sahel village have been replaced with the small and somber rooms of the couple's new apartment. The books that cover the walls constitute a mere decor that obscures the home and do not evoke the fulfillment of having mastered the written world and being an intellectual. At this moment, her new status as a Westerner does not seem to provide any sentiment of satisfaction. The "cri collectif, the you-you multiplié" [collective call, the echoing 'you-you'] (109) that accompanied Brada, the Mazouna bride, has disappeared and given way to "ces épousailles [qui] se dépouillaient sans relâche: de la voix stridente féminines, du brouhaha de la foule emmitouflée, de l'odeur des victuailles en excès" [these weddings (which) were indubitably stripped: of the strident feminine voices, of the humming of the muffled crowd, of the odor from the food in excess] (126). All the physical marks of communal activity, of group solidarity and of enjoyment emerging from group experience seem to have vanished. At that moment, Paris constitutes a very restricted space: for the nostalgic narrator, freedom has the taste of solitude.

The very notion of a home seems to have evaporated in her flight from house to house with a fiancé hiding; the freedom of movement she gained by leaving the Algerian village now resembles fleeing. The traditional dowry patiently created piece by piece by a whole community in Algeria is, in her case, a mere mercantile act: bought "en une fois, dans les Grands Magasins" [all at once in department stores] (121). This "semblant de trousseau," [a poor excuse for a dowry] will not constitute the symbol of other women's support as the bride enters the unknown of a new life; it will not be the shared gift of time and patience attached to the traditional dowry. The "ensemble pied de poule bleu-ciel" [the light blue checkered suit] she wears for the ceremony replaces the layers of elaborate costumes and jewelry Brada wore, and the institution for deaf and dumb located across from one of the fiancé's apartments emphasizes the couple's isolation and distance from the resounding voices of the village and is a metaphor for her overwhelming loneliness. The ceremony itself attracts a few guests: the mother, one sister, and a few friends exiled in France, pale token of the past ceremonies. The bride's nostalgia goes beyond the loss due to geographical displacement. The weight of French influence, she realizes, had, even in Algeria, slowly dissipated traditional rituals, such as the father carrying the bride over the doorstep, or the women's dance with the blood-stained sheet on the morning after the wedding night.

The sense of estrangement from her community so manifest in the evocations of the wedding is also felt by Djebar's narrator whenever she is in contact with her family in Algeria. Never integrated to the harem, she remembers that her body "s'occidentalisait à sa manière" [occidentalized itself in its own way] (148). Her emotions appear ambivalent when she realizes that "dans les cérémonies les plus ordinaires [elle] éprouvait du mal à s'asseoir en tailleur" [in the most banal ceremonies she had trouble sitting cross-legged] and that the ancestral call of Arab women "ne sortait de [sa] gorge que peu harmonieusement . . . il [la] déchirait" [came out of (her) throat with but little harmony . . . it tore (her) (148). She is now a nostalgic outsider to the women's people, forever unfit to the life that was designed for her by generations of continuity: "Sous le poids des tabous que je porte en moi comme héritage, je me trouve désertée des chants de l'amour arabe." [Under the weight of the taboos I carry in me as my heritage, I find myself deserted by the Arab love songs] (244). But from this feeling of desertion, from what she often perceives a helplessness, rises a new kind of communication with this heritage. *L'Amour* is in many ways her own love song for this lost heritage.

Ironically, writing, a skill the narrator directly acquired from the French colonists (212), constitutes for emigrant privileged Algerian women like Assia Djebar a means to reconnect with the community.[12] She finds in the French language a way to subvert the colonialist's agenda of breaking down the Algerian coherence. In this way, "La langue adverse" [the adverse tongue] (245) becomes the very tool for a new coherence: "Cette langue était autrefois le sarcophage des miens; je la porte aujourd'hui comme un messager transporterait le pli ordonnant sa condamnation au silence, ou au cachot" [This language was once my people's sarcophagi; I carry it today as a messenger would transport an envelope containing his condemnation to silence, or to jail] (245). Highlighting the distortions made by French soldiers and colonialist discourse in general on Algeria, and on the historical events they in which they were involved, she now allows the voice of women, "la première réalité-femme" [the primary woman-reality] (207), the forgotten actors of Algeria history, to be heard. She gives them visibility, makes them alive for herself and for her readers, casting a new light upon them by praising, not denouncing, the customs and specificities of their life in Muslim environment. Indeed, in *L'Amour*, writing, which has empowered the narrator and the author, also empowers and gives voice to Algerian women.

Djebar is conscious, though, of her privileged position as sole translator of all the voices contained in her text, and perceives a real danger in her written manipulation of women's experiences. The danger of betraying her community and her sisters lies in great part in the fact that now she writes in French for a French audience. Indeed, examining and representing these communities, even in fragments, both in her past and in other women's past, puts her in danger of doing what the colonial gaze did: romanticizing a life she would not want to live. One wonders if this specter of betrayal has not been the reason why the critics of Djebar's texts have kept away from examining the significance of the different aspects of women's group lives that the novelist includes in *L'Amour, la fantasia*.

However, textual fragmentation and the revelation of ambiguities attached to Muslim women's communities constitutes an important alternative to the colonizing gaze Djebar is in danger of casting upon her own cultural background. No one gaze, no one voice, the text implies, can account for the complexity found in Muslim homes which have so often been objects of monolithic readings from Western observers. *L'Amour, la fantasia* deconstructs this kind of reductive reading by de-victimizing women and recognizing the control they have been able to have over their lives.

L'Amour, la fantasia can therefore be read as an evocation of harmony among women's communities in rural Algeria. The narrator's evident nostalgia for a way of life Westerners like to describe only in confining terms, a nostalgia which seems to echo a common concern in many Arab women now exiled from their traditional communities, clearly invites approbation and recognition of values the Western world has been slow or reluctant to accept. Readers of texts like *L'Amour, la fantasia* are able to consider these communities—so different from our own—in a different light, and to recognize that the dynamics of Arab women's communities were not just repressive. The narrator's compassion for her women ancestors' and mother's contemporaries' restricted field of action combines with the evocations of pleasurable moments of group harmony, and weaves itself into a vision of relative contentment. Djebar's ambiguous gaze upon women's lives in rural Algeria thus enables readers to trade pity for more esteem toward the not-so-silent members of the communities she introduces to us.

NOTES

1.   Among the numerous scholars who examine this notion, see Mireille Rossello; Lisa Lowe; and Leila Ahmed. Ahmed's historical approach focusses on various discourses that Arab women have been subject to and corrects some Western misconceptions (including feminist ones) of Islamic customs. Of particular interest to the issue discussed are the introduction, "Discourse on the Veil," and "Divergent Discourses."

2.   One will recognize such stereotyping in the following statements found in books separated by twenty-two years. According to Harold Nelson's edited collection, *Algeria, a Country Study:* "The bride then often goes to the household, village, or neighborhood of the bridegroom's family, where she lives under the critical surveillance of her mother-in-law. A great deal of marital friction centers on the difficult relationship between mother-in-law and daughter-in-law," (100). John Ruedy mentions that "men knew their mothers as parents who doted on them and derived pride and status from the fact of their existence; later, they knew women as wives, who satisfied their sexual urges and produced sons for them. Other than in these two relationships, there was little communication between the sexes" (126).

3.   Denise Brahimi, recognizing the value of texts like *La Répudiation* by Rachid Boudjera which denounces polygamy, proposes "de faire émerger ce que (d'autres textes) nous disent un peu mystérieusement, des liens qui se créent, contre toute apparence, entre des femmes dont on a longtemps résumé la situation d'un seul mot: rivalité" [to bring out what [other texts] tell us, a little mysteriously, about links which are created, against general assumption, between women whose

situation has, for a long time, been summarized with one word: rivalry] (125).

4. For the purpose of this study, I have chosen not to formally identify the main narrator with Assia Djebar, the author.

5. The ambiguity between tradition and modernity regarding the Islamic Law has been discussed by Issa J. Boullata. Her chapter "Voices of Arab Women" (119-137) overviews three different positions of Arab women scholars on this issue.

6. One thinks, for example, of the series of postcards representing women in harem situations which Malek Alloula has collected and annotated in *The Colonial Harem*.

7. Albert Hourani, 105. Also helpful regarding the physical configuration of the home is the chapter "The Kabyle House" in Pierre Bourdieu, *Algeria 1960*, 133-153.

8. Moroccan feminist activist Ghita El Khayat reproaches Arab women's compliance with century-old ways of life as a major obstacle to the Maghreb's progress in *Le Maghreb des femmes*: "La précarité de la condition féminine des maghrébines est très largement tributaire de pratiques, de colportages et d'à-priori féminins, je dis bien féminins, qui empêchent l'ensemble de la nation maghrébine d'avancer, d'être heureuse et d'accueillir bébés garçons et bébés filles dans la même bénédiction et la même allégresse." [Precariousness of the feminine condition is greatly dependent on practices, gossips and feminine a-priori, I insist on the fact that they are feminine, which prevent the Maghreb nation to advance, to be happy and to welcome baby boys and baby girls with the same grace and the same joy] (99).

9. The vision of backwardness found in this French comment concerning the Arab population, is examined in Ahmed as a justification of colonialism. For her, "anthropology, as is often said, served as a handmaid to colonialism" (155).

10.   Seduction between the same sexes in sex-segregated social
        structures is analyzed by Fatima Mernissi in *Beyond the Veil:*
        "in a country like Morocco, in which heterosexual encounter
        is the focus of so much attention, seduction becomes a
        structural component of human relations in general, whether
        between individuals of the same sex or between men and
        women" (140).

11.   The English translation of "chez moi" into "at my home" does
        not account for the association of a place with the person,
        since in French "moi" is a reference to the speaker, and "chez
        moi" a reference to his / her home.

12.   The narrator's refections of writing in the colonizing tongue
        would be worth a separate and specific study.

WORKS CITED

Achour, Yadh Ben. *Politique, religion et droit dans le monde arabe.* Casablanca: EDDIF, 1992.

Ahmed, Leila. *Women and Gender in Islam: Historical Roots of a Modern Debate.* New Haven: Yale UP, 1992.

Alloula, Marek. *The Colonial Harem.* Minneapolis: U of Minnesota P, 1986.

Boullata, Issa J. *Trends and Issues in Contemporary Thought.* Albany: State U of New York P, 1990.

Bourdieu, Pierre. *Algeria 1960.* Cambridge: Maison des Sciences and Cambridge UP, 1979.

Brahimi, Denise. *Appareillages.* Paris: Deuxtemps Tierce, 1991.

Djebar, Assia. *L'Amour, la fantasia.* Casablanca: EDDIF, 1992.

El Khayat, Ghita. *Le Maghreb des femmes.* Casablanca: EDDIF, 1992.

El-Sohl, Camillia Fawzi, and Judy Mabro. *Muslim Women's Choices.* Providence, RI: Berg Publishers, 1994.

Fanon, Frantz. *Sociologie d'une révolution: l'an V de la révolution algérienne.* 2nd ed. Paris: Maspero, 1982.

Hourani, Albert. *History of the Arab Peoples.* Cambridge, MA: Harvard UP, 1991.

Lowe, Lisa. *Critical Terrains: French and British Orientalisms.* Ithaca: Cornell UP, 1991.

Mernissi, Fatima. *Beyond the Veil.* Bloomington: Indiana UP, 1987.

Nelson, Harold, ed. *Algeria, a Country Study.* Washington, DC: American UP, 1979.

Pellow, Deborah. "Solidarity among Muslim Women in Accra, Ghana." *Anthropos* 82 (1987): 488-495.

Random House Webster's College Dictionary. New York: McGraw-Hill, 1991.

Ridd, Rosemary. "Separate but more than Equal: Muslim Women at the Cape." El-Sohl, *Muslim Women's Choices* 85-107.

Rossello, Mireille. "Du bon usage des stéréotypes orientalisants: vol et recel de préjugés anti-maghrebins dans les années 1990." *Esprit créateur* (Summer 1994).

Ruedy, John. *Modern Algeria: The Origins and Development of a Nation.* Bloomington: Indiana UP, 1992.

Tucker, Judith, ed. *Arab Women.* Bloomington: Indiana UP, 1993.

Woodhull, Winifred. *Transfigurations of the Maghreb.* Minneapolis: U of Minnesota P, 1993.

14

Spices

Ama Ata Aidoo

—for Pandi (Mutuma)

I

Actually,
I could handle the matter of
peppercorns
really well since
I can still see Mother
leaving them to ripen
on the odupon.

A proper parasite if ever there was one
who vinely and shamelessly
sprouted by giant roots
secured itself to massive ancestral trunks and
wove thin firm tendrils
singing a long and difficult solo
through the dappled undergrowths
                    then
lay queenly and luxuriantly on the branches and
on each wider, greener, thicker leaf,
until up and up and up
it reached its highest crescendo and kissed
the glorious sun
gloriously.

II

My Sister,
we shall not even discuss
ginger,

wild mint or
its more delicate kin
which acquired
the anti-chicken name akoko-besa
meaning fowls-end:
when grown in
old chamber- and water-pots, and
other closed-in spaces behind the bedroom wall.

Can you believe that?

III

On the other hand,
The Pepper-master's and
The Pepper-mistress's
pepper
is another story.

There was a time when it was known only to
priests, priestesses, prophets and
sundry holy ones
who ate the sacred stuff to sharpen
their tongues
their visions of the future and
the immediate and urgent matter of
their sexual prowess.

Which name do you know it by, My Sister?

Shito
Pripiri
Miripiri
chili
cayenne
agoi
???

We speak of
the beginning and end of all heat. . . . .

Where I come from
we called it muoko
its etymology
completely lost in
millennias into which
harried wives
ground and ground and ground
the precious stuff. . . .

If we insisted on counting,
we could end up with one hundred species, and
still not be done.

My Sister,
when The Pepper-person's pepper moved out of
the shrines and the temples,
it stayed for a thousand more years
in near-by habitations known only to locals in
Africa and Asia . . .

—another ancient and spicy secret,
valued in equal parts with gold dust
then, but soon to be

just one more Third World exotica
variously liked and apologised for.

These days,
between the mildest and the most abrasive,
green, red, yellow, thin, squat, full or hollow,
peppers
grace supermarket stalls from
Atlanta through London to Zurich . . .

from which places
we zero in
on the issue of how
we take care of our bourgeois palates.

IV

When you first dropped your
artful reproof,
startling me with
its delicious wit and sweet censure,

I first and
guiltily
saw clear evidence of
my westernization,
or rather
the ease with which
the food-lover in me had taken to
"foreign cuts" of meat:
the steaks, the chops and

the briskets
duly cased in
condiments of exotic names and flavours:
—never mind their origins—

cardamon
origanum
rosemary and thyme. . . .

But then, because
we try never to quite give in without a fight
I quickly recall that from
sweeping airports,
driving taxis and
cleaning rich old folks' bodies,

Cousin Kwaku, Bro Kofi, Sissie Yaa
and the rest of the extended family
go home to

New York's Flat and London's Shepherd's Bushes
Amsterdam and Hamburg to
eat
more authentically and richly

than the kings and queens
we left at home.

So whose bourgeois palate
are we talking of
taking care of?

Eh, My Sister,
whose
bourgeois palate?

10/11/94

TO WHOM IT MAY CONCERN

I have noticed over the last few years that every now and then, some
editor would approach me for a contribution to an anthology, a
volume of essays, etc. In response, I would send what I considered to
be an appropriate piece of work. Then the volume would come out
for me to only realise that my piece is next to the last page or
somewhere towards the end of the book. Since this kept happening
for no other reason that I could figure out, I have concluded that may
be, *it's the same old wahala*: either because I am an African (black)
or a woman or both.

I am sending you my poem / short story / essay, in the hope that it
would be judged by you or whoever edits this volume solely on its
merit, like all other entries. I am not asking that story is put first:
only that it is placed somewhere in the anthology in relation to some
editorial logic other than my nationality / the color of my skin / or
and gender.

Otherwise, frankly, I am not even interested.

Ama Ata Aidoo

15

Relocating Home and Identity in
Zami: A New Spelling of My Name

Jennifer Gillan

As fifteen-year-old Audre Lorde pounds spice with her mother's Grenadian mortar and pestle, preparing a special dish to celebrate her first menstrual cycle, she feels a "new ripe fullness" awaken in the "molten core" of her body:

> That invisible thread, taut and sensitive as a clitoris exposed, stretched through my curled fingers up round my brown arm into the moist reality of my armpits, whose warm sharp odor with a strange new overlay mixed with the ripe garlic smells of the mortar and the general sweet-heavy aromas of high summer. (78)

This image of taut and sensitive threads radiating from a vibrant center associates Lorde's heightened awareness of sexuality with her African Caribbean ancestral history, especially her newly forged relationship with her mother's island home. In transforming the simple and mundane act of pounding spice into an experience of sexual, familial, and ancestral awakening, Lorde's biomythography, *Zami: A New Spelling of My Name* creates an empowering vision of home which lessens the alienation of marginality and exile.

Grinding the Grenadian pestle against the Lenox Avenue West Indian Market spices, Lorde feels a temporary sensation of intergenerational and intercultural unity different from her usual feelings of dislocation and disconnection from her mother and her stories. Although Linda Lorde often affectionately recalls Grenada, Audre and her sisters have trouble visualizing it: "She told us stories about Carriacou, where she had been born, amid the heavy smell of limes. She told us about the plants that healed and the plants that drove you crazy, and none of it made much sense to us children because we had never seen any of them" (113). Weaving these elaborate tales about Carriacou, Linda comes alive: "out of my mother's mouth a world of comment came cascading when she felt at ease or in her element, full of picaresque constructions and surreal scenes" (32). Looking back in this way, the island that Linda left many years earlier becomes a sweet place, more desirable because of its unattainability and perfect because of its distance. What appeared commonplace and ordinary when there, becomes extraordinary now that it is out of reach. Likewise, in *Imaginary Homelands*, Salman Rushdie describes how India seemed to have undergone a similar magical transformation during his years of exile: "The shards of memory acquired greater status, greater resonance, because they were *remains*; fragmentation made trivial things seem like symbols, and the mundane acquired numinous qualities" (12).

As Linda pieces together the fragments of her memory, they displace her disillusionment with life in New York, filling her apartment with the numinous presence of Carriacou. That these stories restore the vitality to their lives is evident to Lorde each time she listens to her mother's tales of home. When her mother talks, Audre hears traces of another world, a world of such sensuality that it eclipses her mother's attitude of mirthless austerity, a world superimposed upon the familiar repressive atmosphere of her Harlem home. The voluptuous beckoning of "home" that seeps into the walls of their apartment and floats in the air above Audre's plain, uncomfortable cot, is part of Linda's sensory production of home, a world of tastes, smells, sounds and sights all linked with Carriacou, "a magic name like cinnamon, nutmeg, mace, the delectable little squares of guava jelly each lovingly wrapped in tiny bits of crazy-quilt wax-paper cut precisely from bread wrappers" (14). Exuding from every pore of Linda's body, home not only is smelled, but also is felt in the air, vibrating from her humming:

> Once "home" was a far way off, a place I had never been to but knew well out of my mother's mouth. She breathed exuded hummed the fruit smell of Noel's Hill morning fresh and noon hot, and I spun visions of sapadilla and mango as a net over my Harlem tenement cot in the snoring darkness rank with nightmare sweat. Made bearable because it was not all. (13)

As quickly as Lorde forges this link with her mother and her ancestry, it is shattered. Her grinding ceremony is interrupted when Linda rushes angrily into the kitchen. Annoyed that her daughter has not even begun to cook the meat, she grabs the tool from her hand and gnashes the last piece of garlic: "Thump, thump, went the pestle, purposefully, up and down in the old familiar way" (80). With each heavy and monotonous thud of wood, Audre's pleasure is diminished along with her feeling of union with her mother and female ancestors. Linda's reaction recalls that the events leading up to this celebratory dinner are marked by a combination of trauma and elation. For the past year, she has dragged Audre from doctor to doctor in order to discover why she has not started menstruating. Because Linda never explains the reasons for the appointments or discusses sex with her, the visits terrify Audre. Even after hours of searching through books from the "closed" shelf of the library, she still does not understand her own body. She does know, however, that she cannot ask her mother questions because she implied that sexual matters were "nasty and not to be talked about by nice people" (75).

Even though she has been taught to suspect the erotic, Lorde still understands it as a source of power and information to which she has gained access through the ritual celebration of menstruation. Linda's stories about home evoke a world filled with bodily pleasures by which Lorde is enthralled. Associating the mortar with a woman-centered sexuality at odds with the negative male-female sexual interactions she already has experienced, she tenderly describes caressing it: "I loved to finger the hard roundness of the carved fruit" (71). The refrain, "Thud push rub rotate up" (77), repeated three times as part of a ceremonial chant, further sexualizes the pounding of spice. The sensual imagery, full of hunger and excitement, links the maturing of Lorde's own body through menstruation, her own "womansmell, warm, shameful, but secretly utterly delicious" (77), with the ripe fruits and the delicious mixture of spices she is pounding: "All these transported me into a world of scent and rhythm and movement and sound that grew more and more exciting as the ingredients liquified" (74). This liquid alludes to the reserve of blood that she now contained inside her: "a tiding ocean of blood beginning to be made real and available to me for strength and information" (78).

The sexual imagery Lorde uses to describe the mortar refers both to her desire to explore her own body and those of other women. Carved on the wooden bowl are a plethora of splendid, succulent fruits: "rounded plums and oval indeterminate fruit, some long and fluted like a banana, others ovular and end-swollen like a ripe alligator pear. In between these were smaller rounded shapes like cherries, lying in batches against and around each other" (71). All of these images lead her back to her ancestors who knew how to tap the magical healing properties of herbs and roots, and forward toward her own development of powerful lesbian relationships. Her affiliation with these women is felt as a potency at the center of her body: "There was a heavy fullness at the root of me that was exciting and dangerous" (78). From this day forward, Lorde associates the combination of smells from her newly transformed body, the garlic, the Grenadian pestle, and the Harlem summer air with her specific womanhood and her particular heritage.

By anchoring the text with this painful and pleasurable kitchen scene, *Zami* complicates the easy romantic evocation of mother and home. Lorde's relationship with her mother is mostly one of contention. But, slipped between the bitter scenes are moments of union like the one with the mortar. She describes other moments of sudden and fleeting intimacy: "The radio, the scratching comb, the smell of petroleum jelly, the grip of her knees and my stinging scalp all fall into—*the rhythms of a litany, the rituals of a Black women combing their daughters' hair*" (33). As her distance from Grenada grows, Linda's austerity often replaces the sensuous and elaborate litanies of storytelling and hair combing, and her relationship with Audre disintegrates.

However, this estrangement does have positive repercussions. Out of the experience of loss, Lorde formulates a portable concept of home as a temporary stopover. Because she envisions this constant movement as the source of her strength, she is not devastated by the number of times she must create new homes for herself. In the spaces between homes Lorde discovers possibilities for change and growth: "We came to separation, that place where work begins. Another meeting" (256). Her mixed heritage provides her with a complicated variety of homes, Harlem, Greenwich Village, Hunter College, Carriacou, and Africa. Parts of these places have affected her, but none totally makes up her psychic territory or even her physical location. Knowing that "home" is always a temporary location, she lives in-between homes, on the border of many different communities.

Scattering and reworking her "journeywoman pieces of self" (5) as she travels between countries, myths, selves and identities,[1] Lorde gains energy from the variety of women she encounters along the way. Women have defined the borders of her voyage, both in the sense that they are her limitations and that they are her structure of support and protection. Whether they have sheltered or excluded her, each woman she has known has enabled her strength and her survival: "To the battalion of arms where I often retreated for shelter and sometimes found it. To the others who helped, pushing me into the merciless sun—I, coming out blackened and whole" (5). By feminizing the traditionally masculine noun, journeyman, Lorde transforms herself into a craftswoman who has finished her training and is working at her trade. In this context, her apprenticeship under "all those feisty, incorrigible, beautiful black women who inhabit her body" (Evans 268) and who have given her the power behind her voice can be read as her attempt to create a home from herself.

By a chronicling of these journeywoman pieces of herself, Lorde creates a "biomythography,"[2] similar in format to Gloria Anzaldúa's *Borderlands / La Frontera: The New Mestiza.* Like Anzaldúa's text, *Zami* is part autobiography, poetry, revisionary history, and narrative which switches between locations and languages, often recalling Linda Lorde's sensual language of home. An elongated poetic metaphor of what Caren Kaplan has called deterritorialized identity,[3] the biomythography tells the story of a self constantly in the process of becoming, of a home which can be relocated at particular historical moments to meet particular needs. By inserting the term myth within the established generic category "biography," she refuses to simply narrate an account of one individual, and instead creates a collective vision through which to articulate the nuances of her personal history. Using this multi-generic format, Lorde tells a collective history of the women who have influenced her.

Paradoxically, Audre has to move away from home to fully appreciate these influences. As a teenager, she feels disconnected from her mother's rule-bound, repressive world, especially because it seems so far removed from the sensuous evocations of her singing and cooking. To toughen them against the pain or disappointment the world would heap upon them, Linda constantly chides her daughters:

> The merciless quality of my mother's fumbling insights turned her attempt at comfort into another assault. As if her harshness could confer invulnerability upon me. As if in the flames of truth as she saw it, I could eventually be forged into some pain-resistant replica of herself. (101)

Paradoxically, it is these bungled attempts at care-taking that make Linda inaccessible to her children.

Audre describes home during high school with the unflattering image of a Blitzkrieg, constant in its fury. She avoids the cramped apartment as much as possible, travelling the streets with her friend Gennie. The girls dress as workers, foreigners, and prostitutes, experimenting with different identities, and imagining themselves out of their ordinary lives: "there were appropriate costumes for every role, and appropriate places in the city to go play them all out. There were always things to do to match whomever we decided to be" (88). These forays into the city provide a space outside her mother's home in which Audre develops her own relationship to the city and its injustices. Unlike her mother who refuses to acknowledge inequalities, Lorde makes herself vulnerable in order to open herself to more possibilities. Raising three small black girls in the pre-Civil Rights 1950s, Linda cannot embrace this vulnerability as easily as her daughter. Instead, she tries to shield her children from the knowledge of racism, by refusing to acknowledge situations which she could not change: "if she couldn't stop white people from spitting on her children because they were Black, she would insist it was something else. It was so often her approach to the world; to change reality. If you can't change reality, change your perceptions of it" (18).

As a child, Lorde is aware only subtly of her mother's awkward position because the woman she knew always carried herself with such self-assurance and authority. Thus, she believes her mother's claims that these incidents—like the time when Lorde and her mother are spat upon in the street because they are black—are purely random acts, unrelated to racism. Lorde, too young to understand the full meaning of the event, does recognize the hostility of the harsh sound that comes just before the spit hits her: "I remember shrinking from a particular sound, a hoarse, sharp, guttural rasp, because it often meant a nasty glob of grey spittle upon my coat or shoe an instant later" (17). It is not until much later that Lorde comprehends her mother's pain at having to transform these instances of humiliation into something less personally offensive like bad manners because she could not stop their occurrence. Although Lorde could not see beyond the harshness until many years later, she realizes that her mother's actions were necessary for her own strength. Moreover, it is only as an adult that she perceives the complexity of her mother's position as a foreign, black female living in New York City, her ambiguous status intensified because she is "quite light enough to pass for white, but her children" are not (17).

Because Lorde has distance from her mother's experience of exile, she is able to forge a different relationship to the United States and Grenada. Hopeful that she can make a space for herself in New York, she creates a new definition of home out of the experience of dislocation, seeking a "more fruitful return than simple bitterness from this place of [her] mother's exile" (104). In doing so, she also acknowledges her mother's influence and the importance of her lessons of harsh survival: "But thanks to what she did know and could teach me, I survived them better than I could have imagined" (104).

This vital homage for a mother's "arrogant gentleness" (9) is reiterated in many books and poems by daughters of first-generation immigrants. In "For the Color of My Mother," Cherríe Moraga speaks for her mother because, as a dark-skinned Chicana worker, she had no power to speak for herself: "I am a white girl gone brown to the blood color of my mother / speaking for her through the unnamed part of my mouth / the wide-arched muzzle of brown women" (60-1). Similarly, there is a long history in African American literature of women speaking for and through their mothers. Dorothy West claims that when she began to write, "All my mother's blood came out in me. I was my mother talking" (1). In "I Sign My Mother's Name," Mary Helen Washington describes the portability of the home-making techniques her female ancestors have taught her: "what these women passed on would take you anywhere in the world you wanted to go" (161). Often, these lessons are learned in the kitchen. Like Lorde's experience pounding spice, the protagonist in Paule Marshall's *Brown Girl, Brownstones* creates a whole sensual world as she kneads dough for coconut bread (108). But it is Marshall's novel *Praisesong for the Widow* that is most explicitly linked to Lorde's text and the description of both the experience of surviving exile and recreating home. While Lorde does not recount her mother's entire history, Avatara Johnson, Marshall's protagonist, tells a story that could be Linda Lorde's.

Also a West Indian from Carriacou, Avatara slowly loses contact with her home as she becomes consumed by the increasing emptiness of her life in New York City and her husband's obsessive drive to get ahead. It is only after her husband dies that she allows herself to reestablish a connection to Grenada. After returning to Carriacou, she feels as if she has become "part of what seemed a far-reaching, wide-ranging confraternity" (249). Avey describes her intergenerational bonds as "hundreds of slender threads streaming down from her navel. . . . And although they were thin to the point of invisibility, they felt as strong entering her as the lifelines of woven hemp that trailed out into the water at Coney Island" (190-91).

Marshall's use of the metaphor of the invisible thread recalls Lorde's intergenerational imagery. The threads link a "strong triad of grandmother mother daughter, with the "I" moving back and forth flowing in either or both directions as needed" (7). In *Zami*, Lorde weaves a connection from her own grandmother, Ma-Liz to the Dahomean female-male sky goddess-god principle, Mawulisa, in order to rejoin the strands of her own cultural heritage. As a Grenadian, Ma-Liz, a root-woman who taught her daughters how to use the power of herbs, plants, and roots, traces her cultural practices to a mixture of Yoruban and Dahomean traditions. Both through her ancestral line and through a mythic connection to Mawulisa, Lorde joins herself to the power source of these strong African women. Because of her desire to encompass the both / and position of man / woman, Lorde also is associated directly with Mawulisa: "I have always wanted to be both man and woman, to incorporate the strongest and richest parts of my mother and father within / into me—to share valleys and mountains upon my body the way the earth does in hills and peaks" (7).

In her poetry collection, *The Black Unicorn*, Lorde clarifies her use of African history. She grounds her work in a mythic origin in Dahomey, an ancient African center of culture and power. By utilizing the story of the warrior women who are enjoined not by the shedding of blood, but rather as creators of life, Lorde claims a usable past from which she gains strength and power. Even more importantly, she uses the myth to fulfill her need as a black lesbian for non-patriarchal familial bonds: "There were no mothers, no sisters, no heroes. We had to do it alone, like our sister Amazons, the riders on the loneliest outposts of the kingdom of Dahomey" (176). She has learned to forge her own relationships with other women outside the nuclear family, to make homes out of the limited materials that she has, and to develop bonds with the variety of women that she meets.

Yet, Lorde cannot understand completely the importance of home until she develops some temporary homes of her own—a rented room in Coney Island where she recovers from a kitchen table abortion, a small apartment on Spring Street which becomes a meeting place for her high school friends, and a back porch in Stamford, Connecticut where she experiences her first lesbian sexual relationship. While these homes may provide refuge, each is only momentarily fulfilling, and none can encompass all her selves or needs. This unsettling of the stability of home evolves from Lorde's recognition of her multiple levels of difference. She is disturbed by the way her difference often is effaced in each community in which she lives. After she moves into her own apartment, she realizes that while the Branded, her collection of outsider friends, provide a community in which she can explore her own needs and desires, they always refuse to discuss her difference from them, despite the fact that they are all white and she is black and banned from their homes. The lesbian community has the same problem dealing with difference; they flatten out the actual material differences between women into an essentialized outsiderness. Lorde knows that her difference from other lesbians is real and important and cannot simply be ignored:

> Being women together was not enough. We were different. Being gay-girls together was not enough. We were different. Being Black together was not enough. We were different. Being Black women together was not enough. We were different. Being Black dykes together was not enough. We were different. (226)

Even the lesbian bars in the 1950s were not a safe haven. Inside, she faced a world only "slightly less hostile than the outer world" (225); as a black woman she could never feel at home in these bars in which the majority of women were white and the male bouncers at the door were positioned to keep out the undesirables, which usually meant black women.

Again, an estrangement from one community brings her closer to another. It is through her recognition of her difference from other women that she learns to reestablish her connections with her mother. By loving women across racial and sexual boundaries, she re-envisions her mother through what Maria Lugones has termed, "the loving eye," the ability to see oneself in other women who are quite different from oneself (279). Identifying with her mother through the outsiderness she experiences as a lesbian, Lorde gains new respect for her mother's struggles, especially when she understands the multiple tensions that a poor, black woman faces in American society. Seeing her mother in this way, Lorde develops a more complex understanding of her. Severity is only one aspect of Linda's personality; she also is a woman of incredible strength:

> All our storybooks were about people who were very different from us. . . . Nobody wrote stories about us, but still people always asked my mother for directions in a crowd. . . . It was this that made me decide as a child we must be rich even when my mother did not have enough money to buy gloves for her chilblained hands, nor a proper winter coat. (18)

Grounding her perceptions in a recognition of difference, Lorde does not see Linda simply as victim or aggressor, but rather as the source of her own flexibility in traveling between hostile and comfortable worlds.

From her mother, Lorde learns to make a space for herself at the juncture of all these identity positions; her place becomes the "very house of difference rather than the security of any particular difference" (226).[4] Her ability to bridge these various worlds, enables her to serve as a mediator between them. A medium through which other women's stories could be told, Audre's life becomes "increasingly a bridge and a field of women" (255). Moreover, this openness to other women's needs is related to Lorde's conceptualization of the erotic: "When I speak of the erotic, then, I speak of it as an assertion of the lifeforce of women; of that creative energy empowered, the knowledge and use of which we are now reclaiming in our language, our history, our dancing, our loving, our work, and our lives" (*Erotic* 55). This formulation of a politics of the erotic circles back to the scene with the mortar and pestle. From her mother's stories which taught her that in Carriacou, "the desire to lie with other women is a drive from the mother's blood," Audre learns to love other women and her own body (256). Her mother's evocations of home serve as a reminder that her capacity for loving other women can be linked with her need to pursue genuine change, instead of settling for simple survival.

By returning to the sumptuous bodily image set up at the beginning of the text, Lorde reveals how her conceptions of home have changed and developed along with her evolving political desire for an enabling politics of difference.[5] In a lesbian bar, she meets Afrekete, a woman who reunites her with her African roots and the sights and smells of Carriacou. In a description of their lovemaking, she employs almost the same language she uses to characterize pounding spice with the Grenadian mortar:

> I took a ripe avocado and rolled it between my hands until the skin became a green case for the soft mashed fruit inside, hard pit at the core. I rose from a kiss in your mouth to nibble a hole in the fruit skin near the navel stalk, squeezed the pale yellow-green fruit juice in thin ritual lines back and forth over and around your coconut-brown body. (251)

As Lorde recalls how she covered Afrekete with a mashed fruit paste, she reiterates her earlier description of the liquefaction of the spices: "The oil and sweat from our bodies kept the fruit liquid, and I massaged it over your thighs and between your breasts until your brownness shone like a light through a veil of the palest green avocado, a mantle of goddess pear that I slowly licked from your skin" (251). This relationship brings Lorde back to her mother's kitchen and she finally understands the relationship among her mother, the other women she has met, and that nebulous place called home. In loving other women, she finally pieces herself and her history together.

While the mortar and pestle forges a bond among Lorde's mother, Carriacou and home, this scene with Afrekete connects the` continuous process of locating and relocating home with the creation of an African American myth. As a Caribbean American, one generation removed from immigration, her remembrance of Carriacou is a creative and imaginative act, based on her mother's stories and not on personal experience. She does not reclaim precisely the home that her mother left and never pretends to have gained access to Linda's past as she had experienced it. Thus, while Lorde associates Afrekete with Africa and the mortar with Carriacou, she also returns to the very specific material conditions of day-to-day life in Harlem:

> It was not onto the pale sands of Whydah, nor the beaches of Winneba or Annamabu, with cocopalms softly applauding and crickets keeping time with the pounding of a tar-laden, treacherous, beautiful sea. It was onto 113th Street that we descended after our meeting under the Midsummer Eve's Moon, but the mothers and fathers smiled at us in greeting as we strolled to Eighth Avenue, hand in hand. (253)

By allowing it to spill out onto 113th Street, Lorde Americanizes this African myth. Yet, despite the romantic overtones of this passage, Audre and Afrekete do not live happily ever after in an idyllic lesbian union. By ending the book with yet another estrangement, Lorde emphasizes the importance of the formation of a variety of communities rather than a single bond. She terms this network of women Zami, "A Carriacou name for women who work together as friends and lovers" (255). By separating Audre and Afrekete, the text also rejects the romance of sisterhood, home and community and insists that these "homes" are far from uncomplicated and certainly not comfortable.[6] Afrekete has taught Lorde to appreciate the nourishing power of the exchange between women and homes: "We had come together like elements erupting in an electric storm, exchanging energy, sharing change, brief and drenching" (253).

By teaching her new definitions of women's bodies, Afrekete finishes Lorde's apprenticeship as a journeywoman and allows her to go off into the world and practice her craft. Read through this metaphor of the journeywoman, *Zami: A New Spelling of My Name* becomes a chronicle of intersections—the meeting points, breaking points, and departure points—that have forced Lorde to grow and change and adapt. The zones of transition in which she has lived and the fragments of self that she has gathered become Audre Lorde's piecework, her craft as a journeywoman who continually locates and relocates her self and her home.

NOTES

1.   In "Playfulness, 'World'-Travelling, and Loving Perception," Maria Lugones argues that women of color must travel between worlds because of the hostility toward them within the Anglo American community. She connects world travelling to cross-cultural and cross-racial loving.

2.   Anzaldúa switches from English to Tex-Mex, to Castilian Spanish to North Mexican dialect to Chicano(a) Spanish to a mixture of all the dialects and languages with which she has come into contact. This discourse indicates Anzaldúa's position as a mestiza, a mixture Indian, black, Hispanic and Anglo backgrounds.

3.   Caren Kaplan uses the phrase "deterritorialization through struggle" to indicate the difficult and ongoing process of locating and relocating one's position at particular historical moments. This process of positionality is enabling in that it allows for many different and often contradictory positions.

4.   This formulation of difference seems similar to Trinh Minh-ha's in "Difference: A Special Third World Women's Issue" in her collection *Woman, Native, Other: Writing, Postcoloniality and Feminism.* Trinh envisions difference as multiplicity, not division: "I / i can be I or i, you and me both involved. We sometimes includes, other times excludes me" (92). For Trinh, the "I" embodies difference, ambiguity, ceaseless change to infinity. If one assumes a single, unified identity, change and difference can only undermine that stability. Once one accepts identity as unstable, then difference

is no longer a threat: "Difference does not annul identity. It is beyond and alongside identity" (104).

5.   The language of Chela Sandoval's formulation of differential consciousness in "U.S. Third World Feminism: The Theory and Method of Oppositional Consciousness in the Postmodern World" is similar to Lorde's poetic articulation of theory of revolutionary political desire within *Zami: A New Spelling of My Name* and *The Uses of the Erotic: The Erotic as Power*: "Its power can be thought of as mobile—not nomadic but rather cinematographic: a kinetic motion that maneuvers, poetically transfigures, and orchestrates while demanding alienation, perversion, and reformation in both spectators and practitioners" (3). The important emphasis in both texts is on movement, change and becoming.

6.   See Biddy Martin and Chandra Mohanty, "Feminist Politics: What's Home Got to Do with It?" Martin and Mohanty criticize the tendency to set up uncomplicated identity positions and comfortable homes within feminism.

WORKS CITED

Anzaldúa, Gloria. *Borderlands / la Frontera: The New Mestiza.* San Francisco: Spinsters / Aunt Lute, 1987.

Evans, Mari, ed. *Black Women Writers, 1950-80: A Critical Evaluation.* New York: Anchor Books, 1984.

Lorde, Audre. *The Black Unicorn: Poems.* New York: Norton, 1978.

____. "Sisterhood and Survival." *The Black Scholar* 17.2 (1986): 5-7.

____. *Sister Outsider: Essays and Speeches.* Trumansburg, NY: The Crossing Press, 1984.

____. *The Uses of the Erotic: The Erotic as Power.* Trumansburg, NY: Out and Out Books, 1978.

____. *Zami: A New Spelling of My Name.* Freedom, CA: The Crossing Press, 1982.

Lugones, Maria. "Playfulness, 'World-Travelling', and Loving Perception." *Hypatia: A Journal of Feminist Philosophy* 2.2 (1987): 3-19.

Moraga, Cherríe. "For the Color of My Mother." *Loving in the War Years.* Boston: South End Press, 1983.

Marshall, Paule. *Brown Girl, Brownstones.* Old Westbury, NY: The Feminist Press, 1981 [1959].

____. *Praisesong for the Widow.* New York: Dutton, 1983.

Martin, Biddy, and Chandra Talpade Mohanty. "Feminist Politics: What's Home Got to Do with It?" *Feminist Studies / Critical Studies.* Ed. Teresa de Lauretis. Bloomington: Indiana UP, 1986. 191-212.

Rushdie, Salman. *Imaginary Homelands: Essays and Criticism 1981-1991.* London: Granta Books, 1991.

Sandoval, Chela. "U.S. Third World Feminism: The Theory and Method of Oppositional Consciousness in the Postmodern World." *Genders* 10 (Spring 1991): 1-24.

Trinh T. Minh-ha. *Women, Native, Other: Writing, Postcoloniality and Feminism.* Bloomington: Indiana UP, 1989.

Washington, Mary Helen. "I Sign My Mother's Name: Alice Walker, Dorothy West, Paule Marshall." *Mothering the Mind: Twelve Studies of Writers and their Silent Partners.* Ed. Ruth Perry. New York: Holmes and Meier, 1984. 142-63.

16

Wild Lessons: Native Ecological Wisdom in Ruby Slipperjack's Fiction

Sylvia Bowerbank and
Dolores Nawagesic Wawia

When I was an infant, it was the custom to name the child after the first animal that came close to the encampment after its birth. I was born at the end of April. As everyone knows the animals are in hibernation. Mother and Grandmother had to wait for a few weeks before any animal life was sighted. It happened one warm afternoon in late June. Mother left the living room door open for fresh air. I was bundled up in a tiknaagan (cradleboard) which was supported by the old armchair. Suddenly, a huge bull frog came bounding into the front room and stopped in front of my tiknaagan and took a good look at me before leaping out through the front door again. My mother was so excited that she ran to my Grandmother's and told her the good news. From that day on I was known as Muk Kee Queh. Frog Lady.

(Wawia, From Teepee to Penthouse)
[in progress]

But I saw, you know, my grandmother skin moose and remember her soft voice talking to that moose's spirit and giving her thanks.

Bannock warm with lard. I taste home.

Calico and hide. Sweetgrass and sage. My fingers touch these things and compare (as my mind so often does) the feel of polyester, styrofoam and keyboard. Fingers then and now.

Gone. Gone as my Grandmother.
But I remember her and she is with me.

(Fedorick, Sense of Home)

A growing consensus is emerging that human beings need to turn away from the modern ideology of domination over nature. We claim that the age of ecology is dawning, but what will this mean in practice? What alternative political, economic, and cultural structures should we develop? In its very etymology, the word "ecology" is connected to knowing and caring for one's home place; it derives from Greek roots, *oikos* (household) and *logos* (discourse) (Williams 1983, 110). Ecology as a social practice, therefore, must be grounded in the good management and preservation of our home habitats. Judith Plant (1990) argues that, in the late twentieth century, the "home" is coming to refer to "the theatre of our human ecology" rather than a bungalow in the suburbs of industrialized society:

> [It] is the place where we can learn the values of caring for and nurturing each other and our environment and of paying attention to immediate human needs and feelings. It is a much broader term, reflecting the reality of human cultural requirements and our need to be sustainably adaptive within our nonhuman environments. (160)

If Judith Plant is right, a new sense of "home" is emerging as a place where we can create new values and behaviors. But how are we to undertake such a fundamental transformation in our ways of thinking and living? Habitual consumers that we are, few of us have the knowledge or the skills to thrive in our own places. As Gary Snyder writes in *The Practice of the Wild*, "for most Americans, to reflect on 'home place' would be an unfamiliar exercise" (25). How are we to learn to become native to our home places?

Despite the pressures of colonialism and capitalism, the Native peoples of the Americas have struggled to keep alive a sophisticated heritage of ecological knowledge and practice. It is a spiritual legacy which was, and remains, embedded in every aspect of Native political, social, and cultural life. One of the ways in which this knowledge has been remembered, passed down, and renewed over successive generations is by means of the ancient art of storytelling. This insight is the main theme of Anna Lee Walter's *Talking Indian: Reflections on Survival and Writing*, which records these words of a hundred-year-old elder:

> "You are longing for something," he continued. "You hunger for it but you can't name it because you don't know what it is.

> You have searched for it everywhere . . . in money, in drink,
> and what else? You really have tried everything to find it,
> haven't you?"
> "It's for the old stories and songs that you grieve," he said.
> "That's what you want and need."(29-30)

Likewise, at a 1987 gathering of women at Brandon University
(Manitoba, Canada), Eva McKay, an Elder from the Sioux Valley
Reserve, explained that she and other elders are the keepers of the
memory of her people's encounters with wild nature. Thus, the
story-telling of the elders is a strategy of survival:

> We are the people with the natural skills because the world
> and everything in it has a story for us. These are the natural
> stories. And this is why our people survived. (347)

During the past decade or so, a new generation of First Nations writers
in Canada has been maintaining, and yet transforming, the traditional
oral art of story-telling by means of writing stories of survival. One of
these writers is Ruby Slipperjack, an Ojibway author and artist from the
Fort Hope Band, now living in Thunder Bay, Ontario. In this essay, we
interpret Slipperjack's two novels—*Honour the Sun* (1987) and *Silent
Words* (1992)—as ecological texts. Both novels teach their readers the
subtle ways in which contemporary Ojibway culture struggles to live
well on the land despite the encroachments of modern industrial culture.
Yet, Slipperjack is not writing for non-Native readers who wish to
misappropriate Native culture once more, this time to serve the
environmental movement. Nor is she purporting to speak for all Native
cultures. Her wisdom is bioregional, that is, specific to contemporary
Ojibway experience in northwestern Ontario. As this essay will explain,
we interpret Slipperjack's novels as partaking in the new cultural project
of homemaking, understood as a transformational strategy for planetary
survival. Slipperjack's understanding of "home" is markedly different
from that of mainstream Western society which separates "the home"
from the nasty, competitive world of politics and feminizes it as a
private site of security and love.[1] Given the present ecological crisis,
surely, it is clear that no home is separate or safe from the disastrous
consequences of the way we work and live. Slipperjack's novels
articulate a Native perspective on ecology as a discourse of the "home"
in the wilderness. Based on the landscape of her childhood in northern
Ontario, her novels celebrate the distinctness of knowing and caring for

one specific place: one's home ground. In a 1990 interview with Hartmut Lutz, she explains that, in writing her novels, she throws out any preconceived ideas about form—so "don't look for plot" (213). Instead, she concentrates on the psychological development of her main characters—Owl in *Honour the Sun* and Danny in *Silent Words*—as they interact with the human and non-human inhabitants of their shared environment:

> Everything is tied with nature. . . . The land, rocks, trees, are part of our history, a part of us. They live longer than we do. If you stay in one place, a tree will watch you crawl, run, walk, shuffle, and eventually see your children also complete the cycle behind you. (Lutz 207)

Our essay will use Slipperjack's fictional accounts of Ojibway ecological wisdom to exemplify how literature might contribute to cultural homemaking, that is, to the reclamation of ways of knowing and living in one's home place. Slipperjack's novels are cultural projects in homemaking precisely because they teach readers to be attentive and to honor the unique opportunities and gifts of our own habitats.

In writing this essay, we are trying to avoid the inappropriate judgmental approach and tone of literary criticism as it is usually practiced in the academy. In the interview mentioned above, Slipperjack explains why Native readers rarely become critics of her novels:

> It is like questioning someone! You don't question people. You don't make comments. That is why the lecture theatres are such a foreign environment in universities, the debates, and the discussions, the panels—those are totally foreign. It is just like pointing a finger at somebody. [Laughs.] (Lutz 213)

Why does Slipperjack find criticism so amusing? Why are Native writers and intellectuals hesitant to take up the role of literary critic? In *Approaches to Studying Native American Literature*, Mohawk teacher Rick Monture explains one reason: "In almost every Native culture, to criticize is to show disrespect for another person, to view another's knowledge, opinions, and emotions as inferior to one's own" (13). Similarly, in a recent essay entitled "'Border' Studies: The Intersection of Gender and Color," Native American critic Paula Gunn Allen (1992) expresses her discontent with the pontificating and power-tripping that characterizes the practice of literary criticism in the academy. She particularly laments the life-alienating practices that are in vogue among elite feminist theorists; such theorists "mistake the menu for the meal and starve thereby" (312). Allen's domestic metaphor is telling. Her argument is that intellectual women should avoid critical practices based on negation—subversion, dissidence, and criticizing from the margins. Echoing Audre Lorde, Allen writes, such practices are "enterprises that support and maintain the master, feeding his household on our energy, our attention and our strength" (312). Instead, says Allen, women should develop life-affirming approaches that are in keeping with their ultimate end to care for human society. Rick Monture calls on Native writers and scholars to develop their own critical paradigm. This Native approach, writes Monture, can "be likened to a 'non' approach, involving much word play, a few inside jokes, self-deprecation, humor, anger, sadness and elation—all in equal amounts in order to bring about a balance of literary voice that speaks to, and for, all people" (14). It is in this "new" spirit of life-affirmation that we write about ecological wisdom in the fiction of Ruby Slipperjack.

For those people who do not have daily contact with wild places and free animals, Native principles of ecological wisdom are difficult to understand. It must be said that Native and non-Native cultures have contrary ways of valuing nature. Unlike Euro-American culture, the indigenous cultures live, not separately, but as part of the wilderness. The Native sense of home place includes free animals, plants, reptiles, and rocks. In *Taking Care of Sibô's Gifts*, an environmental treatise by the KéköLdi Indigenous Reserve in Costa Rica, Gloria Mayorga criticizes Euro-American values that lead to the destruction of human community with non-human species:

> [White man] works very hard, but he destroys Nature. He chops down all the trees to make his big cities, and where he lives . . . there are no trees, no rivers, no animals. . . . The indigenous people don't work so hard. We plant corn, raise animals and live in the forest. We like to see the plants and the animals, the birds and the rivers around us. We don't like to destroy Nature, we like to live in Nature. (Palmer 36-7)

All Native ecological beliefs and practices follow from the basic condition of making one's living on the land, surrounded by wild animals and plants.

Ruby Slipperjack's ideal of home insists on the necessity of living with animals and plants as a part of daily life. Her novel *Honour the Sun* celebrates the early life of "The Owl," a girl who lives with her mother and the other children in a log cabin in the woods. Time passes in the novel, but the plot is not as important as character development, as the unfolding of Owl's understanding of her own and her people's place in nature. The Ojibway community shares a complicated kinship with animals and plants. This kinship is ritualized, for example, in the Ojibway custom of naming the newborn child after the first animal which it encounters. In *From Teepee to Penthouse*, Dolores Wawia, who comes from an Ojibway community just north of Slipperjack's home, describes the amusing forms the custom can take:

> Many of the children had beautiful and noble names such as Gookookhoo (Owl) and Mkwa (Bear). Mother wasn't so lucky though. She was born in the early part of December, and the neighbour down the road also had birthed a boy that same week. The boy's father saw a muskrat (Wzhashk). Lo! The boy became known as Wzhashk. Eventually the same muskrat meandered down the road during that night to Mother's place and sight unseen laid a huge deposit near the front door. My grandmother noticed the tracks and the unsightly deposit; ergo, my baby mum became Wzhashk Mo! Muskrat turd.

The girl in *Honour the Sun* got her name because an owl hooted several nights in a row outside the cabin just before her birth. She was born with big round eyes and her nightly crying kept everyone awake. So she was called "The Owl." The log cabin, the Owl's habitat, is closely integrated into the habitats of other creatures. There is no clear demarcation between the inside and the outside of the home. Cooking is largely done outside the cabin; washing and bathing are done in the lake. Blueberry picking, for example, is the delightful pastime of the girl Owl and the other children, but it is also a serious economic activity, undertaken to gain a tradable commodity.

For indigenous cultures, economy and ecology are one. The wilderness interconnects the human and nonhuman inhabitants of a place in ways that benefit all forms of life native to that place. The wilderness is not separate from where we work and live; it is the home of the people. Even many environmentalists, it seems, fail to understand this principle. Marie Wilson, elder of the Gitksan Wet'suwet'en of northwestern British Columbia, worries that, after her people defeat the developers on the issue of appropriate land use, they will have to take on the environmentalists. Although environmentalists think of themselves as allies of the Native peoples, Marie Wilson points out that their attitudes towards the wilderness are contrary to those of her people:

> [T]he environmentalists want these beautiful places kept in a state of perfection: to not touch them, rather to keep them pure. So that we can leave our jobs and for two weeks we can venture into the wilderness and enjoy this ship in a bottle. In a way this is like denying that life is happening constantly in these wild places, that change is always occurring. Human life must be there too. Humans have requirements and they are going to have to use some of the life in these places. (83)

According to Marie Wilson, the Gitksan people have developed cultural practices to help them to avoid the over-use of natural resources. Over the generations, they have learned to conform to nature's patterns, fitting themselves to its cycles and changes, its checks and balances. The Gitksan concept of nature limits and regulates the people's scope of activity. Knowing that the well-being of their children and their grandchildren depends on their taking care of the land, the Gitksan maintain a covenant with the earth: "The land is the skin of the Earth—without it, we die" (78). Self-discipline is required in order that the tribe as a whole will live appropriately on the land, preserving the sacred place which sustains the life of that tribe over time. The limits and controls on behavior are not enforced from the outside, but are learned by the careful practice of elaborate customs, ceremonies and taboos, developed by the tribe, over hundreds of years, as they learned to live appropriately in a home place. As Marie Wilson points out, ancient practices, which may now seem outdated, are rooted in a deep understanding of a tribe's duty to the earth. Fasting, for example, not only heightens the body's sense of gratitude and sensitivity to life; it is also a ritualized way of returning to the survival mode of existence, in which need, not greed, is the principle of life (83).

In *Honour the Sun*, the Owl must learn to live ambiguously between two cultures. She is required to attend school where she learns the cultural values and language of English-Canadians. When she gets older, she knows that, by Canadian law, she will be forced to leave her community to go to residential school. As she sits in the classroom, she daydreams of the freedom of life in the bush. She remembers that on a winter day when there was no school, she went deep into the bush with her mother to check the rabbit snares and to ice-fish. Her mother chopped two holes in the ice of the lake:

> There we sat and fished, facing each other about twenty feet apart. She told me stories about Indians of long ago and the magic people who lived inside the rock cliffs. Mom caught three large jackfish and I caught one. Oh, that was great. Afterwards, we built a fire and had some tea and bannock. (125)

For Slipperjack, the home in the woods is not an oasis, a sweet refuge from the cold, unsafe world of work. Neither is it a sentimental return to the Never-never land of commodified "Indian" legends. The mother of Owl is not the delicate angel of the house, but a witty and resourceful woman, living precariously in the bush with her kids. She outwits drunken men who break down her door. Her style of homemaking includes not only food-preparation but also fishing, trapping and hunting. She can kill a moose with a .22 gauge rifle. She can skin it and preserve its hide; she can pound its meat into pemmican. Yet, such are the changes threatening her way of life that, by the end of the novel, even Owl's mother is drinking and neglecting her home. Owl, however, remains determined to find a way to follow her mother's saying: "Honour the Sun for shining on your face". . . (182).

In both of her novels, rather than focussing on a critique of white culture, Slipperjack struggles to bring about positive change: to reclaim Native American ways of knowing and living on the earth as home, despite the encroachments of an alien culture. In *Silent Words*, she uses the story of one boy's apprenticeship to the ways of his ancestors to teach the code of self-discipline and self-reliance that defines Ojibway ecological practice in the bush. The first chapter of *Silent Words* depicts the social ills that afflict many of the Native peoples living in towns in northern Ontario. As the materialistic values of white society impinge on daily life, the Ojibway community is losing its bearings and is becoming plagued by alienation and violence. The central character is a boy named Danny whose family is caught in a cycle of abuse: the father has taken to drink and has run off with another woman; the mother is nowhere to be found; the white stepmother cheats on the father and beats the son; the boy, in turn, kicks the baby's crib. Emblematic of the family's degeneracy and despair, their house is choked by weeds and filth. The boy—addicted to junk food and cruel pranks—has all but lost contact with Ojibway ways of life. He is even forgetting how to speak Ojibway. This negative image, however, is confined to the first chapter of *Silent Words*. The novel is chiefly a journey of healing: the boy runs away from the counterfeit home and eventually recovers a true home. Through a series of encounters with Ojibway elders and with animals, Danny comes to understand for himself how to survive in the woods of northern Ontario. By indirection, the reader too learns the wild lessons of the novel.

As the title suggests, *Silent Words* is, in good part, about the problem of language as a bearer of cultural values. Ruby Slipperjack is well aware of the difficulty of translating her cultural wisdom into English. She first writes her novels in Ojibway and then struggles to find a good way to express an equivalent meaning in English. Even so, she knows that the spirit of what she is saying might not be translatable (Lutz 207); fluency in Ojibway is somehow connected to fluency in the old ways of living. In *Silent Words*, to illustrate the problematic relationship between culture and language, Slipperjack has Mr. Old Indian (the elder from Savant Lake) speak in broken English: "To honour da Eart, boy, you mus'un'erstan dat it is alibe. Da men wit da machines are like lice dat feed on da libin' scalp o' Mudder Eart" (55). The broken English of Mr. Old Indian also allows Slipperjack to represent the process by which one elder assimilates Christian stories to his Ojibway way of thinking. Thus, Mr. Old Indian claims that Jesus, the Son of God, agrees with Ojibway attitudes towards nature; Jesus gave a sign of this by being born "in the open air" with animals around him, as all children of the earth "should be born" (55-6).

Ruby Slipperjack and other First Nations writers often raise their concern about writing in English. They do not feel at home in the dominant language of Canada. The process of translating one's cultural values into the literary forms and language of English-Canadian culture is fraught with difficulties and dangers. The English language may not be able to convey the subtleties of Native culture. The potential for misunderstanding is especially great in writing about Native ecological wisdom. This barrier of language is overwhelming even when both non-Native and Native ecologists are trying to understand each other. An amusing anecdote, told by Métis writer Lee Maracle, captures the nature of the problem:

> Recently, there was a conference at Opitsit (Meares Island) to discuss and shape thoughts on the importance of trees to the environment. Native and European environmentalists both

attended. The morning consisted of presentations made by "prominent" environmentalists, who droned on about p.b.m.'s, chloroform counts, soil erosion, and so forth—none of which was understood by the Native people there. All of our people spoke and understood English, but none had a background in Latin, so the presentations by the environmentalists went over all their heads. At the end, an old man got up and said he would like to give an Indian point of view. Gratefully, the environmentalists bent their ears to listen. The old man spoke for three hours in his language, then sat down. The Natives cracked up. The environmentalists sat confused. (90)

Every language bears the long-established attitudes and habits of its users. That is why, as Okanagan writer Jeannette Armstrong explains, it is near impossible to convey her people's understanding of nature in the English language. Armstrong gives the example of the English word "tree," which has come to refer, in the extreme case, to a mere natural resource, the lumber and paper of consumer culture. The Okanagan language expresses a totally different sense of trees as "living relatives in spirit":

> To the person whose direct survival depends on trees, the *tree* has a deeper cultural meaning—steeped in an essence of gratitude toward the creation of the tree, and therefore enveloped within a unique cultural expression of reverence toward creation. . . . Thus, even though I might translate *tree* into an English word, my cultural meaning remains intact as though spoken in my language while your cultural understanding of the word remains locked within the context of your culture. Unless you also speak my language, or permit me to fully interpret my meaning, the *tree* of which I speak remains a *tree* cloaked in my culture and language which excludes my meaning. (76)

Thus, differences of culture and language make it difficult for non-Natives to understand, let alone live, Native ecological skills and values. These values are passed down through the generations by means of narratives of one's ancestors' (and one's own encounters) with animals and plants, told in detail in the traditional languages. How does one learn, in contemporary times, the ways to be at home in nature? *Silent Words* mediates on that question by studying the initiation of one

Ojibway boy. For Slipperjack, wise words must be "silent," grounded in practice. In order to understand and to respect the Elder's words, the boy Danny must undergo his own experiences among the wild lakes, plants, and animals. Danny learns to exercise a complicated code of self control that ensures that he will respect the earth and take only what he absolutely needs for sustenance. In the silent language of the body and spirit, he discovers how to become native to his own place.

To dramatize Danny's education in wilderness values, Slipperjack uses a powerful narrative thread: he must learn a subtle code of conduct in regard to food. In the beginning of the novel, Danny often feels desperate about getting food. His chaotic home-life means that he has to get to the store, past the town bullies, to get something to eat. After he runs away, he continues to subsist on store-bought stuff, mostly pop, bubblegum, and candy; later, he is even given the nickname "Chips." Other Ojibway people laugh at him for being a "city Indian" because he is unable to kill and to butcher his own meat (84). During his adventures, however, he slowly learns how to feed himself. He catches his first fish, a good-sized pickerel, and experiences the pleasure of providing food for Charlie's family's dinner (44). His friend Henry teaches him how to cook on an open fire (77). A severe look from an elder lets him understand that playing with meat is shameful and disrespectful (85). In his travels, Danny observes Ojibway attitudes that are new to him: kids studying minnows, caterpillars, and frogs (30); Bobby carving his own spoon instead of just buying one (32); Henry and Jim discussing the meaning of a fish's life (72-73).

To become an Ojibway adult, Danny must learn about the sacredness of animals and plants; he must learn the respect and gratitude due to life forms that, although they might serve him as food, shelter and medicine, have their own integrity. His most important teacher is the elder Ol' Jim who takes him on a canoeing trip. Separated from the conveniences of town-life, at first, Danny worries about starving. One evening while Ol' Jim is setting up camp, Danny approaches the grub box:

> I had not looked in it before and did not know what was in there. I didn't know if I could keep myself from eating everything in sight—that's how hungry I was! I opened the lid, but what was this? There was nothing in there! No food! . . . There was a bag of flour, oats, the can of tea, sugar, lard, and something called baking powder. Where was the food? (111)

Later, he remarks that he can't get over what Ol' Jim can make out of so few supplies (122). By observing the elder's wilderness skills, Danny learns not only how to cook bannock and porridge tea, but also how to handle a canoe and to find his way; how to set up camp; how to prepare a balm for mosquito bites; how to set a rabbit snare and to skin the rabbit. He comes to understand that the meat, fish, and berries which the Ojibway harvest from the land are healthier than store-bought food. He comes to appreciate the spiritual advantages of being without modern conveniences, such as hospitals and electricity. In the bush, he begins to recover the ancient art of herb-collecting and healing. Danny learns that, if a man kills a moose and there is no refrigeration, the man will not hoard the meat, but bring the community together to share his good fortune. For the Ojibway, land is life; food, shelter and even human community are all gifts of the land.

We want to describe one incident in Danny's journey of healing at length because it illustrates the distinct and complicated attitude of the Ojibway towards life and the taking of life. One morning when he is on the canoe trip, he arises before Ol' Jim and finds that he has caught a duck in his snare. He is elated because, for the first time, he will be able to cook Ol' Jim fresh duck for breakfast:

> I tried to pounce on him, but my hands kept slipping to the left and to the right, amidst flying feathers, slaps to the face, and scratches to the hands. I finally got a hold of him and we rolled around in the sand and thrashed in the bush, then he slipped away from me again. That was the most slippery, agile critter in the world! I landed on him again and, finally, my hand came around a leg and I hung on, and then my other hand found the neck. I laid down on it twisted the neck around like Ol' Jim had when he showed me how to kill a rabbit. Suddenly, all was still. My heart was thumping so loudly in my ears I could hardly hear anything. I felt like laughing for joy. I did it! I killed it! Breakfast! (153-54)

The duck is still not dead; it flaps and thrashes around desperately for some time before Danny, in agony and ignorance, wrestles it down and finally pounds and shreds its neck with a stone. The passage ends with Ol' Jim's burst of laughter at Danny who is covered with feathers, but nevertheless proud of the duck he is roasting.

What is so funny about killing a duck—especially given the earnest way in which we have been discussing Native people's respectful attitude towards animals? At a conference at McMaster University in October, 1992, most of the audience laughed when Slipperjack read aloud this passage about Danny's killing of the duck. In the question period, however, one person in the audience protested the prolonged suffering of the duck and the cruelty of the passage. It was not a surprising response given that mainstream culture is generally sentimental about pets and pictures of wildlife. For most of us, our culture's slaughter of animals and birds remains an invisible and depersonalized process. As we enjoy that roast duck, we are not mindful that we have killed it. In Danny's encounter with the duck, the personal responsibility for killing for food is made manifest; Danny's duck is not a meat product, but a worthy adversary who fights for his life. In the context of the novel, this is a significant moment in Danny's education. He is learning not only a survival skill, but also a complicated code of etiquette in relationship to animals. Ol' Jim's laughter at Danny's fumblings and the pleasure they both feel about breakfast is a great and personal tribute to the duck who has died to feed them. The death of one creature is the life of another. The novel is full of gestures of gratitude to the animals, the land, and the spirits of ancestors who nurture and care for Danny and his circle of friends. The boy learns his sacred duty to leave tobacco offerings for the great wolf who protects him during a storm and for the Memegwesiway [magic people] who dwell among the rocks. He does this in tribute to the wisdom of his ancestors, even though as Ol' Jim regrets: "We have lost the level of thought and knowledge to be able to see and talk with them" (97).

As the killing of the duck episode reveals, Native ecological wisdom cannot easily be understood and put to good use in a very different cultural milieu. There may be some Native values and feelings towards nature that are resistant to translation into English-Canadian and American culture. As Anna Lee Walters says in *Talking Indian*, when the hundred-year-old Elder speaks of the source of the wisdom of his tribe, his words are *not* in English, even though Walters renders them in English:

> It is important and curious to remember that everything we two-leggeds know about being human, we learn from the four-leggeds, the animals and the birds, and everything else in the universe. None of the knowledge is solely our own. (29-30)

The challenge for the new generation of First Nations writers of Canada is to transform their oral traditions into a literary form without violating the original meaning. In her novels, Ruby Slipperjack remembers the ecological wisdom learned from living in the bush as a child; she is developing textual strategies that will re-teach that wisdom for both Native and non-Native readers. Her novels suggest that the wisdom and skills needed to live appropriately in our home places can be preserved and rehabilitated. Above all, her novels suggest that all peoples—whether Native or non-Native—can learn to practice a mindfulness in our relationships with each other and with the non-human inhabitants of our home places.

NOTE

1.   In *Discrimination by Design*, professor of architecture Leslie Kanes Weisman links the ecological crisis in Western society with the schism between the work place as a space of male power and the home as a space of woman's nurturance and care-taking. "Healing this schism through new spatial arrangements that encourage the integration of work and play, intellect and feeling, action and compassion, is a survival imperative" (20).

WORKS CITED

Allen, Paula Gunn. "'Border' Studies: The Intersection of Gender and Color." *Introduction to Scholarship in Modern Languages and Literatures.* Ed. Joseph Gibaldi. New York: The Modern Language Association, 1992.

Armstrong, Jeannette. "Racism: Racial Exclusivity and Cultural Supremacy." *Give Back: First Nations Perspectives on Cultural Practice.* Vancouver: Gallerie Publications, 1992.

Bowerbank, Sylvia, and Dolores Nawagesic Wawia. "Literature and Criticism by Native and Métis Women in Canada." *Feminist Studies* 20:3 (Fall 1994): 565-81.

Fedorick, Joy Asham. "Sense of Home." *Canadian Woman Studies* 10:2-3 (Summer/Fall 1989): 57.

Lutz, Hartmut. *Contemporary Challenges: Conversations with Canadian Native Authors.* Saskatoon: Fifth House, 1991.

Maracle, Lee. "Oratory: Coming to Theory." *Give Back: First Nations Perspectives on Cultural Practice.* Vancouver: Gallerie Publications, 1992.

McKay, Eva. "We Are Here." *Our Bit of Truth: An Anthology of Canadian Native Literature.* Ed. Agnes Grant. Winnipeg: Pemmican Publications, 1990.

Monture, Rick. "Commentary." *Approaches to Studying Native American Literature: An Annotated Bibliography.* Compiled by Rick Monture and Sylvia Bowerbank. Indigenous Studies Programme, McMaster University, Hamilton, Ontario, 1995.

Palmer, Paula, Juanita Sánchez, and Gloria Mayorga. *Taking Care of Sibô's Gifts: An Environmental Treatise from Costa Rica's KéköLdi Indigenous Reserve.* Asociación de Desarrollo Integral de la Reserva Indígena Cocles/KéköLdi. San José, Costa Rica: Editorama, 1991.

Plant, Judith. "Searching for Common Ground: Ecofeminism and Bioregionalism." *Reweaving the World: The Emergence of Ecofeminism.* Ed. Irene Diamond and Gloria Feman Orenstein. San Francisco: Sierra Club, 1990.

Slipperjack, Ruby. *Honour the Sun.* Winnipeg: Pemmican Publications, 1987.

_____. *Silent Words.* Saskatoon, Saskatchewan: Fifth House, 1992.

Snyder, Gary. *The Practice of the Wild: Essays by Gary Snyder.* New York: North Point Press, 1990.

Telling It Book Collective. [Sky Lee, Lee Maracle, Daphne Marlatt, Betsy Warland, Eds.] *Telling It: Women and Language Across Cultures.* Vancouver: Press Gang Publishers, 1992.

Walters, Anna Lee. *Talking Indian: Reflections on Survival and Writing.* Ithaca, N.Y.: Firebrand Books, 1992.

Wawia, Dolores Nawagesic. [Work in Progress] *From Teepee to Penthouse.*

Weisman, Leslie Kanes. *Discrimination by Design: A Feminist Critique of the Man-Made Environment.* Urbana: U of Illinois P, 1992.

Wilson, Marie. "Wings of the Eagle." *Turtle Talk: Voices for a Sustainable Future.* Eds. Christopher Plant & Judith Plant. Philadelphia: New Society Publishers, 1990.

Williams, Raymond. *Keywords: A Vocabulary of Culture and Society.* London: Fontana, 1983.

17

Nature, Spirituality, and Homemaking in Marjorie Kinnan Rawlings' *Cross Creek*

Carolyn M. Jones

From the syndicated feature, "Songs of a Housewife," a series of poems about homemaking that, as one editor put it, explores the "romance of the dishpan and kettle,"[1] to her memoir *Cross Creek*, Marjorie Kinnan Rawlings' works emphasize the importance of homemaking as a spiritual act. Rawlings believed that from the complex relationship of human to place emerges identity and meaning. Therefore, she explores the universal truths that can be drawn from a profound sense of location—for Rawlings, her home within the life of the Cross Creek community—and from acting within that located space.

This involvement in the world challenges traditional forms of spirituality that often urge separation from the world. Traditional spirituality, in the modern and post-modern world, now finds itself, Ursula King says, at a crossroads at which it either must choose to engage the world or become insignificant (5). Women's spirituality, in contrast, has located itself at that crossroads and has begun to transform this place of dislocation into one of mediation, vitality, and power through the concrete activity of homemaking. To explore spirituality and homemaking in Rawlings' work, I want, first, to look at how the inclusion of women's voices and women's writing about their modes of approaching and defining the holy have changed definitions of spirituality. Then, I would like to turn to *Cross Creek* to see how Rawlings' concentration on the details of making a home—particularly, her attention to nature, to the Creek community, and to the preparation and serving of food—opens up, for her, new forms of spirituality. Finally, I want to comment on location and identity and the politics of homemaking.

Geoffrey Wainwright defines spirituality as the combination of prayer and living—that is, the way in which we relate the contemplative inner life to the active outer life. Spirituality is the way that we conduct the search for meaning and significance in our reflection on the totality of human experience; thus, it is fundamentally about defining the self in relationship to the "other" (Jones et al. xxii-xxvi). Spirituality is linked traditionally to mystical or ascetic experience and to finding a relationship to the "wholly / holy other," to God within the framework of the church. For some women, however, spirituality has come to mean something different—often, a search for individual meaning and identity outside of traditional religious structures. Various critics, beginning with the work of Carol Gilligan, Carol Christ and Judith Plaskow, and Alice Walker, have located this search for individual meaning for women to what bell hooks calls the "homeplace"; it is not just a house, but a space in which autonomous and receptive subjects live and interact. For women, recent critics have argued, spiritual meaning and identity may be found, as they are for traditional religious expressions, in relationship to various "others"—to other humans, to nature, and to the holy "other," but these meanings are expressed in forms that have been discredited in and ignored by the master narrative.

Significant spiritual relationships, for women, are not generally in the form of a one-on-one encounter with a holy "other." Women find themselves in a web of relations, each interdependent on the other, that must be negotiated daily. That negotiation reveals the presence of what women consider holy, and self-definition emerges from successful and ethical negotiation of these relationships, and also from the articulation of those negotiations in story. In *In A Different Voice*, Carol Gilligan says that for women, identity is defined within the context of relationship and judged by a standard of responsibility and care. Similarly, morality comes from the negotiation of the experience of connection (1-4; 150-174). In their introduction to *Weaving the Visions*, Carol Christ and Judith Plaskow agree. There is, they argue, the "pull to relation among women—relation particularly to others, to communities of origin and choice, and to a wider web of connectedness that encompasses the earth" (11). Thus, the experience of women is entangled and embedded.[2]

Alice Walker, in *In Search of Our Mother's Gardens: Womanist Prose*, argues that for women, and particularly for black women who have been denied access to "high" art forms by oppression, creativity and spirituality are expressed in everyday tasks and forms. Walker asks how a woman is to make known the "unknown thing" that is in her, either when the form to express it has not been invented or when she is denied access to the traditional forms of expression (233). Walker finds the representation of that "unknown thing" in a "living creativity," symbolized by her mother's garden. She argues that in the repetition of these acts of homemaking, generations of women recover their histories and find their identities and strengths: "Guided by my heritage of a love of beauty and a respect for strength—in search of my mother's garden, I found my own" (243).

This emphasis on connection, this privileging of the particular, and this valuing of a living creativity redefines spirituality for women. Carol Ochs, in *Women and Spirituality*, reminds us that spirituality traditionally has been associated with mysticism and located in an "otherworldly" space. That is, spirituality is associated with disconnection and dislocation, the seeking after ecstatic experience rather than the understanding of lived experience. Ochs argues that the daily routine of human existence and the working through of human pain can also open us to spiritual wholeness (3). If religion is insight into the common experiences of mankind, ecstatic experience is "the ordinary [becoming] the vessels of the extraordinary" (11). Thus, the "active, conscious, and deliberate process of coming into [relationship to our everyday experiences and reflections] is the beginning of spirituality" (3; 138).

Spirituality, therefore, is something that permeates all human activities and that is a process of transformation and growth; it is, as Ursula King puts it, "an exploration into what is involved in becoming human" (5). Building on Gilligan, Christ, and Walker's emphasis on context and on living creativity, King and Ochs argue that women's everyday experiences can be and are the "occasions for the disclosure of meaning" (5). Love,[3] work, and community are the central concerns of women's spirituality, but these concerns are explored and defined from the foundations up, beginning with and valuing the preparation of food, the making of clothing, the arrangement and maintenance of house space, the pain of childbirth, and other "women's work." Women's spirituality undercuts the idea of, to use Susan Glaspell's phrase, the "insignificance of kitchen things" (440). Like the women in Glaspell's story, "A Jury of Her Peers," in which two women come to understand why a woman murdered her husband through the evidence of a misplaced rocker, a half-cleaned kitchen table, and the nervousness in a missed stitch, the spirituality of homemaking has that "look of seeing into things, of seeing through a thing to something else" (446).

The attention and creativity, the "seeing through," required for fully living the everyday life become, in women's spiritual practice, therefore, modes of negotiating crisis and of bringing about recovery of the self and of community. Rawlings, we see, is not alone among either critics or writers in her concentration on the organization of private space as a form of spirituality. May Sarton's journal, *Recovering*, for example, explores the confluence of physical space and psychic space and the re-formation of both in time of illness. The issues of the journal, which is filled with photographs of Sarton's home, are those of solitude, writing, housekeeping, love, and recovery and the relationship of those. Similarly, Madeleine L'Engle's *Two-Part Invention: The Story of a Marriage*, is also the story of a house. L'Engle uses the symbol of the house to explore marriage, illness, and loss. Crosswicks, the name her mother gives the house, means "where two roads meet" and is "a symbol of family and community life" (3). L'Engle reminds us of the "deep rhythms" (231) of a house, which come from the convergence of physical structure with lived experience. In the details of the household are revealed the lives of those who people it. The position of the furniture reflects the relationships of the inhabitants; the decorations reveal the workings of the soul; and the order and disorder reveal the sense of community or its absence.

No one understands the intimacy and revelational power of homemaking better than Marjorie Kinnan Rawlings. Cross Creek, too, is a place of convergences. It is a meeting place of land, "a bend in a country road," and water, "the flowing of Lochloosa Lake into Orange Lake" (1). It is also the crossroads, the meeting, of the "house of language," the physical home, and the life of a woman (Davidson 169). At Cross Creek, Rawlings writes her self, in her work and in her home, and writes the relationships of the Creek residents; through this act, she comes to both self-understanding and to the acceptance of her place in the community and in nature. Rawlings' memoir, *Cross Creek*, is, like L'Engle's, the story of a house and, like Sarton's, the search for identity and community. Rawlings seeks, in *Cross Creek*, a definition of and relationship to the self that allows her to establish nurturing and intimate relationships with others and a space in which to conduct the relationship with the self and the "other." This definition, relationship, and space May Sarton calls solitude:

> If one does choose solitude it must be for a purpose other than mere self-seeking; the search for "identity" is a fashionable concept these days, but sometimes at least it looks like pure self-indulgence. How does one find one's identity? My answer would be through work and through love, and both imply giving rather than getting. Each requires discipline, self-mastery, and a kind of selflessness, and they are each lifetime challenges. (32-33)

Sarton's definition could be a textbook expression of the concerns of women's spirituality: the love, work, self-reflection, and discipline that lead to communion with self, other, nature, and the holy. These are the elements of spirituality and of homemaking in Marjorie Kinnan Rawlings' *Cross Creek*.

Initially, Rawlings goes to nature in search of distance and solitude, focusing on the connection to nature to define her spirituality. Like Thoreau in *Walden*, on which she models her Pulitzer Prize-winning memoir, Rawlings goes to the woods to "live deliberately and to front the essential facts," and she uses Thoreau's seasonal organization for the fundamental structure of her work. Nature provides for Rawlings, as it did for Thoreau, symbols of the spiritual and a process of reconnection both to the "other" and to the "self." Rawlings searches, like Thoreau, for the eternal, the good, and the beautiful—the constant and essential sources of life and of the holy that are an immanent part of the now, if we can see them. She brings to nature the human ethical imagination that reveals in the natural world a reference to and a commentary on human morals and existence.[4] She finds that "a [human being] may learn a deal of the general from studying the specific, whereas it is impossible to know the specific by studying the general. For that reason, our philosophers are usually the most unpractical of [people], while very simple folk may have a great deal of wisdom" (Rawlings, *Cross Creek* 359).

Rawlings' is not to be, however, a contemplative life. Living at Cross Creek, Rawlings quickly discovers, demands more than a relationship with the natural world. She finds herself involved in a group of complex relationships with Creek residents as she tries to make her farmhouse habitable and to make her orchard productive. These relationships force Rawlings, when she moves to Cross Creek, on Hawthorne, Route 1, Florida, and when she writes her memoir, to take Thoreau's second step to spiritual wholeness and to combine distance, what Sarton calls solitude, with an intimacy in her Creek life—intimacy not only with nature but with other human beings. Rawlings bought Cross Creek orchard and farm in 1928 and lived there for the rest of her life—first, alone for thirteen years following her divorce from Charles Rawlings and, later, after her marriage to Norton Baskin, on and off until her death in 1953.[5] Rawlings was farmer and orchard hand, as well as neighbor to a group of interesting and often contentious individuals. She creates an intimacy with nature, neighbor, and self that establishes a physical as well as a spiritual home.

Rawlings had a strong sense of the relationship of the human to place. She says that "much human unhappiness comes from ignoring the primordial relation of man to his background" (31), and, for her, Cross Creek was the context for her soul. This acceptance of a place brings with it both joy and terror, "for the joining of person to place, as of person to person, is a commitment to shared sorrow, even as to shared joy" (9). Rawlings commits to restoring her dingy and ramshackle farm house, to entering a web of relationships of Creek residents, and to writing that life in her fiction and her memoirs.

These commitments to land, house, and human beings, as well as to her own writing, create the themes of Rawlings' memoir early in the narrative. She shares with Thoreau an organization around the changing seasons, but Rawlings' journal is also organized around the theme of individuality and community and its unique balance at Cross Creek. She and her Creek neighbors, she says, require, above all, "a certain remoteness from urban confusion" (3) and a vital relationship to the earth: "We cannot live without the earth or apart from it, and something is shrivelled in man's heart when he turns away from it and concerns himself only with the affairs of men" (3). Cross Creek was a working farm, containing an orange grove, from which Rawlings made her living for a time, and livestock. Hence, Rawlings' relationship to nature is a combination of artistic delight and practical life. One beautiful example is Rawlings's deep pleasure in the magnolia tree she sees from the particular vantage point of her kitchen window every day as she works in her kitchen:

> The tree that has nourished me in lean times is still here and will be as long as I can protect it from everything short of lightning. It is not conspicuous when walking through the grove. It comes into its own from the west kitchen window beside the sink. The high window frames it, so that its dark glossy top is singled out for the attention of one standing there, washing dishes, preparing vegetables, rolling pie crust on the table under the window, putting a cake together. The sun sets behind it and is tangled in the branches. . . . I have been alone a long time, and the magnolia tree is still here. (30-31)

The convergence of housekeeping, the tree, and time of day open spiritual meaning for Rawlings. Rawlings' spiritual relationship to nature, therefore, is shaped by her immersion in it and by work. For Rawlings, the transcendent and the immanent are inextricably entwined, if not one. Thus, she moves toward the articulation of a moral and ethical structure that comes to terms with human suffering and loss through human action in the context of the creation.

The source of this structure is Martha Mickens, an old black woman who has lived at the Creek all her life and who welcomes Rawlings to the community. Martha's acceptance of Rawlings and Martha's drawing "aside a curtain and [leading Rawlings] in to the company of all those who loved the Creek and had been tormented by it" (19) makes her the presence who, to use Christ and Plaskow's term, "weaves the vision," both in the community and in the narrative:

> Old Aunt Martha Mickens, with her deceptive humility and her face like poured chocolate, is perhaps the shuttle that has woven our knowledge, carrying back and forth, with the apparent innocence of a nest-building bird, the most revealing bits of gossip; the sort of gossip that tells, not trivial facts, but human motives and the secrets of human hearts. Each of us pretends that she carries these threads only about others and never about us, but we all know better, and that none of us is spared. (5)

Though Rawlings herself comments in a letter to Max Perkins that Martha did not truly have the central role at the Creek that the memoir gives her, there is a moral and ethical reason to make Martha a center (*Letters* 209).[6] Rawlings uses Martha as a symbol of true individuality and of community. As an individual, Martha has no "residue," to use Rawlings' term. She is someone who has been sifted "through the great sieve of circumstance" (122) to the degree that only her essential self remains. Martha is one of the poor who have found through their experiences the "substratum of the world" (Albanese 170). They "have been put through the sieve and stand nakedly for what they are" (Rawlings 122). From an unexpected source, therefore, a poor black woman, flow freely the values and the qualities that are necessary for community.

In a sense, Martha is the Creek. Far from a Mammy figure, Martha possesses that aristocratic quality of the Creek residents, their dignity in the face of difficulty and their innate goodness, but also their individuality and essential aloneness. Martha and her family lived and worked at Cross Creek throughout Rawlings' life and after.[7] In her letters, Rawlings often complains of Martha (*Letters* 256), but theirs was a relationship that lasted from Rawlings' move to the Creek until her death. For Rawlings, Martha's essential quality is that she can see people for what they are and love them in their strengths and weaknesses. She represents loving the neighbor as the self, and, thus, she is the foundation of community at Cross Creek:

> When Old Martha Mickens shall march at last through the walls of Jericho, shouting her Primitive Baptist hymns, a dark rock at the core of the Creek life will have shattered to bits. She is nurse to any of us, black or white, who fall ill. She is midwife and layer out of the dead. She is the only one who gives advice to all of us impartially. She is a dusky Fate, spinning away at the threads of our Creek existence. (17)

Martha articulates and represents for Rawlings the relation of self to "other" and a sense of virtue that Rawlings explores throughout the rest of the book (*Letters* 170). The first component of that relation is the need to find one's place in the grove, in relationship to nature: "They was wild grove here as long back as tongue can tell. . . . And they'll be grove here right on, after you and me is forgotten" (Rawlings 21). Hearing Martha's statement, Marjorie articulates the second component: the need to struggle to define the self in the context of the cycle of life and death. Rawlings thinks that "if others could fight adversity, so might I" (21). The final component of relationship is that of love represented in Martha's presence as the supportive neighbor. On their first meeting, she tells Rawlings, "'I won't keep you . . . I jes' wanted to tell you I was here'" (21). Rawlings explores these three principles throughout the rest of her work.

Rawlings seeks to define a vital relationship to the world. Violence and death are part of life at Cross Creek, yet Rawlings does not find horror in death. When she begins her love affair with the Creek, Rawlings immerses herself in every part of its life. She hunts, though she admits that she does not enjoy the kill; she fishes, and she deals daily with snakes and other pests, with the illnesses of her animals, and the sickness and death of friends. She goes hungry in the early, lean years on the Creek. Violence and death frighten Rawlings: ". . . time frightens me, and I seek, like a lonely child, the maternal solace of timelessness" (243). Yet, she is able to subsume the ego and to overcome her fears. Realizing that the distance that is required for selfhood must be balanced with involvement with the "other," Rawlings seeks, not the reduction of the self that is called for in traditional spirituality, but participation: to join the earth.

To join the earth means loving the creation, accepting suffering and loss, but also struggling against the enemies of disease, poverty, and death. Rawlings has communion and community with nature. The whippoorwills call her one night to dance in the orange grove. She paints loving portraits of Jib, her cat and of Moe, her beloved Pointer, who is named after her dear, human friend Moe who died. She says of Old Joe, her mule, that he deserved to have companionship at his death because he was faithful and because they made their living together (339). Rawlings does not observe nature; she embraces it. George Bigelow contrasts Rawlings to Thoreau in this respect, saying that she does less "observing, classifying, cataloguing" than Thoreau and that she writes "more as a person determined to communicate personal experience" (36-37). Both nature and community are involved in this articulation. We must, Rawlings asserts, "hold tight to the earth and its abundance" (21), but, we must also hold tight to one another.

Mixed with Rawlings' "cosmic optimism" is an "earthy realism" (Bigelow 96). Rawlings has a deep communion and strong community with other human beings, and her relationship to other humans is, at once, both one with and in tension with her relationship to nature. She and her neighbors need the land for a sense of self. Rawlings believed that we are all born with an attachment to the earth and that the closer one's intimacy with the natural world, the fuller and happier one's life. Though strong and solitary individuals, however, the Creek inhabitants also need each other. Their intimacy is expressed materially, in a system of exchange, not verbally:

> We know one another. Our knowledge is a strange kind, totally without intimacy, for we go our separate ways and meet only when new fences are strung, or someone's stock intrudes on another, or when one of us is ill or in trouble, or when woods fires come too close, or when a shooting occurs and we must agree who is right and who must go to jail, or when the weather is so preposterous, either to heat or cold, or rain or drought, that we seek out excuses to be together, to talk together about the common menace. . . . And when the great enemies of Old Starvation and Old Death come skulking down on us, we put up a united front and fight side by side, as we fight the woods fires. (4-5)

The residents of the Creek, black and white, are woven into community by the tacit ethic of the Creek. Creek life is one of working with the cycles of nature, planting and harvesting. It is also one of sharing: of giving some of what you have to those less fortunate—money, food, and shelter. The union, she says, "is vital" (365).

Yet there is also tension. Life, says Rawlings is a balance and a battle "between the forces of destruction, between love and hate, between life and death" (364), both human and natural, and we must "fight on the side of the creative forces" (365). Human life is risky and uncertain, and that uncertainty is contained in Rawlings's understanding of God:

> We know that as human beings we are very stupid and that somewhere beyond us are forces unintelligibly wiser or cleverer or more fixed than we are. The forces may concern themselves with us or they may not, but it seems, to me . . . that people live or die, thrive or pine, quite beyond human reason. (70)

Given that death is inevitable, we must not seek reduction and separation; the forces of destruction reduce us enough and separate us in death. We must seek connection with and love one another in order to live well and to be whole. When Rawlings goes to her neighbor, Old Boss, whose wife is ill, she finds not the tyrant who controls the Creek, but a fragile human being whom she holds in her arms:

> I put out my hand to touch him. The next moment he had reached out his arms to me, and Old Boss was crying on my shoulder. I held his small old body close to me and was astonished by his frailty. He was not now the giver of laws, but a lonely little old man weeping for his beloved. I knew in that instant how fragile a defense are pride and authority against the common enemies.
>
> I thought, "How can any of us be cruel to one another? How are wars possible, and hate, when we must all face such things? Death is the enemy, and life itself is inimical, for all its bounty. We must hold one another close against the cosmic perils." (340)

Loving nature and loving human beings means the acceptance of the fact that while there might exist a Parmenidean oneness, we cannot know it. Human life is a continual coming to crossroads, change and loss, made meaningful by love and a commitment to struggle and to work.[8] To accept the cycle of life and death—in short, to accept and to honor mystery—and to act anyway is to develop the virtues and to define the character. To achieve contentment in life, under adverse circumstances, Rawlings says, "requires first an adjustment within oneself . . . and after that, a recognition that one is not unique in being obliged to toil and struggle and suffer. This is the simplest of all facts and the most difficult for the individual ego to accept" (19). Since human life is suffering and loss, we must struggle where we can and accept where we must:

> I am something of a fatalist, in that I believe in a fatalism that stems from one's own adjustment, or lack of it, to circumstance. The Chinese call this "luck character," and it is the same thing. (169)

Virtue is expressed and is represented in the work that we do, the effect that we have on the world while we are here: "We [at the Creek] know above all that work must be beloved" (365). Beauty and meaning are found in the combination of mind and muscle (Bigelow 124). In this combination, beauty is and is made real. Beauty exists and is created when and where we "join with the earth and [are] comforted" (Rawlings 8).

The most important example of this joining is the hospitality that Rawlings extends to guests at Cross Creek; the essential space is the table, and the essential activity is Rawlings' one vanity: her cooking. She tells us that her "vanity about [her] cooking is known and pandered to" (110) and that she is "a slave to any guest who praises [her] culinary art" (205-206). Rawlings continues: "For my part, my literary ability may safely be questioned as harshly as one wills, but indifference to my table puts me in a rage" (206). To be a good cook is to have science, art, and instinct (207); thus, cooking becomes a metaphor for homemaking, for life on the Creek.

The longest chapter in *Cross Creek* is called "Our Daily Bread," from the Lord's Prayer, and it both shares recipes and discusses cooking. Cooking links Rawlings to her mother and grandmother and makes them present in Rawlings' home; cooking was their "garden," to use Walker's phrase, theirs and Rawlings' "great art" (206). It also links Rawlings to the men and women of the Creek, who teach her recipes, and to the nation that read her book. In 1942, soon after *Cross Creek* was published, Rawlings published, by popular demand, *Cross Creek Cookery*, a cookbook and commentary on cooking and eating. The recipes in the volume are interspersed with stories about the Creek and about Florida in general, about where and from whom Rawlings learned a recipe, about the various members of the Creek community, and about Rawlings' own history, particularly with her mother.

The relationship to her mother is symbolized in the recipe that is lost forever—the recipe for her mother's watermelon cake. The cake brings back memories of Rawlings' fifth birthday and leads her to a speculation on the ingredients, the way to prepare the cake, and what it looked like. Rawlings says that her memory of its appearance and taste and speculation about its ingredients are enough; she will not make the cake herself: "I have never had the courage to try to make it, fearing adult disappointment. If it is as good as I remember it, it is worth a trial by any curious cook" (*Cookery* 155).

Memory, nostalgia, and need for community surround *Cross Creek Cookery*. This book prompted service men to write to Rawlings both complimenting her and complaining that her descriptions of food made them yearn for home. Women and men from around the country wrote to share memories of food and of people whom they loved who prepared special foods. Rawlings finds that food, its smell and taste and the ritual that surrounds its preparation, are part of memory, and that the desire for food, especially in a time of war, is a symptom of spiritual need:

> "Bless us," I thought, "the world must be hungry." And so it is. Hungry for food and drink—not so much for the mouth as for the mind; not for the stomach, but for the spirit . . . Country foods . . . have in them . . . the peace and plenty for which we are all homesick. (*Cookery* 2)

The preparation, serving, and enjoyment of food become the deepest source of Rawlings' spirituality. In "Our Daily Bread," Rawlings begins by comparing Fanny Farmer to a prayer book (207) and ends with how a disagreement over pilau, a meat and rice dish which, in this case, has the squirrels' eyes still in it, breaks up a prayer meeting (207).[9] Indeed, cooking becomes spiritual; it is the metaphor for the remaking of her personality, the establishment of her house at Cross Creek, and for community. Cooking in Florida makes Rawlings redefine cooking itself. The making of a foundational food, bread, and the matter of a foundational metaphor like "bread," have to be relearned and rethought in the context of the Creek and of her activities there. Rethinking "bread" becomes rethinking the self and the possibilities of the self. For example, "bread" to a Floridian is not white bread, which is not only disliked but disparaged, but cornbread (*Cookery* 19). The highest form of cornbread, on the hunt and the fishing trip, is the hush puppy: "Fresh-caught fried fish without hush puppies are as man without woman, a beautiful woman without kindness, law without policemen" (*Cookery* 28). Rawlings finds that making bread in its numerous varieties defines the community and can create sacred space anywhere. Her best rolls are made in a fish camp; they rise by the sun and are baked in a Dutch oven (212). Bread is not just filling for the body; it is, she says, "heart-warming" (*Cookery* 19). *Cross Creek Cookery* is a community volume, emphasizing the communal act of cooking and eating. Food is not appreciated simply for its taste; it becomes a part of memory and of self-understanding as where she serves it, to whom, and in what season are recounted. As Maggie Kilgour reminds us, taste is part of intimacy: "[As] a model for knowing, taste is not only the most basic and bodily way of making contact with the world outside of the individual but also the most intimate and intense way" (9). Rawlings emphasizes community and intimacy when she discusses serving meals. Rawlings serves meals in the context of her home and of nature, on the veranda of her house where her visitors can see both her pecan trees and her orange grove; in winter, she serves in the farmhouse by the fireplace. Hospitality, both the gracious preparation and serving of food and the gracious receiving of the gift of food, emerges as the supreme expression of spirituality. Rawlings returns to the metaphor of "our daily bread," writing:

> Two elements enter into successful and happy gatherings at table. The food, whether simple or elaborate, must be carefully prepared; willingly prepared; imaginatively prepared. And the guests—friends, family or strangers—must be conscious of their welcome. . . . The breaking together of bread, the sharing of salt, is too ancient a symbol of friendliness to be profaned.

She continues, emphasizing that table is a sacred space:

> At the moment of dining, the assembled group stands for a little while as a safe unit, under a safe roof, against the perils and enmities of the world. . . . The delight of friends and family in being together is the thing. (*Cookery* 217-218)

Cooking and hospitality become metaphors for spirituality and are moments of self-expression and self-understanding in the flux of existence. Made almost mythical in human memory, the memory of food shared and loved reveals the ritual dimension of cooking: that cooking is understanding proportion and creating order, the transformation of matter through work of the hands.

These recurrent ritual moments make the transience of existence meaningful as food and shared meals signify interdependence, community, and vulnerability (Kilgour 214-215). Spiritual openness and shared existence help Rawlings to negotiate the sense of sadness she feels facing her own mortality. As she contemplates, in spring, her pecan trees that were not supposed to bloom, but did, she thinks: "And the old comfort came, in the recurrence, and on the heels of the comfort, despair, that there was no end to seasons, but an end to me" (244). Love, work, and community, however, define her place within the cycle of creation and death:

> A knowledge brushed me as briefly as though a bird had flown past me from the tree. Lives are only one with living. How dare we, in our egos, claim catastrophe in the rise and fall of the individual entity? There is only Life, and we are beads strung on its strong and endless thread. (244)

That thread is what binds Rawlings to Cross Creek: "And after long years of spiritual homelessness, of nostalgia, here is that mystic loveliness of childhood again. Here is home. An old thread, long tangled, comes straight again" (8). As Rawlings writes her self in her memoir, she, ironically, gives up the pre-eminence of the individual; her life is working to see the "other" and to join the rhythm of the Creek:

> The universe breathed, and the world inside it breathed the same breath. This was the cosmic life, with suns and moons to make it lovely. It was important only to keep close enough to the pulse to feel its rhythm, to be comforted by its steadiness, to know that Life is vital, and one's own minute living a torn fragment of the larger cloth. (39)

Rawlings accepts her finitude. Thus, she can see and can love, like Martha, the self and the "other." Having located herself in the context of Cross Creek, her final act of attention is to the Creek, not to the human self. She does not claim ownership or cry out for attention.

Indeed, when faced with the question, "Who owns Cross Creek?," she recognizes that, to the creek, she is no more important than, but just as important as, the redbirds, the blue jays, and the black snake who lives under her bedroom. Creation and destruction are relative, she argues, and we cannot know the purposes of the creator. We can, however, and must, make our place here for the time that we are here: "Houses are individual and can be owned like nests, and fought for" (368), but the earth is not ours:

> It seems to me that the earth may be borrowed but not bought. It may be used, but not owned. It gives itself in response to love and tending, offers its seasonal flowering and fruiting. But we are tenants and not possessors, lovers and not masters. Cross Creek belongs to the wind and the rain, to the sun and the seasons, to the cosmic secrecy of seed, and beyond all, to time. (368)

We do not go our way, but the way of the spirit.

For Rawlings, the issue of community and solitude is at the center of her memoir. Rawlings both writes and lives Cross Creek.[10] For Rawlings, Cross Creek is the acceptance of loss and the definition of the self in relationship and over time to the "other"—to nature, to community, and to the holy—expressed in concrete activity in the home. Cross Creek fills a need that Rawlings has had since childhood, a need for reconnection:

> It is necessary to leave the impersonal highway, to step inside the rusty gate and close it behind. By this, an act of faith is committed, through which one accepts blindly the communion of beauty. One is now inside the grove, out of one's own world and in the mysterious heart of another. (8)

The grove is an earned Eden, worked with the hands and loved with the flawed human heart. Through her memoir, Rawlings gives us Cross Creek, to use her own words, with "deepness and intimacy and revelation" (*Letters* 195). Rawlings accomplishes Thoreau's desire: to explore the relationship between nature and human community. Her work also illustrates the aims of women's spirituality: to reveal and to mark the importance of the web of our interconnections and to join contemplation and action in a meaningful way.

In this, Marjorie Kinnan Rawlings finds spirituality to be compatible with, and emergent from, life in the world. Rawlings illustrates that solitude can exist with community, mind with body, and human with nature. She is able to envision an existence that reconciles the seemingly irreconcilable dualities that patriarchal definitions of masculine and feminine modes of being set forth as true and to find the expression of that existence in love and work.[11] Spirituality can mean that, in seeking the self, one has to exclude all "others," except the holy, in order to be. Rawlings shows us that, to paraphrase May Sarton, we cannot withdraw our selves or our love without damaging ourselves (Sarton 245). Her emphasis on homemaking reminds us that the "other world" is not our true home and that eternally seeking the gap, as Annie Dillard calls it, the ecstatic experience that becomes the space through which we may slip from this world into the "other, better" one may make us, at least, neglectful of the significance of kitchen things and, at worst, cruel.

Thus, Rawlings, through the idea and activity of homemaking, offers a challenge to the post modern idea that dislocation, despite its costs, offers the capacity to be able to speak about the universal. As Talal Asad, in *Genealogies of Religion*, reminds us, "all people most of the time are 'local' in the sense of being locatable" (8). He warns that the privileging of dislocation in post modernism can be another way to reinscribe categories that have been used to oppress "others":

> To say of people that they are local is to imply that they are attached to a place, rooted, circumscribed, limited. People who are not local are thought of either as displaced, uprooted, disoriented—or more positively as unlimited, cosmopolitan, universal, belonging to the whole world (and the world belonging to them).[12] (8)

Living her life in a rural community, Rawlings also offers a challenge to the post modern romance with the city, whether as an actual place or as a metaphor for the multiplicity of possibilities of identity choice and, potentially, formation.[13] The universal voice, dislocated in time and space, is, perhaps, only another name for Enlightenment reason that, ultimately, has failed to negotiate, in a meaningful way, the modern dilemma; multiplicity is possibly only another name for confusion and homelessness. The movement from the "meta-narrative" to the local narrative, to homemaking, offers a sense of self that is contextual. Rawlings, along with Sarton and the poet Adrienne Rich, suggests that home as a location is a space from which we can think about community and difference, self and other, simultaneously. Home does not mean homogeneity; "homeplace," as bell hooks defines it, is a space that celebrates and tolerates difference, that promotes relationships between complete selves, and that becomes a foundation for political action. Home is "the site of speaking, the place of a shared language and of meaning, the place to find a voice to speak for those who have no home or voice" (Davidson 176). Thus, homemaking, the attention to the details of physical and spiritual existence of both the self and the other, not only grounds us in reality but becomes an activity that allows us, at the same time, critically to examine it, as Rawlings says, in an attitude of love (365).

NOTES

1. *Selected Letters*, 34-35. These poems, published when Rawlings was a reporter for the Louisville *Courier-Journal* and the Rochester *Times-Union*, brought the writer great success.

2. Gilligan and Christ and Plaskow have been criticized for their "essentializing" of women's experience. They have been charged with reinscribing patriarchal definitions of woman's role, with separating women's experience from men's experience, and with applying results gained from poor methodology to all women. See, for example, "On *In a Different Voice*." Two things make Gilligan's and Christ and Plaskow's approach interesting to me: the emphasis on story and the idea of interdependence, imagined as a web. The connection, the formation of identity through story-telling is essential in postmodern thought. Toni Morrison's novels and criticism offer a significant example of the importance of story for the understanding and making of self. See her essay, "The Site of Memory." Connected to the importance of story is interdependence, which recognizes that we are bound to others and that we tell stories about relationality. Interdependence is an important element of the so-called "liberation" theologies of Martin Luther King, Gustavo Gutierrez, and others, and the image of the web and / or of a story woven is one that writers

like the Cherokee poet / essayist Marilou Awiakta use as a metaphor for understanding and writing the self in relationship to others. Nina Pelikan Strauss argues that, while Gilligan has limitations, her claim that "images and the narrations we use can destroy or create values" (288) and her belief that "the efficacy of ordinary communication . . . is a form of reciprocity" (291) offer a significant beginning towards feminist negotiation of the humanist tradition.

3.   By love, I mean what theologian Dorothee Soelle says when she talks about sexuality and love. In *To Work and to Love*, she says that love has four dimensions: wholeness (to be multidimensional and to make the integration of our physical, psychical, intellectual, aesthetic, emotional, and spiritual potencies), trust (to have a home for oneself with others), ecstasy (to love the other, both human and holy, and to risk the self in that love), and solidarity (to know others, to take seriously the inseparability of love and justice and of the public and the private, and to understand the political dimensions of eros and agape) (144).

4.   George E. Bigelow notes how Rawlings conceives nature in terms of personality and beauty in terms of character and adds that her work "might have been written by Thoreau or one of the other transcendentalists with ethical imagination" (84).

5.   See Silverthorne, 56. Cross Creek, purchased by Rawlings and her first husband, Charles Rawlings, consisted of 74 acres, an eight-room farmhouse, a tenant house, a barn, and orange, pecan, grapefruit, and tangerine trees. Rawlings purchased the farm for $9,000.

6.   The critics record Rawlings' notes: see, for example, Silverthorne, 66-67 and Bigelow, 142-143.

7.   In her will, Rawlings provided the tenant home and a weekly income to Martha for life. See Silverthorne, 352.

8.   Bigelow says that Rawlings believed that "The secret of human happiness is to commit oneself in love to that portion of the earth with which one can feel a bond of harmony, and this will

flood life with joy and give strength to withstand whatever adversities life might bring" (126-127).

9.   For the relationship of food to spirituality, see, for example, Louis Bouyer: "To recognize the sacredness of a meal as being the highest form of human activity is to recognize man's total dependence, both for his creation and his continued existence, upon a God who is at the same time apprehended as the one who possesses the fullness of life" (84).

10.   I am indebted to my Women's Spirituality class, Louisiana State University, Spring 1992, for this formulation.

11.   For two excellent lists of the oppositions, see Sheila Ruth, 47; 126.

12.   In other words, if dislocation is privileged, two extremes can appear. Either the dislocated (universal) may be able to use the discourse of authority to determine what "difference" is and therefore continue to reconstruct itself in its own terms by this self-defined difference. Or the privileged dislocated can argue that there is no difference: that "all human beings live in the same cultural predicament. . . . Everyone is dislocated; no one is rooted. Because there is no such thing as authenticity, borrowing and copying do not signify a lack [in the self]. On the contrary, they indicate . . . creative human agency" (9-10). Either position may become tyrannical.

13.   For an excellent critical study of postmodern ideas about the city, see Robins. He explores the possibilities of multiplicity and identity formation even as he argues that the new urban ideal is a Romantic form that "seems to want a cozy and cleaned-up version of city life, one which avoids the real conflicts and stresses of urban life" (321).

WORKS CITED

Albanese, Catherine. *Nature Religion in America: From the Algonkian Indians to the New Age.* Chicago: U of Chicago P, 1990.

Asad, Talal. *Genealogies of Religion: Discipline and Reasons of Power in Christianity and Islam.* Baltimore: The Johns Hopkins UP, 1993.

Awiakta, Marilou. *Selu: Seeking the Corn Mother's Wisdom.* Golden, CO: Fulcrum Publishing, 1993.

Bigelow, George E. *Frontier Eden: The Literary Career of Marjorie Kinnan Rawlings.* Gainesville: UP of Florida, 1966.

_____ and Laura V. Monti, eds. *Selected Letters of Marjorie Kinnan Rawlings.* Gainesville, UP of Florida, 1983.

Bouyer, Louis. *Rite and Man: Natural Sacredness and Christian Liturgy.* Trans. M. Joseph Costello, S.J. Notre Dame: U of Notre Dame P, 1963.

Christ, Carol P. and Judith Plaskow, eds. *Weaving the Visions: New Patterns in Feminist Spirituality.* San Francisco: Harper and Row, 1989.

Davidson, Harriet. "Adrienne Rich's Politics and Poetics of Location." *Contemporary Poetry Meets Modern Theology.* Eds. Anthony Easthope and John O. Thompson. Toronto: U of Toronto P, 1991. 166-76.

Gilligan, Carol. *In a Different Voice: Psychological Theory and Women's Development.* Cambridge: Harvard UP, 1982.

Glaspell, Susan. "A Jury of Her Peers." *Murder Without Tears: An Anthology of Crime.* Ed. Will Cuppy. New York: Sheridan House, 1942. 433-57.

hooks, bell, and Cornel West. *Breaking Bread: Insurgent Black Intellectual Life.* Boston: South End Press, 1991.

Jones, Cheslyn, Geoffrey Wainwright, and Edward Yarnold, eds. *The Study of Spirituality*. New York: Oxford UP, 1986.

Kilgour, Maggie. *From Communion to Cannibalism: An Anatomy of Metaphors of Incorporation*. Princeton: Princeton UP, 1990.

King, Ursula. *Women and Spirituality: Voices of Protest and Promise*. University Park, PA: The Pennsylvania State UP, 1993.

L'Engle, Madeleine. *Two-Part Invention: The Story of a Marriage*. New York: HarperCollins, 1989.

Morrison, Toni. "The Site of Memory." *Inventing the Truth: The Art and Craft of Memoir*. Ed. William Zinsser. Boston: Houghton Mifflin, 1987. 101-24.

Ochs, Carol. *Women and Spirituality*. Totwah, NJ: Rowan and Allanheld, 1983.

"On *In a Different Voice*: An Interdisciplinary Forum." *Signs* 11:21 (Winter 1986): 304-33.

Rawlings, Marjorie Kinnan. *Cross Creek Cookery*. New York: Charles Scribner's Sons, 1942.

_____. *Cross Creek*. New York: Macmillan / Collier, 1987.

Robins, Kevin. "Prisoners of the City: Whatever Could a Postmodern City Be?" *Space and Place: Theories of Identity and Location*. Eds. Erica Carter, James Donald, and Judith Squires. London: Lawrence and Wishart, 1993. 303-30.

Ruth, Sheila. *Issues in Feminism: An Introduction to Women's Studies*. Mountain View, CA: Mayfield Publishing Company, 1990.

Sarton, May. *Recovering: A Journal*. New York: W.W. Norton, 1980.

Silverthorne, Elizabeth. *Marjorie Kinnan Rawlings: Sojourner at Cross Creek*. Woodstock, NY: The Overlook Press, 1988.

Soelle, Dorothee. *To Work and to Love: A Theology of Creation.* Philadelphia: Fortress Press, 1984.

Strauss, Nina Pelikan. "Rethinking Feminist Humanism." *Philosophy and Literature* 14 (October 1990): 284-303.

Walker, Alice. *In Search of Our Mother's Gardens: Womanist Prose.* San Diego: Harcourt Brace Jovanovich, 1983.

18

Guest to New York City

Cheryl Fish

Can you sleep inside my elbow?
That's where I'll put you.
My apartment is very small.

Man on the Terrace

The man on his terrace
doesn't see me

on the 35th floor he can't place
my dulcimer, gesturing

River's out there, he's rocking
drops his novel

My window overlooks a place to touch
every building a monument
but will we keep them?

Inside, a piping jig
from independent public radio
I called in my pledge today

Terrace man goes inside
who is there with him?
How easy it seems, to share a home

Roofs across the glance hold gardens
vacated factories
Empire State's needle-in-camera
sharp shooting in the wild, wild East

Slowly he rocks
I want my passage delivered

Why is it silent on the blue-grey pier
changing color with that angle of sun?

Who is the one against, across?
Stranger in the elevator carries food,
a child, address book underlined.
Our boundaries start and stop, on terraces.
Each day relinquishes intangible lives.

19

Jewish Women in the Diaspora

Gabriele Kreis

Translation and Introduction by
Ingeborg Majer O'Sickey

Introduction

The selection translated on page 269, "Jewish Women in the Diaspora," is an edited excerpt of a chapter from Gabriele Kreis's 1984 study, *Frauen im Exil* [*Women in Exile*]. For this book Kreis researched the expatriation of more than thirty Jewish women who fled from the wide destructive swath the Nazis cut across Jewish communities in many parts of Europe. She visited the women in their homes in exile in New York, Zürich, Los Angeles, and Ascona. There she spoke to them about their early years in the Diaspora.[1]

A survey of the literature written about Jewish exiles during the 1930s creates the impression that women were simply supporting actresses to their leading men. Kreis's is the first study that takes Jewish women in exile as its object. Her book's subtitle, *Fiction and Reality*, refers to her method of contrasting the actual lives of Jewish women in exile to portraits as they appear in the novels by male authors, such as Lion Feuchtwanger's Anna Trautwein in *Exile*, Bruno Frank's Susanna Rotteck in *The Passport*, Hans Habe's Nora Geldern in *Across the Border*, and Gustav Regler's Lisbeth in *Crossfire*. The women that we meet in these novels live through their husbands or lovers and derive their identity from the reflections they find in the eyes of men. They are portrayed as dependent, helpless, psychologically feeble childwomen; or, they are painted as voracious temptresses, who devour men in their quest to fulfill their narcissistic desires; or, they are characterized as whimpering, self-sacrificing handmaidens to their mates, convinced "of the overwhelming significance of his personage and works" (25). However various the authors' images of women in exile, they are always accessories to the male lead.[2]

Kreis calls her research for *Women in Exile* "Spurensuche," or "search for traces." "Traces," however, is somehow inadequate as a translation of *Spuren*. The semantic range of *Spuren* is vast; it resonates with "marks," "signs," and "imprints." *Spurensuche* also locates itself in the metaphoric field of *footsteps*: Kreis's book re-traces the women's early years in exile, re-marking the imprints they have left. Kreis describes their accomplishments oxymoronically: colossal and quotidian at once. Kreis's *Spurensuche* results in a colorful tapestry that, however disparate its individual strands, nevertheless reveals a pattern: while there is no typical Jewish woman emigrant, of course, there are many similarities in the ways Jewish women faced the challenges of life in the Diaspora. Reading Kreis's conversations with these women leaves us with a tremendous respect: respect for their enormous energy and their will to survive; respect for their determination to learn the languages of the countries they adopted as their refuge; respect for their ability to cross class lines, for enduring "downward mobility" in order to ensure that their husbands could continue to engage in the practice of philosophy or literature; respect for their determination not to let their privileged upbringing and education block them from taking any job at all in order to keep themselves and their family from starving; and respect for the way they combined creativity with practicality in order to forge a materially secure existence for themselves and their families.

But also this reaction: some readers may come away from reading about the emigrants' accomplishments with impatience (as I did) for the way most of them tolerated generally demanding, rigid, whiny and often burdensome husbands or lovers. As Gabriele Kreis emphasizes, her interviews with the women reveal that becoming independent and self-reliant did not grow out of their conscious desire for emancipation but was the result of the need for survival in the Diaspora. Role reversals of traditional husband-wife relationships were common. One has to wonder whether these women would have so radically refashioned their identities had their husbands continued in their traditional roles as providers and heads of family. Many readers of these testimonies may feel bewilderment to read that decades later, speaking of the changes they made, most women still justify their husband's behavior and shield them from criticism.

Clearly, not all husbands and lovers were incapable or undesirous of adapting to the new circumstances. Elsbeth Weichmann's husband is a case in point. But Mr. Weichmann was an exception. The comparison of the women's success in forging new existences in exile with their husbands' unwillingness and / or inability to contribute equally, compels me to ask whether the fact that these women were always already expatriated in "their" home country was decisive to their ability to re-make themselves. Margot Ruben, cited in the essay that follows, believes that

> It was so much easier for women to adjust. They accepted any kind of work. And also, because they were women, they were used to menial work anyway. For the men this was often much more difficult. For them these kinds of jobs meant a social degradation. Women just feel more responsible that the daily things are taken care of.

Hers seems an intuitively acceptable answer. "Social degradation" is, one could argue, something women are used to. But there are degrees and kinds of social degradation, mostly class-based ones, of course. When one looks at the professions many of the women trained for (lawyer, architect, poet, journalist), and when one understands that many of them came from upper middle-class families, it becomes clear how enormously privileged they had been before they became exiles.

The reasons for the women's willingness and / or ability to adjust to a new culture may not have to do with the fact that they were used to social degradation in the sense of having to perform menial work. For this kind of work was done by their more oppressed sisters: maids, cleaning women, laundresses. Perhaps the answer to questions about their ability to adjust in the foreign cultural and linguistic zones had to with the reality that they did not experience "their" German culture as their own before being *expatriated*. Shari Benstock's remarks illuminate the point I wish to make:

> For women, the definition of patriarchy already assumes the reality of expatriate *in patria*; for women, this expatriation is internalized, experienced as an exclusion imposed from the outside and lived from the inside in such a way that the separation of outside from inside, patriarchal dicta from female decorum, cannot be easily distinguished. (20)

I suggest that it may have been easier (not less painful, however) for women to leave a culture they did not experience as produced by them and belonging to them; I suggest that it may have been easier for women to leave a country where they did not have equal status with men, to let go of social power they derived solely through association with men, that is, primarily through fathers and husbands.

This speculation leads me to another question which must be asked: does the women's willingness and / or ability to learn new languages bespeak the way they had been socialized as borrowers rather than forgers / owners of language? I suggest that the overshadowing *nom du père*, which for many women represents a cultural *"non"* du père, recedes into the background for women who communicate in a foreign language. Speaking a foreign language, a language that did not directly articulate the feminizing and imprisoning messages internalized from infancy, may have been liberating. As an expatriate since the age of nineteen, who has lived in four different language zones outside Germany, the country of my birth, I find this explanation convincing. Conversely, it may follow that the fact that the husbands (especially the intellectuals) often refused to learn the language of their chosen exile, and refused to write in the foreign language, betokened that they experienced German as *their* language. It may also follow that the fact that the husbands often desperately clung to the culture they had lost, betokened that they experienced *their* culture unmediated; I am well aware of the risks and the cruel irony such a proposition entails.

One final word. When I first read Kreis's book I felt that it was important that the stories of the Jewish women should be published not only in their former homeland, but in their country of refuge as well. Many of the women Kreis spoke with were very elderly, and I was eager to translate their stories so that the Jewish women living in the diaspora could see that their history was not buried. I am therefore very pleased to offer a small part of their history in these pages.

[Editors' note: While Gabriele Kreis's essay does not deal directly with women *writers*, we think it provides a significant contribution to *Homemaking*. "Jewish Women in Exile" contrasts real women with their representations in novels written by men; the essay shows how Jewish women fashioned new and workable partnerships with their husbands and lovers in exile, often shielding the men from the difficulties of work-a-day life. Kreis describes her essay as a "search for traces," an exploration of the buried stories of Jews in exile. Whether these women were themselves writers, or whether they worked at menial jobs to allow their men the time and energy to write, all of them created, through imagination and hard work, home in an unfamilar environment.]

Jewish Women in the Diaspora

The small heroic actions of the Jewish women in the Diaspora should not be forgotten. And I'm not only talking about the actions of the wives of well-known intellectuals but of the many unknown women who emigrated. They have done more than is known. In these difficult times they learned to become independent, self-sufficient. And it was often with a great sense of humor that they took up the fight for their families' and their own survival.

Elsbeth Weichmann and I sit in her apartment in Hamburg. It is Spring 1983. Exactly fifty years before, she had been forced to leave Germany. In 1933, together with her husband—he was later to become the mayor of Hamburg—she fled first to Czechoslovakia, then to France and finally in 1940, after the Germans invaded that country too, to the U.S.

I look around me: generously sized rooms with plenty of space for books and people; furniture that tells stories. It's hard for me to imagine that these stories don't begin until 1948—the year after their return from New York.

Eighteen years of exile. That means: eighteen years of fear and anxieties; eighteen years of fear of persecution; ousted: tracking from country to country; worries about where the next meal would come from; an acute sense of social degradation and displacement; the loss of familiar surroundings and of one's own language. The life of the emigrant is a life at the precipice of an abyss: it is a life of contingencies.

I had asked her on the telephone whether she wanted to talk to me about her years in exile. "Of course!" she had answered, and: "should my husband be there?" I had told her no, that I'd like to speak to her alone. And explaining my reasons, I told her that I was interested in the lives and accomplishments of the women who lived in exile. I told her that since these were the buried stories, I was looking for lost traces and wanted to preserve them; that I wanted to know about the everyday life in exile. She liked my plan. More than that: she said that it was long overdue. We made a date and then we met. When I arrived she quickly came to the point:

I know about the many, let's say, not famous women, who managed their emigration creatively and independently. One friend, whose husband—he was an intellectual—couldn't adapt, turned a talent she had for drawing into their livelihood. She hand-painted blouses and hired another woman to sell them. Another friend opened a dry cleaners and used her capable hands to cut cost by doing the work herself. She got her husband, who had become helpless in the U.S., to take in the dirty clothes and work at the cash register.

I had heard similar stories from all the women emigrants with whom I had spoken in the last three years. I had talked to over thirty women and each one told of the women's energy and their will to survive. They all told of creative entrepreneurship and unconventional ways to land a job. Women with all sorts of backgrounds: intellectuals and non-intellectuals, famous and unknown women. For instance: the lawyer Ruth Fabian worked as a waitress and ran a newspaper clipping service; the journalist Charlotte Beradt colored hair; the singer Hilda Bondy sewed gloves; the poetess Vera Lachmann cleaned houses; the jurist Gisela Graf repaired zippers; the actress Elisabeth Viertel-Neumann gave courses teaching make-up techniques; the philologist Hertha Haas became a nurse; the writer Lili Körber sewed brassieres; the drama and theater scholar Elisabeth Freundlich took courses in library science.

These are some of the women in exile. They told stories about themselves and other women. Elisabeth Freundlich: "I knew a wealthy woman who was very interested in painting and who collected paintings. In exile she worked as a domestic and had to become interested in how many paintings she had already dusted. . . ".

"And you, Mrs. Weichmann, what did you do?"
"Oh," she smiles, "I had so many jobs. . . ."

In France she and her husband operated a news agency that supplied eleven newspapers with news items. Compared to other emigrants they lived well. But this changed once they arrived in America:

That's when were we really began at the bottom. The difficulties were these: you introduced yourself and said, "this is what I learned in Europe, this is what I did"; and they said "you're too qualified, we don't have any jobs for people like you." And when we asked for jobs in inferior positions, they asked about our American work experience.

Later Elsbeth Weichmann trained as a statistician because it was easier to find a job with an American diploma. She began working in all kinds of offices: once she was hired by a State farm for "sinful girls." Her job was to gather data that would document the successes of the State's reeducation program. Another job consisted of typing bills and tabulating long columns of numbers. Her husband, who at first wrote for the German-language paper *Aufbau*, retrained to work as a tax consultant.

From journalist to typist. I ask her whether she suffered from this downward move. "No," she answers, "I took things with a certain calmness because I told myself that it's I who has to adjust to America, not the other way 'round. I said to myself that now I'll have to learn the American way of life, learn how to get along with the people, and learn to relate to the childish ways the girls have that work here, and if I can do that, I believed, then I'd get closer to the people in that country. And I managed to do it in the end."

Elsbeth Weichmann was successful. She was promoted to the position of manager of a division in the Rockefeller Foundation in New York. After the war, the office relocated to Washington and she had to look for work again:

> By that time I had become so bored with American office life that I went out and bought six machines for sewing fur—I had met a fur dealer and since sheep-skins were cheap at the time I had the idea that I could make toy animals out of them. I asked myself, why not do something with my hands for a change. . . ?

Indeed, why not? But it was a question that didn't readily occur to these women's husbands. In a retrospective comment about his life in American exile, Ernst Bloch writes:

> At first we lived in the country, then in New York, and later in Cambridge near Boston. I was happy to be able to write uninterruptedly in German, in a language that no one spoke around here and that therefore could not be trivialized. I wrote in a scientific and philosophical language. While I worked day and night my wife supported me. In this way I was not exactly

a model of masculinity in the American sense. "If your husband can't earn any money here," an American once asked my wife, "why doesn't he change jobs? To work means to make money and if he doesn't make any doing philosophy, he should do something else!" But I could not do anything else. Anyway, I didn't speak English . . . what should I have done? Become a dishwasher?

This notion was unthinkable to his wife, too. In the first place her Ernst had "two left hands," as she put it, and in the second place, he had more important things to do than worry about the survival of his family. She would never have permitted this "exceptional philosopher" to do anything else but philosophize. Whether an interlude as a dishwasher would have had a negative influence on Ernst Bloch's work, we'll never know. Karola Bloch, for her part, did everything to keep distractions from her husband and his work. There was no job that the highly accredited architect Karola Bloch would not have taken. She worked as a waitress and, unsuccessfully, as an insurance agent before she finally landed a position in her field.

The actress Dorothea Gottfurcht had similar experiences. In 1933, she and her writer-husband Fritz Gottfurcht emigrated to Paris and in 1935 they went on to London. She recalls:

My husband, who couldn't speak a word of English at that time, found the first years in emigration very difficult, especially in financial terms. In Paris I had learned to sew leather gloves, to cut them and design them. At first I only began with this work reluctantly. But after I received a work permit for this unusual profession I became successful quite rapidly. Very soon I had contracts with the large fashion houses and I employed a number of seamstresses.

Fritz Gottfurcht wrote cabaret programs for the "Free German Cultural Organisation," of which he was a founding member. Since he was not paid for this activity, it was up to his wife to support them with her earnings.

The literary scholar and critic Margot Ruben, too, worked for the poet's Karl Wolfskehl and her own survival. She tutored students in Latin in New Zealand. There is no doubt: without her income, Wolfskehl—forty years her senior—would not have survived the time in exile. Even then, his assessment of her role lacks generosity:

> I don't know many people, and of course even fewer with
> whom I have interests in common. But, as you know, I am not
> alone here, of course. My time for dictation is extremely
> limited, the girlfriend Margot, who is tied to her work as a
> language teacher and similar things, can barely grant me more
> than two mornings of her time. She does this sweetly and
> faithfully, but the amount that has to be crammed into these
> hours!

What had to be crammed into them is his correspondence and his
literary work. In the morning Margot Ruben was at the typewriter as his
secretary. At noon she was in the kitchen cooking their meal. In the
afternoon she tutored students to earn money.

In 1943 she separated from Wolfskehl. She writes in her
memoirs:

> Wolfskehl was older and had become less self-sufficient, he
> needed a regulated daily routine and I couldn't give it to him
> any more. "Margot has left me," he wrote in one letter. He
> didn't want to see, in fact, he couldn't see, reality . . . and as
> a poet he had every right to this. He had to be surrounded by
> his own world, people with his kind of temperament, he had
> to create his own ambience in order to live in a dignified way.

She needed much less in order to live with dignity. When, in 1979, I
accidently ran into her in the Literature Archives in Marbach, she gave
me her interpretation of the reasons why:

> It was so much easier for women to adjust. They accepted any
> kind of work. And also, because they were women, they were
> used to menial work anyway. For the men this was often much
> more difficult. For them these kinds of jobs meant a social
> degradation. Women just feel more responsible that the daily
> things are taken care of.
> That's the way it is.

How deeply ingrained this feeling of responsibility is, is revealed in
some articles that appeared in the few women's magazines that were
published in exile. Karola Bloch and her colleague Friedel Brandeis, for
instance, wrote an article titled "How Can I Best Reorganize My
Apartment?" in which they give advice on how to optimize the small

space of a one-room-emigrant apartment. Other articles give hints on how to make a delectable dinner out of practically nothing; still others provide information about what sort of jobs offered a good income. Even fashion advice could be found in these magazines. Erna Muller, for example, wrote in the magazine *Woman* that was published in Paris: "I recommend a Bolero type jacket for this problem because it is especially elegant. A woman with a slender figure can make her waist and hips seem even smaller and the jacket creates the impression of lightheartedness, something we are all in need of in these times."

These accounts are moving and awe-inspiring; up to now they have been buried in the archives. In my research of the existing narratives about life in exile, exile means a "man's world." Women, with the exception of Anna Seghers, are depicted only as "the woman at his side." That without the women "most of our great authors would have perished in exile" as Alfred Kantorowicz puts it, is usually not mentioned. One of the few self-conscious men, Kantorowicz wrote in his autobiographical text *Everyday Reality in Exile*:

> The day began promising. For a week now his brave and attractive young wife had a temporary job in an office. They gave her documents to type. Yesterday she was paid an advance and she left him ten francs on the night table before she went to work—for the night—as he cynically commented. It was already after nine o'clock. With a bad conscience he jumped out of bed.

This kind of self-criticism is the exception. The norm is rather like this:

> She stuck it out it for two years. One day was worse than the next and one night worse than the following. In those two years she became a parody of the earlier Anna, but she didn't let herself go, she stuck it out. Now she can't go on any longer. And now she doesn't want to anymore. Almost with pleasure she feels her energy drain. She had put up an artificial facade and behind it is a woman who is helpless, incapable of action, crying, disintegrating.

The woman is Anna Trautwein. Her creator, Lion Feuchtwanger. The text cited here comes from Feuchtwanger's novel *Exile*. Her daily fight for survival for herself and her husband, the composer Sepp Trautwein, who has neglected his family and profession for his political activities, has finally eaten Anna Trautwein up. She kills herself by turning on the gas on the stove. For her husband her death becomes a personal and artistic catharsis. He finally composes his masterpiece—in honor of Anna: "Because suffering makes only the strong stronger, the weak, on the other hand, it makes weaker."

I ask Elsbeth Weichmann whether she knows Feuchtwanger's novel. No, she says, there wasn't time to read such books. I tell her the story. She listens attentively. I ask her whether Anna Trautwein's life could be seen as typical for the lives of women in exile. Without hesitation, she says

> No. This is the typical life of a woman who is able to give up everything for another but who isn't able to find her way back to herself. Of course, there were some women who lived like this. But as far as I can remember, the majority of the women were able to manage their own and their husband's life. They did it either by leaving their husband or they created a different kind of partnership.

I'd heard many such statements from other women I talked to during my search for the traces of their lost history. I didn't find their stories in the novels of exile. These emigrants were not lost without their husbands, as Anna Trautwein was. They were women who took on whatever work there was in order to feed themselves and their families; women who could deal with the realities of exile and who managed to adjust to it; women who faced the challenge of life in exile with courage and optimism; women whom we need to ask about their lives to get the real story. Questions like, how was it really back then? Why did you emigrate? With whom? What were the circumstances in which you lived and worked? How did you manage the deprivations, the change of your social position? Love and life in exile—how did the two work together?

In *After Midnight, a Novel about Life in Exile*, Irmgard Keun's heroine Susanna "solves" the question of love and life in exile by reverting to deception: "I have to seem weaker than I am so that he can feel strong and so that he can love me." One thing is clear: the women in exile were able to adjust to the changed circumstances more easily than the men. For many women it meant their first attempt at independence; often it meant that they had to leave their husbands so that they could survive.

Women who formerly provided care and emotional support for their families had to make drastic changes to enlarge their traditional spheres of responsibility. But it would be a mistake to see this as an emancipatory act; after all, the role change with their husbands was forced by the pressures of the new reality of life in exile. Still, as many emigrants pointed out to me, countless possibilities for shaping a new identity opened up for them. Elsbeth Weichmann summarizes:

> What remains in the end is the achievement. A certain satisfaction that one has faced a challenge and that one has managed it well. Because most of these women were middle-class women, who had led a fairly satisfying life as the Mrs. to their Mr. They found their own strengths within themselves and by mobilizing them, they created truly equal partnerships with their husbands.

I ask Elsbeth Weichmann how the men liked these changes in their wives. "Well, yes," she says, "I think that they were very happy about it since they suddenly needed them."

Charlotte Beradt, when I asked her the same question some years ago, had a different answer: "these German gentlemen, with their doctorates, well, they sat at home and were depressed and didn't understand the world any more." The truth, I would say, lies somewhere in the middle. And we can find it between the lines of the novels of exile.

In a period of the loss of all values, a woman remained for the man what she had always been: a social and emotional place to escape to. Klaus Mann calls a woman "the home in exile." 'Home' here doesn't only mean comfort, trust in another, and love; it also means common experiences, the same language and similar cultural backgrounds. And this is the way that one can look at the literary image of the woman in exile: Anna Trautwein emerges as the reminder of a time in which the men were strong and the women weak. At least at first glance. . . . The reminder points to a reaction to life in exile; it points to the real and the fictional place that women have in it. It's a dangerous place—an ejection seat into an erased past.

NOTES

1. Most exiles stayed in their country of exile. An exception is Elsbeth Weichmann, who with her husband returned to Hamburg after the war.

2. An exception is Klaus Mann's Marion von Kammer in his novel, *The Vulcano*: ". . . intelligent and very independent she seems an anomaly in the series of women who are defined through their relationships to men. She is one of the few strongly defined women in the literature about exile. We have to thank a homosexual man for this. Klaus Mann describes a strong woman, free from the experiences of the traditional man-woman relationship" (25).

WORK CITED

Benstock, Sheri. "Expatriate Modernism." *Women's Writing in Exile*. Eds. Mary Lynn Broe and Angela Ingram. Chapel Hill and London: U of North Carolina P, 1989.

Home

Velina Hasu Houston

Whenever I travel to Hawai'i or to any other destination that requires me to be in an international airport terminal, a certain experience occurs. It is both sociological and political in nature. A recent trip to Honolulu provides an excellent example. As I checked my baggage at Los Angeles International Airport, a young woman standing behind me in line kept smiling at me as if we shared a special, unifying covenant. I smiled at her, perhaps out of a sense of fragmented community for, in a way, she was like me. She was clearly Amerasian, a mixture of Asian and American (usually non-Asian) ethnicities. (The term was coined by Pearl S. Buck to refer to children born of World War II liaisons or marriages between native Japanese women and American military men.) Encouraged, the young woman then smiled even more broadly and, as if I would automatically share her relief at leaving behind the ethnic whiteness of the U.S. mainland for the colorful ethnic polyglot of Hawai'i, asked, "Going home?" For a moment, I did not answer and she quickly assumed the affirmative. "Me, too," she said. "I'm from Pearl City. Are you from Oahu, too?"

She looked surprised when I told her that I was not from Hawai'i at all. Perplexed, she declared, "But you look so local." ("Local" is the term that citizens of the state of Hawai'i used to refer to resident persons of mixed race.) I thanked her for recognizing my multiethnicity and admitted that I felt "at home" in Hawai'i because its ethnic diversity included so many multiethnic persons. In addition, I noted that people from various [foreign] countries—usually South Pacific or Latin—tell me that I look local to their respective regions. She understood. She, too, knew. It was a circumstance of looking like "everybody's exotic other." In other words, I am a chameleon. To the worldly eye, sometimes I look South American, sometimes Polynesian. This is because each of those cultures historically has included persons of mixed ethnic ancestry. My airport friend said that I was lucky for looking like I belonged in many places. Maybe. But it also means that "home" does not exist. It means that I am not truly "local" to any place.

On that same trip, inside the jet as it headed toward Hawai'i, an African American couple stared at me as if I were a new and interesting exhibit in a zoo. I smiled at them and they smiled back, summoning the courage to have a conversation with me. "Headed home?" they asked. They were mistaking me for a Polynesian. I pondered whether or not I ever "head home" in that ethnocultural vein that the nature and context of such questions imply. Where, after all, does an Amerasian go? To Japan? To America? To neither, or both?

A Japanese can (at least physically) go home to Japan. A European American can go home to America. A Mexican can go home to Mexico, the Irish to Ireland, and so on and so forth. As an Amerasian who is native Japanese, Blackfoot Indian, and African American, I am without the luxury of state ("home"). I am, however, often besieged by the politics of many nations or communities that want me to adopt a narrow categorical identity. To adopt just one, however, eradicates my true identity, my multiethnicity, which means compromising my ethnic integrity. This is not a compromise that I am willing to make. Many do. I, however, cannot pretend to be what I am not.

Often when people hear the word "home," they think of home as a physical site, a building in which things can be collected to mark it as one's exclusive territory. They also may think of it as an individual country, state, city, or community. On the basis of ethnic, cultural, economic, religious, sexual similarities or on the myth of a homogeneous national identity, these places believe that they offer unified territories that can tender a sense of belonging to diverse populations. This is "home," then, as domicile and as haven.

As a person whose ethnocultural background is composed of two nationalities, three ethnicities, and four cultures, the true essence of "home" for me cannot be located in one country. The idea of a geographic place defining home to a first-generation Amerasian is ludicrous. Although I am a U.S. citizen, I am both Japanese and American in nationality because my mother is a native Japanese born in Matsuyama and raised in Imabari; and my father was an American of African and Indian descent. My three ethnicities are native Japanese, African American, and Native American Indian. My four cultures include those of my three ethnicities plus a hybrid, multiethnic, multicultural culture that is distinct from my ethnicities and yet an amalgam of them. Furthermore, with regard to membership in any given ethnic community, "home" is neither wholly Japanese or Native American Indian or African American. It is *all* those things, a fusion.

In addition, as an Amerasian, I am infrequently wholly comfortable in either America or in Japan.

In America, cultural politics and societal politics that define the artifice of race create discomfort and exclusion. Asian Americans often want me, as an Amerasian, to identify with being Asian American, perhaps because my cultural identity is so Japanese (by virtue of being reared and culturally educated by a native Japanese mother) and / or because the governmental definition of a Japanese American (according to Executive Order 9066) is any person who is one-eighth Japanese ancestry or more.

African Americans expect me to adhere to the societal one-drop theory, which states that one drop of African blood makes one African American. This theory was created and proliferated by slave owners to maintain psychological and physical control over their slaves. This was especially true in circumstances in which slaves had more white or Indian blood than African blood. Today, African Americans remain enslaved by plantation owners' controls. They demand that multiethnic persons who have any African blood must turn away from their other cultures and exclusively embrace African American culture.

Most of the Native American Indians whom I meet are half or three-quarters white; they are so defensive about their struggle to be recognized as Indian that they do not recognize their own racism in denying identity to Indians who also have African blood. The governmental definition of a Native American Indian is one-quarter ancestry or more, if one has papers to qualify that ancestry. This conveniently excludes Indians who intermarried with African Americans, thereby leaving their reservations and becoming disenfranchised from their tribes, thus being "paper-less." None of these communities can offer me a sense of "home."

Unfortunately, these traditional ethnic groups' desire to have me or other Amerasians as members of their fold amounts to crass politics. For the invitation to the fold is not based on a desire to share fellowship or genuine interest in the sociopolitical needs of Amerasians, but on a political desire to alter the perception of the size of their communities, to use Amerasians as statistics for the U.S. Census Bureau, thus superficially increasing their numbers. Such increases are superficial because, while they demand we enter their fold, our political needs and agenda are disregarded.

Amerasians are in a struggle to be heard as a small international and intercultural minority in a sea of more vocal and aggressive minorities who have been around a lot longer than we have.

The reasons they want to include us in their groups are not born of fraternity or sorority. Rather, the reasons amount to political extortion, and the attempted murder of identity and spirit. It is another kind of ethnic cleansing. No heart exists in a home laid with that kind of foundation.

I have challenged the various ethnic communities of which I am composed to address even a single issue of Amerasian politics, such as stateless Amerasian orphans in Japan, the Philippines, Korea, and Vietnam, many of whom are of partial African ancestry. These communities on the whole, however, remain uninterested in the issue and an "issue" only does it remain. Such Amerasians (myself included) never become flesh and blood to them, only potential statistical fodder that is physically and mentally disposable in between each U.S. Census tabulation.

In Japan, I am always the exotic other, never perceived as an American, but always as Brazilian, Venezuelan, Colombian, or South Pacific Asian (Pacific Islander). This provides me with a buffer that people who are clearly recognizable as Americans do not have. Many Japanese have a low tolerance for or suspicion of North Americans. If they believe that I am South American, I am more of a novelty. Since the turn-of-the-century, the Japanese have been fascinated with South America and many of them emigrated to that continent in the hope of making their fortunes and returning (including two of my uncles and several cousins).

On the other hand, it is better to be mistaken for Latina than Pacific Islander because the Japanese public stereotypes Southern and Southeast Asian women as prostitutes or potential prostitutes, the "dirty exotic" versus the clean and possibly educated exotic of a South American. In Japan, however, everyone who is not native Japanese is a foreigner, so, sooner or later, the shield of objectification as "exotic other" comes down and I am just a *gai-jin* (shortened from *gaikoku-jin*, which means foreign or "outside" person).

When I was five years old, I had some vague notion of home based on a pot holder that I saw at our neighbor's house that read: "Home is where the heart is," which, for me, was staked in my mother, the nurturing parent. That meant that home was a Japanese place, a place where shoes were removed at the door and sprayed with disinfectant to ward off the diseases of the demons of the streets, where incredibly scorching baths were taken every evening, and foods included things such as *o-tsukemono*, *maki-zushi*, and *tatsuta age*. This was sanctuary from the foreign world outside called America, which I quickly found out was neither a land of the free—because I was not free in being Amerasian or female—nor a land that welcomed the world-weary with open arms, at least when it came to brown-skinned, sloe-eyed Amerasian girls with thick, wavy black hair. In kindergarten, I remember standing with several other Amerasian children as a group of white and African American children stared at us and our mothers and laughed. An African American boy stepped forward boldly and said, "You all stink. Go back to your own country." Even then, the question of whether or not America was "home" for Amerasians was terrifying, insulting, and infuriating. They wanted me to choose one and I was determined to have both countries and all of my ethnicities, not to be a half, but a double; indeed, a triple.

Early in my life, I had no patience for exclusionary politics because, of course, they had a direct impact on part of my family's presence in America. I felt it was no accident that the Statue of Liberty stood away from the Pacific Rim, arms extended to Europe, with only her back and rear end facing Asia. This view, however, only made me more resolved and determined to accomplish and succeed.

As old as the "home is where the heart is" maxim is, I still find truth in it today. Home is sanctuary from the world, but it is not found in one physical place or in a particular community. It definitely is found where the heart is, which, for me, results in a fragmented definition of "home" that includes Matsuyama, Kyoto, Tokyo, Honolulu, Santa Monica, San Diego, and San Francisco; and wherever the few great passions of my life—my son, my significant other, my family, and friends—may be.

21

Untitled Letter

Charlotte DeClue (Kawashinsay)

I met a young woman this morning while jogging in the park.
She had two babies plus one on the way. Her husband was
pacing back and forth worried about where their next meal
was coming from.

She told me she was just happy they had a room at the
homeless shelter.

So I took off some silver I was wearing and gave it to
her to either feel pretty or pawn, whichever came first.

That woman is going to have to make it through this day
without a lot of things that we with homes take for granted.

I am a free agent who has been hired by the Creator
to speak out about the things I see going on in this
world . . . we are all free agents of the Creator, we
all have that right.

Because I remember living in parks and the backseats
of cars, and remember calling the place where I stand
"home" and blessing it with the same sacredness as I
would any lodge the Creator provided us with.

Many women I talk to feel like the young women in the
park . . . that these are their last days. My mother's
generation would have called these times "the twilight
years." And taken the Willow as their symbol.

In that spirit I contribute this letter to support
the struggle of those of us entering those years.

Enclosed is some willow bark to celebrate ceremonial season.

Willow sister, bend but do not break!

22

Yes, Something *Did* Happen in My Childhood

Margaret Randall

I am a cook for others, a shameless feeder
of lovers, children, friends.
I plead guilty to this destiny or daily task
this knowledge running from the succulent pores
of a pork roast
lodged in the aftertaste of curry stew
rising in weekly dough of warm bread.
I give food as sustenance, stake well my territory,
unnerving tempers I spoon advice
to challenge hearts and minds.
On cold mornings I sit with recipe books,
The Joy of Cooking lived and died
five lifetimes in my hands.
There are full-color gourmet photographs
I preview heady scrapings from a bowl or pan
my energies rush to the fore
when no one waits or wishes to be served.
I am that woman over-filler of mouths
that plate-heaper leaning late
to let my eaters serve themselves
come back for seconds on their own terms.
My food is not for thought
but for the belly, belt unbuckled,
every diet plan on hold.
I am the writer, teacher, political activist
who dreams of high praise for my apple pie
a note in the *Times Book Review*
for my oven-baked chicken enchiladas.
Yes, something *did* happen in my childhood.
No, I can't remember what it was.

23

Imagined Communities in the Novels of Michelle Cliff

Meryl F. Schwartz

It is not a question of relinquishing privilege. It is a question of grasping more of myself. I have found that in the real sources are concealed my survival. My speech. My voice. To be colonized is to be rendered insensitive. To have those parts necessary to sustain life numbed. And this is in some cases—in my case—perceived as privilege. The test of a colonized person is to walk through a shantytown in Kingston and not bat an eye. This I cannot do. Because part of me lives there—and as I grasp more of this part I realize what needs to be done with the rest of my life. (Michelle Cliff, "If I Could Write This in Fire, I Would Write This in Fire," 71)

Where human subjects politically begin, in all their sensuous specificity, is with certain needs and desires. Yet need and desire are also what render us nonidentical with ourselves, opening us up to some broader social dimension; and what is posed within this dimension is the question of what *general* conditions would be necessary for our particular needs and desires to be fulfilled. Mediated through the general in this way, particular demands cease to be self-identical and return to themselves transformed by a discourse of the other. The feminist, nationalist, or trade unionist might now come to recognize that in the long run none of their desires is realizable without the fulfillment of the others'. (Terry Eagleton, "Nationalism: Irony and Commitment," 37-38)

A fundamental assumption of many contemporary narratives of political awakening, indeed of much resistance literature of all genres, is the notion that one can—and ultimately must—choose one's political allegiance. As Barbara Harlow explains in *Resistance Literature*, one of the important issues oppositional texts consider is the "social and political transformation from a genealogy of 'filiation' based on ties of kinship, ethnicity, race, or religion to an 'affiliative' secular order" (22). In choosing to affiliate with others on the basis of political perspectives and goals instead of on the basis of identity, we create what Chandra Talpade Mohanty, drawing on Benedict Anderson's work, calls "imagined community." Explaining the usefulness of this concept for her analysis of the relationship of Third World women to the politics of feminism, Mohanty writes:

> The idea of imagined community is useful because it leads us away from essentialist notions of third world feminist struggles, suggesting political rather than biological or cultural bases for alliance. Thus, it is not color or sex which constructs the ground for these struggles. Rather, it is the *way* we think about race, class, and gender—the political links we choose to make among and between struggles. Thus, potentially, women of all colors (including white women) can align themselves with and participate in these imagined communities. (4-5)

Mohanty notes that "our relation to and centrality in particular struggles depend on our different, often conflictual, locations and histories" (5), and indeed, the tension between identity politics based on inherited or otherwise fixed social locations and chosen political alliances must not be underestimated, but the attempt to develop imagined communities is nonetheless a crucial expression of utopian desire and resistance.[1]

Jamaican American novelist, poet, and essayist Michelle Cliff has shown a sustained interest in the concept of imagined community, representing attempts to forge such communities in three novels containing political awakening narratives. In exploring the theme of imagined community, Cliff indirectly draws attention to the political function of her texts. We may view the readers of any given political awakening novel, or readers of the genre in general, as members of an imagined community, linked through their imaginative sympathy and engagement with the protagonists and concerns of such novels. Cliff's representations of imagined communities make palpable the strength of the utopian desire for such alliances, a desire that can be read as an example of the search for the home that has never been, as described in Ernst Bloch's utopian opus, *The Principle of Hope*.[2] However, as Cliff's experiences and narratives illustrate, the strength of the desire for such coalitional homelands cannot easily counter their vulnerability to dismemberment along established lines of social division.

As both epigraphs to this essay suggest, an individual's political awakening results from a psychological imperative. Material conditions create the needs and desires individuals experience, and material conditions must be changed in order for those needs and desires to be met, but the motivation to work for this change is based in personal need and dissatisfaction, not disembodied political analysis. In the passage above from "If I Could Write This in Fire, I Would Write This in Fire," Michelle Cliff is implicitly addressing the distrust members of both dominant and subordinate groups express towards those who make a commitment to struggle against the material and ideological bases of their privileged positions within a particular social structure. Cliff has repeatedly explored the phenomenon of the radical individual who is a "traitor to her class."[3] As her autobiographical essays and interviews make clear, this interest emerges from Cliff's own experience as a favored daughter of colonialism who has aligned herself with anticolonialist politics.

Originally from Jamaica and educated in Jamaica, the United States, and England, Michelle Cliff is a light-skinned descendant of both slave owners and slaves, with African, English, and Arawak ancestors. Her family were landowners, thus positioning them, in the Jamaican context, as economically privileged. In the United States, where they lived for extended periods during Cliff's childhood, they were light enough to pass and thus had access to economic opportunities unavailable to darker Jamaicans. Cliff is herself apparently "white," recognized as a person of color only when she identifies herself as such. Given this background, Cliff does not want her oppositional position to be viewed as altruistic self-sacrifice; indeed, she insists that she does not perceive herself as making a sacrifice. Her own "needs and desires," as Eagleton puts it, are what have led her to a radical critique of the "*general* conditions" that are a consequence of the colonial past and neocolonial present. Cliff's claim that her identification with the anticolonialist struggle is necessary to her own wholeness is also a way of legitimizing her oppositional position. Her statement seems to emerge in part from an underlying assumption that struggle in one's own name has more legitimacy than struggle in the name of "the other," a position which was occupied, in Cliff's formative experience, by the darker, poorer peoples of the Caribbean.

Cliff's assertion of personal investment in the struggle for decolonization is also rooted in painful experience, as revealed in a 1992 interview. Her self-identification as a woman of color and her commitment to radical politics have not always shielded her from the distrust and anger of darker people, particularly in the West Indian context. When asked about her personal experiences with such distrust, Cliff speaks of the "nasty swipe" at her in the introduction to *Her True-True Name*, an anthology of West Indian women writers edited by Pamela Mordecai and Betty Wilson:

> They say something to the effect that I am light enough that I might as well be white, which is not true. It's one thing to look x and to feel y, rather than to look x and feel x, and that's part of the difficulty being light-skinned: some people assume you have a white outlook just because you look white. You're immediately met on that level. . . . I felt I was included in that anthology because they couldn't exclude me, but to put me in they had to make a crack about me. The introduction ends with something like "not many of us are called Clare Savage," words to that effect. It was just plain bitchy, if you want my reading of that remark. And it goes back to very old and very painful stuff. (Schwartz 607)[4]

Against this context, Cliff seeks in her non-fiction and fiction to examine, among other things, the route by which individuals may come to disrupt assumptions about the correlation between social position and political alliance.

To date, Michelle Cliff's most sustained analysis of political development is in her first two novels, *Abeng* (1984) and *No Telephone to Heaven* (1987). Cliff's mixed heritage is shared by the protagonist of these novels, the first of which is largely autobiographical, the second rather less so.[5] The two-volume narrative of Clare Savage's political awakening may be read as Cliff's analysis of her own commitment to opposing the conditions that would sustain her comparative wealth. Clare's oppositional stance, like Cliff's, is not conceived "as a question of relinquishing privilege." Rather, Clare's development leads her to oppositional activism because it is only through the anticolonialist struggle that Clare can grasp more of herself. This insight is the result of a long struggle to understand her own needs and desires; as Eagleton suggests, this struggle necessarily involves transformation of Clare's conception of her needs through encounter with a discourse of "the other." In Clare's case, however, the role of "the other" in her awakening process is particularly complex, as Clare is the product of both colonizer and colonized, though she has been trained to identify with the former. "None of [her] desires is realizable without the fulfillment of the other's," in part because "the other" is a repressed part of her own identity.

In addition, each novel represents figures of "the other" whose stories fragment the narrative of Clare's development, and whose history and discourse have an impact on Clare's experience. Indeed, both *Abeng* and *No Telephone to Heaven* are highly fragmented narratives, a structure which simultaneously mirrors Clare's fragmentation and expands our attention from an exclusive focus on Clare's *Bildung*. The fragmentation works as an estrangement device that subverts the individualist ideology of the traditional *Bildungsroman*, signalling that Cliff's texts are ultimately narratives of a collective history as well as meditations on the task of creating new forms of community.[6]

Abeng, for example, is fragmented by narrative leaps backwards and forwards in time. The story of Clare's tenth through twelfth years, 1956-1958, is interrupted by narratives that provide the reader with information Clare lacks about Jamaica's history, her own family history, and the histories of several additional characters. *Abeng*'s most prominent representation of "the other" is Clare's girlhood friend Zoe, dark-skinned daughter of a woman who squats on Clare's grandmother's land. The representation of the relationship between the two girls stresses the power of social structures to determine even the most intimate of relationships. Cliff highlights the way the island's dominant ideologies of class and race differently affect the lives of the two girls; in its positioning of Zoe as darker, poorer other, the colonialist system offers certain economic and social opportunities to Clare alone but also alienates Clare from crucial elements of herself: her developing lesbian desires and her matriarchal African heritage. Clare's successful *bildung*, the text strongly suggests, depends upon her confronting the social divisions and self-division created by the social structure which ultimately determines her estrangement from Zoe. Through its fragmented structure, emphasis on history, and illustration of social determinism, *Abeng* suggests that orientation to the collective is the only cure for the fragmentation of its protagonist and her society. *Abeng* draws to a close when Clare is fourteen. Emphasizing the interdependence of the "personal" and the "political," the novel's conclusion connects Clare's sexual development with her political development; the text ends on the day she first menstruates, shortly after she has experienced sexual desire for Zoe, and as we leave Clare, she has just learned some of her country's suppressed history and had a dream, discussed below, with important political implications.

Like *Abeng*, *No Telephone to Heaven* jumps back and forth in time, spanning the period between 1960 and 1982, from Clare's adolescence in America and graduate education in Britain to her death, at thirty-six years old, during a guerrilla action in Jamaica's Cockpit Country. The novel repeatedly shifts its attention from Clare to characters whose experience is contemporaneous with her own. Though her story forms the novel's major, unifying narrative, Clare's centrality is significantly displaced by chapters devoted to her mother and to a character named Christopher, whose story serves as an important counterpoint to Clare's. Significantly, Clare never meets this "other" whose story most prominently fragments her own, although their paths twice cross. Christopher is an itinerant laborer in the gardens of the upper class, product of Kingston's shantytowns. His pain and rage eventually erupt in gruesome murders of his employers and their maid. Cliff has explained that Christopher's particularly brutal murder of the maid is an expression of his self-hatred, a condition that connects him with Clare Savage.[7] Supporting Eagleton's assertion, the narrative structure implies that Clare's self-hatred can by resolved only if she is transformed by the discourse of figures such as Zoe and Christopher; this discourse is an anguished expression of impotence and disenfranchisement represented in its most raw form by Christopher's howl at the end of *No Telephone to Heaven*. Though Clare's social position allows her to choose whether or not she is going to listen to the discourse of "the other," she will remain divided against herself until she decides to do so. Ultimately, Clare seeks wholeness through a return to Jamaica, claiming it as her home. She recognizes that Jamaica, the land her now-dead mother loved, is her true motherland, not Britain, the land she had been taught to revere as the "mother country." Back in Jamaica, Clare researches and teaches the suppressed history of Jamaica, the history that Cliff shares with the reader in *Abeng*. She becomes increasingly committed to a nationalist resistance movement, letting its members use her grandmother's abandoned farm and eventually joining their armed struggle against the forces of neo-colonialism. Though her grandmother's land is the site of maternal filial ties, Clare consciously *chooses* it as her home, and so it is fitting that this family property supports the resistance group's attempt to create an imagined community based on an ethic of chosen political affiliation.

In joining the resistance movement, Clare has both recognized her implication in the history that produced Jamaica's social divisions and accepted the burden of agency that accompanies her dual heritage. As the title of *Abeng* emphasizes, Clare, like the island of Jamaica, is heir to two opposed discourse communities. The title page tells us that:

> Abeng is an African word meaning conch shell. The blowing of the conch called the slaves to the canefields in the West Indies. [But] the abeng had another use: it was the instrument used by the Maroon armies [which waged a sustained resistance against the colonizers] to pass their messages and reach one another.

Like the abeng, Clare has the capacity to be an instrument of oppressive or resistant forces, and the narrative of her maturation is the story of her coming to recognize that the choice of allegiance is hers to make.[8]

The theme of choice recurs over and over in both novels, sometimes, as above, as a choice between complicity and resistance, sometimes as a choice between victimization and resistance. The latter dichotomy can be seen in one of the early descriptions of Nanny, the legendary Maroon warrior whose story is repeatedly alluded to in these texts. Cliff tells us in *Abeng*:

> In the beginning there had been two sisters—Nanny and Sekusu. Nanny fled slavery. Sekusu remained a slave. Some said this was the difference between the sisters. It was believed that all island children were descended from one or another. All island people were first cousins. (18)

Despite the stark dichotomies suggested by this passage, Cliff's representation of her characters often stresses their multiple positionality; individuals may simultaneously occupy positions of victimization, complicity, and resistance.

Like most Jamaicans, Clare is of mixed race, mixed heritage, the product of a British colonial education and colonialist values as well as the Jamaican culture which has evolved from the encounter of West African and indigenous cultures with slavery and European colonization. Cliff recognizes that after centuries of British colonialism, followed by American neo-colonialism, there can be no simple decolonization of the mind or the economy. Her novels are concerned with the ways in which the colonialist race hierarchy intersects with the class system, the gender system, and heterosexism in such a way that it is sometimes difficult to distinguish clearly between acts of oppression and resistance or between signs of privilege and victimization. Clare's mother's silence, her refusal to share herself, her history, and her knowledge with her daughters, particularly the lighter-skinned Clare, is traced to her sense of the inevitability of her people's victimization and her position in the gender system. The narrator of *Abeng* tells us that Kitty "felt Black people were destined to labor under the oppression of whiteness, longing for a better day." Her "love of darkness became a love conceived in grief" (128), and she wears this love "in silence, protecting it from her family, protecting the depth of this love from all but herself" (127). While sympathetic to Kitty's grief and to the challenges she has faced in her marriage and her family of origin, the narrator shows us how Kitty's silence functions as a form of complicity with the forces of oppression. Such political complexity is also evident when, near the end of *Abeng*, Clare exploits her class privileges in order to protect herself and Zoe from sexual harassment. Nonetheless, these novels stress that neither the complexity of the social structure nor the difficulty of radical intervention negate the imperative for Clare of making a conscious decision about her relationship to the social system into which she was born. From childhood on, Clare follows a troubled, non-linear path towards resisting the dominant ideology and claiming the community of "others" as her home, but her dual heritage and centuries of betrayal make Clare suspect to those with whom she chooses to identify. Clare cannot simply go home; rather she can only create a home by participating in the struggle to forge imagined communities of political allies. This struggle is Michelle Cliff's as well, and its importance to Cliff's vision is evident in her repeated attempts to conjure imagined communities in and through her fiction.

In *No Telephone to Heaven* and *Free Enterprise*, Cliff describes more or less intentional communities of people marked by diverse racial, class, and cultural backgrounds, bound by a common commitment to oppositional politics. In *Abeng*, a novel of girlhood, the friendship between Zoe and Clare is not a political alliance in the same sense but may still be read as an exploration of the challenge of forging coalition—in this case based on shared interests of age and gender. The relationship between Clare and Zoe forms the heart of *Abeng*, enacting in microcosm the novel's primary concerns. The development and destruction of this friendship demonstrate that there is no pure relational space that transcends history and social structures, a lesson that is crucial to Clare's political development. The ultimate failure of this relationship illustrates the loss Clare will experience if she fails to listen to the discourse of those positioned as other to her in Jamaican society.

Significantly, Clare's closest relationship is set in St. Elizabeth, the rural village where her mother feels most at home and where Clare spends summer vacations with her maternal grandmother, Miss Mattie.[9] Miss Mattie is a small property owner, and Zoe's mother, Miss Ruthie, squats on a piece of Miss Mattie's land. The summer that both girls are ten, Miss Mattie asks Miss Ruthie to send Zoe to be her granddaughter's playmate. Zoe has no choice but to comply, and so from the first Zoe and Clare's relationship is bound up with the class system.

In a narrative move typical of the associative patterns that determine *Abeng*'s fragmented structure, the description of Zoe and Clare's relationship is interrupted by an anecdote that reveals how race and class divide girls from a young age, determining one's "place." During prayers at the private school Clare attends in Kingston, a dark-skinned scholarship student, Doreen, has an epileptic seizure. The headmistress insists that the girls continue singing a hymn, and it is some time before one teacher, herself dark-skinned, goes to the aid of Doreen. Doreen loses her scholarship and everybody acts as if she had never existed at all. But Clare is troubled by the fact that her teachers failed to help Doreen, and she asks her mother about it. Kitty evades the truth, telling Clare that the English mistresses are "ladies," and thus afraid of sickness. Clare wonders what her mother would have done if she had been one of the teachers at the school. She is quite certain Kitty would not have come forward, but because everyone around her conspires to deny the omnipresence of racism, Clare has trouble thinking the matter through:

> It was easy to lose sight of color and all that went with it within the imitation-English quadrangle of brick buildings. A school with a tuck shop that sold English sweeties and copies of *School-Friends*, stories of English girls in English boarding-schools. It was so easy to lose sight of color when you were constantly being told that there was no "colour problem" in Jamaica. Or anywhere in the Empire, for that matter—Her Majesty's Government had all that under control. Apartheid, for example, was only a way of keeping the peace—Black

people in South Africa, the geography mistress told them, had as equal chances as the whites. Just like in Jamaica. (100)

As the placement of this anecdote implies, the denial of the centrality of race that Clare experiences in Kingston has important consequences for her relationship with Zoe back in St. Elizabeth.

Escaping into a world of fantasy play, Zoe and Clare try to ignore the class and race differences between them, but even in the relatively unregulated space of rural summer vacations the differences between the girls occasionally surface in such a way that they cannot be avoided, leading to fights. During the second summer of their friendship, they have an argument over a new bathingsuit that represents Clare's economic advantages. During this struggle, Clare denies her privileged position, and we see in Zoe's report of the incident to her mother that Zoe has also invested in the idea that her relationship with Clare can transcend their social differences. She responds to her mother's assertion that "De buckra people dem is fe dem alone" by insisting that "Clare is fe me friend" (102).[10] By the following summer, however, Zoe has achieved a much more mature understanding of the forces that will inevitably divide her experience from her companion's, while Clare's privileges enable her to continue refusing to acknowledge the differences between her life and Zoe's.

The crisis in their relationship occurs towards the end of the summer when Clare and Zoe are twelve years old. Clare devises a plan to steal her grandmother's gun and hunt down a famous wild pig known as Master Cudjoe. This plan emerges from Clare's desire to prove herself by succeeding in a traditionally male enterprise that her community respects. Her immediate motivation is the feeling of exclusion she experienced earlier that summer, when she was not allowed to participate in the slaughtering of a hog. Her sense of exclusion was exacerbated when she found her male cousins sharing a secret feast of the hog's genitals. Zoe has agreed to participate in the hunt, but after a long morning of cutting through the bush, she tries to discourage Clare from continuing on:

> Wunna know, wunna is truly town gal. Wunna a go back to Kingston soon now. Wunna no realize me have to stay here. Wunna no know what people dem would say if two gal dem shoot Massa Cudjoe. Dem would talk and me would have fe tek on all de contention. Dem will say dat me t'ink me is

buckra boy, going pon de hill a hunt fe one pig. Or dat me let buckra gal lead me into wickedness. (117-118)

Claiming St. Elizabeth and the community of dark-skinned Jamaicans as her home, Clare responds, "Me not town gal. And me not buckra. Me jus' want to do something so dem will know we is smaddy" (118). To which Zoe replies:

> Wunna is town gal, and wunna papa is buckra. Wunna talk buckra. Wunna leave here when wunna people come fe wunna. Smaddy? Wunna now is smaddy already? Gal Smaddy. Kingston smaddy. White smaddy. Dis place no matter a wunna a-tall, a-tall. Dis here is fe me territory. Kingston a fe wunna. (118)

Still Clare denies the truth of Zoe's assertions, insisting "No, Zoe, dis is as much fe me place as fe wunna" (118).

During this argument, we see Clare once again denying her privileged status. Only Zoe recognizes that while transgression of gender roles is dangerous for both girls, the punishments they risk are inflected by their different class positions. Later, while relaxing in the sun after she and Zoe have bathed in a pond, Clare begins to acknowledge the truth in what Zoe has said, and she tells herself she has been at fault for not adequately considering her friend's precarious social position. However, she insists on seeing this incident as an isolated instance of her individual selfishness. These thoughts occur during a scene that has a distinctly homoerotic element, suggesting how much easier it is to love and desire across class lines than actually to negotiate cross-class relationships. Because she has come so close to losing it, Clare recognizes how important Zoe's friendship is to her; she wants to kiss her as an expression of remorse for her foolish behavior. But before any apologies can be tendered, the day's adventures come to a tragic conclusion.

A passing cane-cutter notices Clare and Zoe lying in the sun and screams out "Coo ya! . . . Two gals nekked pon de river-rock" (122). Responding quickly to this sexual harassment, Clare uses the gun and her class privilege to assert herself. Pointing the gun at the cane cutter, she shouts, "Get away, you hear. This is my grandmother's land." As the narrator points out, Clare "had dropped her patois—she was speaking *buckra*—and relying on the privilege she said she did not have" (122). Clare shoots, but at the last minute she jerks the gun upward. The bullet fatally wounds Miss Mattie's bull. For this crime, Clare is forbidden ever to see Zoe again, banished from her grandmother's farm, and sent to live with an autocratic, explicitly racist, elderly white woman who, Clare's parents decide, will rid her of her rebellious ways and prepare her for the upwardly mobile life that her light skin makes possible. In effect, Clare is sent into exile, and the rest of her life may be read as a sustained attempt to return "home." With increasing consciousness, Clare recognizes that the pursuit of whiteness places her in exile from herself. While living in the United States, she feels closest to her mother and by extension "home" when identifying with black Americans, and while studying in England she feels solidarity with the community of dark-skinned immigrants, although her appearance exempts her from the persecution they suffer. Clare's return to Jamaica and commitment to the battle against cultural imperialism are her most deliberate claims to a home in the black community.

For the young Clare, however, Zoe functions as the synecdoche for all she has lost through banishment into the world of light-skin privilege. At the very end of *Abeng*, before waking to her first experience of menstruation, Clare dreams that during a fist fight with Zoe she hits Zoe in the face with a stone and then apologizes and attempts to heal the wound. As Belinda Edmundson has noted, this dream is a mirror image of the scene in Jean Rhys's *Wide Sargasso Sea*, in which the young Tia throws a rock at her white "friend" Antoinette. Significantly, Cliff's version reverses the characters' roles. As Edmondson notes:

> What is important about this scene is that Cliff does not simply repeat the doubling of black and white female identities but actually reverses the scene, so that 'white' Clare Savage is the one who inflicts damage on black Zoe. If we consider this scene within the context of its literary history, Cliff is rewriting an *historical* relation of black and white West Indian women not only to link their cultural identities but to acknowledge the white woman's relation to power. (182-3)

The confluence of this dream with Clare's biological entry into womanhood suggests that she is in the process of developing into the adult who will be able to confront the power dynamic between herself and Zoe, and consequently create a political home: "Something had happened to her—was happening to her" (166). She is not, however, ready to understand the dream at the point where *Abeng* concludes.

While Zoe never reappears in the narrative, she nonetheless functions importantly in Clare's subsequent development. Though never mentioned by the adolescent or adult Clare Savage of *No Telephone to Heaven*, the loss of this connection is arguably a significant contributor to her sense of fragmentation and rootlessness. External evidence for the importance of this relationship comes from Cliff's non-fictional autobiographical narrative, as told in the fragments of prose and poetry that make up *The Land of Look Behind* (1985). In the essay "If I Could Write This in Fire, I Would Write This in Fire," Cliff remembers her girlhood friend Zoe. The circumstances and details described are all precisely consistent with those in *Abeng*. The difference is that where the adult Clare Savage never explicitly recalls this relationship or attempts to reconnect with Zoe, as a young adult Michelle Cliff visits Zoe, and she later recalls the relationship with great pain in both autobiographical fiction and non-fiction. Cliff writes in her essay:

> *Looking back:* Through the last page of *Sula*. "And the loss pressed down on her chest and came up into her throat. 'We was girls together,' she said as though explaining something." It was Zoe, and Zoe alone, I thought of. She snapped into my mind and I remembered no one else. (LLB 63)

Memories of their girlhood times together are followed by a recollection that reveals the dramatically diverging paths the two women's lives have taken, confirming the fictional Zoe's prophecy. At twenty-seven, Cliff visits Zoe during a trip back home. She finds:

> Her front teeth are gone. Her husband beats her and she suffers blackouts. . . . She is given birth control pills which aggravate her 'condition.' . . . She is being taught by Peace Corps volunteers to embroider linen mats with little lambs on them. . . . (63)

Cliff concludes this memory: "I can come and go. And I leave. To complete my education in London" (63). Through confrontation with the memory of Zoe, Cliff addresses her acute sense of the paradoxical confluence of her homelessness and her privilege.

Still stressing the impact of her friendship with Zoe during an interview conducted when she is in her mid-forties, Cliff says in response to a question about the ways in which she was marked by a colonialist education:

> How can you not be marked? But you work with it. I was
> quite privileged in my education, in a sense, but I will always
> be marked by the fate of people like Zoe, who were my
> friends and whom I loved and whom I saw damaged and
> deeply hurt. That's another kind of colonial education.
> (Schwartz 606)

In so far as the narrative of Clare Savage is autobiographical, the
implication of this intertextual evidence is that Clare's girlhood tie to
Zoe—and its abrupt disruption—is an important piece of the personal
experience that leads Clare towards oppositional politics. While she
represses the discourse of this "other" for many years, her encounter
with Zoe—and the sense of loss and exile resulting from the conclusion
of their relationship—accounts in part for the adult, literally exiled
Clare's eventual repatriation to Jamaica and assertion of her Afro-
Caribbean heritage. This decision includes a return to her grandmother's
land, site of the crucial friendship as well as her tie to mother,
grandmother, and by extension the matrilineal heritage of resistance
recorded by the historian-narrator of *Abeng*. Though the location for
Zoe and Clare's alliance is ultimately utopia—literally no place, it
represents a desire for transcendence of enforced social divisions that
fuels the far more deliberate effort to build an imagined community in
No Telephone to Heaven. Participation in this community is the only
way for Clare to return "home."

    No Telephone to Heaven opens with a description of a
community of twenty people who are united by their commitment to
armed struggle against the forces of neo-colonialism in Jamaica. Cliff's
description highlights the fragility of a community that challenges the
usual bases of alliance in Jamaica. As we are introduced to them, the
members of the community are on a truck, headed for the site of a
guerrilla action:

> These people—men and women—were dressed in similar
> clothes, which became them as uniforms, signifying some
> agreement, some purpose—that they were in something
> together—in these clothes, at least, they seemed to blend
> together. This alikeness was something they needed, which
> could be important, even vital to them—for the shades of their
> skin, places traveled to and from, events experienced, things
> understood, food taken into their bodies, acts of violence
> committed, books read, music heard, languages recognized,

ones they loved, living family, varied widely, came between them. (4-5)

Because of her light skin and the material privileges it has afforded her, thirty-six-year-old Clare Savage is one of those whose presence on this truck contradicts the logic of identity politics. We do not learn her name until later in the text, but Cliff here describes her as a "light-skinned woman, daughter of landowners, native-born, slaves, emigres, Carib, Ashanti, English, [who] has taken her place on this truck, alongside people who easily could have hated her" (5).

In explaining how Clare came to be on this truck, the narrative consistently refers us to Clare's psychological needs and personal process, though that personal process is connected to its political context. Thus the text repeatedly draws us back to Eagleton's thesis that "human subjects politically begin . . . with certain needs and desires." Clare explicitly acknowledges her personal investment in anticolonialist politics when she first seeks to ally herself with an organized resistance movement. During an introductory interrogation, Clare is asked "what drew you to this work . . . this place." She responds, "Nothing pure and simple. . . . My own needs, for the most part." Asked to elaborate, she says:

> I returned to this island to mend . . . to bury . . . my mother.
> . . . I returned to this island because there was nowhere else.
> . . . I could live no longer in borrowed countries, on borrowed time. There is danger here—in sounding . . . seeming foolish. (192-3)

While Clare is embarrassed by the confessional nature of her answers, it is apparently her statement of personal need that gains the trust of her interrogator. Nonetheless, Clare's strong personal desire to belong to the imagined community of anticolonialist guerrillas cannot in itself compensate for the long history that divides her from those members whom history has placed in less privileged positions than hers.

The eventual betrayal of the resistance group by a quashee—an informant—is figured in *No Telephone to Heaven* as historically inevitable, an unavoidable parallel to the historic betrayal of Nanny. Commenting on this history of betrayal and Clare's precarious position within the anticolonialist community Cliff has said:

I really wanted to show that she makes this choice and she wants to be part of this group, but she will never feel that she's really part of it, and they will never quite accept her either. The problem is that all these people on the truck represent different parts of Jamaican society and they've been brought up to distrust one another. And so that's why the revolutionary act at the end of the book is sabotaged by somebody and you never know who's done it. Somebody betrays them because they've been colonized to be betrayers of one another and they haven't managed to deal with that. (Raiskin 64)

While Cliff represents this betrayal and its tragic consequences as inevitable, Clare's decision to commit herself to the anticolonialist resistance is represented as a necessary path towards her personal fulfillment. Contesting readers' perceptions of the conclusion of *No Telephone to Heaven* as an "unhappy ending," Cliff argues in "Clare Savage as a Crossroads Character" that "[i]n her death [Clare] has complete identification with her homeland; soon she will be indistinguishable from the ground. Her bones will turn to potash, as did her ancestors' bones" (265). Joined in death with the other casualties from the guerrilla group as well as her ancestors, Clare's final moments find her closest to the end of exile. In identifying herself with an imagined community of the ancestral and living victims of colonialism, Clare has achieved significant reconciliation of the fragments of which she is composed.

The two-volume chronicle of Clare's development into oppositional subjectivity stresses the relationship between Clare's psychic fragmentation and the historical ignorance engendered by colonialism. As noted earlier, Clare's fragmentation is reflected in the form of the texts. In *Abeng*, the separateness of the narrative's many parts is emphasized by lines and spaces between sections of text. The parts of this novel that focus on the protagonist are presented in an episodic fashion, and these episodes are themselves divided by narrative fragments that provide historical information to which Clare has no access. In providing the reader with information that Clare and other Jamaicans lack, the narrator stresses its importance: this is information Clare will need in order to occupy the position of the resistant subject. When in adulthood Clare becomes a historian and teacher, she both demonstrates her recognition of the political and cultural importance of knowing one's history and begins to glue together the many pieces of her identity. In highlighting Clare's psychological need to learn of Jamaica's multicultural history of slavery, colonialism, and resistance, Cliff seeks to effect in the reader an awakening process that will lead her to adopt a political position similar to Clare's. We are invited both to react to the compelling historical information presented in the narrative and to identify with the protagonist, thereby perceiving commitment to anticolonialist politics as our own psychological necessity. The narrative's consistent connection between the personal and the political thus functions simultaneously as political argument and narrative strategy with important implications for reader response. For Cliff's strategy in her novels is to invite us to become members of an imagined community bound by a common, deeply experienced response to the knowledge they pass on. Stories, Cliff explicitly suggests in her third novel, *Free Enterprise*, are our most important resource and connective thread. It is through the telling of their stories that different groupings of characters in *Free Enterprise* seek to forge imagined communities that can sustain the struggle against slavery, racist ideologies, and the disappointments of the post-Civil War years.

Spanning roughly a century, from the antebellum era to the 1920s, *Free Enterprise* portrays the experiences of several resistant women, both historical and imagined and born to a range of economic and social circumstances. Juxtaposing against each other a series of short vignettes, Cliff explores the revolutionary commitment of Mary Ellen Pleasant, a historical African American woman who funded the attempted slave revolt that came to be known as John Brown's raid on Harper's Ferry; the anguish of the light-skinned, mixed-race Annie Christmas, who joins the anti-slavery resistance in the United States, having despaired of fighting the colonialist ideology of her own relatively elite Jamaican milieu; and the nuances of privilege and pain experienced by the aristocratic white abolitionist cousins, Alice and Clover Hooper, the latter married to Henry Adams.

The text records a series of attempts at connection across differences: of age, class, race, era, political perspective. Clover Hooper seeks communion with a homeless African American woman who makes the alley outside Ford's theatre her home. Tenuous connections are effected between the Hooper cousins and Mary Ellen Pleasant. Mary Ellen Pleasant seeks out Annie Christmas, who becomes her protege and the daughter she never had. Malcolm X, presenting himself as a hologram, reaches out to Mary Ellen Pleasant across the decades between their revolutionary programs. Mary Ellen Pleasant and John Brown forge a powerful bond despite important ideological differences.

Pervading the narrative of these encounters is a deep sadness, an awareness of bridges impossible to build, coalitions unequal in strength to the forces they resist, or spirits broken by the strain of battle. Hope, in this narrative, is situated in the revolutionary potential of knowledge. In the passing on of these women's stories lies the possibility of creating imagined community; resistant narratives create a bond among the tellers and the listeners, revise histories that have distorted or removed oppositional figures and movements, and thereby sustain the communities and knowledge that are a necessary if insufficient condition for radical change. Cliff illustrates this point most powerfully in her representation of U.S. Public Health Service Station #66, a leper colony on the banks of the Mississippi River in Louisiana.

"In the colony," the narrator of *Free Enterprise* tells us, "new kinship was forged" (43). Many of the inhabitants of the colony are people of color or members of other marginalized groups; many have histories of oppositional activism. Storytelling becomes their main pastime, and through sharing their stories of colonialist oppression and anti-colonialist resistance they both form a community among themselves and nurture future generations. Beginning their narratives with the stories that have been passed down to them, each individual reaches back centuries. An unnamed Hawai'ian begins his story with the landing of Captain Cook; the Jewish woman Rachel DeSouza begins hers with anecdotes from the Spanish Inquisition. The community formed through this sharing of oral history is mutually supportive and sensitive to the common threads and significant divergences among oppressive histories and ideologies. The storytellers are conscious of their collective and individual experiences of marginalization and therefore approach their task with particular vigilance and attention to detail; recognizing that their stories are likely to be muted by dominant historical narratives, the members of the community seek to increase their stories' survival rates through repeated recountings.

Cliff uses the character of Annie to address the doubt that readers may feel about the value of oral history. Though not a prisoner of the colony herself, Annie lives nearby and has made the storytellers her community. During one of the oral transmission sessions, Annie addresses the group: "Sometimes, too much of the time, I think all we have are these stories, and they are endangered. In years to come, will anyone have heard them—our voices" (58-9)? Rachel affirms the significance of their activity: "Once something is spoken, it is carried on the air; it does not die. It, our words, escape into the cosmos, space." Annie asks, "Who will take responsibility for these stories?" Rachel replies, "We all do, Annie. It's the only way." And then Rachel self-consciously begins her story by saying "I, Rachel DeSouza, am sending this story into the ether, on a Sunday afternoon, 1920, from the banks of the Mississippi River" (59).

As the readers of Cliff's novel we are among the designated receptors of Rachel's story, the stories of the other members of the leper colony, and the several other stories included in *Free Enterprise*. The conversation between Annie and Rachel suggests that all of us in the audience for this text must take responsibility for these stories, that through accepting this shared burden of historical knowledge we form an imagined community of allies across difference. Cliff's representations of imagined community both here and in her earlier novels support the contention that we have the power and responsibility to make political choices, that inherited identity need not determine our alliances. In effect, Cliff's novels support the conclusion June Jordan reaches in her essay "Report from the Bahamas," an extended meditation on identity politics. After examining a series of both failed and successful attempts to connect across difference, Jordan finds that it is not who we are that matters but what we know and what we are prepared to do about what we know (49). Home, in Michelle Cliff's vision, is ultimately to be found in the imagined communities we create through taking responsibility for both hearing suppressed stories and acting on what we have learned.

NOTES

1. For a different definition of "identity politics," see Linda Alcoff, for whom the notion of identity politics includes the concept of chosen positionality.

2. Bloch concludes *The Principle of Hope* thus:
    > But the root of history is the working, creating human being who reshapes and overhauls the given facts. Once he has grasped himself and established what is his, without expropriation and alienation, in real democracy, there arises in the world something which shines into the childhood of all and in which no one has yet been: homeland. (1376)

3.   This phrase appears in Cliff's 1994 novel, *Free Enterprise*.
        Alice Hooper, a wealthy New England abolitionist, distressed
        by the fact that her wealth stems from "the traffic in human
        souls" and troubled as well by "the question of property in and
        of itself," notes that she risks being seen as a "traitor to her
        class" (78).

4.   Mordecai and Wilson say the following about Cliff in their
        introduction:

> The only one of the recently published Caribbean
> writers who does not affirm at least aspects of being
> in the Caribbean place is Michelle Cliff, who along
> with Rhys could be regarded as being more in the
> alienated tradition of a 'francophone' than an
> anglophone consciousness. Personal history perhaps
> provides important clues: like Rhys, who also felt
> isolated, Cliff is 'white'—or as light-skinned as
> makes, to the larger world, little difference. Also like
> Rhys, she went to the kind of school—quite
> comprehensively described in *No Telephone to
> Heaven* which promoted the values of the metropole.
> Like Rhys, she left her island early and never really
> came home. One of the prices she has paid is a
> compromised authenticity in some aspects of her
> rendering of the creole. (Interestingly enough, the
> name of her heroine of both *Abeng* and *No Telephone
> to Heaven*, Clare Savage—'White Chocolate'—
> suggests in reverse the meaning of *La Negresse
> blanche*, title of an early francophone Caribbean novel
> by Mayotte Capecia, harshly condemned by Fanon for
> its heroine's alienation.) (xvii)

Their concluding paragraph adds in patois:

> Maybe is true some name is Clare Savage, but not
> plenty; not everybody stay like the woman in "Let
> Them Call it Jazz" what manage to find a room near
> Victoria; but some like Mama King (*Frangipani
> House*), and Clare ('bright', 'true', 'clean') and Gem
> (*Whole of a Morning Sky*), and Angel (*Angel*), and

Telumee Miracle (*The Bridge of Beyond*) done find them true-true name. (xviii)

See Françoise Lionnet for a discussion of these comments in an extended analysis of the question of Cliff's alleged "compromised authenticity." I would add to Lionnet's critique of Mordecai and Wilson a query about the latter's nearly explicit demand that "true" Caribbean heroines experience no feelings of alienation. Wouldn't authenticity be compromised if Caribbean writers were to bow to political pressure to silence such feelings? Cliff represents her heroine's experience of alienation—and her name—as a consequence, both directly and indirectly, of imperialist geopolitics. Do Mordecai and Wilson want to deny the varied effects of the region's history? Further, their comments seem based on a willful misreading of the text. After all, Clare returns to Jamaica, expressing her retrieved sense of connection to her homeland through acts of intellectual and armed resistance that demonstrate deep commitment to "the Caribbean place." Mordecai and Wilson seem ultimately to be speaking out of a parochial nationalism, angry with Cliff for having left Jamaica and for refusing to sentimentalize it. See Schwartz for Cliff's comments regarding her permanent exile from Jamaica. Cliff insists that as a gay woman there is no place for her in Jamaica. Mordecai and Wilson's silence on the sexuality of their women writers suggests their participation in the region's intense homophobia, and by extension another reason for their slap at Cliff.

5.   See Lionnet for a discussion of *Abeng* as autobiography. Her evidence is primarily the correlation between features in the novel and in Cliff's essays. Additional evidence for the autobiographical elements in both *Abeng* and *No Telephone to Heaven* may be found in the interviews conducted by Schwartz and Raiskin.

6.   See Fiona Barnes and Maria Helena Lima for discussion of Cliff's subversion of the *Bildungsroman*, contextualized in each case within a consideration of the function of the genre in postcolonial literature. See Françoise Lionnet for discussion of *Abeng*'s fragmented structure, as well as for her argument regarding the centrality of the collective in *Abeng*, which she

sees as typical in this regard of postcolonial autobiography. Simon Gikandi examines *Abeng*'s fragmented structure in his study of Caribbean modernist discourse, *Writing in Limbo*. He argues that:

> the uniqueness of Cliff's aesthetics lies in her realization that the fragmentation, silence, and repression that mark the life of the Caribbean subject under colonialism must be confronted not only as a problem to be overcome but also as a condition of possibility—as a license to dissimulate and to affirm difference—in which an identity is created out of the chaotic colonial and postcolonial history. In writing about the ways in which Caribbean subjects strive to subjectify themselves within the commodified space and time of colonial modernity, Cliff finds discursive value in the very fragmentation that other commentators have seen as the curse of West Indian history. (234)

In support of this argument, Gikandi quotes Cliff's essay "A Journey into Speech," in *The Land of Look Behind*, where she writes of her "struggle to get wholeness from fragmentation while working within fragmentation, producing work which may find its strength in its depiction of fragmentation, through form as well as content," and describes this approach to writing as characteristic of writers originating in colonialist cultures (14-15). While granting the point that Cliff has indeed approached fragmentation as "a condition of possibility" and noting Gikandi's acknowledgment that "the goal of narrative is to overcome [fragmentation]" (234), I would argue that Gikandi understates the extent to which Cliff's narrative interest in fragmentation emerges from a tragic sensibility; she finds fragmentation sadly inescapable. Discussing the ending of *No Telephone to Heaven*, Cliff has said "I see Clare's return [to Jamaica] as tragic. She's a fragmented character, and she doesn't get a chance to become whole at all" (Schwartz 600-601). This conclusion seems to reflect Cliff's sense of the futility of resisting neocolonialism under current geopolitical conditions (Schwartz 611).

7.   See Schwartz 612-14.

8.   Wendy Walters discusses the issue of Clare's choices in an unpublished paper on *No Telephone to Heaven*.

9.   Most critics of *Abeng* and *No Telephone to Heaven* have noted the association, frequently stressed in the narrative, between Jamaica as motherland, Clare's literal mother, and the symbolic, historical mothers, notably the maroon warrior Nanny and slave woman Mma Ali, both symbols of resistance. See Fiona Barnes's dissertation, Maria Helena Lima, and Françoise Lionnet.

10.   In the glossary to *Abeng* Cliff defines "buckra" as "white person; specifically one representing the ruling class. British. (also *backra*.)."

WORKS CITED

Alcoff, Linda. "Cultural Feminism Versus Post-Structuralism: The Identity Crisis in Feminist Theory." *Signs* 13:3 (1988), 405-436.

Barnes, Fiona. *Explorations in Geography, Gender and Genre: Decolonizing Women's Novels of Development*. Diss. University of Wisconsin-Madison, 1992.

____. "Resisting Cultural Cannibalism: Oppositional Narratives in Michelle Cliff's *No Telephone to Heaven*." *Journal of the Midwest Modern Language Association* 25:1 (1992): 23-31.

Bloch, Ernst. *The Principle of Hope*. Cambridge, MA: MIT P, 1986.

Michelle Cliff. *Free Enterprise*. New York: Dutton, 1993.

____. *No Telephone to Heaven*. New York: Dutton, 1987.

____. *Abeng*. New York: Crossing Press, 1984.

____. "If I Could Write This in Fire, I Would Write This in Fire." *The Land of Look Behind*. New York: Firebrand, 1985.

____. *The Land of Look Behind*. New York: Firebrand, 1985.

Eagleton, Terry. "Nationalism: Irony and Commitment." *Nationalism, Colonialism, and Literature*. Terry Eagleton, Frederic Jameson, Edward Said. Minneapolis: U of Minnesota P, 1990.

Edmundson, Belinda. "Race Privilege and the Politics of (Re)Writing History: An Analysis of the Novels of Michelle Cliff." *Callaloo* 16:1 (1993): 180-191.

Gikandi, Simon. *Writing in Limbo: Modernism and Caribbean Literature*. Ithaca: Cornell UP, 1992.

Harlow, Barbara. *Resistance Literature*. New York: Methuen, 1987.

Jordan, June. "Report from the Bahamas." *On Call: Political Essays.* Boston: South End, 1985.

Lima, Maria Helena. "Revolutionary Developments: Michelle Cliff's 'No Telephone to Heaven' and Merle Collins's 'Angel.'" *Ariel* 24:1 (1993): 35-56.

Lionnet, Françoise. "Of Mangoes and Maroons: Language, History, and the Multicultural Subject of Michelle Cliff's *Abeng.*" *Decolonizing the Subject: The Politics of Gender in Women's Autobiography.* Ed. Sidonie Smith and Julia Watson. Minneapolis: U of Minnesota P, 1992.

Mohanty, Chandra Talpade. "Cartographies of Struggle: Third World Women and the Politics of Feminism." *Third World Women and the Politics of Feminism.* Ed. Chandra Talpade Mohanty, Ann Russo, Lourdes Torres. Bloomington: Indiana UP, 1991.

Mordecai, Pamela, and Betty Wilson. *Her True-True Name.* Oxford: Heinemann, 1989.

Raiskin, Judith. "The Art of History: An Interview with Michelle Cliff." *Kenyon Review* 15.1 (1993): 57-71.

Schwartz, Meryl. "Interview with Michelle Cliff." *Contemporary Literature* 34:4 (1994).

Walters, Wendy. "A Coalition Is Not a Home: Identity Strategies in Michelle Cliff's *No Telephone to Heaven.*" unpublished paper.

24

Refusing the Poisoned Chalice: The Sexual Politics of Rita Ann Higgins and Paula Meehan

Karen Steele

On February 13, 1993, the *Irish Times* published a survey of five hundred Irish women conducted in order to produce "a vision of how women see themselves in Irish society today" (1). When asked what they saw as a woman's most important role in life, seventy-four percent responded that "motherhood / providing for family" ranked highest. At the same time, sixty-six percent said they most admired not a stay-at-home mom but President Mary Robinson, a career woman who has been active in politics for twenty years. This ambivalent attitude of Irish women is more remarkable when one considers some of the issues for which Robinson was known before her election to the presidency: as a lawyer in the 1970s and 1980s, she campaigned for the right to divorce, freedom of reproductive choice, and equal rights for homosexuals, issues which are often represented by conservatives as a threat to Catholic morality and Irish social customs. Robinson's presidential victory in 1990, moreover, represented a dual achievement: for women, a release from the image of Woman as a passive and pure dispossessed nation; for the Irish, a liberation from the Arnoldian stereotype of the Celts as quaint, effeminate, backward people. As Ailbhe Smyth argues,

> It was a positive vote for a new force capable of breaking the strangle-hold of the historical narratives of Ireland and Irishness. It was a vote for disruption and disturbance of the myths on which we have fed ourselves for longer than we now want to remember. ("Great Day" 62)

Mary Robinson's election by a constituency that reveres motherhood as deeply as the motherland or the Mother of God, and her continuing popularity (ninety percent approval ratings in 1995) speaks volumes about her finesse in the politics of home. For, while she is an influential advocate for progressive social change, her constituency and her circumscribed powers require careful, symbolic acts rather than bold legislation or radical speeches.[1] Contemporary female poets in Ireland face a similar challenge: they need to break free from a stifling idea of Irishness while still working in a lyric tradition largely influenced by W.B. Yeats. This essay examines the way poets Rita Ann Higgins and Paula Meehan have symbolically reshaped Irish identity, indeed refashioned the Irish homeland, through disrupting and disturbing the old myths of the Yeatsian imagination, and so destabilizing what Eavan Boland names the poetic and political "tendency to fuse the national and the feminine, to make the image of the woman in the pretext of a romantic nationalism" (*A Kind of Scar* 23). In revising some of the most revered and persistent images of Irish femininity, Higgins and Meehan effectively assert a radically new Ireland by challenging traditional Irish representations of sexuality and motherhood.

Paula Meehan has observed that because poets naturally look back to their literary predecessors as they struggle through a long apprenticeship, "the big lessons are learned from the dead," the vast majority of whom are men (Dorgan 269). Eavan Boland has also written frequently about her minority position as an Irish female poet among the poets of the overwhelmingly male poetic ascendancy, noting that "a hundred years ago I might have been a motif. Now I could have a complex self within my own poem" (*A Kind of Scar* 23). Despite her ascent from object to author, however, she still finds herself in a "bruising struggle" with W.B. Yeats, whose poetry she characterizes as "the poisoned chalice" (Battersby, "An Irishwoman's Diary" 11). The perilous allure of Yeats's poetry is venomous for women writers, Boland argues, because of his emblematic portraits of women—especially those of his unrequited love, the political activist Maud Gonne. Indeed, though Yeats's attitudes towards and writings on women were complex and changed throughout his life, his nationalist play *Cathleen ni Houlihan* and his early love poems allegorizing women as Ireland have profoundly affected Irish national and female identities, especially among female writers. As a result, Boland asserts, Irish women poets have found it more difficult to establish themselves as autonomous creators.

Yeats is of course only partially responsible for the tendency in Irish culture to equate women with the idea of the nation. Although Yeats made dramatically memorable the myth of Ireland as a nurturing or devouring woman, he was not original in invoking the stereotype. Proinsias MacCana observes, "In Irish tradition it would be hard to exaggerate the importance of the idea of the land and its sovereignty conceived in the form of a woman" (7). In Irish culture, the representation of the female body in a political context has been limited to only a few forms: a chaste woman who is a victim of or in need of protection from mad Fenians (Hibernia); a fiercely patriotic or weeping mother who has lost her sons in battle or to emigration (Mother Ireland); or a sexually dangerous female demanding the blood of her lovers as sacrifice for her confiscated lands (Cathleen ni Houlihan).

The 1937 Constitution—seeking to emphasize Irish cultural difference from the colonizer, Britain—legally inscribed and culturally enforced the nationalist and Catholic ideas of femininity as chaste maternity.[2] Article 41, Section 2 states, "By her life within the home, woman gives to the state a support without which the common good could not be achieved." Women who fought for the country's right to self-determination lost their own power and liberty, as they were directed out of the political scene and into the home.[3] Under the guise of chivalrous, masculine protection, Eamonn de Valera's Constitution worked effectively to keep women out of the labor market. Endeavoring "to ensure that mothers shall not be obliged by economic necessity to engage in labor to the neglect of their duties in the home," the State in reality curtailed women's opportunities in the workforce, although it offered little economic support for their maternal "place in the home."[4] Contrary to de Valera's romantic vision of the "romping of sturdy children . . . [and] the laughter of comely maidens,"[5] the woman rigidly defined as wife-mother has little protection and few legal rights under family law. As Nell McCafferty has observed, "There's no place like a courtroom to dismiss the nonsensical notion entertained by housewives that they are in any degree independent of their husbands" ("Housewives" 93). Even outside of marriage, Irish women are not treated as equal citizens. In education, employment, politics, and the tax and welfare systems, women are discriminated against; in the few areas where sex-based discrimination has been banned, pervasive residual attitudes remain.[6] Moreover, as Gerardine Meaney argues, when women are forced into this role as "bearers of national honour and scapegoats of national identity," inevitably they are reduced to emblems, "the territory over which power is exercised" (7). The most compelling example of how women have become this territory is the use of the Constitution to attack women's most fundamental right, the control of their bodies. As abortion-rights activist Ruth Riddick has observed, using the Constitution to deny women the right to reproductive control closely follows the spirit of the document and the will of its framers (148).

The genre of poetry provides perhaps the most persistent images of Ireland as a woman, from the *aisling* of eighteenth-century Gaelic verse to Yeats's love poetry and Heaney's bog poems.[7] Thus, because the Irish national mythos—Yeats's poisoned chalice—silences women, Irish female poets have developed several strategies in order to refuse the cup. One tactic is to reject the old images and to adopt a new subject matter that examines, for example, "real" history and "real" women: something Boland has tried to do in poems such as "Self-Portrait on a Summer Evening," a poem which discusses a painting by Jean-Baptiste Chardin and the ordinary life:

> Jean-Baptiste Chardin
> is painting a woman
> in the last summer light.

> All summer long
> he has been slighting her
> in blotched blues, tints,
> half-tones, rinsed neutrals.

> What you are watching is light unlearning itself,
> an infinite unfrocking of the prism. (*Outside History* 80)

Here Boland places herself as "Chardin's woman," the domestic subject of his composition. The negative language, the "slighting," and "blotched blues" of the second stanza, is not a critique of Chardin's attitude toward his subject; like the "bruised summer light" of "The Oral Tradition" and the "kind of scar" in "Miss Eire," this disfigured vocabulary reflects "a sense / suddenly of truth," a perspective that refuses the unblemished, false nature of myth (42). This canvas, indeed, reveals not a formal pose designed to recall myths or history but rather the "simple colors of / her ankle-length summer skirt" and "the sky that odd shade of apron" (81). The images that fill the poem are detailed and suburban. The woman is depicted:

> crossing between
> the garden and the house,
> under the whitebeam trees,
> keeping an eye on the length of the grass
> the height of the hedge,
> the distance of the children. . . . (81)

Throughout, Boland as subject and poet is motivated by "the need to be ordinary," a compulsion to reorient the reader away from emblematic portraits of women towards representations of the common and ordinary aspects of female life.

Where Boland's "need to be ordinary" entails meditating on eighteenth-century art, such "common" subjects seem alienating for others, such as working-class poets Rita Ann Higgins and Paula Meehan. Moreover, Boland's practice of altering the subject matter of poems from stereotyped feminine nationalist images to depictions of her private domestic experiences in suburban Dublin is also problematic. As Clair Wills has argued in *Improprieties: Politics and Sexuality in Northern Irish Poetry,*

> There is a danger not only that such an approach will tend to reconfirm the view that women's concerns are focused on the home and the family, but also that the radical dislocation of the private sphere in modern society will remain unacknowledged. (49-50)

If we believe Meaney's assertion that "in post-colonial southern Ireland a particular construction of sexual and familial roles became the very substance of what it meant to be Irish" (191), then the most powerful refusal of the old myths would be through radically rewriting women's sexual and familial past through verbalizing previously silenced or taboo topics. As Willis claims, "Representations of alternative and 'improper' forms of sexuality may not only suggest alternatives to the national representations, but also deflate the debilitating ideal of purity and perfection on which they are built" (3-4). Higgins and Meehan dismantle the myth of Ireland as a woman through discussions of sexuality, especially "unspeakable" desires such as lesbianism, adolescent sex, and maternal sexuality.

Rita Ann Higgins's poems about sexuality operate to undermine traditional images of Irish femininity by playfully breaking the silence surrounding the taboo subject of Irish women's sensuality. Irish poet Nuala Ní Dhomhnaill has facetiously observed that living in a puritanical Irish social setting has made it difficult even for heterosexuals to come out of the closet.[8] In her poems about sexuality, Higgins writes out of a similar frustration, disregarding cultural practice by writing about human and animal libido with frankness and humor. Celebratory discussions of sex, in fact, characterize a number of her poems: "Sunny Side Plucked," "It's Platonic," "No Balls at All," "Light of the Moon," "I'll Have to Stop Thinking of Sex," and "I Want to Make Love to Kim Basinger." As a group, these poems enable the poet to challenge Irish social mores that silence discussions of or reflections on passion and desire.

For example, in "I Want to Make Love to Kim Basinger," Higgins writes about the closeting effect of compulsory heterosexuality in Irish culture:

> I'm terrified
> of hairdressers
> who always say
> Are you going
> to the dance
> tonight love?
>
> I always say yes
> even though
> I'm never going
> to the dance
> tonight love.
>
> They say the dance
> I say the dance
> we all say the dance
> we say, the dance.
>
> They think
> I should be going
> to the dance
> and what they think goes.
>
> I always have my hair done
> so I can look good
> in the bath
> in case
> Kim Basinger
> calls round. (*Philomela's Revenge* 80)

Higgins's use of location is particularly effective, for she demonstrates the ubiquitous power of heterosexuality and patriarchy even in all-female spaces. Like the ladies' room or the bridal boudoir—places where no man may enter in case he discover the secrets of female charm and beauty—the hairdresser in the West of Ireland is dedicated to reinforcing traditional femininity and values: look good and you'll catch that man. And so, as she seats herself before her hairdresser Consumpta, a woman who "talks in scrunch and blow-dry" and obsesses about split ends, the speaker must endure Consumpta's assumption that the feminine world primps only for testosterone-pumped males. As Consumpta observes,

> No split ender
> ever shifted
> the bull of the ball
> and we do want
> the bull of the ball
> don't we
> otherwise why bother
> getting our hair done
> in the first place. (82)

As in many of Higgins's poems, there is a great deal of fun here in the character sketches of Consumpta and her closeted client; the poem's humor, however, also conveys a serious message about the silent rage and repressed desire associated with being gay in Ireland. When she is continually asked, "Are you going to the dance tonight love?" the speaker tells us:

> I always say yes
> I start to shout,
> I say yes Consumpta yes

and her shout both releases her pent-up anger at having to play the role of a heterosexual hopeful going to the dance and suggests her delighted cry if Kim Basinger did take,

> the further
> of five lefts,
> two rights
> and three straight aheads

when she called round so that the speaker could make love to her.

In a more serious poem, "Mothercare," Higgins combines issues of class and feminism in her depiction of the consequences of adolescent sexuality.[9] The subject of the poem—babies having babies—is a favorite among social and political conservatives who preach the message of sexual abstinence. But Higgins doesn't moralize; rather, she portrays the damaging effect of romanticizing motherhood. At a poetry reading at the University of Texas at Austin in the spring of 1994, Higgins explained that among her teen-age daughters' circle of friends there were a number of girls who had babies; many of these girls were travelers and all were working-class. As Higgins watched the young girls gather with their babies and the babies' many accoutrements, this poem began to take shape as a kind of admonishing song to her daughters:

> The girls came over
> to see the new buggy,
> the rainbow buggy
> with the sunshine stripes.
>
> O.K. it was expensive
> but it was the best
> and welfare pitched in.

For the young mother and her friends, the buggy becomes a metaphor for their girlish views of motherhood. The rainbow buggy, for example, seems as much chosen for the lively sunshine stripes as for its many features:

> It had everything—
> she listed its finer points
> under belly things we hadn't seen.
>
> A little touch here
> and it collapses
> a little there
> and it's up like a shot,
> you barely touch this—
> and you're in another street
> another town.
>
> A mind of its own

a body like a rocket
it's yours to control—
just like that.

Implicit in Higgins's focus on a buggy that "had everything" is the sobering knowledge that motherhood for a young, poor, single woman will not resemble the bright new pram for long. The twenty-four hour job of minding a demanding infant entails denying or delaying one's own needs, as this mother is surely learning. One cannot trigger the role with "a little touch here" or "a little touch there."

Further, a baby can hardly be compared to a buggy. While "welfare pitched in" to purchase the pram, a baby's many basic needs—food, diapers, clothing, doctors' bills—are not fully covered by monthly support from the state. Moreover, while a baby has "a mind of its own" (if only regarding a sleeping and eating schedule), a child cannot be managed like a buggy that is "yours to control." Unlike her finely-tuned piece of equipment, her baby cannot be handled and cared for with such ease of command. As a dependent and extremely needy individual, the child requires constant care, and depletes both financial and psychological resources quickly and exhaustively.

Higgins's emphasis on control is important, though. As a working-class Irish female—one who has been disenfranchised and disempowered by virtue of her economic status and gender—Higgins recognizes the desire for power, if only over a helpless individual. As she writes in "Some People," she knows what it is like

to be second hand
to be second class
to be no class
to be looked down on
to be walked on
to be pissed on
to be shat on. (*Witch* 63)

Mothers, also, know what it is like. Young girls who have babies in order to control or be needed by someone else, therefore, rarely gain the kind of respect or power for which they hoped. As any new parent soon finds out, there are few occasions that engender impotency more than trying to soothe the cries of a colicky or teething infant.

Higgins also employs irony in her focus on the buggy. As a vehicle, the buggy provides transportation: out of the house, out of the yard, perhaps even out of the neighborhood. It is still, nevertheless, a piece of equipment that moves at a walking pace. Unlike Tracy Chapman's fast car that she hopes "is . . . fast enough so you can fly away," the buggy not only fails to offer flight from a life of poverty, it symbolizes her ever-decreasing chances of escape. In the final lines of the poem, Higgins focuses on the economics of single motherhood in Ireland:

> She swears she'll keep it well
> immaculate she says
> immaculate.
>
> When she's nearly eighteen
> it will still be new,
> Tomma-Lee will be two and a half
>
> she can sell it then
> and fetch a high price,
>
> almost as much as she paid.

The mother's unrealistic pledge to keep her pram "immaculate" especially resonates for an Irish Catholic audience: it reminds one of every Catholic schoolgirl's vow to emulate the sexually pure Virgin Mary. As sure as the buggy will get sullied by rain and mud, baby spitup and cracker crumbs, so too we can foresee the futility of an Irish populace that refuses to acknowledge sexual desire. Higgins's somber close also brings the poem back to issues of welfare and class politics. Implicitly, this young mother has paid for motherhood with her future: without the middle-class benefits of childcare and playgroups, she will presumably forego school and job prospects and instead live on the dole while raising a child. Higgins thus dismantles the idyllic vision of glowing motherhood and exposes the sham of de Valera's promise of economic stability for all Irish mothers who remain in the home.

Where Higgins replaces images of Irish national purity with modern portraits of lesbian desire and teenage motherhood, Paula Meehan also disturbs traditional images of Irish femininity. Challenging the representation of chaste maternity and examining the effects of religion and religious politics, Meehan's "The Statue of the Virgin at Granard Speaks" comments on two events from 1984-5 that symbolized women's social and religious status in Ireland: the death of Ann Lovett and the phenomenon of the moving Marian statues. By juxtaposing these two moments where Irish Catholicism and Mariolatry have worked so effectively to subordinate women and define their roles as solely maternal and chaste, Meehan criticizes the Church's prescription of feminine modesty and virtue via a statue of the holy mother who is an outspoken detractor of Christian faith and purity, and neither a willing nor believing participant in the cult of the Virgin Mary.

To appreciate Meehan's poem fully, one must first understand the circumstances behind and the significance of the death of Ann Lovett, a fifteen-year-old single girl who died giving birth in an open-air grotto in Granard on January 31, 1984. Giving birth to an illegitimate baby is not uncommon in rural Ireland, nor was Lovett's premature death due to childbirth complications. Rather, her death became significant because she labored and died at the feet of a statue of the Virgin Mary. The symbolism of a young mother's death before a statue of the Church's most revered figure of nurturing maternity stirred the consciousness of the nation. Moreover, in the wake of the Kerry Babies Tribunal in 1984,[10] Ann Lovett's death brought together again the issues of infanticide, women's lack of reproductive control, and the debates surrounding the 1983 abortion referendum.

Meehan juxtaposes Lovett's haunting death with the phenomenon of the moving statues to comment further upon the conservative effect of popular Catholic belief on women's social and religious role in the community. In the spring and summer of 1985, numerous witnesses recounted seeing Marian statues move, change appearance, create visions, or light up the sky in Ballinspittle, Carns, Camolin, Glenbrien, Munster, and outside Wexford.[11] Some people interpreted the moving statues as a sign of the "terrible things that were being dragged to light" locally, such as the Kerry Babies Tribunal and increasingly common reports of incest. One father whose children witnessed moving statues inside the Church in Asdee noted,

> There've been two murders in the Listowel area and over in Tarbert there was a case of a man who was having sex with his two nieces and got one of them pregnant. That's why some of the people here think that what's happened is a sign. (O'Toole 89)

Where some viewed the moving statues as an admonishing message from God to fix the troubled state of affairs in their local area, others sought to explain them as a warning symptom of national or global problems. In his introduction to *Seeing Is Believing: Moving Statues in Ireland*, Colm Tóibín provides a list of causes:

> The Kerry Babies Tribunal, the bad weather, the Air India crash, the death of Ann Lovett, the national debt, facts and divisions which came to light during the [abortion] Amendment debate, unemployment, the hunger strikes in the North, . . . the failure of Garrett FitzGerald to improve the lot of anyone in the country, simple piety, nostalgia for the happiness and harmony induced by the Papal visit, fear that the church has moved too far away from things of the spirit. . . . (7)

Dáithí Ó hÓgáin observes that there is historical precedent for public sightings of moving Marian statues. These occurrences seem to have two things in common: first, they accompany impending disaster, such as plague or outbreak of fire. Second, the moving Mary, who is perceived as the great intercessor and protector, becomes the one comfort and aid to the whole community under threat (73). In all cases, however, a wave of conservative sentiment follows the event. Ó hÓgáin thinks that some contemporary causes of community angst or apocalyptic thought in Ireland which have accompanied the sightings of the moving statues could range from the threat of nuclear war to attacks on traditional attitudes. The most influential factor, in his opinion, was the "assault on traditional mores of sexual conduct by consumerist culture" (73). Not surprisingly, the vision of the moving shrines was interpreted by many as a re-affirmation of conservative politics and social practices.

Meehan strategically uses this occasion, which produced a conservative impulse, not to support but rather to subvert the message of sexual restraint and religious piety. She, moreover, refuses to allow Mary her traditional role of comfort and aid. Unlike the moving images, the statue in Meehan's poem cannot move; she speaks. Encased in her "stony robes," she longs to break loose of her vestal image "pure blue, pure white" to be "incarnate, incarnate / maculate and tousled in a honeyed bed." Instead, she is stuck up here in this grotto, "shivering in the bitter November winds" (*Man* 40-1). This Mary, then, not only resists emblematizing purity, she longs for its opposite.

Meehan strategically uses this occasion, which produced a conservative impulse, not to support but rather to subvert the message of sexual restraint and religious piety. She, moreover, refuses to allow Mary her traditional role of comfort and aid. Unlike the moving images, the statue in Meehan's poem cannot move; she speaks. Encased in her "stony robes," she longs to break loose of her vestal image "pure blue, pure white" to be "incarnate, incarnate / maculate and tousled in a honeyed bed." Instead, she is stuck up here in this grotto, "shivering in the bitter November winds" (*Man* 40-1). This Mary, then, not only resists emblematizing purity, she longs for its opposite.

In writing about the death of Ann Lovett, Nell McCafferty observed that the grotto where Lovett died was "not accessible to the public gaze" as it was tucked in at the end of town ("Death" 105). As the most secluded spot in Granard, it was the place where students went when playing hookey, where young lovers retreated for discreet time alone, as well as where Ann Lovett chose to give birth without being seen. For Meehan's statue, the location is neither cozy nor evocative of intimacy. The statue's physical and emotional anguish at being the sequestered object of veneration reveals how the Catholic Church has effectively sought to control all Irish women by defining femininity exclusively as chaste and / or procreative. Her stony seclusion serves as a metaphor for Irish women trapped by church doctrine and laws heavily influenced by the Catholic Church, notably those affecting women's reproductive choices within and outside marriage. The laws of church and state regarding women's knowledge of and access to contraception and abortion restrict not only women living in the Republic: the bitter November wind "sweep[s] across the border" (40), connecting the twenty-six counties of the Republic with the six counties of the North. Meehan reminds her audience that unwanted pregnancy is a problem regardless of who controls the state. Indeed, while contraception has been legal and more widely available for a longer period in the North, the 1967 Abortion Act, which legalized elective abortions for social and medical reasons in England, Scotland, and Wales, was not extended to Northern Ireland (Hooley 40). Thus, for Irish women with an unwanted pregnancy, there are very limited options on both sides of the border: stigmatized illegitimacy, adoption, or abortion abroad.

Meehan's statue of the Virgin not only discloses her disenchantment with her lonely spot in the grotto, she exposes herself as a Christian skeptic when she admits, "They fit me to a myth of a man crucified" (40). She also sardonically notes, "They name me Mother of all this grief / though mated to no mortal man" (40-1), ostensibly disdaining her contradictory role as a model of maternity and virginity. The statue's frustrated rejection of what the Catholic Church has always worshipped as miraculous underscores the difficult position of Irish women who are measured against the same unreal achievement. Indeed, as we observe the statue's despondency over her own asexual existence, we can see how much more acute is the plight of real Irish women who are expected to model their lives after Mary's despite the fact that they—like the statue—delight in the sensual allure of nature. The statue tells us,

> It can be lovely here at times. Springtime,
> early summer. Girls in Communion frocks

> pale rivals to the riot in the hedgerows
> of cow parsley and haw blossom, the perfume
> from every rushy acre that's left for hay
> when the light swings longer with the sun's push north.
>
> Or the grace of a midsummer wedding
> when the earth herself calls out for coupling . . .
> ....
>
> Even an autumn burial can work its own pageantry.
> The hedges heavy with the burden of fruiting
> crab, sloe, berry, hip; clouds scud east
> pear scented, windfalls secret in long
> orchard grasses. . . . (41)

These lines, which echo Keats's ode "To Autumn" in describing the abundance of the rustic landscape, suggest the natural origins of sexuality; like Keats's depiction of the bending apple trees, swelling gourds and overbrimming honeycombs, Mary's portrait of the hedgerow in blossom and, later, ripe with autumn fruits stirs a physically tangible and olfactory response that all creation feels. The seasons are also a metaphor for the stages of fetal development; like the flora in nature, Lovett's body blossoms and expands with ripening life. When "winter" comes early, however, both mother and child die tragically because no one will assist in the "harvest," no one will provide aid in the birth of an illegitimate child. Trapped as a figure of the Church and as a religious model for society, the statue refuses to intervene on behalf of Ann Lovett who "cried out to me in extremis." Silently, passively, the statue stood:

> I did not move,
> I didn't lift a finger to help her,
> I didn't intercede with heaven,
> nor whisper the charmed word in God's ear. (42)

So, too, Ann Lovett's family, the villagers of Granard, the Church, and the sisters who taught Lovett at the Convent of Mercy School refused to act on Lovett's behalf because they "did not know" she was pregnant, "could not intervene" because it was not their place, or "would not help" a girl who was no longer innocent.

In a recent interview, Ailbhe Smyth—editor of the Irish feminist Attic press—explained her rationale for titling a collection of Irish women's poetry *Wildish Things*: "Irish women's voices were wild voices, not because women are essentially wild but because *historically* we're wild—we have been maintained outside what passes for the story, the narrative, the one and only narrative of our nation" (Gray 106). Indeed, while Irish women's writing is increasingly visible and more female poets are getting published, the St. Peters of the Irish poetic canon—publishers,[12] academics, and critics—are overwhelmingly male.[13] Few women make it into the best known anthologies. For example, the recent *Field Day Anthology of Irish Writing*, which purports to be an exhaustive collection of 1,500 years of Irish writing, included only six female poets in its third volume (to redress this "omission," Field Day is putting out a fourth volume of just women's writing).[14] Further, the poetic audience is still largely under the spell of Yeats and, increasingly, his heir-apparent Seamus Heaney. Yet, if Mary Robinson can call Áras an Uachtarán (the Irish Presidential Residence) home, Rita Ann Higgins and Paula Meehan can also claim a space for Irish women writers, inviting "wild" voices that could only be heard on the margins to a prominent place in mainstream Irish culture. For, as Robinson maintains a powerful (if symbolic) position in the previously male-dominated sphere of Irish politics, so, too, Higgins and Meehan have the imaginative force to reshape the Irish imagination both inside and outside of the academy, in their homeland of Ireland as well as beyond.

NOTES

1. Because of the ceremonial function of the Irish non-executive presidential office, the President cannot make policy and is constitutionally barred from speaking out directly on political issues.

2. I am indebted to Kathleen Kane's unpublished paper on the 1937 Constitution for providing an insightful theoretical framework for approaching women and the constitution.

3.   In *Husbandry to Housewifery: Women, Economic Change, and Housework in Ireland, 1890-1914*, Joanna Bourke shows that during the turn of the twentieth century, rural Irish women in the thousands switched from paid work on farms, in houses, and in factories to unpaid labor in the home. Bourke argues that many women left public employment opportunities willingly and relished the change because this new role as housewife allowed them to increase their status and to improve their quality of life. These women, however, did not always benefit from these improvements. Bourke notes that sometimes "economic growth exasperated inequality within the household, making women worse off *in relation to men* than they had been in 1891" (264).

4.   The 1935 Conditions of Employment Bill set a limit on women workers in industry and banned married women from most jobs. Although the bill was lifted in 1973 and women now compose over one third of the workforce, residual attitudes and structural discrimination remain, as is evidenced by sex-stereotyped teacher expectations and curriculum, lack of career orientation for girls, discreet bars from traditionally male-held jobs, denial of proper training and deserved promotions, and unequal pay. See Eugene McCarthy, Ailbhe Smyth ("Women"), and Evelyn Mahon.

5.   Quoted in the *Irish Press* March 18, 1943.

6.   See Jenny Beale (139-163).

7.   See Elizabeth Butler Cullingford for an historical explanation and a critical discussion of the allegorical identification of Ireland as a woman in Irish poetry.

8.   Remarks made at the Seventh Annual Graduate Irish Studies Conference, March 20, 1993.

9.   I am grateful to Rita Ann Higgins for her generosity in sending me a copy of this poem before publication. She read "Mothercare" at *Remapping the Borders: The Eighth Annual Graduate Irish Studies Conference* held at the University of

Texas at Austin in March 1994. The poem was recently published in *Feminist Review*.

10.   Conducting a highly publicized gynecological inquisition, the Kerry Babies Tribunal sought to uncover the murderer (mother) of a newborn that had been stabbed twenty-seven times, placed in a sack, thrown into the sea, and washed ashore in Kerry in 1984. Lacking evidence, the Tribunal nonetheless charged a woman, Joanne Hayes, with the murder despite proof that she gave birth to a different child (who was born prematurely, died, and was buried around the same time that the Kerry baby was found). See Nell McCafferty, *A Woman to Blame*, for a full account.

11.   For more information on the phenomenon of the moving statues, see Colm Tóibín.

12.   A few notable exceptions re the feminist publishing house Attic Press, and Salmon Press, which has a reputation for publishing female poets, especially those living in the west of Ireland, such as Angela Greene, Rita Ann Higgins, Anne Kennedy, Anne Le Marquand Hartigan, Catherine Phil MacCarthy, Áine Miller, Mary O'Donnell, Mary O'Malley, and Eithne Strong.

13.   See, for example, Ailbhe Smyth, "Letters to the Editor" (*Irish Times*, June 12, 1993) in which she responds to poet Derek Mahon's assertion that "living white females" run the poetry show in New York: "The gatekeepers of American poetry (publishers, academics, critics) are still a massively solid male phalanx. And of Irish poetry, too, for that matter. Which reminds me, the rarity of books by women, poets or others, reviewed in the *Irish Times* ought to be a matter of embarrassment (to the *Times* itself), although I am afraid it is not."

14.   See the debate over the exclusion of women in *The Field Day Anthology of Irish Writing*, especially Edna Longley's detailed critique (qtd in Battersby, "Field Day") and the heated debate between Nuala O'Faolain (July 20, 1992) and Tom Paulin (July 25, 1992) in the letters section of the *Irish Times*. The

British TV company Channel Four also ran a program entitled "Bandung File," which discussed the absence of women in the new anthology. Few women, moreover, feature as editors or selected poets in the major Irish poetry anthologies. *The Faber Book of Contemporary Irish Verse* (ed. Paul Muldoon) includes one woman, Medbh McGuckian, and *The New Oxford Book of Irish Verse* (ed. Thomas Kinsella) has no women from the nineteenth or twentieth centuries. Feminists have responded by putting out their own collections, such as *Pillars of the House: An Anthology of Verse by Irish Women from 1690 to the Present* (ed. A.A. Kelly); *The Female Line: Northern Irish Women Writers* (ed. Ruth Hooley); *Voices on the Wind: Women Poets of the Celtic Twilight* (ed. Eilís Ní Dhuibhne); *New Irish Women's Writing* (ed. Ailbhe Smyth).

WORKS CITED

Battersby, Eileen. "An Irishwoman's Diary." *Irish Times* July 15, 1992: 11.

_____. "Field Day under Heavy Fire from Academics." *Irish Times* August 18, 1992: 7.

Beale, Jenny. *Women in Ireland: Voices of Change.* Bloomington: Indiana UP, 1987.

Boland, Eavan. *A Kind of Scar: The Woman Poet in a National Tradition.* Dublin: Attic Press, 1989.

_____. *Outside History, Selected Poems 1980-1990.* New York: W.W. Norton, 1990.

Bourke, Joanna. *Husbandry to Housewifery: Women, Economic Change, and Housework in Ireland, 1890-1914.* Oxford: Clarendon, 1993.

Cullingford, Elizabeth Butler. "'Thinking of her . . . as . . . Ireland': Yeats, Pearse, Heaney." *Textual Practice* 4 (1990): 1-21.

Deane, Seamus, ed. *The Field Day Anthology of Irish Writing.* Derry: Field Day Press, 1991.

Dorgan, Theo. "An Interview with Paula Meehan." *Colby Quarterly* 28 (1992): 265-269.

Gray, Kate Martin. "The Attic LIPS: Feminist Pamphleteering for the New Ireland." *Éire-Ireland* Spring (1994): 105-122.

Higgins, Rita Ann. *Goddess of the Mervue Bus.* Galway: Salmon Press, 1986.

_____. "Mothercare." *Feminist Review* 50 (1995): 67-8.

_____. *Philomela's Revenge.* Galway: Salmon Press, 1992.

_____. *Witch in the Bushes.* Galway: Salmon Press, 1988.

Hooley, Ruth, ed. *The Female Line: Northern Irish Women Writers.* Belfast: Northern Women's Rights Movement, 1985.

Innes, C.L. *Woman and Nation in Irish Literature and Society, 1880-1935.* New York: Harvester, 1993.

Kelly, A.A., ed. *Pillars of the House: An Anthology of Verse by Irish Women from 1690 to the Present.* Dublin: Wolfhound, 1987.

Kinsella, Thomas, ed. *The New Oxford Book of Irish Verse.* Oxford: Oxford UP, 1986.

MacCana, Proinsias. "Women in Irish Mythology." *Crane Bag* 4.1 (1980): 7-11.

Madrigal, Alix. "Ireland's Women, Finding Their Way." *San Francisco Chronicle* October 3, 1993: 4+.

Mahon, Evelyn. "Women's Rights and Catholicism in Ireland." *New Left Review* 166 (1987): 52-68.

Mahoney, Rosemary. *Whoredom in Kimmage: Irish Women Coming of Age.* Boston: Houghton Mifflin, 1993.

McCafferty, Nell. "The Death of Ann Lovett." *The Abortion Papers: Ireland.* Ed. Ailbhe Smyth. Dublin: Attic Press, 1992: 99-106.

____. "Housewives' Independence Notions Disappear in the Courtroom." *The Best of Nell.* Dublin: Attic Press, 1984.

____. "Virgin on the Rocks." *Seeing Is Believing: Moving Statues in Ireland.* In Tóibín. 53-58.

____. *A Woman to Blame: The Kerry Babies Case.* Dublin: Attic Press, 1985.

McCarthy, Eugene. "Women and Work in Ireland: The Present, and Preparing for the Future." *Women in Irish Society.* Eds. Margaret MacCurtain and Donncha Ó'Corrain. Westport: Greenwood Press, 1979. 103-117.

Meaney, Gerardine. *Sex and Nation: Women in Irish Culture and Politics*. Dublin: Attic Press, 1991.

Meehan, Paula. *The Man Who Was Marked by Winter*. Oldcastle, Co. Meath: Gallery Press, 1991.

Muldoon, Paul, ed. *The Faber Book of Contemporary Irish Verse*. London: Faber, 1986.

Ní Dhuibhne, Eilís. *Voices on the Wind: Women Poets of the Celtic Twilight*. Dublin: New Island Books, 1995.

Northern Ireland Abortion Law Reform Association. "Abortion: The Case for Legal Reform in Northern Ireland." *Abortion Papers: Ireland*. Ed. Ailbhe Smyth. Dublin: Attic Press, 1992. 40-46.

Ó hÓgáin, Dáithí. *A Manifestation of Popular Religion*. In Tóibín. 67-74.

O'Toole, Fintan. "Seeing is Believing." *Seeing is Believing: Moving Statues in Ireland*. Ed. Colm Tóibín. Mountrath, Co. Laios: Pilgrim Press, 1985. 89-95.

Phillips, Andrew. "A Woman of Substance." *Maclean's* October 19, 1992: 46+.

Riddick, Ruth. "The Right to Choose: Questions of Feminist Morality." *A Dozen LIPs*. Dublin: Attic Press, 1994. 140-61.

Smyth, Ailbhe. "'A Great Day for Women of Ireland . . . ': The Meaning of Mary Robinson's Presidency for Irish Women." *Canadian Journal of Irish Studies* 18.1 (1992): 61-75.

____, ed. *Wildish Things: An Anthology of New Irish Women's Writing*. Dublin: Attic Press, 1990.

____. "Women and Power in Ireland: Problems, Progress, Practice." *Women's Studies International Forum* 8 (1985): 255-262.

Tóibín, Colm, ed. *Seeing Is Believing: Moving Statues in Ireland*. Mountrath, Co. Laois: Pilgrim Press, 1985.

Wills, Clair. *Improprieties: Politics and Sexuality in Northern Irish Poetry*. Oxford: Clarendon P, 1993.

25

Zehra Çirak: Foreign Wings on Familiar Shoulders

Marilya Veteto-Conrad

In Zehra Çirak's 1994 volume, *Foreign Wings on Familiar Shoulders,* the book cover shows a figure by Jürgen Walter. A light-skinned male clad only in faded green underwear stands on a brick-colored wedge instead of a left foot, his face and head almost completely concealed by a disproportionately large hand clasping the forehead. The right foot is on tiptoe as if to lift off from the motion of the large silver-colored airplane wing sprouting from the right shoulder.

This figure is an apt symbol for Çirak's position in her adopted homeland of Germany, the country that she has chosen to call home and in which she has made a home for herself on both the personal and literary levels. Sometimes she despairs of making an impact with her work, of being able to live by her art, of finding the words to describe her perceptions. Other times she is *beflügelt,* up-lifted or, literally, bewinged. In the poem, "Notwehr" [Self Defense], Çirak's ambivalent relationship with her adopted homeland is exposed in metaphors of violence that is paradoxically feathered and winged:

"Notwehr"

> Knüppel und Knüppel gesindelt sich gern
> egal wohin sie sich verschlagen
> wohin und wen sie treffen
> ein Knüppel verlängert den Arm
> ein anderer verkürzt das Leben
> Arme schlagen aus wie Flügel
> und heben ab zur Knüppelfahrt
> auswärt fliehen Dortige
> und seitwärts reisen Hiesige
> arme Arme Knüppelhalter
> immer unterwegs treffen sie sich zu
> und winken sich Arme ab

die Erde ist ein Dorf ein rundes
auf unser Dorf schauen Nachbarsdörfer
sie halten sich andere Arme
mit anderen Knüppeln
uns liegt nichts fern
uns liegt nichts nah
wir sind erst übermorgen dran.[1] (*Vogel* 72)

"Self Defense"

clubs of a feather mob together
no matter where they hit it off
wherever they go and whomever they meet
one club extends the arm
another shortens a life
Arms flail like wings
and lift off for a club flight
away flee people from there
and sideways travel people from here
poor arms club carriers
always underway they meet up
and wave their arms off
the earth is a village a round one
at our village look neighboring villages
they keep other poor arms
with other clubs
nothing is far off
nothing is close
it's not our turn 'til tomorrow.

Berlin's Istanbul-born Çirak is typical of her generation and so might
easily represent children of *Gastarbeiter*—menial laborers recruited by
the Federal Republic of Germany between the 1950s and 70s—by dint
of her biography alone. Her politics of home, that is, the manner in
which she has come to address in her poetry the socio-political issues
of racism and nationalism in her adopted home of Germany, also place
her in the role of spokesperson. When she first began writing, these
issues were still dormant; in recent years they have taken center stage
both in newspaper headlines and in Çirak's work. As the above poem,
"Notwehr," illustrates, she criticizes not only the way nationalism is

destroying the world but also the complacency that permits it to flourish.

As Germany's standard of living increased in the decades following World War II, so did the need for laborers willing to fill unskilled and frequently low-prestige jobs, such as garbage collection or street sweeping. Recruitment in the poorer, southern European countries such as Italy, Greece, and Yugoslavia as well as in Turkey was a huge success, and in 1964 the Federal Republic welcomed its one-millionth *Gastarbeiter* with a much-publicized ceremony and the gift of a moped. The gift was to prove telling: the recruited workers were invited with the tacit understanding (at least on the part of the host) that these so-called guests would one day return to their native country. In actuality, the work opportunities and the living conditions proved in many cases to be so much better than in, for instance, Turkey, that many of the recruits stayed in Germany, much to the chagrin of the German government, who had not foreseen this eventuality. Today over seven million non-native Germans reside in Germany; Turks are the largest non-European minority.

In Çirak's case, her parents came to the Federal Republic when she was only three years old; hence, her knowledge of her original homeland was restricted to holiday visits and the stories her parents told. Çirak's generation has come to be known in Turkey as *Almanciler* [Germanites]. This derisive name was coined by Turks for their countrywomen and men abroad who are perceived as Turks in name only after living away for a long span of time or having been born and raised outside of Turkey. Like most of their uneducated, rural compatriots in Germany, Çirak's parents clung to the pious Islamic faith and time-honored Turkish traditions, despite the distance to their home, or perhaps precisely because they felt so far removed from the familiar.

The eldest of three children, Çirak bore the brunt of the family's lack of roots in the new country. Like many women of her generation, she was overly protected and sheltered by her family, guarded carefully until the day that a marriage could be arranged for her and the family honor thus perpetuated. Nonetheless, concessions to the new surroundings were made within the family regarding the eldest daughter: Çirak was permitted to attend German school, but she was admonished to keep her head covering on and not to wear makeup like her German peers did. Çirak tells of the typical teenage behavior of waiting until she was out of sight and then hastily hitching up the unfashionable below-the-knee skirt to mini-length, and tapping a secret cache of lipstick and eyeliner before making an appearance at school.

But there was something different about Çirak, something that set her apart from her peers, German or Turkish: she turned to writing as an outlet. Taking advantage of her parents' meager knowledge of the language, she kept a secret diary in German. That way, she reckoned, even if they did find it, they couldn't read her private thoughts. At first, she recounts in *Freihändig auf dem Tandem* [*With No Hands on a Tandem*], the diary was merely a diary, an outlet for teenage frustrations, and she makes light of it. As time passed, the jotting down of daily experiences evolved into something more reflective, more multi-layered, more condensed: Çirak was becoming a poet. Her material remained the same for some time: reflections and commentary on her dual existence. An early example is the semiautobiographical text "Kopftuch" [Headcloth], anthologized by *deutscher taschenbuch verlag* (Ackermann 197), in which the protagonist and her sister resort to deceptions in order to achieve some balance between the restrictiveness of her parents' guidelines and the mores of a liberal German society. The main problem for the sister is the ubiquitous kerchief worn by pious or conservative Muslim women to cover their hair. The sisters rebel against this symbol of their homeland even as they are scheming to undermine another tradition—arranged marriages. The short prose piece illustrates the tension between the older generation, which is determined, even desperate, to adhere to the customs of the homeland, and the younger one, which is equally firm in its resolve to either change or discard those very customs.

Like the protagonists of "Kopftuch," Çirak maintained a Turkish façade at home to please her parents, yet found herself being someone neither Turkish nor German away from home. This sometimes fulfilled her and sometimes confused her. In retrospect, one wonders what kind of an identity could be formed while performing such a tight-rope act? Independence—from her parents, from her homeland, from family life—was clearly necessary for the development of her adult self, and equally important for the further development of her muse.

In the early eighties, when Çirak was working in Karlsruhe as a cosmetician, she casually mentioned to one of her clients that her private pastime was writing. The woman asked a friend, Dr. Beatrice Steiner, to read a sample. Reluctantly, Dr. Steiner complied and as she relates in the afterword to *flugfänger* [*flightcatcher*], she was so captivated by Çirak's work that she became her patron. Steiner's aid was invaluable in the production of Çirak's first volume of poetry, *flugfänger*. The volume is illustrated with art by a sculptor named Jürgen Walter, whom she had met a short time previously. The two found kindred spirits in one another, and in 1982, Çirak left home with Walter to live in Berlin. The story of their clandestine meetings and secret flight to Berlin is the stuff of movies. The text "Geflüchtet" [Fled] is a poignant commentary on the process of distancing that Çirak initiated when she ran away from home; it is the first of her texts to deal overtly with the dualities inherent in her situation. The text can be read as both a description of her personal life and a portrayal of her political life as an expatriate Turk who has become more German than Turkish.

"Geflüchtet"

und dann
bin ich einfach nicht mehr da
ihr schaut euch nicht um
nach mir
werdet selten sagen
wie schön es war
alles wird bleiben
für euch
nehme nichts mit
dafür bin ich fort
fühle mich jetzt schon so sehr
verlaufen
möchte den weg zurück
doch es ist die einbahnstraße
vor der ich mich fürchtete
die ich umgehen wollte
in die ich geriet (Ackermann 204)

"Fled"

and then
i was just no longer there
you don't look around
for me
seldom will say
how nice it was
everything will stay
for you
take nothing with me

but i am gone
feel already so very
lost
want to find the way back
but it is the one-way street
that i had feared
had wanted to avoid
have ended up in

The poem is less sophisticated or less multi-layered than most of Çirak's work. The reader is struck by the simple, almost confessional nature of the poem which conveys the impression that here Çirak has abandoned her usual wiliness vis à vis language in order to present the heart-wrenching schism her departure of Berlin entailed. Perhaps abandoned is not correct: in the chronology of events in Çirak's life, running away was the first real step toward her self-realization as a person and as a poet. The unadorned, artless voice of this poem is meant to convey her own image of herself as not yet fully matured as a daughter *and* a poet.

Once in Berlin, Çirak felt at liberty to devote her energies to writing in earnest. In 1987 she was awarded an artist's stipend by the Senate of Berlin, which enabled her to reduce her hours at a cosmetics salon in favor of her art. She and Walter also worked jointly on performance art and poetry readings. When interviewed in 1988, she commented that her status as a Turkish-born writer living in Germany had both advantages and disadvantages. In the early eighties, when Germany was just discovering that "its foreigners could write," as Eberhard Seidel-Pielen caustically remarked in the Berlin magazine *zitty*, one of its largest and best-known publishing houses—deutscher taschenbuch verlag or dtv—produced a series of anthologies of non-native German writers. Çirak was included in *Türken deutscher Sprache* [*Turks of German Language*] and *Über Grenzen* [*Across Borders*], but she had misgivings about the results. Many of the texts were of questionable literary quality, and her inclusion in the anthologies typecast her, as she found in her dealings with the mainstream literary world. A text from the dtv anthology *Über Grenzen* speaks eloquently of both her situation as a foreigner in Germany and the ambivalence often demonstrated by publishers interacting with writers of non-German extraction. The following text metaphorizes her status as a foreign writer even as it speaks to the position of non-Germans in general. Although the speaker expresses the hope of being accepted and integrated, the experience of being in limbo—here, one a bridge between one place and another—undermines that hope by its very lack of predictability:

"Sich Warm Laufen"

weil man weiß daß auch brücken ein ende haben
braucht man sich beim übergang nicht zu beeilen
doch auf brücken ist es am kältesten. (Esselborn 220)

"Warming Up"

since you know that bridges too have an end
you do not need to hurry while crossing
yet on bridges is where it's the coldest.

"Sich warm laufen," along with other earlier texts, brought Çirak the 1989 Adelbert von Chamisso Förderpreis for her contribution as a young non-native German author to German-language literature. She was nonetheless fiercely determined not to be categorized by dint of nationality alone, since she found such a definition too confining. She coined a phrase for this typecasting, *verschubladisieren* [drawerifying], derived from her sense of being categorized and shut off in the drawer labeled "foreign author," thus never being given the chance to be judged on her own merits. Other foreign writers, especially those of the *Gastarbeiter* generation in the early eighties, were often engaged in bellybutton gazing and pathos-filled ruminations on the plight of foreign workers and their unfriendly or unjust treatment at the hands of Germans. Çirak distanced herself from this type of literature, which came to be known as *Betroffenheitsliteratur* [victimization literature], saying in 1988 that "ich bin eben nicht betroffen!" (I am simply *not* victimized!)[2]

Texts by Çirak from this time period deal only rarely with the dichotomy of homeland / adopted country, familiar / other. Çirak chose for herself the role of the cosmopolitan *Weltbürgerin* [world citizen], even while accepting invitations from publishers and literary societies to write, speak, or read texts that the publishers or societies expected to be typical of *Gastarbeiterliteratur*, or at least of *Ausländerliteratur* [foreigners' literature]. Çirak almost gleefully recalls how she would accept such an invitation and then use the opportunity to "smuggle" in texts she'd written that were of a broader nature with more universal appeal, in the hopes of enlightening her hosts and her audience.[3] One text that she chose frequently for reading was her literary answer to the inevitable question of whether she felt more Turkish or more German. The text is quintessentially Çirak. It appears at first to be a rather superficial quip-like response, but with closer inspection or reflection, one realizes that Çirak is a shrewd judge of human foibles; she catches us in our own trap as we realize we are nodding inwardly rather than rejecting the stereotypes she lists. At the beginning and end of the text (she prefers the broader term *text* over what she considers the older, more rigidly defined term *poem)* she points out that she is not seeking to define herself but that others continually attempt to do so.

"Kulturidentität"

Ist das etwas, womit ich mich wiedererkenne, oder ist das etwas womit andere mich einordnen können?

Ich bevorzuge weder meine türkische noch meine deutsche Kultur. Ich lebe und sehne mich nach einer Mischkultur. Zwangsweise lebe ich so, weil ich weder in Alaska in einem Iglu noch in Anatolien tief in einer Hütte lebe. Es gibt Kulturgegenstände, die ich trotz meiner—(Zitat Strauss) "Zugehörigkeit zum europäischen Hygienekreis"—verweigere. Z.B. Fernsehen. (Als Kind und Teenager blieb mir nicht viel anderes übrig als fernzusehen. Die TV-Serie DALLAS lernte ich einige Zeit, bevor sie in Deutschland gesendet wurde, in der Türkei kennen.) Berauschen lasse ich mich lieber von anderen Kulturen, z.B. durch Musik von Bach und Mahler, durch Filme von Tarkowski oder Bunuel oder Akira Kurasawa.

Ich erkenne mich wieder.

Also würde ich am liebsten japanisch aufwachen auf einem Bodenbett in Räumen mit transparenten Scheintüren. Dann würde ich gerne englisch frühstücken, danach mit fremder Gleichgültigkeit chinesisch arbeiten, fleißig und eifrig. Am liebsten möchte ich französisch essen und tierisch satt römisch baden, gerne will ich bayrisch wandern und afrikanisch tanzen. Am liebsten würde ich russische Geduld besitzen und mein Geld nicht amerikanisch verdienen müssen. Ach, wie möchte ich gern einen Schweizer Paß-ohne in den Verdacht zu geraten,

Inhaber eines Nummernkontos zu sein. Am liebsten möchte ich indisch einschlafen als Vogel auf dem Rücken eines Elefanten und türkisch träumen vom Bosporus.

Will ich also etwas, womit ich mich wiedererkenne, oder etwas womit andere mich einordnen können? (*Vogel* 94)

"Cultural Identity"

Is that something I use to recognize myself, or is it something with which others categorize me?

I prefer neither my Turkish nor my German culture. I live and yearn for a cultural mix. I am forced to live like this, because I live neither in an igloo in Alaska nor in Anatolia deep in a hut. There are cultural objects, which I reject, despite my (quote from Strauss) "Allegiance to the European circle of hygiene," i.e., television. (As a child and teenager I had no choice but to watch TV. I got to know the TV series *Dallas* in Turkey some time before it was broadcast in Germany.) I would rather get high on other cultures, i.e. on music of Bach and Mahler, or on films of Tarkowski or Buñuel or Akira Kurasawa.

I recognize myself.

So I would most like to awaken japanesely on a futon in rooms with transparent pretend doors. Then I would like to breakfast englishly, afterward work chinesely with strange indifference, zealously and ambitiously. Most of all I would like to eat frenchly and bathe romanly, enormously satiated, gladly would I hike bavarianly and dance africanly. I would like most to possess Russian patience and not have to earn my money americanly. Ah, I would like to have a Swiss passport without coming under suspicion of being the owner of an unnumbered bank account. Most of all I would like to fall asleep indianly as a bird on the back of an elephant and dream turkishly of the Bosporus.

Do I therefore want something with which I can recognize myself, or something with which others can categorize me?

The final line of the second stanza, in which Çirak speaks of herself as a bird on the back of an elephant, is an apt metaphor to describe her role as artist. Indeed, Çirak's 1991 book of poetry is so entitled. Although the bird in the text sleeps, the description nevertheless embodies how she views herself: a small but insistent voice on the monolith of German-language literature, sometimes uncovering the debris of German culture in the same way that a bird picks at the vermin on the skin of an elephant, and sometimes annoying the great beast with its presence.[4]

Çirak hops around and flies through the complexity of the German language, thus offering a different perspective, a bird's-eye view, so to speak, that allows the reader fresh insights into both language and culture. Like the elephant bird, Çirak is often a salutary influence but can also be an irritant. In her earlier texts, she performed the function of irritant, of the Brechtian sand in the gears of society vis à vis such topics pertinent to her life in contemporary Germany as multi-culturalism, consumerism, individuality, and a vision of the future. As will become evident, her more recent work has sharpened its focus to confront both racism and nationalism.

The few early texts by Çirak that do address the issue of foreigners in an adopted homeland are distinctively Çirak in their unique, subtly satirical, gripping tenor. The first, whose title translates as *On the Borders of Hospitality*, begins innocently as a reply to the question often put to guests of whether they had trouble finding their way. The poem satirizes the term *Gastarbeiter* [guest worker] by playing upon the relationship between guest and host in a biting manner; the second-to-last strophe is a slap in the face of the reader, who has been lulled into a sense of complacency during the apparently disingenuous exchange in the text, of which only the guest's response is heard. The poem then lapses back into its pleasant mode, but the reader is purposefully left with the urge to question the actual pleasantness of the entire exchange and the underlying societal structures that caused it.

"An den Grenzen der Gastfreundlichkeit"

danke schön
nein es war nicht
schwer
hierher zu finden
bitte schön

ihr könnt uns mal
demnächst besuchen (*flugfänger* 17)

"On the Borders of Hospitality"

thank you
no it wasn't
hard
to get here
by all means
you can just go and
visit us sometime

The following text also speaks to the duality of foreigners in a land
other than home, and bears a title difficult to render in translation. The
best approximation is "Double Nationalitymorality."

"Doppelte Nationalitätsmoral"

die socken
rot mit weißem stem im sichelmond
die schuhe schwarz rot gold
für viele ist es
wie ein warmer fuß
im kalten schuhwerk
für andere
ein doppelknoten
in einem nur schnursenkellangen leben
aber das
auf heißem boden (*Vogel* 91)

"Double Nationalitymorality"

the socks
red with white star and sickle moon
the shoes black red gold
for many it is like
a warm foot
in cold footwear
for others
a double knot

in a merely
shoestring-long life
but that on a bed of coals

The text avoids affectation by focusing on the footwear rather than on
the shoes' wearers. Setting the reader at a distance permits Çirak to
address topics that might otherwise be too full of pathos. She touches
upon potentially clichéd subjects like patriotism, aspirations,
perseverence, and difficulty only obliquely via the symbols and colors
in the text. The colors and icons of the Turkish and German flags are
juxtaposed chiastically; warm flesh is contrasted with cold shoes, and
the simile of the feet and metaphors of shoes are rounded out with the
mention of knots and shoe-strings. Just when the reader has a pleasing
sense of this new set of referents—shoes, feet, and their
attributes—Çirak interjects a new variant on the theme of feet: hot
coals. This image is so much more intense than the previous ones that
it is jolting, as shockingly new as much of Germany once was for
newly-arrived Turks.

    Although Çirak confronts the topic of her countrymen's and
women's fates, there are very few texts that thematize her country of
origin, Turkey. Those that do discuss the subject are less remarkable,
perhaps because her relationship to her actual home is distant and even
strained. She knows her native country and home town as vacation
destinations only, hence the rather touristic images in the text. In the
following poem she articulates both a yearning for a place and a
yearning for a definitive manner of viewing her own origins:

"Istanbul"

von istanbul bis istanbul
ist weit
ist weit geworden
mein weg wohin nach istanbul
ist schmal ist breit wie istanbul
und bosporus fließt in mir
in meinen adem nur blut
salzig und ohne ein blau wie das meer
die windmühlen drehen sich nicht mehr
in istanbul ist
windstille
in mir ist weit geworden

istanbul
wie sonnenblumenfelder
sich der sonne zuwenden
drehe ich mich im kreise
    und suche istanbul (*Vogel* 91)

"Istanbul"

from istanbul to istanbul
is far
has become far
my path to where to istanbul
is narrow is broad like istanbul
and bosporus flows in me
in my veins only blood
salty and without a blue like the sea
the windmills no longer turn
in istanbul
the wind is still
in me has become far
istanbul
like sunflower fields
turn their faces to the sun
i turn in circles
    and seek istanbul

Her origins occupy her thoughts and manifested themselves in her
writing only fleetingly, for that topic is far less immediate than her life
in her real home of Germany. In *flugfänger*, Çirak first touched upon
a topic that would later occupy her more and more—nationalism in its
ugliest form, fascism, was again becoming conspicuous in her adopted
homeland. The text commenting on the continuing presence of this evil
in Germany is biting in its critique, despite its brevity:

"Jahrestag"

das siebente reich
dem himmel in diesem stockwerk nahe
und der fahrstul bleibt im vierten hängen
schaut auf das dritte hinunter
bis die finger an der hand

wieder sind was sie waren
und wer hat zuerst gelacht? (*flugfänger* 59)

"Anniversary"

the seventh reich
close to heaven in this storey
and the elevator gets stuck on the fourth
look down at the third
until the fingers on the hand
are once again what they used to be
and who laughed first?

Before the publication of *Vogel auf dem Racken eines Elefanten* [*Bird on the Back of an Elephant*], Çirak was becoming even more overtly political in her work and in her choice of texts dealing with Germany's political milieu for readings and performances. Although most recent texts deal with the increase of rightist radicalism in the Federal Republic, the following unpublished text, written prior to the publication of *Vogel*, addresses an aspect basic to Çirak's politicization: the use of the written or spoken work—in her case, poetry—as a tool and an outlet in times of political unrest.

Anna wird abgeholt
und hat doch nie gedichtet
Ägar schreibt heute sein fünfhundertstes Gedicht
Bernardo schrieb gestern sein letztes
Cornelius hat auch schon einmal eines geschrieben
Danica dichtet sich auf der bestsellerliste herum
Elke bemüht sich seit jahren vergeblich
Frank kanns nur im wald bei herbstlicht
Gautier hat häuserwände vollbekrakelt
Helmut macht immer nur titel ohne die gedichte dazu
Isaac kritzelt tausend notizen für ein einmaliges gedicht
Jusuf schreibt im knast über leiden und verbotene hiebe
Kamil wird vor seiner todesstrafe noch schnell etwas schreiben
Luise liegt und reimt im bett was sie so fühlt
Manjulaniti versteckt jeden morgen ihr täglich gedicht
Nicolai schreibt ein gedicht über sich selbst und seinen anderen
Otto kennt viele Gedichte nun wird er selber eins
Özlem kämmt und reimt sich die sehnsucht aus der stim

Pedro unterschreibt mit einem dreizeiler
die Queen hat ihren dichter bei hof
Roberto schweigt seitenlang
Said wirft mit gedichten umwickelte steine botschaftsfenster
ein
Tschamano schreibt weiß auf schwarz von apartheid
Umut ist ein wiederkauer in zeilen
Ülena weint buchstaben auf spiegelndes papier
Verena bietet ein selbstgemachtes
Wanja schreibt was er liest und liest was er schreibt
Xanthippe schrieb sokrates ein streitgedicht
You-chan sitzt ein gedicht über einen staatsanwalt ab
Zühre hat mit nur einem gedicht sich den teufel ausgetrieben.[5]

Anna is taken away yet never has she written
Ägar wrote his five hundredth one today
Bernardo wrote his last one yesterday
Cornelius also wrote one once
Danica poems around on the bestseller list
Elke has worked on it for years in vain
Frank can only do it in the woods by autumn light
Gautier has scrawled whole walls full
Helmut writes only the titles without the poems to them
Isaac scribbles a thousand notes for one poem of a lifetime
Jusuf writes in jail about suffering and forbidden blows
Kamil will quickly write something before his execution
Luise lies and rhymes in bed whatever she feels
Manjulaniti hides every morning her daily poem
Nicolai writes a poem about himself and his other
Otto knows many poems now he is one himself
Özlem combs and rhymes his yearning from his brow
Pedro signs with a couplet
the Queen has her poet at court
Roberto is silent for pages at a time
Said throws stones wrapped in poems through embassy
windows
Tschamano writes white on black of apartheid
Umut is a ruminant in stanzas
Ülena weeps alphabets onto mirroring paper
Verena offers a homemade one
Wanja writes what he reads and reads what he writes

Xanthippe wrote socrates a debate poem
You-chan is sitting out a poem about a district attorney
Zühre exorcised his devil with but one poem.

Common to each of the fictitious poets in the text is a need to write, be the text grounded in politics, romance, or ego. Çirak is giving us here her own credo: just as each of the above lives revolves around writing, so does hers.

Realizing that her own literary expression is not created in a void, however, she began about five years ago to speak out against the injustices and dangerous attitudes she sees in Germany and in her larger home, the world, for she had always viewed herself as a *Weltbürgerin*. As she was quoted in the *New York Times* (June 6, 1993):

> My father is worried because I'm giving interviews and making public statements about what happened in Solingen. He's afraid something might happen to me, and he would like me to stay quiet. But my generation feels that we have a right to participate in every aspect of German life. We aren't as timid as our parents. (6)

Her more recent texts continue in a style similar to earlier works, a style described by literary critic Marcel Reich-Ranicki and by the author Hilde Domin as:

> full of melancholy charm and sensitive
> subjectivity, in her poems
> she plays with familiar words and
> sentences that appear in a surprisingly new light.
> Zehra Çirak's verse teaches us to be amazed again.[6]

Part I of *Vogel auf dem Rucken eines Elefanten* is appropriately entitled *Streckphase* [Stretching Phase], in which she begins with the text "ich will versuchen zu berichten" [I will try to tell] (10), a list of poems that, like Hans Magnus Enzensberger's wartime poem "Inventur," skim the surface of what they describe and thus lend greater poignancy than would an in-depth analysis of the same subject. The text begins "About the easiness of wishing for a place"—a home—and continues with the effort, the joy, the struggle, the fear, the greed, the sorrow, the anger, and the pride involved in achieving, keeping, giving up, and of the inability, the forbiddenness, of sharing of a place or home. Every emotion, every aspect of putting down roots is described. Of the twenty-three lines of the poem, well over half address the difficulties involved in making a place—a home—for oneself. The text makes no reference to the location, no allusion to any geographical location. Indeed, Çirak could have been speaking of some inner sense of connection as easily as any actual national or cultural allegiance, for the elements she lists pertain to both levels of belonging. She ends the text with a fragmentary sentence "about the attempt," and with this fragment she expresses the one element that is not contained in the preceding lines—insecurity. She has tried to describe the factors involved with having a place, whether it be within the self or in the world, but cannot fully do so. So she attempts to tell what she can and ends by attempts to tell the attempt. The repetitive nature of the text conveys perseverance and optimism in the face of the adversarial aspects she has just enumerated. Like Enzensberger, she realizes that some things must be left, if not completely unsaid, then merely intimated.

Çirak often expresses herself in subtle intimations and obliquely articulated thoughts when offering her political opinions. To her manner of thinking, directness is not only boring, but unimaginative, and thoroughly unpoetic. Rather than boorishly indulging in finger pointing and pathos-filled ranting over the state of world affairs, she instead refers to a personal favorite pastime, making prophecies by reading coffee grounds, and ruminates in "Fragebogen" [Questionnaire] about the uselessness of lying about what she sees in the grounds. Why, she asks, should one inquire about where the coffee is from, what it costs, and how it tastes, when [she] can read lips and see from them how long it tastes good? The second stanza in the poem extrapolates from coffee to nations, and to other forms of prophecy; reading from the cards and crystal balls (*Vogel* 13):

> seit wann ist Mystik im Spiel
> wenn Staaten sich ihre Karten zustecken
> offen und durchsicihtig für jedermann
> wo ist die Hand
> aus der man sprachlos lesen könnte
> und wie rund die Kugel
> die gläseme
> worauf wir stehen
>
> since when is mysticism at play
> when states pass each other their cards

openly and transparent for everyone
where is the hand
from which one could read speechlessly
and how round the ball
the crystalline
on which we stand

The crystal ball is the globe, and the final stanza clarifies that it is a reference to the global village, for she asks, "why should each one be concerned over each one's question," and answers pithily with a sentence reminiscent of the maxim stating that whoever does not learn from history is doomed to repeat it: "and why should not the blind take part at a convention for clairvoyants?" (13)

For this 1993 winner of the prestigious Hölderlin-Förderpreis, her *Wahlheimat* [home of choice]—Germany—has become the site of increasing xenophobia and nationalism. Since the fall of the Berlin Wall in 1989, the formerly separate Germanies have been plagued by rightist sentiment and race-related violence. The texts that follow testify to a progression in Çirak herself: where once she saw no reason to comment on the socio-political stage in Germany, now she has come to realize the necessity of commenting on what she sees around her.

In "Eigentum" [Ownership] she laments the human foibles that lead people to be at best, grasping and at worst, xenophobic. It also illustrates Çirak's new-found voice, which speaks ironically to the social unrest and political myopia in Germany and the world. Like many of her texts, it begins in a leisurely and innocuous fashion, then gathers momentum at the same time the reader becomes aware of the linguistic set-up constructed by the poet. She begins with "home," a justifiable, even honorable object with which people often identify intensely, then moves via a seeming free association through other instances related to identity such as country, people, language, wife, child, goods, future, and opinion. Suddenly, the words hint at something darker—war, victory, right—come to the fore when "neighbor" is followed by "enemy." Then the undercurrent of the sentiment is revealed: the narrative voice has progressed (or should one say, regressed) from a natural stance of self-pride to reactionism. The reader is left to conjecture about the final line: is "oh my goodness" merely another appeal to a higher power to be on the speaker's side? Since it is marked by the only use of punctuation in the entire text, however, it instead appears to be a comment from another perspective. The last line comments on the appalling direction this line of thinking has taken.

"Eigentum"

Meine Heimat mein Land
meine Landsleute meine Sprache
meine Geschichte mein Krieg mein Sieg
meine Sehnsucht mein(e) Frau (Mann) mein Kind
mein Haus mein Hab und Gut meine Zukunft
meine Meinung mein Recht meine Person
mein Nachbar mein Feind in meiner Zeit
mein Gott steh mir bei daß mir alles bleibt
da kommt einfach ein anderer mit seinem mein
und nichts bleibt mir mehr
nichts von mir—ach du meine Güte (*Vogel* 86)

"Ownership"

My home my country
my people my language
my history my war my victory
my desires my wife (husband) my child
my house my goods and chattels my future
my opinion my right my person
my neighbor my enemy in my time
my god, stand by me so all stays mine
another one comes along with his mine
and nothing
remains for me
nothing of mine—oh my goodness

In "Kleine Geschichte über Helden" [Little Story about Heroes], Çirak
points to the historical recurrences of tyranny and to the dangers of its
recurrence today. The scrambling of dictators' names, though playful,
has a serious intent: by combining the otherwise typically French,
German, Italian, or Iranian syllables, Çirak constructs names devoid of
direct national allusions. In this manner, she avoids pointing an accusing
finger. Instead, her neologisms indicate that fascism is a potential
danger everywhere; the "grandchildren" of the dictators can live in any
country. The laughter she ascribes to them shows how sure they are of
their power, regardless of their venue. The text is a call to wakefulness
against the insidious character of fascism:

"Kleine Geschichte über Helden"

Napoler und Hitleon Musomeini und Khomelini
sie ruhen sanft sie ruhen tief
und unter uns
ihre Enkelkinder leben
sie brüllen um Namen
und schlagen um Gebiete
um die werten Namen ihrer Gebieter
an den kleinen Fingern
in den tiefen Rachen
unter den stählemen Mänteln
in allem was heute noch gilt
wiederfindet sich
das Lachen
von Napoler und Hitleon
von Musomeini und Khomelini
und ihre Enkelkinder lachen mit (*Vogel* 80)

"Little Story of Heroes"

Napoler and Hitleon Musomeini and Khomelini
they sleep softly they sleep deep
and among us
their grandchildren live
they roar for names
and fight for mastery
for the worthy names of their masters
on the little fingers
in the deep breasts
under the steel-like coats
in all that matters yet today
can be found again
the laughter
of Napoler and Hitleon
of Musomeini and Khomelini
and their grandchildren laugh along

In her latest volume, *Fremde Flügel aug eigener Schulter* [*Foreign Wings on Familiar Shoulders*], Çirak continues the flight motif that marked her first and second volumes of poetry. She takes up the themes of xenophobia, of home, of the Other. She also continues her allusions to famous German poets whom she admires for their works and their ideas about humanity. "Kein Sand im Getriebe der Zeit" [No Sand in the Gears of Time] takes its title from Brecht's poem and projects his ideal of political and social friction as a means of curing society's ills. Çirak once again plays with readers' expectations: only in the final section of the poem does she reveal that the first person voice is that of a bicycle and not, as the reader initially construes, a foreigner. The poem is at once a criticism and an appeal: no one comes to the aid of the maligned or the victim. No one is playing the role of social redeemer. The humor of the poem—readers' relief that the victim is a mere bicycle—only partially alleviates the underlying critique. But the humor allows for the necessary distancing so the readers can take stock of their own reactions in a similar situation. Thus, Çirak is subtly appealing to readers to evaluate and perhaps modify their own involvement in the cogs of German society, even as they have modified their attitude toward the narrator of the poem and no longer see "just a bicycle":

> "Kein Sand im Getriebe der Zeit"
>
> Ich stehe in der U-Bahn an die Wand gelehnt
> schweigend schaukle ich in der U-Fahrt
> fünf Jungs und zwei Mädels kommen auf mich zu
> schwankend im Laufe der Geschwindigkeit
> festen Blickes fixieren sie mich
> und grinsen sich immer näher
> ich versuche die sieben zu ignorieren
> die anderen Fahrgäste sind alle
> mit sich selbst beschäftigt
> die sieben stehen nun
> kaum noch einen Schritt vor mir
> der eine und die andere holt aus
> zum Schlag
> die anderen johlen begeistert
> jetzt bin ich Neger—Jude—Ausländer—
> Penner—oder anderswer
> nein sie sehen nicht was ich wirklich bin
> jetzt nur noch ein geschlagenes Ding
> ich höre noch ein kleines Kind
> das ängstlich Mama ruft

und die anderen Fahrgäste machen sich
bereit zum Aussteigen
ich falle um
ich bin ein Fahrrad
mein Besitzer ist
ein Neger—ein Jude—ein Ausländer
der mit Vorausahnungen
schon eine Station früher ausgestiegen war
von nun an bin ich
nicht mehr—nur ein Fahrrad (*Fremde Flügel* 44-45)

"No Sand in the Gears of Time"

I stand leaning against the wall of the subway
silently I rock with the sub-ride
five boys and two girls come toward me
swaying in the course of the speed
with firm gaze they stare at me
and grin their way closer and closer
i try to ignore the seven of them
the other passengers are all
occupied with themselves
the seven now stand
scarcely a step away from me
one and one other hauls back
to hit
once again
the others howl with glee
now I am Negro—Jew—foreigner—
Bum—or someone else
no they don't see what i really am
only a beaten up thing now
i hear a little child
who anxiously cries mama
and the other passengers get
ready to get out
i fall down
my owner is
a Negro—Jew—a foreigner
who, having a premonition,
had gotten out a station earlier

from now on i am
no longer—just a bicycle

It may be expected from Çirak's recent and consistent treatment of the related topics of prejudice and nationalism in her adopted home country of Germany that she has found a subject worthy of her attention for some time to come. Indeed, her manner of approaching an issue with subtlety and finesse is perfectly suited for what she has but lately begun to do overtly: exploit the potential of literature as a tool or even as a weapon. She takes clever aim at the ignorance, myopia, ethnocentrism, and speciousness that characterize Right-wing groups in Germany. In this final text, she looks at various reasons for nationalism and racism in Germany, analyzes the reasons for the popularity of these movements— disenfranchisement, need for recognition—and then she points out their evils—the potential for harm and the danger of hatred.

The broom of the eponymous poem can be read as a symbol for Germany's Right, against which Çirak has set her tool of literature. The reader initially perceives the homeless broom as deserving of sympathy; it has no door in front of which to sweep and therefore is deprived of its function in life. But on closer reading, the word *eigens* [to itself] stands out and sets the tone for the rest of the text.

"Der Besen"

Ein heimatloser Besen
hatte keine Tür mehr da
von der er eigens kehren könnte
jetzt fegt er waagerecht
in verhexten Lüften
sein Stiel ist stählern und geladen
doch seine Borste sträuben sich
ihm fehlt schon jeder Grund
und daher jeder Boden (*Fremde Flügel* 49)

"The Broom"

a homeless broom
had no door to itself
to sweep in front of anymore
now it brushes perpendicular
in bewitched heavens

its stick is steely and loaded
but its straws bristle
it's lacking any basis
and therefore any grounds

Like Germany's nationalistic Right wing, the broom has caused its own problems by refusing to allow others to share its space. The result is a charged atmosphere—*verhexten Lüften* [bewitched heavens]—of xenophobia and hatred. Çirak's reference to brushing perpendicularly is at once a Celan-like upending of a common household item (Celan colored usually white milk black in his famous *Todesfuge* to indicate the perversion and evil of concentration camps) and at the same time, an allusion to the position of arm and hand in the notorious Hitlerian salute. The text goes on to describe the military elements that the Right wing and the broom share: steel as metal *and* as mettle, a willingness to be bristly. Finally, the text concludes with a forceful Çirakian play on words: "it's lacking any basis and therefore any grounds," denouncing the presence of the extreme Right in her adopted homeland.

In "The Broom," as in her other texts cited here, Çirak evidences her finesse with language and her ability to put commonplace words and objects to new uses. Only recently, however, has she utilized her talent to express her political ideas. Çirak's growth as a poet and as an inhabitant of her actual, albeit second, home, has born significant fruit. In addressing the issues of xenophobia and racist violence, she has found a topic that lends itself to her unique voice and style. No longer does Çirak speak to topics that are exclusively personal nor even exclusively German. Her scope, though it takes its origins from her special circumstances as a Turkish woman in Germany, reaches beyond the national level that spawned it to a universal message. Çirak will not use her textual wings to take flight from or hover above the destructive politics of nationalism; rather, she has truly gone *über Grenzen*, beyond the borders of her personal history and her homeland, whether Turkish or German, to make a statement about the world. And the gist of that statement—that no society may be exclusionary—contributes to making the world a more suitable home for all people.

NOTES

1. All translations are my own, with permission from Zehra Çirak.

2.   Zehra Çirak, personal interview, January 18, 1988.

3.   Ibid.

4.   Initially loathe to dignify this upstart literature with a label, Germanists have been hard-pressed to categorize the new phenomenon, but those who study it are unanimous in the judgment that the term "German literature" smacks of nationalism and is too narrow. The broader, more appropriate "German-language literature" is now widely recognized and used.

5.   Zehra Çirak, letter to the author, February 4, 1989.

6.   The German original as taken from the prize certificate awarded to Çirak on June 7, 1993 is as follows:

> Voll melancholischen Charmes und sensibler
> Subjektivität spielt sie in ihren Gedichten mit
> vertrauten Wörtern und Sätzen, die überraschend
> in einem neuen Licht erscheinen. Zehra Çiraks
> Verse lehren uns wieder das Staunen.

WORKS CITED

Ackermann, Irmgard, ed. *Türken deutscher Sprache*. Munich: dtv, 1984.

Çirak, Zehra. *flugfänger*. Karlsruhe: edition artinform, 1987.

-------. *Fremde Flügel auf eigener Schulter*. Köln: Kipenheuer und Witsch, 1994.

-------. *Vogel auf dem Rücken eines Elefanten*. Köln: Kiepenhauer und Witsch, 1991.

Esselborn, Karl, ed. Über Grenzen. Munich: dtv, 1987.

Hölzl, Luisa, und Elena Torossi, eds. *Freihändig auf dem Tandem*. Kiel: Neuer Malik Verlag, 1985.

26

Helena María Viramontes' Homing Devices in *Under the Feet of Jesus*

Cecelia Lawless

Under the Feet of Jesus begins with a question: "Had they been heading for the barn all along?" (1). This interrogation introduces the idea of a journey and its potential destination, which is a fundamental and often-forgotten aspect of the idea of home. *Under the Feet of Jesus* explores the barn as home site, and as a barn-dweller for some years, I appreciate the home-like qualities of this living space. In the warp of boards and slant of roof, a history of communion between architectural structure and function exists. Although an integral part of the indigenous architecture of the United States, the barn is a structure no longer in much demand and often abandoned to time and the weather. As a home site, then, the barn evokes irony.[1] Even this one in *Under the Feet of Jesus* is a dangerous place that is no longer solid on the ground. Thus this symbol for home represents a fragile and perhaps outdated home at best.

In this essay I will map the topographical meanings of silence and the barn, and the spaces in between where I read the shadows of a house-building project in this story of a migrant family. The idea of home in *Under the Feet of Jesus* is not compatible with a traditional home icon complete with white picket fence pictured in the American dream nor an invincible home with the stability of four walls and a roof; rather, this home is a linguistic gesture of refuge for all those marginalized and disenfranchised by a socio-political system intent on silencing dissonant voices. The mythic home of the American dream functions as a useful rhetorical device for both those on the political Left and Right. However, for many, in particular for people of color, owning a house remains merely a dream. With the lack of a home-site and the supposed stability which that place implies, come a lack of voice in the community, in nation-building, and history-making. Estrella's family in *Under the Feet of Jesus* is emblematic of a Chicano migratory family, nomadic in their wanderings from job to job, whose voices do not participate in the continuing process of redefinition of national identity. But even though they do not own a house, they do begin to explore the possibilities for home-building within different sedimentary layers of language.[2]

In *Under the Feet of Jesus* characters do not speak to one another. Although words might overlap in the speakers' presence, no contact between people is made with them. Words follow their own path chiselled from stone, bone, and blood where meaning must be culled from surrounding gestures. Yet it is from the words uttered by the migrant workers in the novel that a home must be constructed, since there is no other material at hand: "It was always a question of work, and work depended on the harvest, the car running, their health, the conditions of the road, how long the money held out, and the weather, which meant they could depend on nothing" (2). Material options for this family are not dependable, and instead they must rely on another level of communicative signs: "The silence and the barn and the clouds meant many things" (2). The barn here becomes marked by its position between two ambiguous phenomena, silence and clouds. Thus framed, linguistic instability threatens to convert the barn into a space "in between."

A home transcends geometric space; a tar paper shack in Mexico or the various pieces of paraphernalia of an American street person can all represent a home, even if not so considered by conventional standards. In his socio-poetic study, Mexican architect Victor Manuel Ortiz capitalizes the word "house" [casa] to give it prominence and in some way establish a link between "casa" and "hogar" in Spanish, where the force of linguistic distinction remains less strong than in the English "house" and "home:" "La CASA ha sido siempre algo más que un techo: el marco físico ha operado como un abanico de posibilidades entre las cuales se hacen elecciones a través de tabúes, costumbres y caminos tradicionales de una cultura" [The house / home has always been more than a mere roof: the physical framework has functioned like a fan of possibilities among which one makes choices through traditional and cultural taboos, customs, and directions] (29). Through capitalization, Ortiz builds in his writing an actual structure for his concept since his form reflects the content of his work: he houses the word "house" at the same time that he analyses and explains it. I would further suggest that when we base our analysis in socio-linguistic, geographic, and architectural studies we can separate out layers of meaning between house and home.

The cover of Ortiz's book displays a naive, child-like drawing of a house. This image of a box with windows, doors, and a chimney crosses cultural boundaries. A house can be a two-dimensional construct. In contrast, a home is a socio-physical construct as well as a cultural icon. A home implies a dynamic tension, a continual dialectic of giving and taking, coming and going, falling away and building up. Thus, for my purposes, the word "house" will refer to structure only, whereas "home" will include the habitable, human implications of the house. This distinction directly relates to the differences already established in sociological studies between space—mathematically oriented—and place—historically oriented. As Yi-Fu Tuan has pointed out in one of his influential geographic studies, "space is a mathematical construct whereas place contains personal, human roots" (98). In other words, space and house are synchronic terms while place and home have diachronic implications.

When viewed through both its structural and existential implications, house / home also represents an institution of power, a defined private space, a middle-class domestic ideal, and hence the term is often manipulated by politicians and nationalists. Home and house have overlapped to such an extent that they have become emptied of meaning; for example, real estate agents no longer sell houses, they sell homes. Thus, these two words form an important linguistic strategy for the framing of social and private lives. But for Estrella in *Under the Feet of Jesus*, and her mother Petra, and many other working-class Chicana women, the house / home conceals as much terror as it projects supposed safety. In the house that the Chicana woman must convert into home, there is pressure to produce and care for children, to work inside and outside the house for economic reasons, and still to remain attractive for one's man. But as Rebolledo suggests, "[Chicanas] . . . have grown up and survived along the edges, along the borders of so many languages, worlds, cultures and social systems that we constantly fix and focus on the spaces in between" (136). If the idea of home, traditionally a central locus point, can be re-conceived as a space in between, rather than merely on the margin, then the home takes on a more powerful and dynamic luster because it becomes less a static space than a place in process. In fact, I would suggest that part of the project of *Under the Feet of Jesus* is to subvert and undermine the claim of the "safe house" so as to make us question the cultural significance of the place that in one way or another we all inhabit. The site of language as home may seem a paltry solace in the midst of the actual poverty of this family, but there is power in language.

Under the Feet of Jesus destabilizes the motifs of the house / home, the journey, and the girl-growing-into-woman, subverting its traditional American counterpart.[3] Such a textual interrogation of language opens the way for readers to review and renew their own participation in the production of discourse on political, racial, and feminist levels by revising cliches and casually held concepts such as "house," "home," "place," "space," "woman," and "culture."

Words are like tools used for building places to inhabit with others. Estrella, the growing thirteen-year-old girl in *Under the Feet of Jesus*, learns this from a man who is not her father, Perfecto Flores. Everyone calls him Perfecto because his work is always "perfecto": he has earned and now lives the word that identifies him. From Perfecto, Estrella connects objects with their function and thus the curves and tails of the worker's tools begin to make sense to her even as the chalky lines on school blackboards become more coherent:

> Tools to build, bury, tear down, rearrange and repair, a box of reasons his hands took pride in. She lifted the pry bar in her hand, felt the coolness of iron and power of function, weighed the significance it awarded her, and soon she came to understand how essential it was to know these things. That was when she began to read. (22)

Reading and telling a story become related here to the act of building. Perfecto's tools are tangible; they lie heavily in Estrella's hands. She can wield these objects and they give her power. In knowing the names of these tools, she increases her independence because she explores simultaneously the use and utterance of language. This knowledge leads her to the place so simply expressed in the phrase, "That was when she began to read." This passage connecting tools to words, Perfecto to Estrella, reading to building, is of fundamental importance in understanding the unfolding story which demands sensitive tools for the interpretation of a home-site.

As Heidegger has shown through his etymological studies in "Building, Dwelling, Thinking," building *is* dwelling, and the idea of being harks back to dwelling as well. What interests me in Heidegger's work is his formulation of home and its connection to language: "Language is the house of Being" (86).[4] If we take this statement literally, we realize that we dwell in language, and in alienating ourselves from language we lose our potential to dwell, to make a home. In learning to build with tools, Perfecto perfects his sense of dwelling, just as Estrella, in seeing words as building tools, will also learn how to dwell with more thoughtfulness. This idea of dwelling, of "homing" oneself, is a touchstone for a family whose emotional and physical life consists of constant movement.

Estrella is the eldest child of Petra, a migrant worker whose maternal feelings extend beyond her own family, as she explains when she takes in the sick Alejo, another young migrant worker: "If we don't take care of each other, who would take care of us? We have to look out for our own" (81). Petra expresses her philosophy of life here, which includes a strong sense of solidarity and community, even amongst transient working people such as Alejo, who is from far away Texas.[5] Petra is a woman constantly on the move from field to field in search of work and food. She has two little boys and twin girls as well as Estrella, and now lives with Perfecto Flores, thirty-seven years her senior. Her husband, the father of her children, left her in search of something he could never articulate, and now Perfecto is also on the edge of leaving, compelled by his yearning for home, for "his real home, not the bungalow. The desire became as urgent as the money he brought in for Petra's family. . . . What would happen if he forgot his way home?" (67). A strong woman who combats varicose veins with large amounts of garlic, Petra has no home to call her own except for her children. At the same time, Estrella the girl-woman explores her potential for making homes through the tentative rapport she builds with Alejo, who will ultimately leave for the hospital because of an illness he has developed from breathing in the poison spray used for fumigation. Each character in the novel finds him / herself on a threshold or in-between space of leave-taking from the promise (or threat) of a traditional home. *Under the Feet of Jesus* relates the implied journeys of these characters, although it refrains from disclosing a final destination.

This migrant family on the border between Mexico and the United States is also on the border between home and homelessness. In the present moment Estrella, Perfecto, and Petra work the fields accompanied by the four younger children. They appear to do this for some months with no thought of school or other less strenuous work options. Perfecto does contemplate tearing down a barn near their desolate bungalow so he can sell the wood for cash, but Estrella refuses to help him because of her strange attachment to the building. The past mostly consists of derelict urban dwellings reminiscent of another Chicana's depiction of transient childhood in *The House on Mango Street*:

> We didn't always live on Mango Street. Before that we lived
> on Loomis on the third floor, and before that we lived on
> Keeler. Before Keeler it was Pauline, and before that I can't
> remember. But what I remember most is moving a lot. Each
> time it seemed there'd be one more of us. (3)

Although these two novels are very different, they both emphasize the
effect of constant displacement on young children and how that
displacement can motivate a desire for expression through language and
story-telling.

   Under the Feet of Jesus interrogates the unique quality of the
traditional house / home that supposedly represents safety for the
woman in flight. For as well as telling the story of a family who
migrates from field to field, from job to job, *Under the Feet of Jesus*
also tells the tale of flight from places. Migration is the working-class
Chicana's journey through "space," and the various bungalows, shacks,
or urban hovels represent the waiting stations or houses not yet homes.
The act of flight reflects these women's despair regarding their sense of
ideological, ontological "place." If migration is a movement towards
some ideal—the house become home—then flight is a movement away
from the fear of the house that has never become home. Thus, on the
physical and existential levels, these women constantly combat the fear
of homelessness that is so directly linked to the problematics of their
cultural female identity.

   Both Petra and her daughter Estrella are in different stages of
flight. Petra, like many working-class Chicanas, finds herself in the
unenviable position of representing the stoic, strong, resourceful
Mother.[6] In fact, she is tired, overburdened with economic problems,
concerned for her five children, and abandoned by her husband. At one
point we do see her in flight from a powerful scene of her children's
hunger and her current despair. By inflicting pain on herself—she bites
through her thumb—and then running out the door, she mentally and
physically leaves the responsibilities of home behind her, but she does
return. In this case, the four walls of the house / home have become a
nightmarish, unsafe prison for her and her children. Because of such
experiences, Petra has learned to shape the shelter of home from the
people, the family that surrounds her rather than to seek stability from
buildings. Estrella's flight, on the other hand, is not so self-conscious.
In this chronicle of her growing from girl to woman, Estrella feels the
pull of something beyond the circuit of migration in which she lives.
The pull is both away from home and towards a reconceptualization of

home, tenuously defined by Alejo, Maxine, Perfecto, and her mother, what an insider observer might call her community. It occurs to Estrella that picking vegetables might not be her life forever (101); words lay a path towards another option. Through Petra we already know that Estrella won a prize for a written essay, and once she has overcome her suspicion of Alejo's questions, his words begin to take on meaning for her, sink into her like the bones in the tar pits that he describes. Estrella is learning that words have substance and weight, like Perfecto's tools, and that with an understanding of language comes the fearlessness and the responsibility to use them.

From these reflections arise certain vital questions for Petra and Estrella: How does the house / home reflect and express their daily life? Do they learn to tell a story the same way that they learn to inhabit a house? Can reconstructed words such as "house" and "home" create a rhetorical foundation for effective social change? And, ultimately, can language act as home?

How do we get from one place to another? We can run, stroll, march, or dance, thus expressing different ways of taking possession of the environment. We can also read. In our lives we move through rooms as we move through stories to reveal and penetrate private realms. As an architectonic object, the text, and implicitly the act of narration, allows a reader or listener a place to inhabit. Many writers have intuited the importance of spatial sequence by playing with the linearity of the stories we read. For example, Cortázar's famous novel *Hopscotch* (1967) tells us explicitly that we can read the chapters in varying order. Ana Castillo's more recent *The Mixquiahuala Letters* (1986) and Sandra Cisneros's *The House on Mango Street* (1984) are two Chicana examples providing freedom of narrative movement. *Under the Feet of Jesus* also is a carefully patterned maneuvering towards an understanding of the Chicana growing into her domestic space, wherever and however that might be conceived. Viramontes' play with borders, with the inside and the outside so fundamental to the traditional notion of home, allows for a re-orienting of space that is not a dichotomy but "the space in between."

Aside from offering story-telling as a model for building a home in the transitory space in between, *Under the Feet of Jesus* demands the participation of the reader. This text does not work on only one narrative plane. Often *Under the Feet of Jesus* reads as a disconnected series of short story vignettes that the reader must in some way assemble. Perfecto likewise assembles his tools in his red tool chest to form a pattern that will help him with the work at hand. Through his knowledge of tools he can semiotically read the value of the walls, the supports, the fixtures and appliances of buildings so as to enter into the language of barter rather than monetary exchange. Instead of paying his bill at the local store, he fixes its run-down freezer. To pay for Alejo's clinic visit, he assesses the various decrepit aspects of the building and offers to fix them. Estrella watches, listens, and learns from Perfecto's "fix-it" lessons and begins to use words as tools to "fix" situations. In learning how to use words forcefully, Estrella also becomes a better reader of others' words. Thus, the give-and-take established in Perfecto's bartering with his tools is also enacted in Estrella's speaking and listening throughout the novel. The same situation of exchange is demanded of the reader of *Under the Feet of Jesus*, where we must use our tools of interpretation to understand the many implications of this story.

A linear time line does not exist in *Under the Feet of Jesus*. The narrative demands an active role from the reader, who must make an effort not to become lost amongst the different time locations framed by blank spaces. Often too, the blocks of text or individual paragraphs will swing back and forth between two characters to express simultaneity. Thus, scenes appearing on the same page, but in different textual places, render time both spatial and parallel. For example, in the beginning of Part II from pages 42-44, the narrative alternates between Estrella in the hot fields picking grapes, her thoughts and tired actions, and Alejo's movements and musings in this same field. We learn here of their different pasts and their reactions to the land. Estrella almost appears defeated by her circumstances: "Her tracks led to where she stood now. Morning, noon or night, four or fourteen or forty it was all the same. She stepped forward, her body never knowing how tired it was until she moved once again. Don't cry" (43). Alejo, in contrast, appears less concentrated on the task at hand, but more grounded in the significance of the land:

> He loved stones and the history of stones because he believed himself to be a solid mass of boulder thrusted out of the earth and not some particle lost in infinite and cosmic space. With a simple touch of a hand and a hungry wonder of his connection to it all, he not only became a part of the earth's history, but would exist as the boulders did, for eternity. (42)

Both characters think of the same themes here—their paths on earth, the act of touching, the sense of hunger—but their views are radically different. Spatially, however, they are in the same place: "Alejo had been working right next to Estrella all along. How could he not have known?" (45). The reader knows this information before Alejo due to the preceding paragraph in which all the different workers are gathered together narratively in a semblance of community, despite their different thoughts and activities, by the evocative call of the train: "The lone train broke the sun and silence with its growing thunderous roar and the train reminded the *piscadores* of destinations, of arrivals and departures, of home and not of home" (45).[7] Time and space converge through the narrative play.

Just after the synchrony of Estrella and Alejo working together in the fields, Estrella decides to walk to her family's bungalow rather than take the truck with Alejo and the rest of the workers. It is almost as if she rejects the physical synchrony of working with Alejo for the mental asymmetry that they also experienced. She opts for independent flight and a potential journey evoked by the railroad tracks she walks. Earlier, the call of home had resonated for the workers from these same tracks, and the reader wonders where these tracks will lead and what division line they mark. As she walks, Estrella encounters a baseball diamond where running boys play the All-American game. She too runs, but her game is a matter of survival due to her tenuous status in American society. She can only observe here; she is not "at home." And then car lights blind her and she realizes that she does not know where home is. The game and its goal: "Destination: home plate" (49), become superimposed on the game of finding illegals and the fear it produces even for people like Estrella who are legal.

While focusing on the nature of home and the relation of Chicanos to home, *Under the Feet of Jesus* also gives the sense of *unheimlich* or "unhomelike" a precise form. As described by Freud, the *unheimlich* is a dis-ease bordering on fear of home. *Under the Feet of Jesus* articulates the *unheimlich's* marginality, whether spatial or temporal, and it recalls an Otherness that lies at the core of the bourgeois world, thus questioning the nature of established, accepted order. Implicitly, questions arise during the reading of this text, such as: why do migrant workers have to live like this? what are their options? what are the "white leaflets with black eagles on them" (72)? Why is there such fear of "la migra" (immigration) if the United States documents for Petra's children are "under the feet of Jesus" in her altar? How can they claim the States as home if they are in fear of its immigration officers? And so on. In this way, the novel functions as historical memory, a site that documents Chicana life in a migrant

American context. The needed tools of interpretation for this text then include a focus on the movement and dislocation of boundaries, both spatial and social; the life-like qualities of the house / home; and the woman's role in the midst of these turbulent problems.

Sometimes words as well as people appear in flight in the novel, particularly when the characters try to speak to one another; like wayward winds their words do not catch onto anything. If Estrella represents a star, as her name indicates, then can she and her words act as a guiding star for others or as a falling star soon lost in darkness? Although Alejo and Estrella have some meaningful conversations, the following represents the apparent lack of connection between the addresser and the addressee:

> -My papa was the one who named me that. . . .
> -What does he call you now?
> -My papa's gone.
> -Dead?
> -Things just happen. (55)

Estrella is suspicious of too many words, too many questions. Alejo asks her a seemingly ordinary question about how many brothers she has and she responds,

> -That's kinda a funny question.
> -You don't like questions?
> -Not really. Only asking maybe.
> -What's your full name?
> -Talk louder.
> -Last name. What's your last name?
> -What's it to you? she snapped back. (56)

In this exchange Alejo is trying to "place" Estrella, and everything conspires against him: Estrella's discomfort with even ordinary conversation, the rumble and noise of the truck taking them to work, and his own nervousness caused by the lack of privacy of the truck filled with a listening and mocking audience.

Between Perfecto and Estrella the lines of conversation do not cross one another either; for example,

> -I'm not your papa. But you're getting me old with
>   your. . . .

-Where did you put the lantern?
-Stay away from the barn, hear me?
-You're right. You're not my papa.
-That should do it. (22)

Such lack of conversation accentuates the homelessness of these characters while pointing towards other forms of home-building, perhaps not always considered by white, anglo, middle-class wage earners. The apparent lack of exchange between characters has been supplanted by a language of gesture that often speaks more strongly than English, Spanish, or the many instances of Spanglish used in this text. Examples of this gestural language abound in the novel, for example: Alejo hardly speaks when he first meets Estrella's family, but he gives them a sack of peaches with no explanation, and Petra quietly returns the sack to him filled with pinto beans (38); in the nurse's office Estrella does not know what to do, or what to say and she holds out her hands, palms up, empty, for all to see (124); the exchanges between Petra's children and Perfecto are nonexistent but the twins love to hold on to his big hands, one on each side (87). All these examples and more speak volumes in a culture where one is judged by one's actions. When one is constantly on the edge of survival, on the border, literal and metaphorical, of becoming invisible to mainstream American society, then the impact and weight of words must shift.

Language as gesture becomes a product of fear and exhaustion and despair. People in this text are so very tired—everyone from Perfecto in his old age, "This was not a time for words . . . He wanted to rest, to lay down and never get up" (137), to Petra and her many burdens—who holds her eldest as if she "was trying to hide her back in her body" (146), and the young Estrella who feels "as if her body had been beaten into a pulp of ligaments and cartilage" (145). Too seldom in the theoretical world of the American academy are these mundane details taken into account in our analyses of textual, potentially innovative linguistic maneuvers.

This silencing of one kind of language and activating another kind is particularly crucial to the understanding of Estrella's growth as a woman when, towards the end of the novel, she appears to abandon language in favor of the use of force. In fact, at this point in her life, she couples language with the only tools (Perfecto's very real tools) she as yet knows how to manipulate. Under her instigation, the family has taken the sick Alejo to a run-down clinic where an insensitive nurse wants to take all their money for a cursory and graceless examination of the young man. Estrella uses her knowledge of the different functions of language—lies, bartering, pleading—but the nurse insists on charging them. Estrella takes up one of Perfecto's tools, a crowbar, and smashes it down on the nurse's desk to make her understand their terrible need. To the nurse such an act might appear like armed robbery:

> Estrella slammed the crowbar down on the desk, shattering the school pictures of the nurse's children, sending the pencils flying to the floor; breaking the porcelain cat with a nurse's cap into pieces. The nurse dropped her purse and shielded her face. Estrella waited. (129)

In fact, this is Estrella's effort to fix the situation. She does not want to hurt anything or anyone, she just realizes that her words coupled with this action will rectify the situation she has concluded is unjust:

> She remembered the tar pits. Energy, money, the fossilized bones of energy matter. How bones made oil and oil made gasoline. The oil was made from their bones, and it was their bones that kept the nurse's car from not halting on some highway, kept her on her way to Daisyfield to pick up her boys at six. It was their bones that kept the air conditioning in the cars humming, that kept them moving on the long dotted line of the map. Their bones. Why couldn't the nurse see that? Estrella had figured it out: the nurse owed them as much as they owed her. (127)

For this nurse, and much of mainstream American society, Estrella and her family represent mere means to an end: they exist as part of a larger labor force, not as individuals with needs and desires. Estrella must have the money back because they need it for gas to get to the hospital. We can see here how Estrella has learned her reading lesson well from Perfecto and Alejo and her mother. For example, it is fitting that Estrella uses Perfecto's crowbar with her own words to pry apart the nurse's prejudices. And in Estrella's position as voiceless and invisible Other, which she is slowly beginning to understand, she must use her knowledge of tools to achieve what she wants and needs.

Estrella's development from girl to woman in *Under the Feet of Jesus* parallels her growing understanding and use of the tools Perfecto, Alejo, and Petra have imparted to her. I have already explained to some extent here Perfecto's tools and the legacy that he leaves with Estrella, but he is a complex character with his own ambivalence concerning home, as he lives a "travesty of laws" (71). Although Petra sees him as part of her family, when Perfecto dreams of home he dreams of his dead wife and their children with whom he has lost contact. Petra believes in him because he has lived his words to her, "trust me" (96) and to Estrella (131), but since they have arrived at the camps, "The desire to return home was now a tumor lodged under the muscle of Perfecto's heart and getting larger with every passing day" (70). This longing leads him to consider tearing down the barn, in some ways a home-site for Estrella: "With or without Estrella's help, he committed himself to tearing the barn down. The money was essential to get home before home became so distant, he wouldn't be able to remember his way back" (71). But Estrella in the end bargains with Perfecto: she will become his tool, and help to tear down the barn, if he will help her to take Alejo to the clinic. And from Perfecto and his knowledge of active tools, Estrella also learns the grace of language. When she thanks him for his help she lays a path for him to follow through her words and her tone which act like the bones in Alejo's tar pit stories. These markers possibly will help him, ultimately, to realize and accept her family as home:[8]

> He had given this country his all, and in this land that used his bones for kindling, in this land that never once in the thirty years he lived and worked, never once said thank you, this woman who could be his granddaughter, had said the words with such honest gratitude, he was struck by how deeply these words touched him. (131-132)

Alejo has a different but related tool that he uses to communicate with and verbally seduce Estrella. In his awkward adolescent fumbling with language to gain Estrella's attention, he tells her stories. These stories are about tar pits and bones and the oil that comes from these historical sites. And these musings resonate throughout the text in powerful ways to explain the situation of this migrant family, particularly the motif of bones that acts as a metaphor for home in the text, the ultimate home for all people, the bones that we inhabit and that we leave behind after death. The story of the tar pits explains Alejo's interests to Estrella and also "homes" her onto his ontological site as person: the story acts as an explanatory analogy of her own family's and others' sense of homelessness, of not belonging in the capital-based market of the United States. Only one of his stories tells of a person, a young girl whose bones were found in a field as if homeless and displaced: "They found her in a few bones. No details of her life were left behind, no piece of cloth, no ring, no doll. A few bits of bone displayed somewhere under a glass and nothing else" (112). This feeling of being lost and "boneless" is how Alejo feels when he breathes in the fumigation fumes: "No fingerprint or history, bone. No lava stone. No story or family, bone" (66). Through Alejo's words, Viramontes clarifies the significant relationship between bone, earth, stone, family story, and finally, home.

With her mother, Estrella learns the language of domesticity, where empty Quaker Oats boxes can be converted into musical drums to appease little children, and the everyday gesture of rolling early-morning tortillas becomes just another appendage of one's body. Rarely do Estrella and Petra speak to one another, but they do exchange glances and embraces. Petra instills in Estrella a respect for the power of home remedies such as garlic for varicose veins and a circle drawn in dirt round a shack to keep away scorpions. Estrella also learns from Petra the strategies of mothering which she constantly uses with the other children in the family. The mother teaches her daughter a home-based language, tools to construct her own home. On first arriving at their bungalow, for example, Petra inspects the cooking grill outside and evaluates the smell of former meals. In this way, the traditionally contained kitchen moves outside, and the art of cooking is established by sensual smells rather than by four walls. Through her language and her gestures Petra enforces the idea of an extended— nontraditional—family and hope for community.

Poet and playwright Cherríe Moraga explains the situation of many Chicana women that applies to Petra as well:

> So we fight back, we think, with our families—with our women pregnant and our men, the indisputable heads. We believe the more severely we protect the sex roles within the family, the stronger we will be as a unit in opposition to the anglo threat. And yet, our refusal to examine *all* the roots of lovelessness in our families is our weakest link and softest spot. (181)

In *Under the Feet of Jesus* the woman acts as participant—not passive object—in the restructuring or redefining of a language laden with "house-bound" ideology. She moves inside and outside the walls of the house to expand domestic intimacy into the public world: she makes the inside become outside. Viramontes gives us an alternative to the borders so glorified in texts such as Bachelard's topophilia studies of the house / home, or an early article by Rivera praising "la casa, el barrio and la lucha as constant elements in the ritual of Chicano literature" (441); *Under the Feet of Jesus* presents an alternative view. It explores "the dialectic of inside and outside, that is, here and there, integration and alienation, comfort and anxiety" that the traditional house / home offers (Olivares 161), and then it questions these dichotomies. Conventional Mexican American texts, especially those written in the sixties and seventies by male writers, implicitly support the idea of the contented woman as the domestic angel, while Viramontes' text explicitly undermines any unthinking acceptance of such ideology. The inside is not necessarily good and safe for the female. Instead the Chicana must explore new layers of language to furnish a home-site, almost as if, using Alejo's motif of bones and stones, she must dig deep into geological layers of language to unearth the bones with which to reconstruct a different home to inhabit.

Unlike the traditional anglo-European view of home, the reader sees here the different cultural approaches that Chicanas from Mexico and Southern California have employed in their reconstruction of a sense of home. The tension between male and female goals in this novel reflects the impasse between individual insight and the unchanging social codes faced by the Chicana heroine. Clearly these clashes are seen in the case of Petra's husband abandoning her, and then Perfecto's more ambiguous leave-taking. And Alejo's courtship of Estrella, though conventional, leads not to her merely mothering him in his sickness but to her letting go of him for his own good and that of her family.

Estrella and her family can barely visualize the kind of home that comes readily to mind for most middle-class white Americans. Estrella and her family are migrant workers—piscadores. The whole premise behind the twentieth century's political rhetoric about a stable and secure home is completely undermined by this family's constant movement, displacement, and potential eviction from both home and country. At one point the little boy comments to Petra, "Maybe we can stay in one place" (130). Even a small child can feel the instinctual appeal of constancy, of not always working, not moving. Hence this story, like so many untold stories, articulates different ways of conceptualizing the home-site. Mohanty and Martin write: "Far too often . . . both male leftists and feminists have responded to the appeal of a rhetoric of home and family by merely reproducing the most conventional articulations of those terms in their own writings" (191).

Under the Feet of Jesus does not reproduce homey nostalgia, nor do its characters long for the anglo version of home. And in this recognition comes a need for, and an acceptance of making space and place available within the diverse layers of the States for various kinds of home. The family in *Under the Feet of Jesus* appears isolated, regardless of whether they are legal or not, for many reasons: economic, racial, linguistic, to name a few. In rejecting a conventional idea of home, they need the practical means to envision another kind of home. In any case, their idea is not a cozy embroidery-stitched picture of "home, sweet, home;" instead, home should be viewed as a vital, thriving reality lived through language, people, and habitable structures. As the sociologist Muntañola explains, "La noción de lugar para vivir es un constante y triple encuentro entre el medio externo, nosotros mismo y los demás, y cada lugar construido es una síntesis y un resultado de este triple encuentro" [The notion of a place to live is a constant and triple encounter between the outside world, ourselves, and others, and every constructed place is a synthesis and a result of this triple encounter] (55). A home cannot be conceived as a private, protected, and individualistic place. Without the interaction with others, and the varieties of religion, race, sexuality, political views that they bring with them, the concept of home as expounded in this paper could not exist.

Future constructions of home sites depend not only on architecture, but in socio-political possibilities for home-building as well. My goal in this study has been to suggest that the act of narration can be a form of "home" where self-identity emerges. Disintegrating language and actual homelessness have become current arenas of debate for many societies. For example, the newly passed proposition 187 in California denies social services to illegal immigrants and in effect denies them a home site in physical and political reality. According to the *San Francisco Chronicle*, the state of California is host to almost half of the nation's undocumented population (11). The proposition has sowed fear and bitterness among many voters. It brings out the xenophobia and racism that often lie just under the surface of the American social fabric. I note that amongst various Other groups who are denied a home-site for racial and / or legal reasons, the "master's tools" are denied them,[9] and an opportunity to found a site of solidarity is missed.

With the passage of proposition 187, people on both sides of the issue lose the potential for home-building. As Martin and Mohanty put it in their example of a women's community:

> The relationship between the loss of community and the loss of self is crucial. To the extent that identity is collapsed with home and community and based on homogeneity and comfort, on skin, blood, and heart, the giving up of home will necessarily mean the giving up of self and vice versa. (209)

Skin, blood, and heart can also stand in for the bones so often evoked in *Under the Feet of Jesus*. These specific, body-structuring details are vital parts of a home community, but laws like proposition 187 forget these human elements in the legal analysis of immigration problems. Identity is related to place, so that when people are denied a place to live, their identity is undermined. The fear that provokes such propositions also acts as a threat to the anglo community because it highlights the presence of the Other instead of incorporating Others in the sedimentary levels of language and society.

Within these layers of sedimentation a Chicana / o discourse is in process. As Rebolledo writes, "I think we would all agree that Chicana criticism and theory are still in a state of flux, looking for a theoretical, critical framework that is our own" (350). In *Under the Feet of Jesus* language in flux and a shifting home are represented by the space in between—the barn. The barn acts almost as another character in the text as well as being a potential home-site for Estrella. Even if not made originally for human habitation, a barn instills a sense of quiet and respect from most people. In its simple and vernacular architectural style, a barn connects the present with the past. Perhaps it is this sense of being grounded that attracts Estrella to the barn from the beginning. It seems to be a structure that will not move, that shelters, that marks time. At the same time, through its holes and cracks it lets through air and light. Estrella personifies the barn when she imagines tearing it down with Perfecto, "pulling the resistant long rusted nails out of the woodsheet walls. The nails would screech and the wood would moan and she would pull the veins out" (63). And this image of destruction, an almost human portrayal of blood and bones, leads her to reflect on a much larger picture: "Is that what happens? Estrella thought, people just use you until you're all used up, then rip you into pieces when they're finished with you?" (63).

In *Under the Feet of Jesus* the barn represents many things: a mysterious place, a refuge, money, a base for flight into other realms, and the home that Estrella has never had. At the end of the novel, after leaving Alejo behind at the hospital, perhaps forever, after her mother verges on collapse as her figure of Christ breaks in two, after Perfecto poises himself in indecisive flight, Estrella goes to the barn in the dark to climb to the roof and feel the power of open skies, stars, and strength in its structure. Grounded, "[l]ike the chiming bells of the great cathedrals, she believed her heart powerful enough to summon *home* all those who strayed" (151, my emphasis). The question arises whether Estrella has the power to be a beacon of home or will fall into disrepair like her barn. In my reading, Estrella finds herself in a discursive exile, on the edge of a threshold, where language becomes the tool to implement an odyssey of self-exploration. Homeless, even within her domestic spheres, this woman will become, I contend, a builder engaged in establishing strong foundations for future homes. I have tried to interweave the ideas of language as home, and the learning of a new language to build a new home, in this essay. An early scene in the novel, between Alejo and Estrella, illustrates this intersection:

> Yeah, and Estrella pointed to the bottle because she wanted to tell him how good she felt but didn't know how to build the house of words she could invite him in. That was real good, she said, and they looked at one another and waited. Build rooms as big as barns. . . . Wide-open windows where she could put candlelights and people from across the way would point at the glow and not feel so alone in the night. (59)

Estrella then takes the empty bottle and shows Alejo how to make music, a different kind of language that they can share and that will house them. By exploring different languages and opening up different silences, Estrella—Star—will be true to her name and thus guide as beacon those around her who need a different kind of home. Such languages of difference act as homing devices in Viramontes' *Under the Feet of Jesus*.

NOTES

1. The fate of the barns parallels the fate of families like Estrella's: both are abandoned by mainstream society after they have been "used up"; both belong to a world in which labor is not depersonalized through mechanization.

2.   I borrow the metaphor "sedimentary layers of language" from Bakhtin's concept of heteroglossia, which he defines as the plurality of voices or discourses and their potentially creative interconnections and overlappings.

3.   *The Grapes of Wrath* is a classic American counterpart to *Under the Feet of Jesus.* Although Viramontes's novel also deals with migrant workers, it focuses more on an interior voyage than does Steinbeck's lengthier novel.

4.   Philosophers and architects such as Heidegger, Bachelard, Le Corbusier, and Norberg-Schulz demonstrate uniformly positive reactions to and interpretations of the idea of home, usually within rather strict terminology. It is only recently in North and South America that the influence of sociological and feminist studies have broadened and deepened the critique of the home site.

5.   The following passage from the novel illustrates the geographic and historical distance of Texas in the minds of the field workers: "-De donde eres? -Del Rio Grande Valle. -Es un estado de México? -Texas ya es parte de los Estados Unidos. -Ay. . . " (53).

6.   Traditionally, the options for Chicanas have included two extremes of the madre santa / wife and the feminist / whore. These essentializing poles have been mitigated by recent theoretical and literary work of such writers as Gloria Anzaldúa, Norma Alarcón, Tey Diana Rebolledo, Cherríe Moraga, Sandra Cisneros, and Helena María Viramontes.

7.   *Piscadores*—fruit or vegetable pickers—is a linguistic marker of a Chicano word entering into the English narrative. A different investigation than mine here would trace the socio-linguistic implications of code-switching in the novel and their effect in producing another level of home through language.

8.   I use "realize" in the Spanish sense of the word *realizar*, to actualize something in the performative sense.

9.   See Audre Lorde's insightful essay, "The Master's Tools Will Never Dismantle the Master's House."

WORKS CITED

Alarcón, Norma. "Making Familia From Scratch: Split Subjectivities in the Work of Helena María Viramontes and Cherríe Moraga." In Herrera-Sobek, 147-159.

Alarcón, Norma, ed. *Chicana Critical Issues.* Berkeley: Third Woman Press, 1993.

Anzaldúa, Gloria, ed. *Making Face, Making Soul: Haciendo Caras. Creative and Critical Perspectives by Women of Color.* San Francisco : Aunt Lute, 1990.

Arthur, Eric, and Dudley Witney. *The Barn: A Vanishing Landmark in North America.* Toronto: McClelland and Stewart Ltd., 1972.

Bachelard, Gaston. *The Poetics of Space.* 1958. Trans. Maria Jolas. Boston: Beacon Press, 1969.

Castillo, Debra A. *Talking Back: Toward a Latin American Feminist Criticism.* Ithaca: Cornell UP, 1992.

Editorial, "The Resonances of Proposition 187 for California," *San Francisco Chronicle,* Sunday, October 23, 1994, sec. TW, 11.

Heidegger, Martin. *Poetry, Language, Thought.* Trans. Albert Hofstadter. New York: Harper Colophon Books, 1971.

Herrera-Sobek, María, and Helena María Viramontes, eds. *Chicana Creativity and Criticism: Charting New Frontiers in American Literature.* Houston: Arte Público Press, 1988.

de Lauretis, Teresa, ed. *Feminist Studies / Critical Studies.* Bloomington: Indiana UP, 1986.

Lorde, Audre. *Sister Outsider.* Trumansburg: The Crossing Press, 1984.

Martin, Biddy, and Chandra Talpade Mohanty. "Feminist Politics: What's Home Got to Do with It?" In de Lauretis, 191-121.

Moraga, Cherríe. "From a Long Line of Vendidas: Chicanas and Feminism." In de Lauretis, 173-190.

Muntañola, Josep. *La arquitectura como lugar*. Barcelona: Editorial Gustavo Gili, 1974.

Norburg-Schulz, Christian. *Genius Loci: Towards a Phenomenology of Architecture*. 1979. London: Academy Editions, 1980.

Olivares, Julián. "Sandra Cisneros' 'The House on Mango Street' and the Poetics of Space," In Herrera-Sobek, 160-169.

Ortiz, Victor Manuel. *La casa, una aproximación*. Mexico: Universidad Autonoma Metropolitana de Xochimilco, 1984.

Rebolledo, Tey Diana, and Eliana S. Rivero, eds. *Infinite Divisions: An Anthology of Chicana Literature*. Tucson: U of Arizona P, 1993.

Rivera, Tomás. "Chicano Literature: Fiesta of the Living." *Books Abroad* 49.3 (1975):439-452.

Tuan, Yi-Fu. *Space and Place: The Perspective of Experience*. Minneapolis: U of Minnesota P, 1977.

Viramontes, Helena María. *Under the Feet of Jesus*. New York: Dutton, 1995.

27

How We Did It
from *Scenes from a Childhood*

Alison Hawthorne Deming

The snowbanks rose taller than the car,
a midnight bobsled run, our ride home—
you asleep under parka and quilt,
home from the sitter, me from the failing

ski resort where the married chef
hustled me nightly, while I shoved
steaming racks of dishes along
the stainless steel drainboard.

The sitter's husband too came onto me,
a wiry deadbeat, metal pin in his leg
from some war. He told me how it
held the cold, taught me to pound

cornmeal and molasses sweet grain
from the freight car walls,
the bunch of us climbing with sacks
up to the backlot siding

where the rusty hulks stood
after unloading at the Richford mill—
free feed for the hogs and hens
you hated me for butchering.

Those were the improvised years
after King and the Kennedys—hopes
humbled down to living with the powerless—
flocks of us, exurbanites, trying to invent

community in the impoverished north

where abandoned shells of homes
lay scattered over hills
as if some sea had backed out and left them there.

Is there a placeless place you came from,
as mystics tell us, where souls drift
inspecting the candidates
they might elect to bring them here?

Those icy mornings in our ramshackle,
wind welcoming house, you twirled on a swing
that hung in the kitchen doorway, singing like the necessary
heat rising from the cast iron stove.

Notes on the Contributors

Ama Ata Aidoo is a Ghanaian writer who has published novels, plays, poetry, short stories, and children's books. She bills herself as a writer, university teacher, and consultant on literature, educational, artistic, and gender issues. Currently, she is Distinguished Visiting Professor in the Department of English, Oberlin College.

Julia Alvarez is the author of two novels, *How the Garcia Girls Lost Their Accents* and *In the Time of the Butterflies*, and two collections of poetry, *The Other Side / El Otro Lado* (Dutton 1995), and *Homecoming* (reissued in 1995). She teaches writing at Middlebury College in Vermont and travels often to her native country of the Dominican Republic.

Fiona R. Barnes teaches literature and composition at the University of Florida in Gainesville. She has published essays on Michelle Cliff, Jean Rhys, and Doris Lessing. She is currently working on Nadine Gordimer's short fiction.

Sylvia Bowerbank started out in a small log cabin in the woods near Baptiste Lake in northern Ontario. She is now an assistant professor of English at McMaster University in Hamilton, Ontario and is writing a book about women and ecology in early modern England.

When she is not at the cinema or reading supernatural fiction, Ellen Brinks is teaching undergraduates and completing a dissertation on gender and sexual deviance in gothic Romantic narratives at Princeton University. Her other publications include essays on gendered cartographies in seventeenth-century France and England, and the economics of sexuality in the film *Single White Female*. She makes her home in New York City.

Amy Benson Brown makes her home in Atlanta, Georgia, where she is a doctoral candidate in English at Emory University. In her dissertation, *Rewriting the Word: Women Writers and the Bible*, she examines feminist biblical revision from Emily Dickinson to Gloria Naylor. At the moment, she is working on a project on literary tradition and American women's poetry.

Alison Hawthorne Deming is the author of *Science and Other Poems* (LSU, 1993), winner of the Walt Whitman Award from the Academy of American Poets, and *Temporary Homelands* (Mercury House, 1994), a collection of nature essays. She is Director of the University of Arizona Poetry Center. Her awards include a Wallace Stegner Fellowship from Stanford University and fellowships from the National Endowment for the Arts.

Clarissa Pinkola Estés, Ph.D., is an award-winning poet, senior Jungian psychoanalyst, and a *cantadora* (keeper of the old stories) in the Latina tradition. She authored *Women Who Run With the Wolves* over twenty years' time. She received a 1990-91 Rocky Mountain Women's Institute fellowship, and for her writing and social justice work, she received the *Las Primeras* award from MANA, the National Latinas Professional Women's Association in Washington, D.C. Estés forged through school, kept the homefires, worked full time and wrote in between at every opportunity. She is married and has three grown daughters. She has definitely "been there / done that."

Rebecca Blevins Faery has indeed given up the house she wrote about in her essay for this volume. She now divides her time between Iowa City and Boston, where she teaches writing at Harvard University. She has also taught literature and writing at Hollins College, the University of Iowa, and Mount Holyoke College. She is a teacher, student, and critic of American cultural history with special interests in feminist theory and the essay as a literary form. Faery is the author, with Carl Klaus and Chris Anderson, of an anthology, *In Depth: Essayists for Our Time*; her essays on the politics of reading and writing and on the work of American women writers have appeared in *The Iowa Review*, *Legacy*, *Mosaic*, *San Jose Studies*, and a number of anthologies.

Cheryl Fish, a resident of New York City, has published poems and prose in journals such as *New American Writing*, *Santa Monica Review*, and *Long News in the Short Century*. She is the author of *Wing Span* (Mellen, 1992) and *My City Flies By* (E.G. Chapbook, 1986). Her dissertation deals with the poetics and politics of reinventing home through the figure of the travelling woman; the project focuses on two black and two white women who travelled in the Americas and Russia in the antebellum period. She teaches at Nassau Community College, State University of New York.

Jennifer Gillan, Assistant Professor of English at Bentley College, is a coordinator of the *Issues in Cultural Studies* and *Performance, Culture, and Subversive Bodies* lecture series. She is the editor with Maria Mazziotti Gillan of *Unsettling America: An Anthology of Contemporary Multicultural Poetry* (Viking Penguin, 1994). Currently, she is completing *Innocents, Indians, and Other American Subjects: Imaginative Historiography in Contemporary Literature.*

Martine Guyot-Bender is Assistant Professor of French language and literatures at Hamilton College. Her primary research is on the representation of war in twentieth-century fiction with an emphasis on the Occupation period in France and the War of Independence in the Maghreb. She is at present completing a book on the Occupation, *Patrick Modiano's dispersed writing* and an article "Seducing Corinne: The Official Popular Press during the Occupation," in *Gender, Fascism and Popular Culture in France* (New England Press, forthcoming 1995). Her interest include genre studies, and narratology as related to gender issues.

Joy Harjo, Professor of Creative Writing at the University of New Mexico, was born in Tulsa, Oklahoma and is an enrolled member of the Muscogee (or Creek) tribe. She received her MFA in Creative Writing from the Iowa Writers' Workshop at the University of Iowa in 1978. She has published five books of poetry, including *She Had Some Horses* (Thunder's Mouth Press) and the award-winning *In Mad Love and War* (Wesleyan). Her awards include the Oklahoma Book Arts award, the American Book Award, and the Josephine Miles Award for Excellence in Literature from PEN Oakland, as well as numerous grants. She has also written a screenplay and a children's book, and plays saxophone with her band, Poetic Justice.

Velina Hasu Houston heads the playwriting program at the University of Southern California School of Theatre. Her signature play, *Tea*, along with many others, has been produced internationally and at regional theaters in the U.S. Her film credits include work with Columbia Pictures, Sidney Poitier, PBS, and Lancit Media. Her most recent book is a play anthology, *The Politics of Life* (Temple) and she has twice been a Rockefeller fellow. Other awards include the California Arts Council, Japanese American Woman of Merit, and the Lorraine Hansberry playwriting award.

Jutta Ittner was born in the Bavarian Alps at the end of the war and lived and taught in Munich until 1989. She received a Ph.D. in German literature from the University of Hamburg with a dissertation on exile literature. Since 1992 she has been living in Oberlin, Ohio and teaching German language and literature at Case Western Reserve University in Cleveland. She is twice married and has one daughter.

Carolyn M. Jones is Assistant Professor of Religious Studies and English at Louisiana State University, where she also teaches in the Honors College. She was a 1993 Ford Foundation Postdoctoral Fellow in the Graduate Institute of the Liberal Arts at Emory University. Her work has appeared most recently in *African-American Review*, *Literature and Theology*, and *In Good Company: Essays in Honor of Robert Detweiler*.

Kawashinsay is the ceremonial name for Charlotte DeClue, a member of the Great Osage Nation of Oklahoma. She is a former child actor whose mentors included her mother, actress Jennifer Jones, and stage sister Virginia Mayo, to whom she credits her work. She is the author of *Ten Good Horses*, a collection of poetry published by Howling Dog Press.

Gabriele Kreis studied French and German literature in Paris and Hamburg. She received her Ph.D. in 1982. After teaching for a short time, she now writes for television and radio. Apart from *Frauen im Exil* [Women in Exile] (Dusseldorf: Classen, 1984), she has written *Irmgard Keun: Was man glaubt, gibt es* [Irmgard Keun: Believing Acts into Being] (Munich: Wilhelm Heyne Verlag, 1993). She makes her home in Hamburg.

Cecelia Lawless is assistant professor of Latin American literature at Hamilton College. A comparatist by nature, she received her Ph.D. in Comparative Literature from Cornell University in 1990. She concentrates her work in the analysis of women's domestic space, cultural studies of food in fiction, and film in Spain in Latin America. She has published on writers such as Laura Esquivel, Cristina Peri Rossi, and Carmen Martín Gaite. She has recently completed a book manuscript, *Homeward Bound: A Study of Home in Hispanic and American Gothic Novels*. Her next project will be a cultural analysis of culinary arts in modern Latin American film and fiction.

Lisa Suhair Majaj, a Palestinian-American writer, is completing a dissertation on Arab American literature. Her poetry and essays have appeared in *International Quarterly, Unsettling America, Food for Our Grandmothers: Writings by Arab-American and Arab-Canadian Feminists, Miscegenation Blues*, and elsewhere. Her critical articles include "Arab American Literature and the Politics of Memory," in *Memory and Cultural Politics: New Essays in American Ethnic Literatures*. She is co-editing a collection of essays on Arab women's literature, and another collection on the Lebanese author Etel Adnan.

Deborah Nelson is a doctoral candidate in English at the Graduate and University Center of the City University of New York and has a Masters degree in English from Columbia University. She currently teaches composition and rhetoric at Queens College while completing her dissertation on confessional poetry and constitutional privacy.

John O'Brien earned his Master's Degree from Trinity College, Dublin, and his Ph.D. from the University of Minnesota. He has published articles on contemporary Czechoslovak, Australian, and Irish literature. Most recently, St. Martin's Press is publishing his *Milan Kundera & Feminism: Dangerous Intersections*, a groundbreaking study of Kundera's problematic representation of women. O'Brien currently teaches at Normandale Community College in Minneapolis, Minnesota.

Ingeborg Majer O'Sickey is an assistant professor of German and Women's Studies at the State University of New York, Binghamton. She has published articles on Ingeborg Bachmann and Marguerite Yourcenar and on representations of race, gender, and sexualities in the New German Cinema. She is currently editing, with Ingeborg von Zadow, *Triangular Visions: Women in Recent German Cinema*, and is at work on a book on cultural and national identity of women in German film of the 1980s and 1990s.

Margaret Randall is a poet and oral historian, photographer and teacher, who lives and works in New Mexico. Among her most recent titles are *This is About Incest, Dancing With the Doe, Gathering Rage: The Failure of Twentieth Century Revolutions to Develop a Feminist Agenda, Sandino's Daughters Revisited: Feminism in Nicaragua*, and *Our Voices/Our Lives: Stories of Women from Central America and the Caribbean*. She is currently writing a book about women and money.

Roberta Rubenstein, Professor of Literature at American University, is the author of *The Novelistic Vision of Doris Lessing* (Illinois, 1979) and *Boundaries of the Self: Gender, Culture, Fiction* (Illinois, 1987), as well as articles on Virginia Woolf, Margaret Atwood, Margaret Drabble, Angela Carter, Rachel Ingalls, and other modern and contemporary women writers. She is currently working on representations of longing and "home" in narratives by women.

Meryl F. Schwartz teaches at Lakewood Community College in Ohio, where she is developing a multicultural literature program. She has published an interview with Michelle Cliff in *Contemporary Literature* and is co-editing, with Fiona Barnes, a collection of essays on Cliff. Other publications include an article on Andrea Dworkin's literary career and an essay on turn-of-the-century African American writer Emma Dunham Kelley. She is currently at work on an article about teaching African American literature from the subject position of a Jewish feminist. Her dissertation is on contemporary women's novels of political awakening.

Karen Steele is a doctoral candidate in English at the University of Texas at Austin, specializing in twentieth-century British and Irish literature. In her dissertation she examines the cultural representation of two Irish nationalist women: Maud Gonne (1866-1953) and Bernadette Devlin McAliskey (b. 1947). Her project concerns the trope of mothering as it is manifested in the nationalist emblem, Mother Ireland, and the Irish Catholic image of the Virgin Mary, and investigates how female sexuality and maternity have influenced the representation of women in a nationalist and (post)colonial context.

Lee Talley is a doctoral candidate and teaches part time in the English Department of Princeton University. Her dissertation is a study of the subversive ways in which the Brontës revised Methodist discourses to challenge dominant secular and religious models.

Marilya Veteto-Conrad, Assistant Professor of German at Northern Arizona University, grew up in the United States, Germany, and Sweden. She received her B.A. in German from Austin College, her M.A. and Ph.D. in German and Swedish from the University of Texas at Austin. Her area of research is minority literature in Germany. Her book, *Finding a Voice: German-language Turkish Writers*, is published by Peter Lang Publishing, Inc.

Dolores Nawagesic Wawia, Frog Lady (Muk Kee Qweh), is an Ojibway grandmother, teacher, and coordinator of Indigenous Studies at McMaster University in Hamilton, Ontario. She is currently writing a book, *From Teepee to Penthouse*, about her experience growing up on the Gull Bay Reserve in northern Ontario.

Catherine Wiley teaches literature and creative writing as assistant professor at the University of Colorado at Denver. She has published essays on playwrights Alice Childress, Brian Friel, Cherríe Moraga, and Elizabeth Robins, as well as on Virginia Woolf. Her poems have appeared in *Kalliope*, *Women's Studies / Thinking Women*, and several anthologies.

Cynthia F. Wong teaches contemporary literature at the University of Colorado at Denver, where she is assistant professor of English. She is the daughter of Chinese immigrants and is researching a book on cultural diversity in American literature. Her essays on other Asian and women writers concern work by Kazuo Ishiguro, Fae Nyenne Ng, and Sandra Cisneros.